0248611

D1765002

Long Loan

This book is due for return on or before the last date shown below

2 0 DEC 2005		
1 2 JAN 2006		
0 4 OCT 2006		
2 1 DEC 2006		
0 7 JUN 2007		
1 7 DEC 2007		

St Martins Services Ltd

Irony, Satire, Parody and the Grotesque
in the Music of Shostakovich

To the memory of my grandfather,
who gave me his sense of humour

Irony, Satire, Parody and the Grotesque in the Music of Shostakovich

A Theory of Musical Incongruities

ESTI SHEINBERG

music engravings by
OFER SHEINBERG

Ashgate

Aldershot • Burlington USA • Singapore • Sydney

Published by
Ashgate Publishing Limited   Ashgate Publishing Company
Gower House   131 Main Road
Croft Road   Burlington
Aldershot   Vermont, 05401–5600
Hants GU11 3HR   USA
England

Ashgate website: http://www.ashgate.com

British Library Cataloguing in Publication Data

Sheinberg, Esti
    Irony, Satire, parody and the Grotesque in the Music of Shostakovich:
    A Theory of Musical Incongruities
    1. Shostakovich, D. (Dmitrii), 1906–1975—Criticism and interpretation.
    I. Title.
    780.9'2

US Library of Congress Cataloging in Publication Data

Sheinberg, Esti, 1954–
    Irony, Satire, Parody and the Grotesque in the Music of Shostakovich:
    A Theory of Musical Incongruities / Esti Sheinberg; musical engravings
    Ofer Sheinberg
        p.   cm.
    Includes bibliographical references and index.
    1. Shostakovich, Dmitræ Dmitrievich, 1906–1975—Humor. 2. Humor in Music
    3. Music—Semiotics.   I. Title.
    ML410.S53S45   2000
    780'.92–dc21   00–041600

ISBN 0 7546 0226 5

This book is printed on acid free paper.

Typeset by Manton Typesetters, Louth, Lincolnshire, UK.
Printed and bound in Great Britain by MPG Books Ltd, Bodmin, Cornwall.

Contents

List of figures

List of plates

Preface

The music of Dmitri Shostakovich has typically been regarded as containing a semantic message, which reflected the political environment in which he composed. Such interpretations inadvertently relegated his works to little more than political propaganda, disregarding not only his artistic skill but the non-political purport of his music. Other studies focused on the music alone, ignoring the multi-dimensional nature of his works. Both approaches neglect an essential point, fundamental to the understanding of the traditional Russian perception of the arts. According to this tradition, an interrelationship between artistic technique and ideological content is the main aesthetic criterion.

This study views music as a form that purports semantic content. As such, it correlates with other, mainly visual and verbal, forms of expression and communication. On the basis of this premise, this study investigates the musical manifestation of four semantic modes – irony, satire, parody and the grotesque – that are related to the comic. These four modes are analysed as specific cases of the overall semantic structure of ambiguity. Subsequently, a correlative structure of musical ambiguity is presented. Thus the correlations between the musical, visual and verbal modes of expression are made principally on the basis of structural parallelism.

Within the greater semiotic web, music has a continuous interrelationship with other cultural units. In order to understand this interrelationship, some appreciation of those cultural units is needed. Therefore irony, satire, parody and the grotesque are explored as philosophical approaches, as creative principles, and as artistic techniques. Special attention is given to particulars that are characteristic of the Russian culture. Therefore, musical examples that correlate with the above modes and their techniques are analysed on the basis of their cultural associations and characteristics. These analyses are then compared with parallel examples from the works of Dmitri Shostakovich, thus clarifying some formerly unacknowledged compositional techniques and characteristics of his music.

Acknowledgements

The theoretical basis of this book is interdisciplinary: while dealing with Russian music and Russian culture, its core lies in the more general field of musical semiotics.

Since the completion of its first version, in 1997, several related books have appeared, three of which are central to its field of study: these are Richard Taruskin's *Defining Russia Musically* (1997), Laurel Fay's recent biography of Shostakovich (1999), and David Lidov's *Elements of Semiotics* (1999). Although I do not directly refer to them in the text, I don't think that any of them contradicts my theories and analyses, as presented here. Moreover, they seem to correlate together into a fuller and more comprehensive picture of musical semiotics in general and the music of Shostakovich in particular.

The book draws its terminology and concepts from a variety of sources. However, the most significant single source for its main theoretical basis is to be found in Robert Hatten's *Musical Meaning in Beethoven* (1994), to which I am greatly indebted for the concept of musical correlation, which became central to my own thought. The ideas I present are meant to continue and develop Hatten's concepts, and perhaps offer some new insights into their application to music in general and to the area of musical ambiguity in particular.

Beyond the inspiration I drew from his writings, I am deeply grateful to Robert Hatten for long and fruitful discussions over the e-mail and for his scrupulous reading of the first version of my typescript. Many of the improvements made from the first version are due to his enlightening comments and unforgiving scrutiny, and for both I am fully indebted and deeply grateful.

Likewise, I would like to express my thanks to Raymond Monelle for his good advice and mind-regenerating discussions, and to Eero Tarasti, whose work introduced me to the field of musical semiotics, for his constant intellectual support. I am also grateful to Stuart Campbell for his useful comments and his help with the translations from Russian, and to Malcolm Hamrick Brown for stimulating correspondence over the e-mail concerning the current state of research on Shostakovich.

My warmest thanks to my son Ofer, who copied and designed all the music examples in this book. I am also indebted to him for his useful comments, and his admirable patience with my many last-minute modifications.

I am indebted to the University of Edinburgh for providing me with financial support to accomplish some of the more complicated technicalities involved in the production of this book, and deeply grateful to my colleagues who covered my teaching duties during the time I was preparing it for publication.

An interdisciplinary research must involve more than one person, and this research is no exception. Many people have contributed to the final result, in various fields of knowledge and in a variety of ways: recommending a particular source that I had missed, providing hard-to-obtain material or correcting my awkward translations from Russian, German and French sources. Others granted me valuable time in discussions that brought up new ideas and refined older ones. The serendipity of these encounters shed sparks of light on a work that otherwise is often quite lonely and secluded.

I am indebted to Nelu Laurian, an alleged non-musician who always seemed to know about music more than I did, for introducing me to the music of Shostakovich and inspiring me to start this research. Many more thanks to Alla Ablova, Emilios Cambouropoulos, Robert Dow, Hans Erhard, Rita Flomenboim, Tony Gilbert, Jenny McLeod, Grant O'Brien, Stephen Priest, Madeleine Şechter, Colwyn Trevarthen, Heather Valencia, John Wexler and many of my students at the University of Edinburgh for stimulating discussions, helpful ideas, valuable research material and technical support.

As someone who is not a native English speaker, I owe special thanks to Mike Turnbull and Jo Towler who proof-read extensive parts of the original typescript and who, following some enigmatic rules that will probably always remain beyond my comprehension, patiently corrected the use and location of my prepositions, my 'alsos' and 'alreadies' which were always, but always in the wrong place, changed my 'thats' to 'whiches' and vice versa, and mercilessly shortened clumsy and complex sentences like this one. Thanks also to the hawk-eyed Kevin Fitzsimmons for his uncompromising final proofreading and his assistance in compiling the Index. Many thanks to Rachel Lynch and Kirsten Weissenberg from Ashgate for their effective and competent support throughout all the publication stages of this book.

Finally, my deepest thank you, Mum, for your financial and emotional support that enabled me to devote my efforts to this research; and my most affectionate feelings of gratitude to you, Ron, for your constant encouragement, for taking over almost full care of our shared life during months on end, and for keeping your good spirits even when I made it really hard for you. Thanks.

Transliterations from the Russian

In transliterating words and names from the Russian I decided to use the popular spellings of composers' names. In other cases I have been guided by *The Grove Dictionary of Music and Musicians*, 1980. In quotations, however, I have followed the spelling chosen by my source. Thus on the same page can be found alternative spellings, e.g. 'Lebyadkin', 'Lebiadkin' and 'Lebiatkin', according to the source quoted.

PART I
INTRODUCTION

Introduction

Ambiguities in the works of Dmitri Shostakovich

Most studies of Shostakovich consist of biographical material. Because he was the major composer of Soviet Russia, Shostakovich's life received unprecedented coverage. Attempts to write his biography were made when he still was in his thirties and early forties.[1] Two further books appeared when he was in his early fifties.[2] However, since the early 1960s the main Russian sources for biographical information about the composer have been supplied by Sofia Khentova, who wrote no fewer than eleven books, which seem to cover every single detail of his life.[3] In spite of this amazingly meticulous coverage there still seemed to be room for more monographs, biographies and memoirs, many of which were probably written as a response to the huge wave of interest that was stimulated in the West with the appearance, in 1979, of Solomon Volkov's *Testimony* about Shostakovich's memoirs.[4] Volkov's book also served as a catalyst for a number of new and forthcoming collections of Shostakovich's correspondence in the West.[5] Analytical studies, either forming part of biographies or published as independent studies, were in no way free of biographical and circumstantial biases. This is true of studies written from the Soviet point of view as well as of those published in the West.[6] The domain of Shostakovich research was so loaded with political and ideological considerations that even works which sincerely aspired to be purely analytical could not entirely avoid ideological preconceptions. These, paradoxically, could often be detected by their manifest lack of any ideological or circumstantial references.[7] Of major importance are those works that fully acknowledge the problems of living under a repressive regime, yet refrain from analysing the music. They aim at the maximum possible objectivity, but nevertheless do not lose sight of the reality, from which those works proceed. Notable among them are articles in the anthologies edited by Christopher Norris and David Fanning.[8] This approach is also indebted to the three large monographs published in Britain within a very short period of time, in which the high waves of the heated political debates began to subside, giving way to more musically substantial research.[9]

Many of these monographs and analytical works mention the high occurrence of musical ambiguities in Shostakovich's music. In Norris's anthology, no less then five articles out of nine mention it as a major factor in Shostakovich's style.[10] Works that are more biographically inclined mention the numerous ambiguous verbal expressions in Shostakovich's speech and in his writings.[11] All these, together with the ongoing discussions around the probable presence of 'forbidden' messages that were allegedly concealed by

the composer in his music, make it almost unnecessary to explain the choice
of his works as a particularly rich source for ambiguity in music.

Expressions of ambiguity were admired by Russian culture in both its
political and artistic aspects. Shostakovich was strongly influenced by this
approach: beside his repeatedly mentioned admiration for the four great
masters of literary ambiguity – Shakespeare, Gogol, Dostoevsky and Chekhov
– Shostakovich constantly mentions writers like Zamyatin, Mayakovsky,
Bulgakov, Akhmatova, Tsvetayeva and Blok and theatre artists like Meyerhold
and Mikhail Chekhov. All of these can be characterized by their consciously
ambiguous artistic language, which at certain points became almost an artistic manifesto. Equally revealing is the relative absence of literary figures like
Tolstoy and Pushkin, of artists like Malevich, Kandinsky or even Rodchenko,
with whom he worked for a while, and of the most famous film director of
the Soviet Union, Sergey Eisenstein. It is highly unlikely that this avoidance
is coincidental, since all these artists have in common their conscious absti-
nence from ambiguities and their commitment to clear-cut artistic
communication that sometimes became straightforward propagandistic art.

Apart from the considerable role that modes of ambiguity play in Russian
culture in general, and in modern Russian theories of literature and art in
particular, it seems that ambiguities also carried a personal significance for
Shostakovich himself. Themes of irony, parody, satire and the grotesque are
constantly intercalated in Shostakovich's biographies as well as in his musical works, speeches and articles. In his brilliant analysis of Shostakovich's
Tenth Symphony, David Fanning quotes ambiguous remarks from the composer's own article about this work.[12] However, besides this study, very few
attempts have been made systematically to explore and analyse Shostakovich's
musical ambiguities. One of these is Richard Taruskin's 1995 article about
Shostakovich's Fifth Symphony, which follows Fanning's ideas, albeit in a
considerably more controversial style. However, both Fanning and Taruskin
each analyse only one work, and as far as I know, no systematic analysis of
the ambiguities in Shostakovich's general musical output has been performed.
Moreover, most of the existing remarks about the ambiguity in his works tend
to regard them, by default, as politically linked. A thorough research of other
possible cultural and historical reasons for the tendency to ambiguous communication is a fruitful field for further inquiry, which may lead the discussion
in new directions.

The theoretical background

Correspondences between musical and non-musical elements appear in a
large number of early analytical and aesthetic studies, and use a multitude of
descriptive labels. An incomplete list of these includes 'representation',

'description', 'expression', 'interpretation', 'content', 'meaning', 'signifi-cance', 'semblance', 'symbol' and 'metaphor'.[13] The abundance and variety of these terms only emphasized the difficulty of defining the semantic import of music. Consequently, many objections were raised against the scholarly use of such terminology, and in spite of some unspecific objections (e.g. Gotuški, 1977) their recurrence in the vocabulary of musical semiotics con-siderably decreased, giving way to purely syntactical methods of analysis that were introduced in the 1960s and the 1970s. These methods, which focused on definitions of syntactical units in a musical work, were regarded as more promising in the conveyance of clear results, and therefore as more suitable for a positivistic approach.[14]

Both trends, when taken to their extremes, had weaknesses that soon became apparent. Each of their major champions, Meyer and Nattiez, subsequently modified and moderated their views. Meyer (1973 and 1989) moved towards a stronger emphasis on syntactical analysis, limiting himself to referential mean-ings based on social and stylistic conventions, while Nattiez, in his *Music and Discourse* (1990), admitted the importance of the referential import of music. As a result, the focus of musical semantics gradually shifted from generalities like 'expression', 'representation' and 'semblance' toward more specific stud-ies, mostly analysing referential meanings in music that are embedded in historical, cultural and social conventions.[15] However, while their importance to research is recognized, these analyses did not give a fully satisfactory expla-nation of many apparent referential meanings, the purport of which could not be clarified solely on the grounds of 'topics' or 'conventions'. Another apparent shortcoming of these applications was that their nearly exclusive focus on various topical units resulted in a tendency to neglect the temporal aspect of music. In extreme cases even temporal traits of music, such as metre and rhythm, were analysed as entities rather than as processes in time.[16]

The need for a new definition of non-musical units, to which music can refer, was made apparent; such a definition should find the balance point that will overcome the rigidity of a theory of topics, yet provide a sufficiently well-defined frame of reference to prevent it from stumbling again into meaningless abstractions. Moreover, a more generalized approach, taking into account both the syntagmatic and paradigmatic axes of music, was needed. Such theories would differ from former structuralist analyses in their focus on the structural *relations* between the units that build up the semiotic structure, be it a semantic or a musical one, rather than on the units themselves.

Cultural units and cultural reality

Such a theory, which proved valuable for musico-semantic applications, is based on Umberto Eco's concept of *cultural units*.[17]

> Every attempt to establish what the referent of a sign is forces us to
> define the referent in terms of an abstract entity which moreover is only
> a cultural convention … What, then, is the meaning of a term? From a
> semiotic point of view it can only be a *cultural unit*. (Eco, 1979a: 66–
> 67)

The complicated problem of unit definition was therefore solved by cutting
the Gordian knot: a cultural unit, according to Eco, is whatever the members
of a culture regard as 'something'. Being culture-bound, cultural units can
come together to create one bigger, more complex unit; on the other hand,
quite a few of them could be reduced to smaller, more specific cultural units.
For example, an 'armchair' is a piece of furniture, considered by certain parts
of society as a necessity and by others as a luxury, due to the surplus comfort
it offers to the person using it. 'Armchair' is a compound cultural unit. It is
made up of two smaller cultural units: an 'arm' is a cultural unit that means
both a weapon and a limb. A 'chair' is a piece of furniture to sit on. An
'armchair' is a chair that provides a support not only for the lower part of the
body but for the arms, too. Historically, it is associated with the 'head of the
family' figure, who was the only one allowed in the sixteenth-century
English rural household to let his arms rest; subsequently, his sitting place
was called 'the armchair'. On the other hand, the cultural unit 'armchair' can
form a part of a larger, more complicated cultural unit. For example an
'armchair detective' which, although connected to both cultural units of
'armchair' and 'detective', is also an entirely new cultural unit, with its own
independent meaning and its own network of associations and semantic inter-
connections.

The fact that anything, regardless of its scope or degree of complexity, can
be a cultural unit might encourage a *laissez-faire* policy that could lead to a
theoretical chaos. This apparent danger should be prevented by inspecting the
function of any cultural unit within its semiotic context, paying particular
attention to its thorough description and analysis. Thus, in order to provide a
valid application of semiotic theories to music, it is imperative both to make
the boundaries of a 'unit' more flexible and to retain explicit frames of
reference that must be rooted in facts.

A triple metre, for example, could relate to the topos of a 'waltz'; a duple
one to the topos of 'march'. However, they also associate, respectively, with a
'circling' and a 'to-and-fro' type of motion. Each one of the topoi, on its own,
has further associations. For example, 'march' is associated with the 'military' whilst 'waltz' brings up the idea of 'amusement'. A lullaby, then, would
be a complex cultural unit, made of at least eight simpler ones: the topos of
'lullaby', the compound metre of 6, and at least the other six cultural units:
'march', 'military', 'to-and-fro motion', 'waltz', 'amusement' and 'circling
motion'. Moreover, the new cultural unit is now attached to two new ideas: a
type of motion that combines the 'to-and-fro' and 'circling' types that charac-

Fig. I.1
The formation of a cultural unit

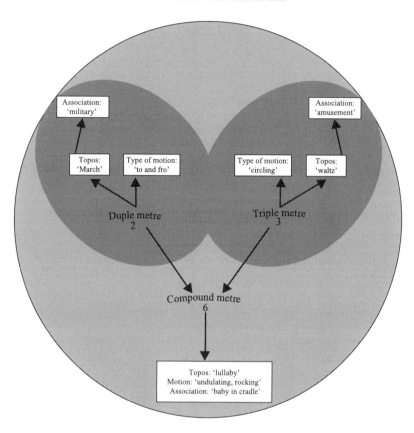

terized its two building-units, resulting in the 'undulating, rocking' motion (which indeed matches the new association of 'baby in cradle') (Fig. I.1).

Given the psychological and socially prevalent function of a 'lullaby', additional cultural units, like 'tenderness', 'night' and 'motherhood', are also immediately incorporated into the unit, creating a stronger tendency toward the mild, arch-shaped line, introverted character and a general softness of expression. The compound unit can bear intact any building-unit the meaning of which does not exclude its main import. For example, the topos of 'march' is expressed by the tempo indication 'andante' assigned by Mozart to his *Wiegenlied* K284[f]. Although 'at a walking pace' does not necessarily mean 'marching', their relatedness, which may lead to the further association with 'the military', must be subdued: the active, choleric import of 'the military' *excludes* the passive and mild character of a 'lullaby', so that their coexistence will certainly create a confusing musico-semantic paradox. Therefore, in a conventional lullaby, all musical elements tend to dissimulate the unit's ingrained topos of 'march' and its association with 'the military'. For example, in the following *Wiegenlied* by Mozart the melodic motion is mildly undulated, moving mainly step-wise. Moreover, the inherent element of duple meter is made less distinct because the melodic scheme groups some of the short phrase-patterns into three (instead of all of them being grouped in twos) (Ex. I.1).

Ex. I.1
Mozart's *Wiegenlied* K284[f]

In certain special lullabies, however, the 'march' topos is indeed enhanced by the use of certain musical gestures, enriching and complicating the final cultural unit. As more components take an active part in a cultural unit, it has more opportunities to include contradictory information, at least by implication. For example, a 'march' will imply a 'non-lullaby'; however, when combined with a clear topos of a 'lullaby' a contradiction will arise, that will open up the stage to a new cultural unit: 'irony'. This happens, for example, in the lullaby that Maria sings to her child in the first act of Alban Berg's *Wozzeck*. Even a mere melo-rhythmic analysis of the theme shows a clear discrepancy between this 'lullaby' and the generally accepted musical balance of this topos. The dotted rhythm conveys the melody with a drive and a defined rhythmic profile, both incongruent with the 'flowing, swaying' rhythm of a lullaby. Moreover, the melody, which in a conventional lullaby would tend to proceed in a step-wise motion, is full of melodic skips, most notably in the interval of a fourth. This interval, in turn, bears strong associations with military trumpet fanfares and with musical hunt-scenes, both in complete contradiction to the normally prevalent semantic import of a lullaby (Ex. I.2).

Ex. I.2
Maria's lullaby from Alban Berg's *Wozzeck*

Han-sel,spann dei-ne sechs Schim-mel an,   Gib sie zu fres-senauf's neu.___   Kein ha - ber fres - se sie,   KeinWas - ser sau - fe sie,

Paradigmatic analyses thus deal with structures of relationship between various referential levels, all of them gathered under the general umbrella of 'cultural units'. These comprise not only cultural and historical referential units, to which musical units could be related as topics, but also social and even psycho-biological elements that might be correlated with musical counterparts.[18] Even the 'topics' analysis in itself widens to include not only the historical and social reality of a culture, but also its *cultural reality*.[19] Raymond Monelle stresses that the referential meaning of music is not rooted in its reference to reality, but to the cultural units that *represent* reality and are therefore bound to certain cultural contexts. In a similar way to Eco's analyses of his cultural units, Monelle emphasizes that our signifieds become signifiers in the instant they have been uttered, thus creating an infinite chain of signification (i.e. of cultural units that signify each other) which does not represent reality but actually *has become* and *is* reality.[20]

> Music deals in cultural units, as do literature and the other arts; these take their place in our apprehension of the real world. Furthermore, they tend to be arrayed in literature according to binary oppositions. This scenario – human cultural units binarily opposed – reappears in music, making it often possible to translate across from music to other media ...
>
> The signifier is not a parasitic 'supplement' to the signified; the world is a dialogue of signifiers and signifieds, each shaping the other. For nothing can be said about the natural world, untouched by signification. Signification *is* the natural world. (Monelle, 1998:13)[21]

Applications of post-structuralist and deconstructionalist ideas

The concern with structures of relationship rather than with the building-units in themselves has considerably affected the contemporary vocabulary, and structuralist-based terminology such as 'discourse', 'narrativity', 'temporality', 'analogies' and 'correlations' now prevails in writings on musical semantics.[22] Far from being a consequence of a mere formal labelling, these changes are substantial and, following deconstructionalist ideas, are eventually more related to the spaces between the units than to the units themselves.

This neo-structuralist approach has affected both syntagmatic and paradigmatic analyses. Syntagmatic analyses, which always foundered on the obstacle of unit-definition and unit-boundaries, seem to be in decline.[23]

Most syntagma-based researches tend now to regard musical time-processes in a more general way, relying mainly on linguistic theories that are more semantically than syntactically oriented, like the writings of Greimas.[24] Eero Tarasti suggests a practically new outlook on musico-semantic analysis, which will conceive music:

> in its original processual meaning as a kinetic event that unfolds in time. Until recently the main task of musical semiotics has been to distinguish the smallest significant units. At the same time, study of *connections* among those units has been neglected; the integrating forces of musical discourse have not been taken into account. Almost all theories of musical semiotics have aimed at transforming the moving character of music to a static one, continuity to discontinuity, *temps de durée* to *temps d'espace*.
>
> In view of the fundamentally processive nature of music, musical logic cannot be based on the logic of a static world, where phenomena are either this or that, but on a logic that depicts the constant changes of phenomena from one state to another. Consequently, musical signification should be based on the continuous becoming and changing of musical figures. (Tarasti, 1994: 18)

While syntagmatic analyses shifted their focus from the segmentation of 'static' units to the inspection of time-relationships between those units, and to the general developmental process in time, i.e. music's 'narrativity', paradigmatic analyses began to inspect closely the kinds of relationship music has with referential units. It becomes more and more apparent nowadays that the question is not so much which are the referential units that should be paired with certain musical ones, but rather how the *structure of their mutual relationship* affects their specific meanings.[25]

The semiotic square

The applications of Greimas's theory of semantics to music were a remarkable breakthrough in this direction.[26] In his *Sémantique Structurale* Greimas presented a 'semiotic square' which outlines the logical structure of signification (Fig. I.2).[27]

According to Greimas, the meaning of each semantic unit depends on its position in a universal structure of signification. This structure, the 'semiotic square', consists of the unit itself, its contextual contrariety, and their two corresponding contradictions. The difference between 'contradiction' and 'contrariety' is therefore a crucial one: a contradiction is the absolute negation, the 'non-unit' of a given unit, which comes as a logical *sine qua non* of the unit itself. A contrariety, on the other hand, is always bound to a given context and therefore is arbitrary, and not the result of any logical procedure. For example, the contradiction of 'red' is 'non-red'. However, its contrariety

Fig. I.2
The semiotic square

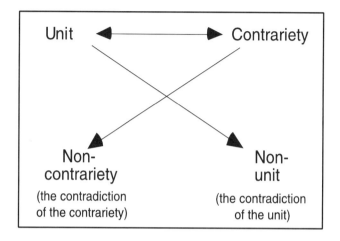

could be 'green', if the context is the physics of light, or 'white', if the context is political. It could even be 'black', in the symbolic context of 'red=love vs black=death' or 'red=life vs black=death'.[28]

This differentiation has major implications for musical semantics.[29] For instance, the word 'march' implies a contradiction with whatever is a 'non-march'. However, the contrariety of a 'march' is more elusive, and depends on the contextual semantic axis, which is arbitrary and therefore subject to the composer's choice. For example, while 'march' could be, in a certain context, contrary to a 'minuet',[30] it still could, in another context, contrast 'pastorale', 'lullaby', 'folk-dance' or 'sarabande', not to speak of its potential to contrast 'static' or even 'non-metric music'. In the first examples the unit will be 'march as topos' and the musico-semantic axis is of 'musical topoi'; in the later examples it is 'a metric unit' positioned on a non-topical axis of 'moving vs static' or 'metric vs non-metric'.[31] Since a contrariety is arbitrary and can include any specificity, as long as it is not the unit itself, one possible choice is the unit's contradiction, positioned on the semantic axis 'existent vs non-existent'. In that case the non-unit functions as a semantic affirmation. For example, 'death' and 'chaos' are symbolized in much of the music of Shostakovich by twelve-tone music. This is due to his use of the correlation between the marked poles in the oppositions 'tonal/non-tonal' and 'existent/non-existent'. The 'non-tonal' is correlated with 'non-existent' and subsequently, by cultural association, with the cultural units of 'death' and 'chaos'.[32]

Besides the obvious usefulness of the semiotic square for topical approaches, it is hard to overestimate the importance, for musical criticism and musical aesthetics, of an idea that introduces an element of arbitrariness to a seemingly purely logical structure. According to this approach, which is actually the main point of the structurally inclined musico-semantic research, there are an indefinite number of semantic axes that each semantic unit can generate, and the major task of the semiotician is to discern those that actually function in the inspected discourse. The next methodological step should be, then, an understanding of the various kinds of possible semantic axes, their functions, and the possibilities they open up for musical interpretation.

Markedness, correlations and musical correlations

A most significant contribution to such a methodology was suggested by Robert Hatten (1987 and 1994a), who applied the concepts of *markedness* and *correlations* to music interpretation. Hatten defined *correlation* as 'the bringing together of sound and content as coordinated by the markedness values of the sound structure' (Hatten, 1987: 411). Thus 'correlation', although style-bound, is supposed to include all the '"varied" kinds of musical meanings', such as 'expression', 'representation', and oppositions like 'congeneric vs extrageneric', 'iconic vs symbolic' etc., suggested in former studies in the philosophy of music (ibid.: 412). Following the linguist Michael Shapiro (1983), Hatten defined *markedness* as 'the asymmetrical value accorded to the relevant feature of a musical opposition, as encoded in a musical style, and by means of which content can systematically be correlated and kept distinct' (ibid.). Hatten then suggested applying the linguistic term of *markedness* to music.

> Markedness is perhaps the most productive concept linguistic theory has to offer music theory ... markedness can be applied to music in a way that helps explain the peculiar organisation and fundamental role of musical oppositions in both specifying and creating expressive meanings ...
>   Markedness as a theoretical concept can be defined quite simply as the valuation given to difference. Wherever one finds differentiation, there are inevitably oppositions. The terms of such oppositions are weighted with respect to some feature that is distinctive for the opposition. Thus, the two terms of an opposition will have an unequal value or asymmetry, of marked versus unmarked, that has consequences for the meaning of each term. (Hatten, 1994a: 34)

Since the primary subject of his inspection is the relationship between the units rather then the units themselves, Hatten gives much thought to the choice of the appropriate vocabulary that will accurately describe it, painstakingly engaging in terminological subtleties, like the differentiation between *musical correlations* and *musical analogies*:

> Correlations should not be equated with analogies, despite their obvious similarities. Analogies help motivate correlations, but correlations have

a different structure ... An *analogy* is a relationship arising from a comparison of relationships: A is to B as X is to Y, where 'as' implies a figural meaning illuminating the nature of one relational pair in terms of another. A *correlation* is a more literal mapping of meaning (literal for a given style) coordinated by the analogous markedness values of the two pairs of oppositions. (Hatten, 1994a: 38)

This differentiation, with all its subtlety, supplies an analytical tool of major importance, particularly when tackling structures of ambiguity such as irony, parody, satire and the grotesque. However, in order to apply it properly, I need to make two slight modifications to Hatten's ideas.

First, correlations are bound to cultural units, and are based on semantic oppositions made out of cultural units (Hatten, 1994a: 30). In this Hatten seems to alternate between *logical structures* and *cultural units*. Yet, since everything can be a cultural unit, and since cultural units can be built into structures, these structures may become cultural units in their own right. Thus cultural perceptions may sometimes be regarded as rational deductions.

Most people, for example, would consider a table shorn of one of its legs as physically unstable, requiring an immediate 'rational' remedy: fixing on a new leg in place of the missing one. This solution, however, is not necessarily the correct one in all cultural contexts. In a series of IQ tests performed in Israel in the 1970s, a number of pictures were given to five-year-old children, who came from various cultural backgrounds. Each picture had something obviously missing, and the children were asked to draw in the missing object in its right place in the picture. One of the pictures showed a mother serving dinner to a young boy, who was sitting at a table that had only three legs, the fourth one obviously missing. To the astonishment of the researchers, a considerable number of children who came from Jewish religious families drew a 'kippa' – a head-covering cap – on the head of the boy, whose head was uncovered in the original picture. It was apparent that, according to the logic of these children, a boy with an uncovered head simply cannot exist at least as much as a table cannot stand on three legs. Their answer had to be accepted as correct within their specific cultural context, in which the analogy 'things cannot float in the air as a head cannot be uncovered' indeed functions as a *logical* proposition.[33] Therefore not only correlations might be bound to cultural units, but analogies, too. Moreover, both correlations and analogies should be considered as cultural units, and are therefore liable to correlative pairings on their own account.[34]

The second modification I would like to suggest to Hatten's theory regards his description of markedness. Hatten accepts Battistella's differentiation between *privative oppositions* (those that have a marked pole) and *equipollent oppositions* (Hatten, 1994a: 34, quoting Battistella, 1990: 2). Markedness occurs only in privative oppositions, i.e. 'presence of A versus absence of A' (ibid.). However, in equipollent oppositions, i.e. 'A vs B, where A=not B and

B=not A' (ibid.), neither pole will have more specified features, nor will it, naturally, be capable of including or of being included in the other pole. Correlations of such oppositions cannot be coordinated by their markedness, and therefore they must rely on other modes of correlation. Hatten's musical interpretations focus on musical correlations of marked/unmarked opposi- tions, while regarding tropes like metaphor and irony, the interrelations between levels of discourse and texts, as being 'beyond the hierarchies of correlation' (Hatten, 1994a, ch. 7). My point is that *equipollent oppositions*, precisely because of their lack of markedness, are the semantic source of irony, and their structure, therefore, can function as the direct model for the correlations of all modes of ambiguity.

Although applicable to all musical analyses, these observations are par- ticularly relevant in the analyses of musical incongruities. In congruous messages correlative meanings will often be doubled or repeated, conse- quently resulting in informational redundancies that are to a certain extent imperative for successful communication (Moles, 1958: 42; cf. Monelle, 1995: 92). However, in incongruous contexts, i.e. in messages containing ambiguities, redundancies tend to function as additional components of infor- mation, and not as mere reaffirmations of the given information. In such messages, every bit of explicit or implicit information is considered and weighed within a 'general balance' that will eventually either point to a preferred meaning of an ambiguous message, or further balance an unresolvable ambiguity. This means that each component of an incongruous correlation bears more responsibility for providing information than any otherwise parallel component in a congruous one, and therefore each one of the various levels of correlations, as well as their motivations (that are actu- ally implicit components of information), should be regarded as a significant addition to the interpretation of the entire message.

Structures of semantic ambiguity

Ambiguity is a problematic concept. William Empson argues that every ex- pression and, in fact, each and every word may be ambiguous, and have several connotations and shades of meaning:

> A word may have several distinct meanings; several meanings con- nected with one another; several meanings which need one another to complete their meaning; or several meanings which unite together so that the word means one relation or one process. This is a scale which might be followed continuously. 'Ambiguity' itself means an indecision as to what you mean, an intention to mean several things, a probability that one or other or both of two things has been meant, and the fact that a statement has several meanings. (Empson, 1930: 7)

Thus ambiguity occurs when two or more meanings coexist in one discourse, and structures of ambiguity will display the different ways in which various meanings function in the context of one specific discourse. According to Empson's description, ambiguity offers the possibility of either choosing one of those meanings as the preferred one, or accepting several or all of them, disregarding their disagreement or even contradiction with each other.

Structures of semantic ambiguity, then, can promote either one of two different discursive functions.[35] In its first function ambiguity is a modifier, a prolongation device in a deciphering process, at the end of which there will be a resolution. In such cases only one of the coexisting meanings of the discourse, usually a 'concealed' one, should be preferred. Here semantic ambiguity conveys an undesirable but temporary state of confusion, while it actually and in principle aims at a state of elucidation, in which the desirable, unambiguous answer will be revealed. In its second function ambiguity is not a device for the conveyance of some other purport, but is in itself the main topic of the discourse. Here ambiguity is a stagnant condition to which there can be neither solution nor clarification. Although two or more layers of meaning, whether concealed or explicit, coexist here as well, it is impossible (as well as undesirable) to tell which one of them should be preferred.

In its first function ambiguity mainly serves the purpose of expressing statements that cannot be uttered directly, due to political restrictions, social conventions or religious reasons. Ambiguity in this function can also add interest and effectiveness to messages that might otherwise be ignored or inadvertently passed by, for example when it is used in jokes, riddles or advertisement-teasers. Ambiguity in its second function is an autonomous reflection on unresolvable paradoxes. This kind of ambiguity has been particularly prevalent in art, music and literature since the beginning of the nineteenth century.

Naturally, an attempt to find correlations between music and these modes of ambiguity raises many related problems. How can a musical message be 'concealed' or 'explicit'? How can we know, given the fact that music does not have 'true' and 'false' statements, which one of two or more simultaneous musical messages should be preferred? The importance of these questions is fully recognized and even dealt with to some extent within this study. However, I am strongly convinced that the key to the problem lies in the understanding of the ways that a *structure*, rather than individual entities, can find a correlation in music. Thus, rather than focusing on ways 'to get to correct solutions' and decide which element of a certain ambiguity is to be preferred, this study examines the various ways in which musical correlations of semantic ambiguities are created and how they work as artistic expressions.

Correlations between structures of semantic ambiguity

The methodological points raised above are, then, particularly significant when musical correlations with *modes of thought, semantic rhetorical devices* or *abstract cultural units* that are structurally more complex are added to correlations between music and non-musical *entities*. For instance, theories of representation and expression that convey one-to-one equivalencies of meaning fail to explain structural interdependencies between music and units that are composed of incongruous layers of meaning, as happens to be the case with all the modes of semantic ambiguity. Thus they could not render musical counterparts for double-layered modes of communication such as irony, parody, satire and the grotesque. It is particularly here that an application of analytical processes rooted in structural semantics could offer substantial help.[36]

Let us imagine two expressions, each consisting of two contradictory units:

1.   Law always forbids murder. Law in wartime demands murder.
2.   God loves the innocent. God kills the innocent.

According to Robert Hatten, if their components are not correlated, they can only be regarded as analogous to each other (because A:B::X:Y, Hatten, 1994a: 38) (Fig. I.3).

However, the *structures* of both, 'A'+'nonA', can be correlated, and since the incongruity between the building-units in both cases is unresolvable, both convey a contradiction or ambiguity (Fig. I.4).[37]

This semantic structure of ambiguity is itself a cultural unit, that could be positioned on the axis 'ambiguity'/'non-ambiguity'. Looking at it as a *component* of a higher-level opposition, there is no reason to deny that even if none of its (non-ambiguous!) components correlate with each other, we could still speak of the correlations between each of these structures and the cultural unit of 'ambiguity'. The fact that the key correlation is in the structure and not in the content allows an easy application to non-verbal modes, such as music. Consequently, a musical structure that encompasses coexisting incongruities can be regarded, by definition, as a correlative to the cultural unit of ambiguity: for example, Maria's lullaby from the first act of *Wozzeck*, which combines incongruous musical elements of lullaby and military march (see pp.8–9 above). It is therefore not only an expression of musical irony, but also a *musical correlative of ambiguity as a cultural unit*. Ambiguity as a subject is, indeed, one of the main purports of Berg's opera.

Ambiguity has several semantic embodiments in semantic structures, most notably irony. In many senses the cultural unit 'irony' is a correlative of the cultural unit 'ambiguity'; their structures are therefore correlative, too, and

Fig. I.3
Analogy between structures of contradiction

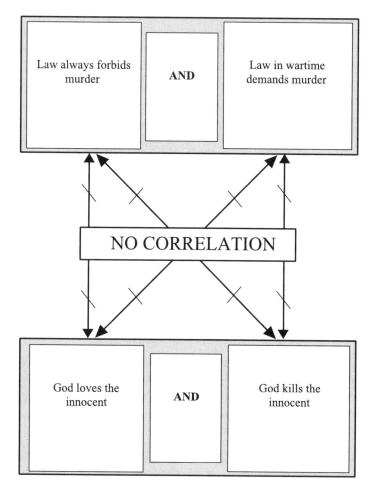

not just analogous to each other. This is a statement of major importance to this study, because it means that there can be musical structures that will *correlate* (rather than be analogous) with irony, parody, satire and the grotesque – all of these being particular cases of the cultural unit of ambiguity. It also means that various constellations of musical elements according to certain musico-semantic axes can provide exact correlations with each one of those particular cases of semantic structures of ambiguity. To prove this point, and to provide examples for its application, is the main aim of this study.

However, a complete dismissal of non-structuralist referential theories and their respective analytical methodologies would not only prejudice a univer-

Fig. I.4
Correlations between structures of contradiction

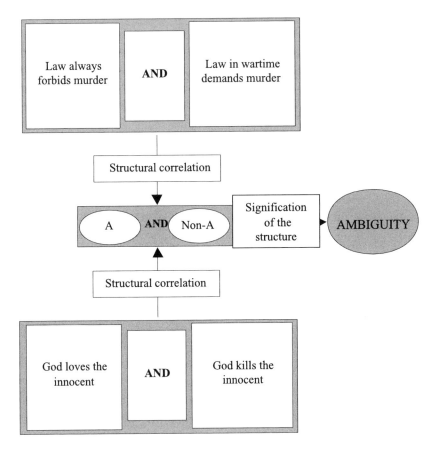

sal phenomenon of musical cognition, but could also undermine the reliabil-
ity of a sheer structuralist analysis. Even the possibility of such an analysis,
devoid of any extra-musical reference, is doubted (Tarasti, 1994: 30). Semiotic analysis is definitely not a one-way process; meaning plays a significant
role from the very beginning. Hatten uses the relationship between units in
order to define better each one of them. After finding the structural oppositions, their poles become entities, or terms, each one of them bearing its
proper meaning (Hatten, 1994a: 34; see quotation above, p.12). A structure
of semantic contradiction cannot be detected unless each one of its building
elements is first identified and semantically understood, since it is only
after such a cognitive process is accomplished that the building elements
can be appreciated as either compatible with or contradictory to each other.
Thus, in order to provide a comprehensive methodology for the analysis of

musical meaning, musical semiotics needs to use both theories of musico-semantic *content* and theories of semantic *structure*, creating a methodological combination that will allow the identification, description and analysis of musico-semantic units of any degree of complexity.

Motivations, correlations of incongruity and musical ambiguity

Hatten's method of musical interpretation through the analysis of correlations between marked poles in privative oppositions posits an all-encompassing, 'single, and more neutral, underlying mechanism' (Hatten, 1987: 412), dis-tilling the rather blurred world of musical semiotics into clearer shapes. Furthermore, the objectivity implied by this phrase separates the nature of the musico-semiotic unit from its genesis, and suggests instead a phenomenological approach of 'here and now'. This approach deals with the correlation as one undivided whole, without differentiating between the various biological, psy-chological and former cultural layers from which it might have evolved and which form an integral part of its present nature. On these theoretical grounds, Hatten presents his methodology for the hermeneutic analysis of musical meaning:

> It is this kind of method that I have called *hermeneutic*: working back and forth between stylistic knowledge and interpretative speculations; grounding those speculations in hypothetical stylistic oppositions; and then moving beyond established correlations of the style to a contextual and thematically strategic accounting of the unique significance of mus-ical events. (Hatten, 1994a: 61)

Hatten's attention is thus focused not on the taxonomy of correlations, but on their function in the act of interpretation as a basis for a further hermeneutic analysis. Hence he chooses to regard *markedness*, which defines particular correlations, as exclusively culture-bound, and claims that the original moti-vation, which 'forms the basis for the association or correlation of musical entity and content':

> may in many cases be irretrievable, since once the association or corre-lation has been made, it may survive in an entity despite change in the code or style. In such cases, the operative motivation defaults to (mere) 'convention'. (Hatten, 1987: 413)

Although its clarity, sharpness and rigour are extremely helpful, some minor modifications will still be needed in order to accommodate Hatten's suggested method to the specific requirements of this study.

A cultural unit, be it a correlation, a metaphor, a person, a nation or a religion, functions within a cultural context, i.e. within history, and therefore it exists within a continuity of development and change. If its past is to be regarded as an inseparable and still functionally active part of its present (as indeed Hatten does regard it – cf. his explanation of the term 'style', 1987: 411), then even if irretrievable, this past still affects, *as an independent factor*, the functioning of the present correlation.[38]

Therefore, a disregard for the differences between various motivations as well as between the various layers of correlations might also impair the very analysis of musical meaning and blur the correlations' actual semiotic functioning. It should be noted that Hatten's apparently unyielding solution does not invalidate the active role of the motivations, nor does it deny their influence on musical interpretation. Hatten himself has acknowledged the importance of what he had formerly called 'lower forms of associations' (ibid.). In his more recent writings on musical gestures, he speaks about their meaning being 'both *immediate and complex*, with iconic and indexical motivation based on human expressive movements and symbolic motivation based on encultured expressive and communicative gestures' (Hatten, 1994b).

The motivation for a specific correlation is an important piece of information, not only because every detail might add something which is either congruent or incongruent with the other details of the message and thus alter its general balance of meaning, but also because it can define the *genus* of a particular correlation, i.e. its level of generality. Furthermore, it also affects the meta-significance of the correlation, which reaches beyond the immediate cultural context of a particular period and/or of a specific style. It is precisely this meta-significance, which is eventually rooted in non-encultured correlations, that grants to a work of art its transcendental meaning and also makes possible its interpretation (indeed, a generalizing one) beyond stylistic boundaries.

For example, the equipollent opposition 'ascending musical line vs descending musical line' can literally be correlated with the equipollent opposition 'ascending vs descending'[39] (and thus also further associated with the 'culturally favoured high vs culturally disfavoured low'). However, since both oppositions are equipollent, the correlation is not a result of coordination of their marked poles but of other semiotic processes: indexicality, iconicity, similarity and projection. None of these processes is based on oppositions, and therefore the 'ascending musical line' does not need to be first opposed to a 'descending' one, but can independently, on the basis of non-encultured motivations such as indexicality and projection, be correlated with 'ascending'. On the next level of interpretation it can be interpreted either metaphorically, imbuing it with encultured ideas about 'high' as 'culturally favoured', or literally, based on the indexical euphoric motion of 'reaching out', therefore leaving its meaning on the literal, correlational level of interpretation.

The incorporation of correlations that are rooted on motivations can enlighten many analyses that would otherwise be cut short at their very first steps. Thus, in order to achieve a full and comprehensive understanding of a musical unit, both privative and equipollent oppositions must be taken into account, and in the latter case, the potential motivations of the opposition's poles, too. For instance, an ascending musical gesture would culturally be correlated with 'aiming', 'aspiring', 'yearning' or 'achieving', mainly depending on contextual – metrical, rhythmical and harmonic – considerations. On a higher level, though, all these musical gestures correlate with the concept of 'reaching out' through a non-encultured, indexical motivation.[40] Thus diverse encultured correlations are associated under one indexically (or iconically) motivated correlation that is related to a larger idea, pointing perhaps to a unifying theme of an artistic whole. Such might be the case, for example, with Beethoven's Piano Sonata op. 2 No. 1, where the first and second movements, as well as the major section of the third movement, all begin with an ascending-leap motion. A purely culturally motivated correlation would point to the first movement as 'minor' in a 'bravura' style, the second movement as an 'aria in a major mode', and the third movement, perhaps, as a 'tarantella in minor' with an intersected 'pastoral in major' section. These semantic correlations seem to be disconnected from each other; therefore, as a next step, the gestural common denominator, i.e. the ascending-leap melodic motion, is added to the data for the analysis. We then obtain the semi-cultural correlations of 'aiming', 'aspiring' and 'yearning' that will be added respectively to the correlations of the first and second themes and the major section of the third movement in the sonata, thus resulting in a 'tragically determined bravura', a 'confidently exposed aspiration' and a 'nostalgic yearning'. Still, these culturally bound correlations do not seem to convey any coherent significance of the work as a whole. However, if we move yet one step higher, to the unmarked, more general opposition of 'reaching out vs complacency', that might be interpreted as the meta-idea of the whole sonata, the whole work then seems to bear its mark, acquiring a new and coherent significance. From this point of view, the exclusively encultured correlation is less complex as well as less capable of conveying complex meanings than correlations that are also based on 'imitative', 'indexical', 'projectional', or 'empathetic' motivations.[41] Thus the motivations for a correlation have a substantial semiotic significance, and a semiotic analysis that overlooked their active impact on the different levels of meaning in a correlation, as well as their contribution to the general meaning of a musical piece, would therefore be incomplete.

I shall try to examine this hypothesis further by analysing the correlations of two more cultural units, both deeply ingrained and highly dependent on cultural and stylistic contexts: the musical topic of the Dance of Death, and the *Der hölle Rache* aria in *The Magic Flute*.

The Dance of Death is a composite cultural unit, and its musical characteristics, one of which is its triple metre, are based on diverse sources – bio-psychological, cultural and stylistic (Sheinberg, forthcoming). However, triple metre has many other associations, some of them connected with other stylistic topics like the minuet or the polonaise, as well as with non-encultured correlatives, such as 'continuity' or 'circularity'. Even when sharing the same metrical component, stylistic topics will tend to exclude each other because of their compound specificity. However, the non-encultured correlatives retain their semiotic potential, and continue to function within the specific topic of the Dance of Death (as well as within the other topics in which the triple meter is a stylistic trait) as independent correlations. Thus any manipulation of the triple meter within a certain topic will also affect the other correlations in which it takes part, i.e. its correlations with 'circularity', 'continuity', etc., and therefore change their own semantic purport. For instance, when Camille Saint-Saëns parodied his own *Danse Macabre* in his *Le Carnaval des Animaux*, he re-wrote it in duple meter, thus caricaturing it by distorting one of its most characteristic traits (Kris and Gombrich, 1952: 189). However, the caricature did not remain exclusively confined to the *topic*, i.e. the Dance of Death, but also invalidated precisely the musical trait that correlates, through a gestural-empathetic motivation, with the 'endless (circular) and uncontrollable (continuous) motion', both of them connected with 'eternity'. Since Death's non-encultured semantic correlatives, 'endlessness' and 'uncontrollability', have also been affected by this manipulation, this musical caricature is not only mocking and degrading of the topic of the *Dance of Death*, but also of *Death itself*, transforming it from an uncontrollable, all-encompassing and eternal power into a mere transitory triviality.[42]

Another case in point is the incongruity, which has puzzled many music critics, in the famous 'vengeance aria' of the Queen of the Night in *The Magic Flute*, between the appalling text and her coquettish coloratura *fioriture*. Its interpretations have ranged from bitter complaints about the sopranos that do not sing the aria 'properly', pointing out, for example, that the Queen's high pitches 'should sound like daggers' (Gammond, 1979: 81), thus denying the existence of any incongruity in the music itself, up to an interpretation of the incongruity as a German satirization of the Italian coloratura style (Batley, 1969: 121). However, a satirization of a cultural unit should: (a) define the satirized unit; (b) choose at least one of its characteristics, in order to ridicule it, and (c) exaggerate this trait to a stylistically abnormal extent. A decodification of such a satire would need a close acquaintance with the Italian coloratura musical style, as well as with Mozart's ideas about it. However, the 'Queen's galactic high notes' (Conrad, 1987: 106) are immediately perceived, regardless of any acquaintance with any stylistic convention, as 'extremely high pitches' that reach far beyond the *normal range of the human voice*. The Queen's voice sounds 'too high' for *any* voice, and its immediate association would not be with the specific style of coloratura singers, but with the non-encultured, non-specific range of the human voice (Sheinberg, 1996a). The sounds are first of all 'inhuman' and 'out of this world'. Peter Conrad is not the only one who needs the imagery of 'outer space' in order to describe this aria, which is perceived as a manifestation not only of 'inhumanity', but also of 'evil', by the correlation of the two oppositions 'human vs inhuman' and 'non-evil vs evil', pointing to the correlation of 'inhuman' with 'evil', as it is manifested in the following description: 'The weird sound of stratospheric coloratura emphasises the mysterious and sinister nature of the Queen' (Branscombe, 1991: 139). However, other correlations with 'evil' are present as well: first and foremost the text itself, but, not less so, the 'tragic' minor mode, sharp melodic contour, clear-cut and short rhythmic patterns, and the ascending-skip gestures (with their 'aiming' and 'reaching' specifiers). The combined correlation of these marked poles with the 'out-of-this-world' too-high pitch marks the final correlation with the complex unit of *Der hölle Rache*, the 'hellish vengeance'.

The satirization mentioned above, even if it holds some truth, could have worked only as a second layer of interpretation, i.e. taking as its starting-point the combined correlation of the projectional too-high pitch, the forte dynamics, staccato articulation and the sharp melodic contour (therefore 'out of this world + violence') with 'hellish'. Only then can the satire function through the incongruity of that correlation with the purely encultured correlation of 'high pitch' with 'Italian coloratura style', letting the audience draw the further implied satirizing correlation of 'coloratura singer' with 'hellish'. The success of this complex correlation is remarkable, if not amazing, since it works in spite of the over-used conventional stylistic and cultural correlation of high pitches with heavenly forces and low pitches with the evil side.

These two analyses demonstrate not only the need for an explicit presentation of the motivations as well as of each and every layer of the correlations, but also that interpreting referential incongruities in music is at least a double (if not a multi-layered) process, thus necessarily following the structure of the specific ambiguity in question. Being based on at least two superimposed structures of correlations, referential incongruities can be discovered only at a second level of interpretation, i.e. only after the first-level correlations have been interpreted and analysed; only then can the meaning be logically deduced from the results of their combination.

Here it is worth introducing yet another point. Many correlations, though seemingly independent, are actually based on implicit equipollent oppositions. Of particular relevance are those based on the opposition 'normative vs non-normative'. All the above interpretations of incongruities were drawn out from the juxtaposition of musical elements, the referential correlatives of which were semantically incongruous. However, there is also another kind of incongruity, in which an implicit or explicit *musical norm* is juxtaposed with an incongruous musical element. In such cases either the element or the norm will be challenged, and its opposition will always be correlated with the implicit opposition 'favoured vs disfavoured', where the norm will be correlated with its 'favoured' pole. This is true even when the norm itself is being challenged, as in the parodies of a musical style.[43] In such cases the norm itself is exaggerated to a point where its explicit manifestation is incongruous with its implicit normativity. The exaggerated norm is subsequently interpreted as a derogatory comment on the norm itself.

The norms can be either stylistic (and thus culturally motivated) or rooted in non-encultured processes like empathetic gestures, projection, imitation, etc. An example of a stylistic norm could be a perfect cadence, which could be challenged either by exaggerating its syntactic impact by too many consecutive repetitions (in which case the norm is implicit, being a stylistic habit), or by a sudden harmonic shift of the tonic chord (in which case the tonal context, i.e. the norm, is explicitly given). Norms that are not motivated by stylistic criteria are reflected in the 'middle', 'comfortable' or 'average' ranges of sound: an average pitch (in the range of the human speaking voice), an average tempo (around 60–80 beats per minute), average dynamics, equally divided rhythms and/or clear rhythmic patterns, etc. These kinds of musical norms include all that we tend to feel comfortable with, without special effort either to perceive or to avoid in order to achieve a sense of comfort and balance. A feeling of 'incongruity' will therefore be correlated with all sounds that are outside this scope of 'comfortable and average sound'. Indeed, it is very hard to affirm the presence of an incongruity solely on such grounds. However, even if we are fully aware of their potential inaccuracy, we should not ignore these incongruities in the final balance of the various musical elements in a musical message, and their purport must be considered in the general interpretation of a semiotic analysis.

An example of a projectional implicit norm could be 'a balanced arch-shaped melodic line' (which is a musical projection of the biologically motivated voice-inflection in a normal spoken phrase) that is implicitly opposed to ascending, descending or static melodic lines. Another implicit norm affects the aria of the Queen of the Night, in which the incongruity results from the challenging of the normal singing pitch-range. One example of an explicit projectional norm is to be found in the first movement of Shostakovich's Violin Sonata, where the violin alternates between its lower pitches, which are parallel with the normal speaking-voice pitch-range, and its highest register, in the c'''' to e'''' range. Since these ranges are used quite separately and do not seem melodically (or otherwise) to connect with each other, their incongruity is apparent not only in the pitch-level. The two extremely high-pitch sections sound 'out of context', i.e. incongruous with the pitch-norm presented in other sections of the movement. A similar incongruity occurs at the end of the second movement, but then the incongruity is a result of simultaneous juxtaposition: the piano conveys the 'normative pitch-range' while the violin is, again, at its highest, abnormal pitch-range.[44]

There is a general tendency to correlate the opposition 'normative vs non-normative' (regardless of whether the norm is culturally motivated or not) with the opposition between 'culturally favoured vs culturally disfavoured' moral and ethical values.

The centrality of value-judgement in the interpretation of satirical modes of incongruity makes this correlation particularly significant in this study of musical ambiguities.[45] For if we accept any sound-range, musical style or musical topic as normative, then oppositions between musical elements that will be congruous with these norms, and elements that will be incongruous with them, will tend correspondingly to correlate with the opposition between culturally favoured and culturally disfavoured ethical and moral values.

This phenomenon has great implications for music criticism. On one hand it has led to critical invectives on music that systematically related culturally disfavoured musical style with culturally disfavoured ethical attitudes and even culturally disfavoured moral values (Slonimsky, 1953); on the other hand, it serves as a device for satires and value-judgements presented by the music itself. For instance, a march is a musical topic that correlates with the military. If some elements of this topic are presented in a way that is incongruous with its stylistic norms, e.g. by their exaggeration, then not only the musical topic of the march will be satirized, but the whole *ethics* correlated with the military (i.e. nationalism, order, obedience, as well as pomp, callousness and showing off) will be highlighted in a derogatory light. Since they are based on the insertion of incongruous elements in musical topics (or norms), even culturally valued traits like 'love' or 'love for your country' can be satirized within a musical work if they are correlated with the particular topic or the specific musical norm that is exaggerated.

An application of Hatten's theory of correlations and interpretations to a semiotic study of musical incongruities would therefore require two main modifications. First, an analysis of musical incongruities, unlike an analysis of congruous musical units, will require a historical analysis of each correlation, i.e. an explicit differentiation between its various layers of meaning, including its motivations. Second, the incongruities will be classified into two main groups: those which exist between referential correlatives of musical elements, and those between a musical element and an existing musical norm, thus implicitly correlated with the particular opposition 'favoured vs disfavoured', with its inevitably attached value-judgement.

All the above kinds of incongruities can furnish either solvable or unresolvable ambiguities. The result depends on the final balance between the various correlations that function in each particular case. The simpler cases usually end up with a satirical message, which can range from a simple caricaturing burlesque to a conveyance of the hopeless human situation, pointing to 'human existential dread'. The more complex, multi-layered correlations will tend to stimulate interpretations of general, 'romantic' irony: a situation in which incongruities will not be solved, but just presented as a phenomenon to an allegedly objective, but actually self-reflexive, spectator. This kind of pluri-vocal discourse develops through self-reflexivity, and is often correlated with the self-awareness of human existence.

The classification of the elements that function in correlations of incongruities is, therefore, double-edged, and depends on the types of correlations on the one hand, and on the type of motivations on the other. Thus the elements can be correlated either through a direct referential relation (for example, a trill for 'birdsong', a fanfare for 'the military' or a minuet for 'nobility' or a high pitch for 'heaven'), or positioned along a favoured/disfavoured normative axis. Such a normative axis is active, for example, when a very quick pace is judged as being *exceedingly* so, and subsequently correlated with the 'disfavoured'. In such a case, where the implicit norm is that 'a steady pace is favoured', a quick pace will be correlated with the ridiculous (as happens in many caricature-arias in comic operas) or with the evil (for example in tarantellas).[46] The other classification of elements that function in correlations of incongruities relates to the types of motivations that led to their present semiotic function. Although in reality most cases are more complex, they can be roughly classified into those that have encultured roots (such as the use of the piccolo for the musical topic of 'a military march') and those whose main roots are non-encultured (like the use of a very quick pace to enhance a *biological* feeling of discomfort, which is subsequently correlated with 'evil'). As can be seen even from the above simple examples, the same correlation can result from both types of classifications. Thus 'an exceedingly quick pace' is correlated with 'evil' both because it is positioned on the 'disfavoured' pole of a cultural axis *and* as a result of the biological projection, in which the normal pulse (e.g. 80 beats per minute), when projected on to the musical unit, cannot synchronize with it.[47] The fact that any of the correlations can be encultured does not exclude their being rooted in a non-encultured motivation. Non-encultured motivations can be related to such projections, often related to biological or psychological norms, or to gestures (for example, in an iconic correlation between a bodily gesture and a melodic line).

Concurrently, each element should also be examined according to its function as a separate entity that either correlates independently, as a pole in an equipollent opposition, or as a pole in a privative opposition, which provides markedness values. Elements from different classifications can be juxtaposed in one musical unit, creating one or more incongruities. Since the number of juxtapositions in a musical message is not limited, some correlations may be congruent with each other, while another group of correlations might display incongruity. For example, a referent of a gesture-motivated correlative musical element can be incongruous with the referent of a topic. For instance, in Berlioz's *Symphonie fantastique* the gestural referent of 'hopping' was juxtaposed with the quotation of the 'Dies irae' to form the grotesque incongruity of the witches' Sabbath. In time, this whole unit became almost a topical referent. The correlation 'major and non-tragic' can be incongruently juxtaposed with 'minor and tragic', with the topic of 'funeral march' and/or with the indexical gesture of 'descending melodic line and sad'. A semiotic analysis of correlation is very often a delicate enterprise, and its process a complicated one, as is the final interpretation of the musical ambiguity. However, the effort is always worth it, because when the interpretation is accurately performed the results often point to new, unexpected and revealing aspects of even the most familiar, apparently 'banal' musical works.

Irony, satire, parody and the grotesque as modes of semantic ambiguity

Incongruities seem to be closely related to humour and to laughter (Clark, 1970 and 1987). Since ambiguities result from incongruities between the components of a cultural unit, it is quite often that literary and artistic modes of ambiguity are classified as comic. Indeed, it is apparent that a considerable measure of the comic effect of satire, parody, irony and the grotesque stems from that instant of bafflement in front of an incongruity. If this incongruity is solved, the result is satirical and its relation to the comic quite apparent. However, even when the incongruity cannot be solved, the resulting ambiguity will still tend to be associated with the humorous, ranging from the amused smile of puzzlement in front of an unresolvable riddle, like Zeno's Achilles, who will never overtake the tortoise, to the despairing laughter that 'originates on the comic and caricatural fringe of the grotesque' in an 'estranged world', suddenly aware of the absurdity of existence in a 'world which ceases to be reliable' (Kayser, 1957: 184–186).

This study examines musical correlations of semantic modes of ambiguity and therefore, to a certain extent, also deals with the comic in music. Although I speak here of musical irony, musical satire, musical parody and the musical grotesque mainly as correlatives of semantic modes of ambiguity, their association with the musically comic should also be borne in mind. The literary, semantic and musical aspects of each one of these modes will be thoroughly explored in the following chapters. However, a short overview and a general inquiry into their mutual interrelationship could be useful at this stage, particularly in order to clarify their choice as embodiments of semantic ambiguity.

Irony, parody, satire and the grotesque all use two or more layers of meaning, and therefore they can all be regarded as manifestations of semantic ambiguity. Irony in its broadest sense, both as a tool for satirical purport and as an expression of the unresolvable, could be regarded as a structural prototype for all other modes of ambiguity (Muecke, 1969 and

1970; Booth, 1974). Its functions are either to provide a temporary state of confusion that needs a solution or to present an unresolvable situation as its main purport.[48]

Satire is a manifestation of irony in its first function: it presents two layers of meaning, of which the concealed one, that should eventually be preferred, can be detected by a distortion of the other, usually by either exaggeration or understatement.[49]

Embodied in a specific case, where the horrifying and the ludicrous are interwoven into one unit of unresolvable contradiction, the grotesque displays irony mainly in its second function.[50] However, sometimes descriptions of the grotesque are also used to satirize, i.e. to express irony in its first function. In such cases the whole grotesque purport, made up of its two layers of meaning, will function as one secondary layer in a more comprehensive structure, in which the concealed message will be its satire (Clark, 1991: 21). Two famous examples are the ball scenes, one in Gogol's play *The Government Inspector* and the other in his novel *Dead Souls*.

Parody is characterized by its structure more than by its content. In all cases the two layers of meaning in parody will be structural, one of them being an item that was ripped out of its original context and the other a new context (Hutcheon, 1985: 12). Usually parody will contain some distortion of the alluded style, mostly by its exaggeration. Since by definition parody's two layers of meaning need not necessarily be contradictory in their semantic purport, it is the most versatile of the four modes. It can satirize, in which case one of the layers is exaggerated or presented in a derogatory light; it can pay a tribute, in which case it uses a contextualized, yet undistorted quotation; and it can point to an unresolvable contradiction, if neither (or both) layer(s) is(are) distorted.

All modes of ambiguity rely on an active reader, and their perception and comprehension depend on the apprehension of their double-layered structure and on its successful interpretation. Their purport is always inexplicit, although the degree of concealment varies greatly between styles and periods and is highly dependent on their purpose.

Being based on logic, the structure of ambiguity is universal. Its various manifestations, however, are culture-bound. Therefore, ambiguities can be regarded as *a set of cultural units that share the same structure*. The following study offers a method for identifying and interpreting musical ambiguities and correlating them with semantic ambiguities. The method is applied to selected works of Dmitri Shostakovich. A further study is then performed in order to reach a yet deeper level of musico-semantic interpretation. On this level the specific cultural unit of 'the grotesque in Russian culture', which is, in many respects, a culmination of the more general mode of ambiguity that is 'the Grotesque', is examined. Musical works and movements by Shostakovich that were apprehended by music critics, musicologists and performing artists as 'grotesque' are then analysed and viewed within their Russian contemporary cultural context. The final result, I hope, will lead to a better understanding of semiotic music criticism and analysis.

PART II
IRONY

CHAPTER ONE

The concept of irony: philosophical background

From its very beginning as an independent concept in the Platonic writings and throughout history, irony was doubly conceived, either as a rhetorical device for the communication of definitive meanings or as an independent phenomenon, a mode of perceiving reality, that exists in and of itself. Most of the theoretical treatises on the concept of irony have their roots in the nineteenth century, particularly in the philosophical writings of Friedrich Schlegel (1772–1829) and Søren Kierkegaard (1813–55). Their ideas, however, developed from quite different vantage points, neither of them purely philosophical: while Schlegel was a literary critic, Kierkegaard primarily considered himself a theologian. In a sense, the various meanings that contemporary thought ascribes to irony emerge from this basic dichotomy that seems to lie at the core of irony's immanent duality: its simultaneous existence as a means and as an end.

The first methodological analysis of irony, Søren Kierkegaard's *The Concept of Irony*, explicitly posed the problem of irony's double nature. He pointed to the existence of 'duplexities' in the Platonic writings, and arrived at the conclusion that Plato had actually presented two different concepts of irony, each of which was tightly connected with a corresponding kind of dialectic (Kierkegaard, [1841] 1989: 40, 121ff.). This form of presentation is of major importance to the understanding of Kierkegaard's two concepts of irony, since it connects irony to the alienation stage of the dialectic process (i.e. the conceptual negation of the original idea). As he does with irony, so also Kierkegaard differentiates between alienation as a device and alienation as an end in itself. The first kind of alienation is the necessary stage of antithesis in a dialectical process which strives to a synthesis, i.e. to a positive solution; the second kind is the creation of an antithesis for its own sake, as avowal of negation *qua* negation, inquiry *qua* inquiry, presenting them as an inherent phenomenon of the human mind. Although Kierkegaard regards both phenomena as manifestations of irony, he is nevertheless conscious of the differences between them; in connecting these two kinds of dialectical process with the two corresponding kinds of irony, he names them *irony as stimulus* and *irony as terminus* (ibid.: 121).

Finite irony: irony as stimulus

The first kind of irony is primarily used to satirize. Bearing a value system, it is teleological, and aims at a 'true' meaning that lies somewhere behind the ostensible meaning of an utterance. Its presupposition is that both the recipient of the message and its sender share the same value systems and communication codes, thus providing the means for the reconstruction of the covert, 'real' message that is to be preferred. It is this kind of irony that is widely described and analysed in textbooks of rhetorics and in literary criticism, from Aristotle's *Rhetorica* and Quintilian's *Institutio Oratoria* to the contemporary *The Compass of Irony* by D.C. Muecke (1969) and *A Rhetoric of Irony* by Wayne Booth (1974). In spite of the vast amount of literature covered and the large span of time between the classical and modern writings, there are no major differences between the theories that are presented. They all speak about 'saying one thing while meaning another', and all stress the aesthetic importance of a correct interpretation of the message by discovering the 'intended' or 'true' meaning behind the ostensible one. Quintilian, for example, stresses the importance of dissimulation and ambiguity in jests and humour, which he defines as irony:

> In eo vero genere, quo contraria ostenduntur, ironia est; illusionem vocant. Quae aut pronuntiatione intelligitur aut persona aut rei natura; nam, si qua earum verbis dissentit, apparet diversam esse orationi voluntatem. (Quintilian, Book VIII, 6, 54)

> On the other hand, that class of allegory in which the meaning is contrary to that suggested by the words, involves an element of irony, or, as our rhetoricians call it, *illusion*. This is made evident to the understanding either by the delivery, the character of the speaker or the nature of the subject. For if any of these three is out of keeping with the words, it at once becomes clear that the intention of the speaker is other than what he actually says. (Quintilian, 1922: 333)

A very similar purport is offered by Douglas Muecke. According to him, the two levels of meaning and the contradictory relation between them are the structural traits of irony (Muecke, 1969: 14ff.). Wayne Booth speaks about the necessity of dissimulation, using other terms than Quintilian, but still bearing the same general idea, saying that 'recently the most popular metaphor has been that of seeing behind a mask or a "persona". In this view the reader is thought of as unmasking an *eiron*, or detecting behind a "mask-character" or persona the lineaments of the true speaker' (Booth, 1974: 33).

One of the major traits of irony is its satirical function. In fact, Aristotle presents mockery as the main purport of irony, although he explains the reason for his evaluation of irony as being more 'gentlemanly' than buffoonery: 'εστι δ η ειρωνεια της βωμολοχιας ελευθεριωτερον. ο μεν γαρ αυτου ενεκα ποιει το γελοιον, ο δε βωμολοχος ετερου' (Αριστοτελους.

Τεχνη Ρητορικη. Book III, ξῶιιι, 1419β, 8. See also Aristotle, 1886: 301).[1] A comparison between various translations of this phrase is revealing. According to R.C. Jebb, the phrase argues for irony's superiority over buffoonery because 'the ironical man jokes on his own account, the buffoon on some one else's' (Aristotle, 1909: 197); J.E.C. Weldon understands that 'the former [irony] is used simply for its own sake and the later [buffoonery] for some ulterior object' (Aristotle, 1886: 301). W.R. Roberts translates it as 'the ironical man jokes to amuse himself, the buffoon to amuse other people' (Aristotle, 1924).[2] Only the last translation does not necessarily include a satirical purport in the ironical message, either in relation to the ironist or the ironized subject; but even in that case the context shows that here irony should be interpreted as a device for a satirical goal.

Irony's satirical function is always combined with its dissimulatory characteristics. Quintilian gives a series of famous satirical quotations that use such devices as 'simulation and dissimulation', 'ambiguity', 'insinuation', 'distortion', 'irony' and 'pretence', all of which clearly locate irony within a genre of jests that mainly use double meaning, emphasizing their dissimulatory character (Quintilian, Book VI, 3, 85–92; 1922: vol. II: 485–489). Wayne Booth describes at length the structure of the ironic message, in which a pretence of innocence and ignorance, that eventually puts to shame the object of irony, plays an imperative role, whilst Muecke stresses the existence of a presupposed 'victim' of the ironic message, who is (or is assumed to be, at least until the message is correctly interpreted) unaware of the hidden meaning (Booth, 1974: 87; Muecke, 1969: 20).

Thus *irony as stimulus* dissimulates one meaning by openly stating another in order to ridicule and debase. It is a rhetorical device that strives to reach a goal that by definition will include a value-judgement – either ethical or aesthetic. However, although Muecke and Booth take great pains to classify kinds of ironies and to describe the communication techniques needed for their creation and apprehension, they still cannot ignore other approaches to the concept of irony, namely those of Schlegel and Kierkegaard. Thus both Muecke and Booth acknowledge the existence of a second kind of irony, and even try to describe it, albeit not with the same amount of success they have achieved with the first kind.

Infinite irony: irony as terminus

The second kind of irony is the embodiment of the dialectical principle of negation. Following Hegel (1770–1831), Kierkegaard called this phenomenon *irony*, also using Hegel's definition of 'infinite absolute negativity' (Kierkegaard, [1841] 1989: 475). It was Hegel who regarded irony as the objectification of the negation stage (i.e. antithesis) of the dialectical process.

Stressing negation's function as just one stage (albeit a necessary one) of a wider process, Hegel wholeheartedly opposed and rejected the transformation of a device into an end in itself, and saw in irony a distortion of his own teleological idea of the dialectical process. Referring to Karl Solger's (1780–1819) ideas about the dialectical process in art, in which irony as 'the supreme principle of art' is coupled with 'eros', the artistic enthusiasm, Hegel writes:

> Hier kam er [Solger] auf das dialektische Moment der Idee, aus den Kunst, den ich 'unendliche absolut Negativität' nenne, auf die Tätigkeit der Idee, sich als das Unendliche und Allgemeine zu negiren zur Endlichkeit und Besonderheit, und diese ebenso sehr wieder aufzuheben, und somit das Allgemeine und Unendliche im Endlichen und Besondern wieder herzustellen. An dieser Negativität hielt Solger fest, und allerdings ist sie ein Moment in der speculativen Idee, doch als diese blosse dialektische Unruhe und Auflösung des Unendlichen wie des Endlichen gefasst, auch nur ein Moment, nicht aber, wie Solger es will, die ganze Idee. (Hegel, 1842: 87)

> In this process he [Solger] came to the dialectical moment of the Idea, to the point which I call 'infinite absolute negativity', to the activity of the Idea in so negating itself as infinite and universal as to become finitude and particularity, and in nevertheless cancelling this negation in turn and so re-establishing the universal and infinite in the finite and particular. To this negativity Solger firmly clung, and of course it is *one element* in the speculative Idea, yet interpreted as this purely dialectical unrest and dissolution of both infinite and finite, only *one element*, and not, as Solger will have it, the *whole* Idea. (Hegel, 1975: 68–69)

Consequently Hegel's attitude to irony in general is one of suspicion and rejection. However, it is important to stress that his rejection has nothing to do with the aesthetic, but relies on ethical grounds:

> So liegt allerdings in der Ironie jene absolute Negativität, in welcher sich das Subjekt im Vernichten der Bestimmtheiten und Einseitlichen auf sich selbst bezieht, indem aber das Vernichten, wie schon oben bei Betrachtung dieses Princips angedeutet wurde, nicht nur wie in der Komik das an sich selbst Richtige, das sich in seiner Hohlheit manifestirt, sondern gleichmässig auch an sich Vortressliche und Gediegene trifft, so behält die Ironie als diese allseitige Vernichtigungskunst wie jene Sehnsüchtigkeit, im Vergleich mit dem wahren Ideal, zugleich die Seite der innern unkünsterlichen Haltungslosigkeit. (Hegel, 1842: 201)

> True, irony implies the absolute negativity in which the subject is related to himself in the annihilation of everything specific and one-sided; but since this annihilation … affects not only, as in comedy, what is inherently null which manifests itself in its hollowness, but equally everything inherently excellent and solid, it follows that irony as this art of annihilating everything everywhere … acquires, at the same time, in comparison with the true Ideal, the aspect of inner inartistic lack of restraint. (Hegel, 1975: 160)

If overcoming alienation achieves self-affirmation and the enhancement of life potential, then irony, that is a manifestation of alienation, is also the embodiment of negation as an independent phenomenon, and consequently an expression of self-annihilation. Concurrently, it also serves as a metaphor for mankind's inherent inability to know, while yet, ironically, of its obsessive striving for knowledge (Kierkegaard, [1841] 1989: 475).

This kind of irony appears in nineteenth-century writings as the basic human incapability to understand essences that are hidden by appearances. Moreover, it represents the human inability to communicate, that is, to emit a message as well as to comprehend it. Friedrich Schlegel devoted an entire article to this aspect of irony, where, in answer to complaints made by his readers, he relates the alleged incomprehensibility of his writings to the major role that irony plays in them (Schlegel, [1799] 1967: 363–372). In his characteristic ironic style he describes the impossibility of genuine communication in a system that necessarily and by definition (since everything contains in itself its own negation) must make use of ambiguous signs. After explaining incomprehensibility, which he sees as an immanent trait of human communication, he puts into doubt the very value attached to communication: 'Aber ist denn die Unverständlichkeit etwas so durchaus Verwerfliches und Schlechtes? – Mich dünkt das Heil der Familien und der Nationen beruhet auf ihr' (ibid.: 370; 'But is incomprehensibility really something so unmitigatedly contemptible and evil? Methinks the salvation of families and nations rests upon it' [Schlegel, 1971a: 268]).

An opposite view is presented by René Schaerer, who points to the final conclusions of Plato's *Cratylus* and *Phaedrus*, in which the question of verbal communication is raised. According to these dialogues, genuine communication is actually impossible, since the intended meaning of the speaker will never be exactly the meaning perceived by his listener; nor is there any possible way of verifying if this is the case. The only mode of communication in which a full understanding can be achieved is therefore the one that explicitly poses the inherent ambiguity of any message: irony. Irony is thus perceived by Schaerer as the only means to communication:

> Si elle [l'ironie] trouve sa principale expression dans le langage, c'est que celui-ci constitue l'instrument par excellence des rapports sociaux ... Elle apparaît partout où deux moi s'épient et s'affrontent. Si ces moi pouvaient communiquer entre eux de façon parfaite ... l'ironie n'aurait aucune raison d'être ... En d'autres termes, chaque individu apparaît comme un monde partiellement clos, qui ne s'ouvre sur autrui qu'en trahissant l'essentiel de lui-même. Nous sommes trop conscients de cette insuffisance pour ne pas tenter d'y remédier. Ainsi s'explique l'ironie. (Schaerer, 1941: 183)

> If [irony] finds its main expression in language, it is due to its being in itself the most appropriate tool for social interchange ... It appears whenever two Is are looking and confronting each other. If these Is were able to perfectly communicate among themselves ... irony would have

no reason to exist ... In other words, each individual appears to be a
partially enclosed world, that can only open up to another by betraying
his own essence. We are too aware of this insufficiency to try to repair it.
That is how irony can be explained.

Schaerer deals with irony almost exclusively in relation to questions of
communication and its ethical concerns. Similar aspects of irony, although
from a more theological vantage-point, are dealt with by Kierkegaard, who
perceives irony as a metaphor for the primeval chaos and as a proof of the
existing moral chaos (Kierkegaard, [1841] 1989: 214). The infinity of irony
as well as the danger of ethical anarchy, when aesthetics and ethics are
intermixed into an amalgam of subjective values, was judged by Kierkegaard
from his own theological point of view as a 'negative freedom' (ibid.: 232–
235). Such a freedom nullifies the boundaries between good and evil, truth
and untruth, in what he apprehended as a chaotic universe, devoid of any
immanent laws. In a world in which 'the reality of ethics has become shaky',
he refers to the Socratic solution of 'obeying the laws' as avoiding the real
problem: 'Here the subject shows itself to be the deciding factor, as that
which arbitrarily determines itself within itself. But the limiting of the universal that takes place thereby is one that the subject himself arbitrarily posits
at every moment'(ibid.: 234).

However, Kierkegaard also asserts that 'moral categories are too concrete
for irony', and deals with what can easily be interpreted as its aesthetic traits.
In a rather Kantian approach, he refers to the aesthetic quality of irony that
'denotes the subjective pleasure as the subject frees himself by means of
irony from the restraints in which the continuity of life's conditions holds
him', and also points to the aesthetic 'independence of all interest' (Kant,
1911: 42): 'Irony ... has no purpose; its purpose is immanent in itself and is a
metaphysical purpose. The purpose is nothing other than irony itself'
(Kierkegaard, [1841] 1989: 256).

In his article 'On Incomprehensibility', Friedrich Schlegel described this
very problem of inescapable subjectivity, and combined ethical and aesthetic
values in a way that Gary Handwerk calls 'a non-Hegelian dialectic of
intersubjectivity' (Handwerk, 1985: 18). Schlegel's approach to irony thus
touches the aesthetic value that he assigns to ambiguity (and consequently to
irony), a value that actually lies at the basis of Romantic aesthetics. He
simultaneously presents irony as an aesthetic goal and as a device, although
here not a device to satirize but to achieve ironic ambiguity, in itself regarded
as an aesthetic goal and value. 'Eine klassische Schrift muss nie ganz
verstanden werden können. Aber die welche gebildet sind und sich bilden,
müssen immer mehr daraus lernen wollen' (Schlegel, [1799] 1967: 371; 'A
classical text must never be entirely comprehensible. But those who are
cultivated and who cultivate themselves must always want to learn more from
it' [Schlegel, 1971a: 269]).

As a purely aesthetic factor, irony can be seen merely as a kind of game, a free play of the creative imagination. Such a view is presented by Vladimir Jankélévitch, who sees the correlation of the first kind of irony with satirical humour, and of the second kind of irony with the free play of the mind:

> Cette ironie, en vérité, n'est pas un humour au sens de Swift, de Sterne et de Voltaire, cette ironie est une ivresse de la subjectivité transcendentale … Du sujet transcendental à la volonté créatrice l'intervalle est le même que de la liberté à la licence, c'est-à-dire du vouloir déterminé par le devoir au vouloir hyperbolique, arbitraire et immoral … [l'ironie romantique] est, chez Frédéric Schlegel, «Verstand», liberté du sujet surplombant l'objet; chez Novalis, elle est «Gemüt», liberté magique et poétique transfigurant le monde, liberté romanesque romantisant la nature; l'univers est un conte de la sublime fantaisie. L'ironie est pouvoir de jouer, de voler dans les airs, de jongler avec le contenus soit pour les nier, soit pour le recréer. (Jankélévitch, 1964: 17)

> This irony, in fact, is not humour in the sense of Swift, Sterne or Voltaire; this irony is an intoxication of transcendental subjectivity … The distance between the transcendental subject and the creative will is the same as the distance between freedom and licentiousness, that is from the will determined by duty to the hyperbolic will, which is arbitrary and immoral … [romantic irony] is, according to Friedrich Schlegel, 'Verstand', the freedom of the subject outweighing the object; according to Novalis, it is 'Gemüt', a magical and poetic freedom that transfigures the world, a romantic freedom that romanticises nature; the universe is a tale told by the sublime fantasy. Irony is the power of playing, of flying in the air, to juggle with the content either to negate it, or to recreate it.

Therefore, what could be perceived by one system of values as a negative perennial process of self-annihilation can be perceived by another as a positive and infinite self-renewal based on endless dialogue with an art work. It is this approach in particular that puts irony and other modes of ambiguous expression in the focus of interest of modern art and places them in a high position in the hierarchy of modern aesthetics.

The major importance Schlegel granted to the interrelation, and sometimes even interdependency, of ethics and aesthetics, is also made clear in one of his fragments, where he asserts that 'ethics [is] the real focal point of art'.[3] Kierkegaard, however, refuses to mix the two, and prefers to see the ironist as beyond ethics: 'It cannot really be said that the ironist places himself outside and above morality and ethics, but he lives far too abstractly, far too metaphysically and esthetically to reach the concretion of the moral and the ethical' (Kierkegaard, [1841] 1989: 283).

This is also the focal point of the clash between the so-called purely aesthetic approaches and those that see themselves as part of a more general ethical system of values, like Kierkegaard's point of view or Marxist aesthetics. It should be remembered, however, that even the allegedly 'purely aesthetic' theories still have their own system of ethical values, although they might be unclearly or poetically expressed. A conscious preference for aesthetics over ethics is an ethical decision in itself, and no system that consciously places aesthetic values above ethical ones should be regarded as free of values, but as bearing full moral responsibility for a value system's hierarchy: no human expression is totally devoid of an ethical background, and prioritizing free or even licentious artistic creation over ethics, or regarding it as a part of ethics, certainly also has moral implications that cannot be ignored.

Irony as terminus is therefore related to ethical as well as aesthetic questions, all dealing with the endless process of nullification that brings the ironist (and the ironized) to the edge of an infinite void of consciousness, often resulting in existential dizziness and feelings of vertigo. The most characteristic expressions of this kind of irony can be found in the romantic literature of Friedrich Schlegel, E.T.A. Hoffmann (1776–1822), Jean-Paul Richter (1763–1825), Ludwig Tieck (1773–1853) and Charles Baudelaire (1821–67). In most of these writings, 'irony's vertigo' is combined with a characteristic human expression of powerless puzzlement: laughter.

Infinite irony and the comic

The absurdity that lies in the concept of a life of self-annihilation immediately relates irony to the comic. Kierkegaard noticed this point, but in the same way that he described the two kinds of irony with the same term, so he did with the comic:

> If it is assumed, therefore, that Socrates' whole activity was ironizing, it is also apparent that in wanting to interpret him in the comic vein Aristophanes proceeded quite correctly, for as soon as irony is related to a conclusion, it manifests itself as comic, even though in another sense it frees the individual from the comic. Neither is the dialectic, of which there are many examples, a genuine philosophical dialectic; it is not the kind of dialectic described earlier as characteristic of Plato but is an entirely negative dialectic. Now, if Socrates had had that Platonic subjective dialectic, it would certainly have been fallacious and it would not have been comic, even though sufficiently funny ... (Kierkegaard, [1841] 1989: 145)

It is obvious that Kierkegaard actually speaks here of two – satirical and existential – kinds of the comic, as is made clear by his differentiation between the two kinds of dialectics (which earlier he correspondingly related to two kinds of irony). Irony, then, can 'manifest itself as comic', and at the very same instant also 'free the individual from the comic'. This can only happen if we think of two kinds of irony, which can result in either a 'manifestation of the comic' or 'freedom from the comic'. The kind of irony that is related to a conclusion, namely the satirical kind, is related to the 'Platonic subjective dialectics', which Kierkegaard emphatically distinguishes from the Socratic. Plato's dialectics, according to Kierkegaard, is teleological and therefore clearly aims at the 'right' answers, systematically rejecting 'wrong' ones. These are regarded as 'funny', thus following the Aristotelian thought, according to which comedy is:

> an imitation of men worse than the average, not indeed as regards any and every sort of vice, but only as regards the Ridiculous, which is a species of the Ugly. The Ridiculous may be defined as a mistake or deformity which produces no pain or harm to others; the comic mask, for example, which induces laughter, is something ugly and distorted, but gives rise to no pain. (Aristotle, 1963: 10–11)

However, it seems that other types of 'wrong answers', also evoking satirical irony, are nevertheless named by Kierkegaard as 'comic' rather than 'funny', apparently because his differentiation between the 'funny' and the 'comic' resides not only in the kind of irony that is used but also in the level of abstraction of the ironized subject. The Socratic irony which, according to Kierkegaard, Aristophanes 'proceeded quite correctly' in using in his play *Clouds*, is the one that confronts us with the absurdity of irony's infinite negation. The irony is still satirical, but here the comedy does not rely on the 'rightness' or 'wrongness' of the conclusion itself, but rather on the absurdity of the very effort of trying to find any conclusion at all in a situation that by definition is an endless process of contradictory propositions. This is definitely a different level of the comic, since it is not the object (i.e. the 'answer') that is satirized, but the subject's entire attitude to reality. The pejoritized target is then the human will and effort to find an answer at all, and the illusory pretension that such an answer can exist at all. It should be stressed, though, that this concept of the comic is still Aristotelian, since it lies within the general framework of a satirical approach.

This meeting point of ethics and aesthetics in irony is closely connected to the process of alienation. At this point alienation is required, either as a dialectic negation which initiates the negative process of infinite irony, as a 'parabasis' with which all critical processes begin, or as a personal Baudelairean act of *dédoublement*, the ability to see himself from the outside, that eventually leads to philosophical laughter:

> Il est dans l'homme la conséquence de l'idée de sa propre supériorité; et, en effet, comme le rire est essentiellement humain, il est essentiellement contradictoire, c'est-à-dire qu'il est à la fois signe d'une grandeur infinie et d'une misère infinie, misère infinie relativement à l'Être absolu dont il possède la conception, grandeur infinie relativement aux animaux. C'est du choc perpétuel de ces deux infinis que se dégage le rire. Le comique, le puissance du rire est dans le rieur et nullement dans l'objet du rire. Ce n'est point l'homme qui tombe qui rit de sa propre chute, à moins qu'il ne soit un philosophe, un homme qui ait acquis, par habitude, la force de se dédoubler rapidement et d'assister comme spectateur désintéressé aux phénomènes de son moi. (Baudelaire, [1852] 1965: 219)

The idea of his own superiority is inherent in Man; and, as a matter of
fact, as much as laughter is essentially human, so it is essentially contradictory, that is to say, it is simultaneously a sign of infinite grandeur and
of infinite misery, an infinite misery relative to the absolute Being that
has the power of conception, an infinite grandeur relative to animals. It
is from this perennial clash between these two infinites that laughter is
released. The comic, the potential to laugh, is in the laughter and never
in the object of laughter. It is not the man who falls that laughs at his
own downfall, unless he is a philosopher, a man that has acquired, by
habit, the power to quickly 'double himself' and participate as a disin-
terested spectator in the phenomena of his own I.

Schaerer develops this notion of the 'doubled' laughing philosopher even
further, showing how the mere recognition of potential inferiority, which is
expressed by laughter, is actually a transformation to a recognition of superiority that is rooted in the very acknowledgement of powerlessness; the superior
position is not powerfulness or powerlessness, but the ability to recognize
them and the courage to admit the human immanent powerlessness (Schaerer,
1941: 188–189).

This version of the comic, then, lies in the infinite embarrassment, the
infinite human helplessness in its confrontation with irony's existential void.
This last 'entirely negative', infinite comedy of the absurd is the human
acknowledgement of its own vulnerability and helplessness. This is the kind
of comic that is referred to by Baudelaire:

Chose curieuse et vraiment digne d'attention que l'introduction de cet
élément insaisissable du beau jusque dans les œuvres destinées à
représenter à l'homme sa propre laideur morale et physique! Et, chose
non moins mystérieuse, ce spectacle lamentable excite en lui une hilarité
immortelle et incorrigible. (Baudelaire, [1852] 1965: 212)

It is curious and truly worthy of attention that this elusive element of the
beautiful is introduced even in those works destined to represent to mankind its own moral and physical ugliness! And, no less mysterious, this
lamentable sight excites in him an immortal and incorrigible hilarity.

Kierkegaard argues that the Socratic questioning, which apparently strives
to discover the truth, actually aims at total destruction and at the humiliation
not only of the questioning subject, but of the very legitimacy of the question
itself – a negation for the sake of negation. In presenting it in this way
Kierkegaard imposes his own teleological system of moral values on the
phenomenon of irony, therefore seeing it as morally negative and even socially dangerous:

One can ask with the intention of receiving an answer containing the
desired fullness, and hence the more one asks, the deeper and more
significant becomes the answer; or one can ask without any interest in
the answer except to suck out the apparent content by means of the
question and thereby to leave an emptiness behind. The first method
presupposes, of course, that there is plenitude; the second that there is

an emptiness. The first is the speculative method; the second the ironic.
(Kierkegaard, [1841] 1989: 36)

According to Kierkegaard, Socrates is not aiming at a true, positive solution of his question. His truth lies elsewhere, in the disclosure of the infinite void of existence. This kind of Socratic irony is always present in the Platonic dialogues by their habitual conclusion with no answer at all; Plato's Socrates never arrives at an answer to any of his queries. Kierkegaard then draws a sharp line between Plato's irony, which is teleological and therefore satirical, and Socrates' aimless, 'absolute infinite negativity'; he takes great pains to stress not only that these dialogues end without any conclusions, but moreover that they end negatively: 'the dialogue is therefore very well aware of this lack of conclusions' (ibid.: 56). There is indeed a conclusion to the Socratic philosophical inquiries, says Kierkegaard, and the conclusion is the void, this 'absolute infinite negativity' that is annihilation itself. Kierkegaard also points out that in this general and all-encompassing annihilation, irony eventually annihilates itself as well (ibid.). Socrates' whole method is destructive, presenting the inability to know, but it does not offer an alternative to knowing, since he does not have one. Kierkegaard condemns it as nihilistic, irreligious and therefore, according to Kierkegaard's system of values, immoral. Schlegel, and the romantic ironists after him, actualize this kind of irony, which culminated in total nihilism. However, this total despair of knowing still has a value, which is precisely knowledge itself. It assumes the existence of a truth, although it cannot be reached. Therefore, even this kind of 'absolute infinite negativity' is not devoid of values, although it does not present a possible solution.

However, the paragraph in which Kierkegaard writes about the two varieties of the comic reveals a point that could perhaps be regarded as a slip of his pen, when he describes this confrontation with the Socratic infinite negativity, 'as long as it is related to a conclusion', as 'comic', yet 'in another sense it frees the individual from the comic'. This last kind of comic, from which the first kind of irony, i.e. the satirical one, can free the individual, is the laughter of powerlessness in front of the absurd fact of infinite negation. Moreover, it is the helpless acceptance of the inexplicable, yet epistemologically phenomenal, existence of non-existence. From this variety of the comic, which perhaps could be regarded as a third type, is generated the third kind of irony.

Existential irony

The first two kinds of irony that were first methodically described by Kierkegaard were later accepted in most of the writings on irony as successfully covering its possible modes of expression.[4] However, further inquiries into the nature of irony, particularly those influenced by phenomenology, point to yet another, third kind of irony, which presents irony as 'a mode of consciousness, an all-encompassing vision of life', that positively accepts the contradictions of reality (Wilde, 1981: 3). According to this view, the phenomenological contradictions of reality do not point to the human incompatibility of knowing the truth, but are in themselves the truth: reality indeed is infinitely contradictory.

The apparent negativity of irony was actually the result of a value system that was arbitrarily forced upon the phenomenon of irony. Lang confronts irony with rhetoric when he regards rhetoric as relying heavily on a clear system of values, shared by both sender and receiver of the message (Lang, 1988: 39–45). The acknowledgement of the inability to know 'the truth that lies behind the appearance' assumes the existence of such a truth; and without such an assumption ironic reality can be positively perceived while still remaining unclear and contradictory. The irony of reality is thus wholly accepted as a phenomenon, as a fact, which does not need or seek a solution. As such, irony does not assume that reality should be without contradictions; actually, it presents contradiction as an integral and even necessary part of reality. We refuse to accept it as such because of our own way of apprehending it, namely what we regard as 'absurd', and what Bakhtin calls 'the carnivalistic laughter'.[5] This perception of reality found expression in Russian literature and theatre at the beginning of the twentieth century, and was undoubtedly inspired by the same cultural environment as Bakhtin's thought. Such a perception of reality's unfinalizability and its relation to the grotesque can be found, for example, in the writings of Vsevolod Meyerhold.[6]

The idea of accepting paradox as a positive value appears in the writings of Schlegel, where it seems to have merely aesthetic implications. Schlegel stressed irony's positive unresolvable nature: 'Die Paradoxie ist für die Ironie die *conditio sine qua non*, die Seele, Quell und Prinzip' (Schlegel, 1957: 114; 'Paradox is the *conditio sine qua non* of irony, its soul, its source and its principle' [quoted in Muecke, 1969: 159]).

However, paradox seems to be the *conditio sine qua non* not only of irony, but also of life itself, therefore leaving irony as the only true *mimesis*, or mirror of life: 'What I call General Irony is life itself or any general aspect of life seen as fundamentally and inescapably an ironic state of affairs. No longer is it a case of isolated victims; we are all victims of impossible situations, of Universal Ironies of Dilemma' (Muecke, 1969: 120).

Although both the second and third kinds of irony see it as a phenomenon, i.e. as *terminus* and not as a rhetorical device, they differ on one important point: the second kind assumes the existence of an ironist (i.e. of an 'intention') who alienates himself from his surrounding reality, assuming a superior position from which he contemplates the absurdities of life, as does Schlegel in his process of 'Parabasis' (Schlegel, 1963: 85). Existential irony, on the other hand, does not necessarily demand the alienation of the contemplating subject from reality, but accepts his consciousness as being an integral part of this reality and accepts the fact that reality does not necessarily play by the rules of logic.

Vladimir Jankélévitch emphasizes the nature of these last two kinds of irony as the outcome of the confrontation of two contrasting ethical attitudes to irony; he begins with the second kind, which is seen by Kierkegaard and Hegel as a morally negative element, i.e. the annihilating potential of chaos, and goes on to the third, which is seen as positive by Jean-Paul, realizing the liberating potential of chaos, that sets human thought free from its boundaries of finitude:

> Le hasard et le destin se rejoignent: cette liberté hyperbolique et fainéante, engloutissant toutes les valeurs de culture, aboutit à une sorte d'indifférence quiétiste pour laquelle il n'est plus de vertu, plus d'objet et même plus d'art! ... Hegel a beaucoup raillé l'autocratie de ce moi ironique qui engloutit toute détermination, dévore toute particularité ... par rapport à notre libre arbitre infini, toutes les choses conditionées s'anéantissent dans le chaos de l'ironie, s'égalent dans le rien. Ce sublime a l'envers, cette négation infinie qui renvoient dos à dos la folie et la sagesse, c'est ce que Jean-Paul appele l'humour; mais, au lieu que le hiatus, selon Schlegel, est entre le moi et le monde. Jean-Paul, rejoignant le concept chrétien du péché, le situe entre Dieu et les choses du monde fini – au nombre desquelles est le moi: l'humour annihile non point le singulier, mais la finitude en général par son contraste avec l'idée de la raison infinie. (Jankélévitch, 1964: 18–19)

> Chance and fate are joined together: this hyperbolic and indolent freedom, that swallows up all the values of culture, reaches up to a kind of quietist indifference for which it is no longer a virtue, an object or even art! ... Hegel jeered quite a lot at the autocracy of this ironic I that swallows up every determination, devours every particularity ... With regard to our infinite free will, all determined things are abolished in the chaos of irony, made identical in nothingness. This sublime in reverse, this infinite negativity that sets back to back folly and wisdom, is what Jean-Paul calls humour; only that instead of the break being, as according to Schlegel, between the I and the world, Jean-Paul, adding the Christian concept of sin, locates it between God and the things of the finite world – one of which is the I: humour annihilates not only singularity but finitude in general, through its contrast with the idea of infinite reason.

Besides its relevance to aesthetics, existential irony has ethical implications. Actually, these two aspects seem to endlessly intermingle with each other. Thomas Mann broadened the scope of irony, claiming that it is not only the result of the human inability to choose between two equally valid moral values, but rather the result of Man's being coerced to choose between life and spiritual values. The question, as Mann poses it, is not which of the two positive moral values to choose, but whether at all to choose moral values which exclusively relate to the human spirit, when they contradict human life. His article 'Irony and Radicalism' inquires into the unresolvable question of general irony, where the individual is disoriented by contradictions of life's realities that are constantly clashing with his customary ways of thought and ingrained moral values. According to Mann, irony is not the result of an impossible choice between two of his moral values, but of the impossible choice between the whole of his spiritual values and his own life, the reality of which often clashes with them. The inevitable exigency – in everyday life as well as in catastrophic situations – to choose between spiritual values and life, when physical existence (or loyalty to it) contradicts the moral one, is presented by Mann as the most unbearable and at the same time inevitable instance of general irony, which is rooted in Man's very existential condition, as he says in the opening lines of 'Irony and Radicalism':

> Das ist ein Gegensatz und ein Entweder-Oder. Der geistige Mensch hat die Wahl (*soweit* er die Wahl hat), entweder Ironiker oder Radikalist zu sein; ein Drittes ist anständigerweise nicht möglich. Als was er sich bewährt, das ist eine Frage der letzten Argumentation. Es entscheidet sich dadurch, welches Argument ihm als das letzte, ausschlaggebende und absolute gilt: das Leben oder der Geist (der Geist als Wahrheit oder als Gerechtigkeit oder als Reinheit). Für den Radikalisten ist das Leben kein argument. *Fiat justitia* oder *veritas* oder *libertas, fiat spiritus – pereat mundus et vita!* So spricht aller Radikalismus. 'Ist denn die Wahrheit ein Argument, – wenn es das Leben gilt?' Diese frage ist die Formel der Ironie. (Mann, [1918] 1968: 423)

> This is an antithesis and an either-or. The intellectual human being has the choice (*as far* as he has the choice) of being either an ironist or a radical; a third choice is not decently possible. What he proves to be is a question of final argumentation. It is decided by which argument is for him the final, decisive, and absolute one: life or intellect (intellect as truth or as justice or as purity). For the radical, life is no argument. *Fiat justitia* or *veritas* or *libertas, fiat spiritus – pereat mundus et vita!* Thus speaks all radicalism. 'But is truth an argument – when life is at stake?' This question is the formula of irony. (Mann, 1983: 419)[7]

The love that Tristan feels for Isolde, lofty as it may be, is not a moral value (as is his loyalty to King Mark) but a life value, a sensual and emotional one, the kind that Mann calls erotic; this term can include Oedipus' love for his wife, children and for his own living, present self, and even Antigone's emotional loyalty to blood relationship. Therefore irony is a direct result of the human condition, in which the choice is to be made between spirit and life: not between two moral values, but between two human values. It is the either/or dichotomy between moral judgement and 'real-life' situations.

Sometimes this existential irony is expressed as an utmost simplicity, a sheer, direct acceptance of reality. Such expressions have been noted in some of the late works of Beethoven, Verdi and Monteverdi (Longyear, 1970: 161–

162); they are described as '"skepticism turned against itself," filled with melancholy born of personal inadequacy, yet showing a smiling serenity of self knowledge that dominates the division between the practical and poetic world' (ibid., referring to Hass, 1967: 30–33). In this light it is revealing to listen to Shostakovich's setting, in the last movement of his Thirteenth Symphony, of Yevgeny Yevtushenko's poem 'Career'. The text presents precisely such a dilemma between professional integrity, in spite of all dangers, and simple human survival: 'Он знал, что вертится земля, / но у него была семья' (Евтушнко, 'Карера'; 'He knew that the earth revolved / But – he had a family' [Yevtushenko, 'Career', translated by V. Vlazinskaya, 1993, RDCD11191]).

Shostakovich begins this movement with a strangely relaxed and naïve music, extremely incongruous with the text of the specific poem as well as with the general atmosphere of the whole symphony. Two flutes float together in an ethereal quasi-waltz, allegedly ignoring its tormented context, but actually contemplating it with that 'smiling serenity of self-knowledge' from some higher level of existential irony. A very similar blissful simplicity also appears in 'Immortality', the last poem of his song cycle op. 145, on the poems of Michelangelo Buonarroti. Located after poems about 'Anger', 'Death' and 'Night', with their appropriately cumbersome musical settings, 'Immortality', with its major mode, duple meter and toy-like simple melody, sounds either stupidly childish or ironic. The musical as well as the poetic context point, doubtlessly, to the second option. This is the peak of existential irony: a simple, direct, childlike acceptance.

> Naiv ist, was bis zur Ironie, oder bis zum steten Wechsel von Selbstschöpfung und Selbstvernichtung natürlich, individuell oder klassisch ist, oder scheint. Ist es bloß instinkt, so ists kindlich, kindich, oder albern; ists bloße Absicht, so entsteht Affektation. Das schöne, poetische, idealische Naive muß zugleich Absicht, und Instinkt sein. Das Wesen der Absicht in diesem Sinne ist die Freiheit. Bewußtsein ist noch bei weitem nich Absicht. Es gibt ein gewisses verliebtes Anschauen eigner Natürlichkeit oder Albernheit, das selbst unsäglich albern ist. (Schlegel, [1801] 1967: 172–173)

> Naïve is what is or seems to be natural, individual, or classical to the point of irony, or else to the point of continuously fluctuating between self-creation and self-destruction. If it's simply instinctive, then it's childlike, childish, or silly; if it's merely intentional, then it gives rise to affectation. The beautiful, poetical, ideal naive must combine intention and instinct. The essence of intention in this sense is freedom, though intention isn't consciousness by a long shot. There is a certain kind of self-infatuated contemplation of one's own naturalness or silliness that is itself unspeakably silly. (Schlegel, 1971b, no. 51)

Naïvety can be, thus, the final expression of existential irony, the attitude we may acquire after all expectations – for the good and for the bad – are forsaken, and all that remains is the contemplation of the phenomenological, of reality as it is. Muecke described the ironic approach to existential conflicts as the abandonment of any a priori attitude to life:

> We cannot escape the irony for as long as we believe or assume that we inhabit a rational or moral universe. We can escape only by finding and adopting a detached position from which we can regard the coexistence of contraries with equanimity, that is to say by abandoning despair as well as hope. (Muecke, 1969: 114)

Irony is a meta-thought, a meta-form of all comic genres. While the Dantesque 'lasciate ogni speranza' leads humans through the gates of hell, the abandonment of both hope *and* despair leads towards the inescapable solution that eventually achieves humour (and through it to all the comic genres, which eventually stem from irony). Whilst satire obviously belongs to the first kind of irony, i.e. to the satirical one, it can express existential irony, too. Parody and the grotesque, whilst still being liable to be used as satirical devices, can equally be embodiments of the second (Romantic) and third (existential) kinds of irony. That is why the carnivalistic laughter of Bakhtin, based on his concept of unfinalizability, can be related either to the grotesque or to existential irony. The interdependency between the various comic genres and irony may be thus best presented by a schematic presentation that summarizes the following argument: if irony can be both *stimulus* (i.e. serve

Fig. 1.1
Interdependence between comic genres and irony

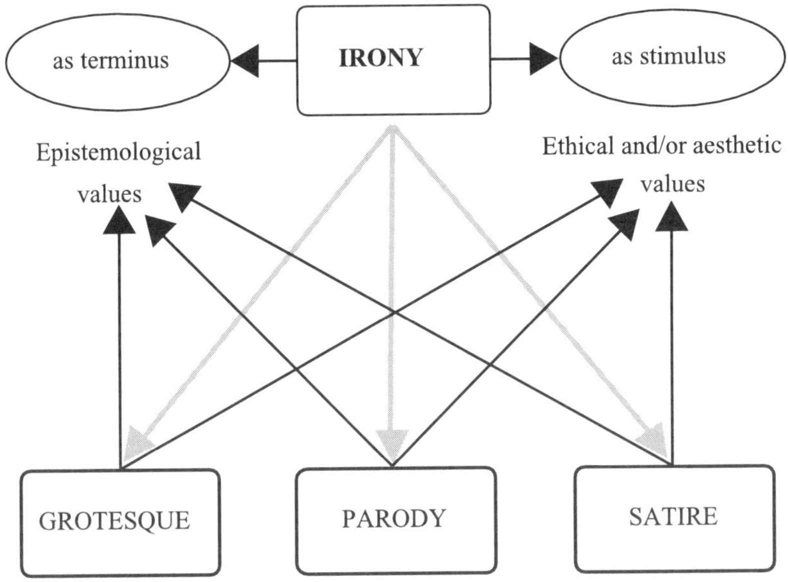

as a device) and *terminus* (be presented as a subject in itself), and if satire, parody and the grotesque are ironical modes, then each one of them can function as either a rethorical device or as a hidden subject of an artistic utterance (Fig. 1.1).

Since irony needs to be based on a distance between the ironist and the ironized (and/or between the contemplating subject and both of them, considering that this contemplating subject can also perform one or both of the other roles), the process of alienation seems to be a prerequisite of all the other ones.

Irony as related to Hegelian alienation: the Marxist approach

Theoretically based on Hegel's dialectics, Marxist thought has largely inherited its positivistic nature. Therefore, since Hegel regarded irony as a distortion of alienation's stage in a dialectical process, when alienation became an end in itself, Marxist thought also regarded alienation as an evil that should be overcome, thus condemning irony as well. Even when irony was accepted by Marxist aesthetics, always with a considerable amount of suspicion and constraint, it happened only when it was used for a 'positive', i.e. 'educational', purpose, in which 'right' was clearly differentiated from 'wrong' and unambiguously preferred. However, when irony was used in an utterance, either polemical, poetical, in art or in music, that instead of being focused on positivistic solutions engaged itself in the rather blurred area of aporic existence, it was always regarded by Marxist theories as negative, destructive and degenerative.

Such a point was easily assimilated by Russian theories that were immersed in mystical thought, formulated within a theocratic frame of mind that preferred to focus on positivistic ethics rather than remain perplexed by the state of existential disorientation in a non-hierarchical system of values or horrified by the infinite void of human life. This remark, however, is strictly confined to Russian literature, philosophy and theory, and does not apply to any practical materialization of art forms. For example, Alexander Blok, in his article 'Irony', written in his early years of mystical self-search, calls it 'a disease' (Blok, [1908] 1955: 80):

Самые живые, самые чуткие дети нашего века поражены болезнью, незнакомой телесным и духовным врачам. Эта болезнь – сродни душевным недугам и может быть названа 'иронией'. Ее проявления – приступы изнурительного смеха, который начинается с дьявольски-издевательской, провокаторской улыбки, кончается – буйством и кощунством ...

Я знаю людей, – которые готовы задохнуться от смеха, сообщая, что умирает их мать, что они погибают с голоду, что изменила невеста. Человек хохочет, – и не знаешь, выпьет он

сейчас, расставшись со мною, уксусной эссенции, увижу ли
его еще раз? И мне самому смешно, что этот самый человек,
терзаемый смехом, повествующий о том, что он вчеми унижен
и вчеми оставлен, – как бы отсутствует.

The liveliest and most perceptive children of our time are afflicted by a
disease unknown to doctors of the body and of the mind. This disease
has an affinity with mental diseases and can be called 'irony'. Its symp-
toms are fits of exhausting laughter which begin with a devilishly
mocking, provocative smile and ends with violence and blasphemy.

I know people that are ready to choke with laughter at the very same
time that their mother is dying, they themselves are starving to death
and their beloved is betraying them. A man guffaws, and you don't
know whether as soon as he leaves you he is going to drink some poison
and you wonder if you will ever see him again. And to me this very
laughter[2] tells about this person, that he despises everything and aban-
dons everything – as if it were nothing at all.

The article ends with a cry of pain, coming out of an ironic heart, explicitly
pointing at the falsity of his mask: 'Не слушайте нашего смеха, слушайте
ту боль, которая за ним. *Не верьте никому из нас, верьте тому,
кто за нами*' (ibid.: 84; 'Don't listen to our laughter; listen to the pain in it.
Don't believe any of us, but those that are behind us').

This article, written long before Blok became a communist, is more influenced by his symbolist mystical way of thought than by any Marxist theories.
It confronts the major trends in art in which he himself had taken part a short
time before. In fact, it seems as if this article was a kind of 'confession of
sins', an apologetic turn toward Marxist views, since only two years before,
in 1906, Blok wrote *Balaganchik*, which features extreme theatrical irony.
The play was produced and performed in the experimental theatre of Vsevolod
Meyerhold, embodying his 'theatrical theory of the grotesque' (Meyerhold,
1911–12 [1969]).[8]

It seems that it is, partly at least, due to their greater interest in the ethical
applications of art rather than in purely aesthetic issues that almost none of
the 'official' Marxist writings on aesthetics contain explicit statements about
irony; however, since irony was looked upon as a result of alienation, the
Marxist attitude towards irony could be deduced from writings about the
concept of alienation in art.

The Marxist aesthetics that glorifies wholeness, consistency and unity seems
to reject whatever is ambiguous, divided, or has more than one facet. This
positivist preference of unity – either of an idea or of a material entity – is a
basic premise of Hegelian thought, as can also be seen in his own critique of
Solger's ideas, mentioned earlier. In the introduction to their anthology of
Marxist writings on aesthetics and criticism, Berel Lang and Forrest Williams
stress the importance that this 'alternative to alienation' has in Marxist aesthetics: 'The self, divided within itself and from others … could become whole

again. The human being would reassert an integrity defying compart-mentalization, reclaiming himself as a unity' (Lang and Williams, 1972: 2–3).

Alienation is therefore regarded by Marxist thought as an element that not only contradicts but actually sabotages unity and wholeness. This Marxist critique was applied particularly to formalist literary writings which flour-ished in St Petersburg in the 1910s and 1920s. The basic formalist aesthetic principle was остранение: estrangement. This term meant, in formalist aes-thetics, the separation and 'alienation' of semantic units from their conventional context in which they became so assimilated as to pass unnoticed, and their re-location in a new (and alien) context; the resulting alienation between the re-located unit and its new context is supposed to create the required aware-ness and distancing that are needed for aesthetic appreciation.[9] The Hegelian accusation about the regard of a part as if it were the whole had thus passed over to Marxist thought. This was one of Leon Trotsky's major accusations against the Formalist School of Poetry, the ideas and methods of which he regards as contradicting Marxism. For example, Trotsky wrote that 'Formal-ism opposed Marxism with all its might theoretically' (Trotsky, 1925 [1972]: 69). His further explanation sounds almost like a paraphrase of Hegel's doctrine against irony:

> The (dialectic) idealism of Hegel arranges ... [the eternal categories] in some sequence by reducing them to a genetic unity. Regardless of the fact that this unity with Hegel is the absolute spirit, which divides itself in the process of its dialectic manifestation into various 'factors,' Hegel's system, because of its dialectic character, and not because of its ideal-ism, gives an idea of historic reality which is just as good as the idea of a man's hand that a glove gives when turned inside out. But the Formal-ists (and their greatest genius was Kant) do not look at the dynamics of development, but at a cross-section of it, on the day and the hour of their complexity and multiplicity of the object (not of the process, because they do not think of processes). This complexity they analyse and clas-sify. They give names to the elements, which are at once transformed into essences, into sub-absolutes, without father or mother; to wit, reli-gion, politics, morals, law, art. Here we no longer have a glove of history turned inside out, but the skin torn from the separate fingers, dried out to a degree of complete abstraction. (Ibid.: 75)

Not only the contradictions engendered by alienation, but contradictions in general seem to be rather unwelcome in Marxist aesthetics. Gyorgiy Plekhanov, one of the founders of Russian Marxism, explicitly stresses the following statement: 'When a work of art is based upon a fallacious idea, inherent contradictions inevitably cause a degeneration of its aesthetic quality' (Plekhanov, 1912 [1972]: 91).

The relevance of ethics to aesthetics makes itself obvious here, as it also does in Hegel's *Lectures on Aesthetics*, referred to above. Since contradic-tions are logically inconceivable, they cannot therefore be part of our ethical or aesthetic system of values.

The Marxist aesthetician Arnold Hauser (1892–1978) describes the basic idea of alienation, the state that enables the presence of irony, as 'the individual's sense of uprootedness, aimlessness, and loss of substance ... the sense of having lost contact with society and having no engagement in one's work, the hopelessness of ever harmonizing one's aspirations, standards and ambitions' (Hauser, [1965] 1972: 393). Hauser refers also to more 'classical' definitions of the term:

> In the classical meanings of the term, from which both Hegel and Marx as well as Kierkegaard and the modern existentialists start out, alienation means disvesture of the self, the loss of subjectivity; a turning inside out of the personality, exteriorizing and driving out what ought to remain within, with the result that what is ejected in this way assumes a nature completely different from the self, becomes alien and hostile to it, and threatens to diminish and destroy it. Meanwhile the self loses itself in its objectifications, faces an alienated form of itself in them. (Ibid.: 395)

Such an interpretation of Hegel's concept of alienation can point to one of the sources of the many prejudices against the comic genres in Marxist aesthetics: since all of them require alienation, thus demanding the 'disvesture of the self' which is actually self-annihilation, no wonder then that it is regarded as negative and even ethically dangerous. The alienated part is not regarded as a source of self-appraisal and objectified self-appreciation, but as a 'hostile' entity that 'threatens to destroy and diminish' the self.

However, Hauser is definitely not satisfied with this simplistic view, since he simultaneously analyses Hegel's concept of alienation as the source of all creation: 'Just as God created the world by an act of self-alienation, so is the human mind confronted by an alien element in his own creations' (ibid.). He acknowledges the necessity of the alienation process in the self-awareness of the human mind, and regards works of art that make use of alienation as expressions of a human quest for real self-identity:

> Whether mannerism presents itself as a positive or negative reaction to alienation, its connection with the social process is unmistakable. In examining its historical and sociological origins it is impossible not to be struck by the parallelism between the loss of personality suffered by the manual worker as a consequence of the mechanization of production and that of the intellectual worker as a consequence of specialization on the one hand, and on the other of the sense of estrangement and loss of self, the doubt about the reality and identity of the self, that are among the principal themes of the literature of the age. Shakespeare's characters ... feel lost in this respect; they are continually wondering what they are, whether they are really what they seem to be, and they talk continually of their sense of going about in changed, distorted, unreal form ... From this idea of man's problematical identity, his failure to appear what he is, partly because he must not and partly because he dares not be what he should be, Shakespeare, Cervantes, Calderón, and

most of the writers of the age, developed the theme that it was his nature
and destiny to conceal and disguise himself, to be always playing a part,
hiding behind a fictitious identity, living an illusion. (Ibid.: 411–12)

As long as and even if presented as an undesirable condition, alienation is
accepted and even appreciated in Marxist art. What does characterize the
Marxist attitude toward irony is that the ethical evaluation that is attached to
irony (and alienation) actually determines its aesthetic evaluation as well.[10] It
is not the way irony is used that is contemplated in those writings, but rather
its ethical value and the way it is used in the ethical context of the work of art
in which it appears. The issue of irony's obvious ethical ground is acknowledged not only in Marxist writings. Vladimir Jankélévitch opens his book
about irony with the following remark: 'L'ironie, assurément, est bien trop
morale pour être vraiment artiste, comme elle est trop cruelle pour être
vraiment comique' (Jankélévitch, 1964: 9; 'Irony, for certain, is much too
moral to be really artistic, just as it is much too cruel to be really comic').

It should be stressed here that the comic genres are underestimated in
Marxist aesthetics not only because they require alienation, but also because
they present a baser, less than ideal, form. Again, it is a moral value-judgement that actually dictates the aesthetic attitude. There is no wonder that
Marxism, following very much the Aristotelian aesthetics, sees in comedy a
materialization of the base that should be rejected. If the 'beautiful' should
equal the 'good', the 'good' equal the 'rational', and the 'rational' equal the
'unity without contradictions', then obviously whatever presents a self-contradictory purport is 'irrational', therefore 'evil' and consequently 'ugly'. The
laughable is, thus, the evil, ugly and base, and it can be identified by the
presence of contradictions in it. Subsequently, comedy is accepted in Marxist
aesthetics only in its satirical function. In such cases the alienation from the
comic will actually be regarded as a 'useful', 'right' one:

> Because all the aesthetic categories are related to man's historical
> progress, all of them are actually confirmation of the beautiful. The
> ugly, for example, is attached to an object or phenomenon which is
> doomed to destruction in the course of historical development and by
> this very fact confirms the beautiful ... The comic has several forms –
> the humorous, satiric, ironic, etc. – although they share a common trait,
> viz. a socially perceivable contradiction, a socially significant lack of
> correspondence of end–means, form–content, event–circumstances, es-
> sence–its manifestations, which are rejected in the name of the beautiful.
> According to Marx, 'History is thorough and goes through many phases
> when carrying an old form to the grave. The last phase of a world
> historical form is its comedy.' By laughing people shed the old form
> easily, seeing in it a hindrance to the newly emergent, life-confirming
> form of society. (Swiderski, 1979: 113)

It is significant, however, that most of the Marxist writings about irony are
written either by writers who are not aestheticians (like Trotsky) or by

aestheticians who are not Russian (like Hauser). It might seem almost paradoxical, but in at least the first three decades of the century, the Russians
themselves were much more influenced by contemporary German art than by
political Marxist writings. Swiderski's excerpt, quoted above, seems rather
an enforced hybrid, the outcome of an effort to make peace between 'official'
Marxist views and an artistic reality that didn't always coincide with it.

The historical facts are that the main artistic trends in Russia of that time
almost glorified the coexistence of contradictions in works of art, which
obviously included irony. The film director Sergey Eisenstein presents his
film theory in a characteristically pamphlet style. His aesthetics is based on
the 'dialectic' superimposition of contradictions, which is perceived as the
main purport of art:

> A dynamic comprehension of things is also basic to the same degree,
> for a correct understanding of art and of all art-forms. In the realm of
> art this dialectic principle of dynamics is embodied in
> Conflict
> as the fundamental principle for the existence of every art-work and
> every art-form
> *For the art is always conflict*:
> (1) according to its social mission,
> (2) according to its nature,
> (3) according to its methodology.
>   (Eisenstein, [1929] 1972: 358)

Meyerhold, Shostakovich's theatrical mentor, who also directed Alexander
Blok's *Balaganchik*, was one of the main theatre theoreticians in Russia, and
his theories had a great influence on twentieth-century theatre beyond Russia
as well. Meyerhold idolized ambiguity and double messages (or rather, infinite messages). In his 'theory of the grotesque' he elaborated many techniques
that are characteristic to irony, like the use of masks and other techniques of
estrangement.[11] Meyerhold consistently tried to insert irony into all his productions, showing a clear predilection for plays that emphasized it. However,
his particular enthusiasm was kept for the third kind of irony that accepts
contradictions and the infinite number of life's facets; Meyerhold's irony is
merged with the grotesque, with which he explicitly deals in most of his
theoretical writings. Meyerhold read Schlegel and often quoted him
(Meyerhold, [1911–12] 1969: 127–128). He coined the expression 'stylized
theatre', which is in accordance with and a result of the formalist attitude and
notion of estrangement, as well as with Schlegel's concept of 'parabasis'.
Meyerhold and Blok influenced each other, and both (particularly Blok)
might have influenced Bakhtin's ideas about the carnival–grotesque.[12] In fact,
Bakhtin regards Schlegel and Jean-Paul, the two great names of romantic
irony, as 'the theorists of the new grotesque' (Bakhtin, [1941] 1984: 37).

Irony, it is true, was conceived as an acceptance of negation, and therefore
as bearing a negative value in the Marxist value system. However, its

educational worth was acknowledged by the Marxists (as was shown in Swiderski's excerpt above) and so it was 'sneaked' into later 'official' Soviet art. Indeed, Blok's *Balaganchik* seems to have, at least as one of his purposes, an ethical, i.e. satirical, function that is typical of the first kind of irony. Only two years before his moralistic attack on irony, referred to above, he writes in a letter to Meyerhold:

В этом смысле я 'принимаю мир' – весь мир, с его тупостью, косностью, мертвыми и сухими красками, для того только, чтобы надуть эту костлявую старую каргу и омолодить ее: в обьятияах шута и балаганчика старый мир похорошеет, станет молодым, и глаза его станут прозрачными, без дна. (Blok, [1906] 1963)

I accept the world – the whole world with its stupidity, obliqueness, dead and dry colours – only in order to fool this bony witch and make her young again. In the embraces of the Fool and the Buffoon the old world brightens up, becomes young, and its eyes become translucent, depthless. (Quoted in Symons, 1971: 29)

It is interesting that this image of irony's potential for eternal renewal also repeatedly appears in Bakhtin's writings, as an immanent potential of the grotesque.

In tireless and desperate efforts to save an inherent quality of Russian art and literature from being abolished, some theoreticians who lived in Soviet Russia tried to twist their writings to accommodate existing Russian art with Marxist aesthetics. Such attempts, which on the surface sometimes seem rather awkward, are in fact manifestations of personal courage and integrity of thought, written in times when people who belonged to the Russian intelligentsia would 'disappear' and be executed on the grounds of expressing 'anti-Marxist ideas'. At the height of Stalin's terror years, the Russian critic Ivan Sollertinsky, Shostakovich's friend and source of intellectual influence, tried to take advantage of this Marxist view in his effort to save and enhance Russian comedy, musical comedy and comic opera, not only stressing the comic as a weapon, but also, according to the required vein of thought, the comic as actual enhancer of realism:

Смех – могущественное оружие, и мировая музыка на своем историческом пути, как мы пытались показать, неоднократно им пользовалась. Советские композиторы не создают свои оперы на пустом месте: они творчески осваивают все мировое музыкальное наследие. В их поле зрения (точнее – слуха) должны войти и охарактеризованные нами выше великие мастера комической оперы, борцы за реализм, в выработке принципов которого комическая опера сыграла столь почетную роль. (Sollertinsky, [1939] 1963: 357)

Laughter is a powerful weapon, and the music of the world, in all its historical pathways, as we have painstakingly shown, has used it many

> times. The Soviet composers do not create their operas in a vacuum. They assimilate their works to their entire musical legacy. Their field of vision (to be more exact, of hearing) must include also the great masters of comic operas whom I have quoted above, for fighters realism, in the elaboration of whose principles [ie. of realism] comic opera has played such an honourable role.

Shostakovich, who worked with Meyerhold (who subsequently became his theatrical mentor) was the closest friend of Ivan Sollertinsky and a fervent admirer of Alexander Blok. He was probably less concerned with Marxist theories than with the real artistic trends of his times. Therefore, although it seems like a natural historical outcome, the 'negative dialectics' of irony within Marxist aesthetics in the West eventually had a very small impact on his art, as well as on art in general within the first three decades of the most Marxist society in the world at that time – Russia itself.

CHAPTER TWO

Incongruities as indicators of irony

There are two possible ways to interpret musical incongruities. One is to resolve them into new congruences by modifying their correlations so that they accommodate each other. Such a procedure would lead either to further hierarchical subsets of correlations or to the creation of musical metaphors (Hatten, 1994a: 161–172). The second way is to acknowledge the structures of incongruities as semantically significant in themselves and interpret them as irony. Thus, on the axis of 'coexisting incongruous elements' that marks both poles within the oppositions 'incongruity vs congruence' and 'irony vs forthright speech', 'incongruity' itself will be correlated with 'irony'. Having a criterion (or a set of criteria) that will indicate the appropriate choice between these two different ways of interpretation is therefore fundamental for this study.

The standard structure of the ironical message, as described by D.C. Muecke, consists of two opposed levels of meaning – one ostensible and the other hidden. The hidden level is evoked by the ironist (and should be detected by the observer) by a hint or a clue that resides within the explicit message. This clue serves to direct the reader's (or listener's) attention to the hidden level of meaning in the message that should be preferred in its interpretation (Muecke, 1969: 17–18). The main difference between irony and metaphor is that irony is a result not only of incongruity based on difference (as is metaphor), but also of incongruity based on negation, i.e. on the impossibility of any accommodation between the incongruous parts of a message (Hatten, 1994a: 172; Elleström, 1996: 205).[1] Therefore it is not just the presence of an incongruity that will hint at the presence of irony, but also its functioning as an indicator of structural negation (Fig. 2.1).

This structural negation, however, is not always present in the message itself, but may also lie within the message's context. A definite identification of irony will thus require not only a consideration of the whole network of meanings and associations of the examined cultural unit, but also of its synchronic and diachronic context. Moreover, since a cultural unit is never finite, such an identification must be based on assumptions, and by definition can never be completely certain. The phrase 'I am a rose of Sharon, a lily of the valleys' is understood as a poetic metaphor and not as an ironic remark precisely because it is assumed that the speaker in this context is a young maiden in love (rendering an incongruity which might be figuratively accommodated) and not one of Mrs Peachum's foremothers (which would result in an unresolvable incongruity with the metaphorical 'first flowering'). Unfortunately, we do not

Fig. 2.1
The structure of irony

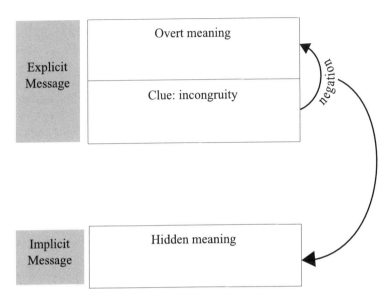

have, and most probably never will have any proof for this assumption, and therefore we shall never know for certain if the *Song of Songs* is a love poem or a parody of one. Infinite irony is rooted precisely in this very uncertainty, since any testimony in one way or another could be suspected as itself being ironical.[2] Any information about the historical, cultural and biographical context of an artistic message can thus be regarded as a reliable source only to the extent to which it assists in the recognition of irony only by reducing the amount of uncertainty. A clearly defined set of criteria might indeed help to increase the chances of a more accurate interpretation, but still it would never render a complete certainty, which will in itself negate the very existence of irony.[3]

Musical irony as a meta-term for modes of musical ambiguity

Attempts to create sets of criteria that will help to establish the presence of an ironic message have been made mainly in literature (Muecke, 1969; Booth, 1974: 49–93). In music, on the other hand, such attempts have been more sporadic. The most serious attempt to formulate theoretical grounds for musical irony was made by Hatten (1994a: 172–188). However, like many others, he focuses on the kind of romantic irony that is related to aesthetic distance, while his attempts to set criteria for satirical irony are not completely convincing (ibid.: 173).

Other studies, although not explicitly regarding irony as their subject, still set criteria that might apply to analyses of musical irony, such as the differentiation between various levels of discourse in music (Kramer, 1990; Abbate, 1991). Several studies enumerate, though not systematically, musical devices for irony; all consider incongruities as first and foremost, either in a purely musical context or in regard to text and other referential elements.

Quite often musical incongruities in themselves, without relying on overt referential context, are interpreted as irony. Thus Hatten speaks about the 'collision of two contexts' (1985: 73) and Rosenberg relates musical irony to a dialectic contrast without synthesis (1988: 9). Musical incongruities as the source of musical irony are also pointed out by Bekker (1911: 556), Cooke (1960: 24, 27, 34), Longyear (1970: 150, 153), Brauner (1981: 274), Fanning (1988: 40, 54, 71, 75), Dill (1989: 174–175), Bonds (1991: 64) and Hatten (1994a: 174–175). The range of musical incongruities is very wide, from incongruities based upon personal idiosyncrasies, through incongruities between topics, and up to those of general correlations which are not always culturally motivated. A specific group of incongruities has to do with music's time dimension. Daverio (1990: 34–37), Jost (1990: 48–50) and Woodley (1995: 175) speak about metrical incongruities. Among other devices, Longyear mentions abrupt shifts, structural and rhythmical incongruities (1970: 157–159). Rosenberg (1988: 9), Daverio (1990: 36–37) and Hatten (1994a: 176–184) analyse syntactical incongruities, where typical 'beginning' and 'ending' gestures are interchanged, while Samuels describes the 'collapse and dissolution at sectional cadences' (1995: 117). Longyear (1970: 154), Jost (1990: 48) and Woodley (1995: 177–178) mention tonal incongruities, either as harmonic shifts, incongruous juxtapositions or as ambiguities in the presentation of tonality. Dyson (1987) describes musical irony that is generated by musical ambiguities of tonal harmonic functions; musical irony created by ambiguities in modes (diatonic/chromatic), melodic gestures and dynamics are referred to by Hatten (1994a: 184–186) and Woodley (1995: 183), who even finds irony in juxtapositions of incongruous timbres and textures (ibid.: 180–182).

Some writers make a specific point of incongruities between musical norms, or between an explicit musical element and an implicit musical norm. This aspect is related mainly to the concept of exaggeration, and will be dealt with separately in the chapter on musical satire (Chapter Four). Several writers incorporate this device in their analyses of musical irony. Although methodically such an approach is not very helpful in clarifying the different strategies and different aims of musical irony versus musical satire, it is still interesting to note that awareness of this type of incongruity exists.

Exaggeration results either from bringing something to an abnormal extreme, as described by Brauner (1981: 270) and Fanning (1988: 43, 71), or as a result of an accumulative process, as pointed out by Dill (1989: 182). In all these instances exaggeration is interpreted as a source of musical irony. Exaggerated simplicity, and particularly the use of cliché, mentioned by Longyear (1970: 161, 162), Dill (1989: 183) and Fanning (1988: 58, 74), are popular devices to create musical irony; Samuels even assigns a whole section to musical irony and musical cliché (1995: 115–119). Exaggerated motion, i.e. the musical *perpetuum mobile*, is perceived as ironic by Cooke (1960: 26–27), Fanning (1988: 71) and Rosenberg (1988: 11).

Exaggeration may serve not as a pointer to ironic reversal, leading to satire, but as an indicator of the very artificiality of the musical work, a distancing device, and thus a sign of romantic irony (Longyear, 1970: 153–154).[4] Authors dealing specifically with romantic irony as a distancing device often analyse the question of different levels of discourse, which are interpreted as indicators of irony by Rosenberg (1988: 10), Dill (1989: 176–179) and Hatten (1994a: 168–170). Other devices are often mentioned in this respect: repetitions, various defined topics, allusions, quotations and rhetorical shifts that reflect shifts between the various levels of discourse.

However, the majority of the writings about musical irony analyse musico-dramatic irony, i.e. irony that is rooted in the relation between music and dramatic events (Noske, 1977: 93–120; Malloy, 1985; Austern, 1986; Dyson, 1987) or between music and texts of *Lieder* (Brauner, 1981; Rosenberg, 1988; Dill, 1989; Jost, 1990).[5] In these cases most of the incongruities that point to irony are set between semantic correlation of the music and textual and/or dramatic instances.

In spite of this apparent abundance, the analyses quite often lack not only explicit criteria for the depiction of musical irony, but also any definition of what they actually mean by 'irony', consequently ending with a confused set of terms that overlap and inconsistently replace each other (Norris, 1982a; 179–183; MacDonald, 1990: 112–116, 145–148). Some use specific examples that illustrate their topic, but without any theoretical framework on which to base their argumentation (Bekker, 1911: 555–556; Cooke, 1960: 24; Fanning, 1988: 70–76; Roseberry, 1989: 49, 61, 285, 335, 348 and 350). Part of the writings about musical irony deal with the question of aesthetic distance, which relates to only one specific type of romantic irony, used as a device for creating artistic distance (Longyear, 1970; Dill, 1989; Bonds, 1991). An exception is John Daverio's article on the writings of Jean Paul and the piano music of Schumann (Daverio, 1990). Daverio confines himself to the exclusive examination of romantic irony in its existential aspect, as 'a musical cipher for the infinite' (ibid.: 37), relating it to Jean Paul's 'intentionally ambiguous structures' (ibid.: 33) that reflect his ideas about the 'annihilating humour' and the 'infinite world' (ibid.: 38). According to Daverio, Schumann follows Jean Paul's literary ideas in creating 'a musical plot that is purposefully ambiguous and richly suggestive because of its very ambiguity' (ibid.: 34).

It is not a coincidence that most of the studies of romantic irony in music are concerned with the nineteenth century, when this kind of irony played a particularly significant role in philosophy, literature and the arts. Studies that analyse romantic irony in twentieth-century music are relatively scarce; an exception is Ronald Woodley's 1995 article on Prokofiev's Violin Sonata op. 80. Woodley brings the traditional approach to romantic irony in music to its self-evident extreme by actually claiming that every form of musical ambiguity could be perceived as musical irony. In interpreting the musical ambiguities in the work as expressions of endless self-questioning, he relates it not only to artistic distancing, but also to the Bakhtinian ideas of unfinalizability and heteroglossia, i.e. to the 'multi-voiced', endlessly self-creating process that is the work of art (ibid.: 171, 178).

Thus the term 'irony' often functions as a meta-term that actually reflects quite a wide range of totally different phenomena. Writers on this subject tend to disregard the various kinds of irony, and their examples of romantic irony are usually interspersed with other examples of existential and/or satirical irony, without explicitly differentiating between them (Longyear, 1970: 156, 161; Brauner, 1981: 274–276; Elleström, 1996: 197, 205; Karbusicky, 1986: 435–436, cited in Hatten, 1994a: 168). Moreover, most of these writers use 'irony' as a general term for all the various modes of musical ambiguity. The problematics of the whole issue is further emphasized by the fact that both the relatively recent publications of Fanning (1988: 73) and Elleström (1996: 205) follow traditional critical paths in their very questioning of theoretical analysis of musical irony, although both recognize musical moments that they describe as indeed conveying irony.

One major obstacle that encumbers the creation of a set of criteria which will allow the depiction of irony is precisely this variety in kinds of irony, ranging from simple puns and satirical remarks to the philosophical levels of existential and romantic irony. Therefore, before any attempt is made to construct a set of criteria for their identification, a clear classification of the different types of irony is necessary.

As mentioned above, there are two kinds of irony: satirical and non-satirical. Satirical irony is attached to a given set of norms and values, and its final aim is to prefer only one of the incongruous elements of the message, i.e. to become a non-ironical message. Non-satirical irony, on the other hand, is more complicated. Often called 'romantic irony', it actually encompasses three different types of irony. These three types are not mutually exclusive; this fact might be, at least partly, the cause of the confusion between them. The criteria for their detection in music, however, are different.

First, romantic irony can be perceived as the aesthetic distance that the artist takes from his work, and that can actually be further developed to an infinite number of levels of discourse. Schlegel refers to this kind when he speaks about 'infinite arbitrariness' (*KFSA, 1797–1799*, [1985] *Atheneum*

No. 305) and 'permanent parabasis' (*KFSA, 1796–1806* [1963]: 85). This kind of irony will often appear in parody and make use of topics, quotations and other stylistic allusions. This will be the only kind of irony that I shall call in this study 'romantic irony'. Romantic irony can result, therefore, from the infinite mutation between levels of discourse, ways of speech, semantic contents, etc., as well as from the infinite shift from one realm of art to another. In this process our 'reality' is just another one of the potential levels of artistic reference.

In negating the difference between reality and art, romantic irony also negates the boundaries of reality *per se*. As such, it relates to the second interpretation of romantic irony as 'infinite negation'. This idea, as well as the consequent condemnation of romantic irony, was developed by Hegel, and then by Kierkegaard (1841: 261). Up to a certain point, this kind can be referred to as 'infinite irony'.[6] The difference in music between this type and the former may be very subtle indeed. It will happen when the various consecutive levels of musical discourse will actually negate each other, i.e. when their correlatives will be contradictory. Another expression of this kind of irony will be all the 'no-win' situations, in which none of the presented incongruous elements could be preferred.

However, this infinite shifting between levels of discourse must not necessarily be an infinite negation based on an either/or criterion. Another possible outcome of the very same potential of irony could actually be the opposite of negation, i.e., the acceptance of coexisting incongruities. Understood in this way, irony is the source of an 'infinite creation', of an eternal process of affirmation. This idea is best formulated by Bakhtin in his theory of the grotesque (1941), as well as in his concepts of 'unfinalizability' and 'heteroglossia' (Morson and Emerson, 1990: 36–40, 139 -145). This approach is also manifested in some of the theoretical writings of Thomas Mann (Mann, [1918] 1983). Musical juxtapositions of apparently irreconcilable incongruities would convey this type of irony. More often than not they would appear simultaneously or with very short-span alternations between two or more musical topics. In this study I shall call this third kind of romantic irony 'existential irony', and deal with its musical manifestation particularly when analysing the musical grotesque.

Indicators of the multi-layered musical discourse

Although not relating the shifts between the various levels of musical discourse to irony, Carolyn Abbate's comprehensive analysis provides a good theoretical basis for such a relation (Abbate, 1991). For example, when she writes about 'oscillation' between various levels of musical discourse, she describes them as 'an ironic voice' and enumerates a series of criteria as indicators for the points of shifting (ibid.: 123–155). The most obvious pointer to such a shift is the 'unmediated juxtaposition of two unrelated musics', a juxtaposition that would often use topics or patterned structures clearly different from the surrounding musical context, as well as 'musical reductions that mark phenomenal song' (ibid.: 144). Such a song would be introduced with an 'exaggerated musical simplicity' which is 'radically unlike the normal musical discourse of the surrounding [musical context]' (ibid.: 138). In such cases, whatever is not a topos would be the first level of discourse, and whatever is a topos or something structured or manifestly simpler would be the secondary level (ibid.: 149). Another indicator is a musical disjunction. Such a disjunction can be achieved by almost any musical element (ibid.: 32, 56–57): a pause; a harmonic incongruity (41); a change in orchestration; a sign for something new, like a sign for a beginning (42); a new character to the music, as if a characteristic of a new speaking voice (48); a change of tempo (58); a change in texture, in tonality, in melodic structure (106); or a sudden shift to a patterned structure like an ostinato (112). Abbate also refers, albeit marginally, to the element of exaggeration as a factor in creating artistic distance. She speaks about repetition that happens 'a few too many times' (56) and about 'exaggerated musical simplicity' (138). Since these are normative statements, and therefore not the focus of her study, she does not analyse them in depth. However, it is interesting to note that any reference to irony does mention, either centrally or marginally, the element of exaggeration.

Existential irony in music

Lawrence Kramer tries to analyse instances in which two contradictory elements nullify each other (Kramer, 1990: 45–46; see also Karbusicky, 1986: 435–436, quoted in Hatten, 1994a: 168). Samuels, on his part, speaks about the 'interpenetration of genres' that creates this kind of irony (Samuels, 1995: 117). In such cases, so it seems, the two incongruous correlations are completely balanced, and there is no way in which one could be considered as 'the context' or serve as 'evidence from a higher level' for the other (Hatten, 1994a: 170). The question is, of course, when should these elements be regarded as 'nullifying each other', and then be regarded as 'negative irony', and when as 'affirming each other', regarded then as 'positive irony'. The answer is incredibly complex, and has to do not only with whether the juxtaposed elements are heard simultaneously or alternately, but also with their length and specific import.

In the following analyses, Shostakovich's biographical and cultural context will be dealt with as one of the implicit levels of his discourse, and will be taken into account as an imperative part of a hermeneutic interpretation of his work. Therefore, the decision as to whether the phenomenon is stylistically congruent or not will be influenced not only by the general context of the 'style', but also, when relevant, by the general context of the cultural and personal background of the composer: his beliefs, convictions and values at the time of the composition of the analysed work.

Criteria for different types of irony in music

On the basis of the former discussion, music that has one or more of the following characteristics will be regarded as conveying irony:

1. Stylistic incongruities within one governing style
2. Stylistic discontinuities within one governing style
3. Incongruities with available information about the composer's set of convictions, beliefs, values, or about his personal characteristics
4. Incongruities based on meta-stylistic norms, e.g. rendering a feeling of 'too high', 'too fast', 'too many repetitions' etc., not when measured relative to a certain style or topic, but *per se*[7]
5. Shifts between levels of musical discourse
6. Juxtapositions of more than one stylistic or topical context, none of which could be regarded as 'governing'.

In order to convey satirical irony, a norm must be invoked. Therefore satirical irony, the subject of the next chapter, will be achieved by any combination of the criteria described above in points 1–4. The latter two points may serve as additional arguments, but *normative* incongruities are imperative for the transmission of a satirical (value-laden, i.e. based on norms) message.

Romantic irony, in which the awareness of the different levels of discourse in a work of art is awakened, must make some use of shifts between levels of discourse. As in the case of satirical irony, other criteria might be used here as well, but in such a case particular care must be taken not to trespass the limits of any norm, since the goal here is not satirical. The stylistic disjunctions must remain, at least in one aspect, within the boundaries of one style.

Negative existential irony, in which any affirmation finds its immediate negation by the use of infinite reversal, aspires to a perfect balance between the incongruous elements. This is the most fragile message, both for the composer and for the interpreter, since an almost perfect balance, which prevents any preference of any of the suggested stylistic topics or contexts, must be achieved in order for the message to succeed. Even more complex would be achieving a successful musical manifestation of positive existential irony. Here, exactly the same characteristics should be used, but somehow they must convey that all incongruous elements are to be accepted without excluding each other. My intention is to show this difference by confronting analyses of musical negative existential irony with analyses of the musical grotesque, which I regard to be a particular case of positive existential irony.

PART III
SATIRE

CHAPTER THREE

The structure of satire

This study is based on a structural premise, and therefore it examines satire mainly from a structural vantage-point. Therefore, satire is regarded here as a subclass of irony: it has two layers of meaning, one ostensible and one hidden, of which the hidden should be preferred. More specifically, though, satire is the only kind of irony that structurally must be bound to a specific set of norms, which should be perceived as its preferred set of values. In this sense, by always pointing at the preferred meaning and never leaving the ironic riddle unsolved, satire is the simplest form of irony.

In view of this, it might be surprising to realize how elusive a definition of satire can be. Books dealing with various aspects of satire abound in recent literature. Most of them, however, examine specific aspects of satire rather than giving a general overview of the genre. Pollard (1970), Nichols (1971), Petro (1982), Fletcher (1987) and Clark (1991) give good starting-points, but Petro is the only one who risks a real attempt at explicit definition of satire. Since he sees satire as an 'umbrella term', like 'mathematics', which includes a great number of trends and genres, he suggests an indirect approach, which starts from satire's essential elements, *criticism* and *humour* (Petro, 1982: 5–7). Late in his study Petro draws a theoretical graph, in which criticism and humour appear as two axes:

> The *horizontal* axis of this diagram is the axis of *humor*, containing a progression from wit to gallows humor, or from Comedy to Tragedy. The vertical axis is the axis of *criticism*, with progression from Reality to Fiction, and it is designed to include the characteristic which distinguishes satirical literature from other types of literature on the one hand, and from non-literature on the other. Satire is the meeting point of criticism and humor in a *literary* work. This meeting point is already expressed in the concept of *ridicule*, but ridicule does not always equal satire. Finally, satire is also situated somewhere between literature proper (Fiction), where the literary text does not necessarily enter into referential relationship with the world, and non-literature (Reality), where, as in everyday speech, there is a clear referential relationship. An ideal satire should be situated closer to, rather than farther from the intersection of the two axes (Petro, 1982: 128)

As in the case of irony, most writers on satire use various and sometimes overlapping terms to describe its specific ramifications: burlesque, irony, the grotesque, parody and even tragedy are constantly interchanged with satire. Within all this variety, however, there is one general agreement: satire relies on a given set of norms, and uses ridicule, often in an aggressive manner, to indicate actual instances of failure to match their standards (Pollard, 1970: 3; Nichols, 1971: 14, 18; Fletcher, 1987: ix). The norms of satire are characteristically (though not necessarily!) related to ethical and social values (Pollard, 1970: 7). Thus satire bears a historical, reality-related character, and is therefore never totally fictional (Petro, 1982: 128). The simplest case of satire would then be a phenomenon that, being incongruous with an accepted norm, is ridiculed. Such is, for example, the condemnation of greed and covetousness in Jonathan Swift's *Gulliver's Travels* or in Nikolay Gogol's *Dead Souls*.

Anything can serve as an object of satire – even the set of norms itself. When this happens, the satirized set of norms is always measured against another, implicit set of norms with which it is incongruous. For example, intellectual apathy is satirized in Gogol's description of Ivan Fyodorovich Shponka:

> Когда был он еще Ванюшею, то обучался в гадячском поветовом училище, и надобно сказать, что был преблагонравный и престарательный мальчик. Учитель российской грамматики, Никифор Тимофеевич Деепричастие, говаривал, что если бы все у него были так старательны, как Шпонька, то он не носил бы с собою в класс кленовой линейки ... Тетрадка у него всегда была чистенькая, кругом облинеенная, нигде ни пятнышка. Сидел он всегда смирно, сложив руки и уставив глаза на учителя ...
>
> Было уже ему без малого пятнадцать лет, когда перешел он во второй класс, где вместо сокращенного катехизиса и четырех правил арифметики принялся он за пространный, за книгу о должностях человека и за дроби ... пробыл еще два года и, с согласия матушки, вступил потом в П*** пехотный полк. (Гоголь, 1832 [1976]: 178- 179)

> When he was still a little boy he went to the local school at Gadyach and I must say he was exceedingly diligent and well-behaved. The Russian grammar teacher, Nikifor Timofeyevich Deyeprichastiye, used to say that if all his other boys applied themselves like Shponka there would be no need for that maplewood ruler of his ... His exercise book was always immaculate, with a ruled margin and not a mark anywhere. He would always sit very quietly, his arms folded, his eyes riveted on his teacher ...
>
> He was nearly fifteen when he entered class two, where instead of the abridged catechism and four rules of arithmetic he grappled with more complex matters, such as the duties of man and fractions. But when he saw that the further one advances, the more pitfalls lie in the way ... he stayed on another two years and then, with his mother's consent, entered the P——— Infantry Regiment. (Gogol, 1832 [1972]: 161–163).

The beginning of the paragraph highlights the explicit set of norms: 'Vanyusha', a 'diligent and well-behaved' pupil at the local grammar school, may be perceived by the reader (particularly if unaware of the Romantic negative aspect of 'diligence', which equates it with 'lack of inspiration') as an exemplary, sweet little boy. Such perception (if also unacquainted with the

Russian intelligentsia's disapproval of physical punishment in schools) may be strengthened by the next sentence, in which the teacher's endorsement of Shponka is mentioned. Even so, the modifier 'exceedingly' in the first sentence does hint at the possible presence of another, though yet implicit, set of norms. The next quoted sentence reinforces such inferences, albeit by using a double-standard terminology: an 'immaculate' exercise book is, indeed, a proof of neatness, as is also the 'ruled margin'; however, an 'immaculate' exercise book with 'not a mark anywhere' lacks precisely what it should have: written exercises. Thus the new set of norms, according to which exercise books should, indeed, be 'marked' (and thus also implying that school children should not 'sit very quietly, arms folded and eyes riveted on the teacher') is taking shape. Still, the structure of the sentence, in which the 'immaculate' and 'with a ruled margin' and 'not a mark anywhere' are put together, leaves the two possible interpretations open, although more weight is given to the pejorative one. After further sentences, however, the truth is revealed: Shponka is simply a blockhead. His quietness is a sign of mental numbness and not of alertness; his compliance an indication of mental torpidity: 'He was nearly fifteen when he entered class two', etc. The rest of the paragraph is a sarcastic description of Shponka's difficulty in coping 'with more complex matters, such as the duties of man and fractions', as well as the inevitable outcome of his joining the army – a symbol (not only in Russian culture) of asinine obedience.

On the other hand, intellectual activity, which is the very contrary of intellectual apathy, can equally be satirized, when measured against another set of norms. In Swift's 'Balnibarbi episodes' of his *Gulliver's Travels*, a whole detailed description of over-intellectualization's absurd results ridicules not only intellectual pretentiousness, but the very scholarly activity itself. Another instance is Goethe's *Faust*, where human aspirations to knowledge are mocked and their futility recognized by the scholar himself:

> Wagner: Verzeiht! es ist ein groß Ergetzen,
>   Sich in den Geist der Zeiten zu versetzen;
>   Zu schauen, wie vor uns ein weiser Mann gedacht,
>   Und wie wirs dann zuletzt so herrlich weit gebracht.
> Faust: O ja, bis an die Sterne weit! ...
> Wagner: Mit Eifer hab ich mich der Studien beflissen;
>   Zwar weiß ich viel, doch möcht ich alles wissen. (abgang)
> Faust: Wie nur dem Kopf nicht alle Hoffnung schwindet,
>   Der immerfort an schalem Zeuge klebt,
>   Mit gierger Hand nach Schätzen gräbt,
>   Und froh ist, wenn er Regenwürmer findet!
> (Goethe, Erster Teil, l. 570 ff.)

> Wagner: I beg your pardon! Engaging the mind with past's spirit is a
>   great pleasure; to behold how a wise man has erstwhile thought, and
>   how we, eventually, have reached such glorious heights.

Faust: Oh yes, as high as the stars! …

Wagner: I have engaged in the studies with great zeal; indeed, I want to
    know, yet my wish is to know it all. (*Exits*)

Faust: How in the mind all hope does not fade, but eternally sticks to
    inane matter, and, greedily grubbing for treasures, is happy when it
    finds earthworms!

The 'glorious heights' to which the human mind has reached are indeed
disparaged by Faust, the scholar who has devoted his life to study. However,
although he does remark ironically, 'Oh yes, as high as the stars', the real
satire lies not in his mockery of Wagner's zeal for learning 'inane matter' and
of his happiness when he 'finds worms', unable to realize that they are far
from anything of real consequence; the real satire is Goethe's, when he
satirizes Wagner's intellectual arrogance, expressed in his wish 'to know it
all', the exaggerated expression serving as a clue to his real set of norms.

Sometimes it is just the distorted perception of a norm that is satirized. In
such cases it often happens that two sets of norms are explicitly confronted,
each nullifying the validity of the other. In his novel *Dead Souls* Nikolay
Gogol satirizes the self-importance and vice of title-bearers, thus indirectly
glorifying the Slavophile values of 'the pure and simple Russian soul'. However, on a higher level, he simultaneously ridicules this very 'pure simplicity'
when it is manifested in a naïve acceptance of the official set of norms (which
is, of course, the very same set of norms imposed by the condemned title-
bearers). In the following monologue Selifan, who is such a 'pure and simple
Russian soul', and serves as Chichikov's valet, speaks to his horse:

Ты думаешь, что скроешь свое поведение. Нет, ты живи по
правде, когда хочешь, чтобы тебе оказывали почтение. Вот у
помещика, что мы были, хорошие люди. Я с удовольствием
поговорю, коли хороший человек; с человеком хорошим мы
всегда свои други, тонкие приятели: выпить ли чаю, или
закусить – с охотою, коли хороший человек. Хорошему
человеку всякой отдаст почтение. Вот барина нашего всякой
уважает, потому что он, слышь ты, сполнял службу государскую,
он сколеской советник ... (Гоголь, 1953 [1842]: 41–42)

You think I don't know what you're up to? No, sir, you must deal fairly
if you want to be treated with respect. Now the servants of the gentleman we visited were good people. I'm glad to talk to a good man. With
a good man I'm always friends, the best of pals: any time I'd be glad to
have a cup of tea or a bite with a good man. Why, if he's a good man
everyone respects him. Take our master, for instance. Everyone respects
him because, you see, he was in government service, a collegiary councillor he is ... (Gogol, [1842] 1961: 49–50)[1]

Here the implicit set of norms is supposedly obvious, a kind of 'common
knowledge' shared by the readers, who know the meaning of the cultural unit
'a good man'. Selifan's set of norms is presented as part of this implicit,
'common' set of norms, his crooked logic being exposed only gradually: if a

man is good, everybody respects him; if a man is in government service, everybody respects him, too. The false deduction, according to which the respect people feel for both 'a good man' and 'a collegiary councillor' equates these two entities, creates the new, explicit and distorted set of norms which is satirized only at the end of the paragraph.

Thus a set of norms can be, by itself, the target of a satire that questions its validity, functioning and relevance. In Voltaire's *Candide*, the damning description of the sly and presumptuous 'Don Fernando d'Ibarca, y Figueroa, y Mascarenes, y Lampourdos, y Souza',[2] who intends to snatch Cunégonde, Candide's sweetheart, still makes no concession to Candide's naïvety:

> Il aimait les femmes à la fureur. Cunégonde lui parut ce qu'il avait jamais vu de plus beau. La première chose qu'il fit, fut de demander si elle n'était point la femme du capitaine. L'air dont il fit cette question alarma Candide: il n'osa pas dire qu'elle était sa femme, parce qu'en effet elle ne l'était point; il n'osait pas dire que c'était sa sœur, parce qu'elle ne l'était pas plus, et quoique ce mensonge officieux eût été autrefois très à la mode chez les anciens, et qu'il pût être utile aux modernes, son ame était trop pure pour trahir la vérité. (Voltaire, 1959 [1758]: 131)

> He loved women frenetically. Cunégonde appeared to him as the utmost beauty he had ever seen. The first thing he did was to ask her if she was not the captain's wife. The manner in which he asked that question alarmed Candide: he did not dare to say that she was his wife, because, indeed, she was not; he did not dare to say that she was his sister, because she was not that either, and although this unofficial lie had been in the past very fashionable among the ancients, and it could be useful for the moderns, his soul was too pure to betray the truth.

Voltaire questions the validity of *any* given set of norms (thus implicitly offering a new set of norms based on pragmatic reasoning). This very questioning becomes, in its turn, the target of a further satirization by Gogol. In the first scene of *The Government Inspector* the protagonists are engaged in a philosophical debate about the various kinds of bribe and the different grades of their moral invalidity. However, just before this ludicrous discussion starts, Gogol defines the implicit target of his satire: the general scepticism about values. In this scene the city mayor has invited his colleagues – the inspector of school, the manager of the charity institutions, the judge, the medical doctor and the two policemen of the town – and reads to them from a letter in which he is told that a government general inspector is due to arrive in their town, incognito:

> Городничий: ... Спешу, между прочим, уведомить тебя, что приехал чиновник с предписанием осмотреть всю губернию и особенно наш уезд. Так как я знаю, что за тобою, как за всяким, водятся грешки, потому что ты человек умный и не любишь пропускать того, что плывет в руки ... (*останавясь*), ну, здесь свои ... (Гоголь, [1836] 1952: 12)

ГОРОДНИЧИЙ: Да я так только заметил вам. Насчет же внутреннего распоряжения и того, что называет в письме Андрей Иванович грешками, я ничего не могу сказать. Да и странно говорить: нет человека, который бы за собою не имел каких-нибудь грехов. Это уже так самим богом устроено, и волтерианцы напрасно против этого говорят. (Ibid.: 14)

The Mayor: ... I hasten to inform you, among other things, that an official has arrived with instructions to inspect the whole province, and especially our district. As I know that you have your little failings like everybody else, for you are a sensible man and don't like to let things slip through your fingers ... (*pausing*) well, we are all friends here ... (Gogol, [1836] 1926: 8)

The Mayor: Oh well, I only just mentioned it. As for the way that the business of the court is conducted, and what Andrey Ivanovitch in his letter calls 'failings', I can say nothing. And indeed, what is there to say? There is no man entirely free from sin ... That is ordained by God Himself, and it is no use the Voltairians disputing it. (Ibid.: 12)[3]

In Gogol's writings it often happens that several layers of meaning, each of which functions under a different set of norms, join together within one utterance. In such cases satire becomes a 'sword flaming and turning' that keeps all parties involved away from the fool's paradise of illusory immunity. One of Gogol's strongest satirical phrases is simultaneously aimed at the protagonists present in the scene; at the Tsarist authorities who relied on heavy censorship and who had every good reason to hate and fear 'scribblers' like Gogol; at Gogol himself, as one of the 'scribblers' mentioned; at the audience that is watching the scene; and finally, perhaps even at mankind, as a general addressee who heedlessly joins in a satirical condemnation of its own self.

ГОРОДНИЧИЙ: ... (*Грозит самому себе кулаком*) Эх ты, толстоносый! Сосульку, тряпку принял за важного человека! Вон он теперь по всей дороге заливает колокольчиком! Разнесет по всему свету историю. Мало того, что пойдешь в посмешище, – найдется щелкопер, бумагомарака, в комедию тебя вставит. Вот что обидно! Чина, звания не пощадит, и будут все скалить зубы и бить в ладоши. Чему смеетесь? – Над собою смеетесь! (Гоголь, [1836] 1952: 95–96)

The Mayor: ... (*Shakes his fist at himself*) Ah, you blockhead! To take a milksop, a rag like that, for a man of consequence! His bells are ringing along the high-road now! He will spread the tale all over the world. It's not enough to be made a laughing-stock – there will come some scribbler, some inkflinger, and will put you in a farce. That's what's mortifying! He won't spare your rank and your calling, and everyone will grin and clap. (*To the audience*) What are you laughing at? You are laughing at yourselves! (Gogol, [1836] 1926: 120)

Although satire seems to demand the rectification of a behaviour that is incongruous with a given set of norms, this is not always the case. When it is realized that faultiness – of human nature as well as of any sets of norms – is an incorrigible given, satire becomes a bitter expression of despair. Mankind is then seen as just one component of an indifferent universe, engineered by an alienated force which ironically bestowed it with a set of norms and values, only to endow it also with the mental capacity fully to grasp this very set's practical futility. Satirical remarks on this subject have been part of human culture since at least the second millennium BCE. The most obvious source for this approach is the answer that the biblical Job gave to his self-righteous friends, who had reprimanded him for his complaints over his unjustified misfortune:

אָמְנָם כִּי אַתֶּם־עָם וְעִמָּכֶם תָּמוּת חָכְמָה. 2

גַּם לִי לֵבָב כְּמוֹכֶם לֹא־נֹפֵל אָנֹכִי מִכֶּם וְאֶת־מִי־אֵין כְּמוֹ־אֵלֶּה. 3

שְׂחֹק לְרֵעֵהוּ אֶהְיֶה קֹרֵא לֶאֱלוֹהַּ וַיַּעֲנֵהוּ שְׂחוֹק צַדִּיק תָּמִים. 4

לַפִּיד בּוּז לְעַשְׁתּוּת שַׁאֲנָן נָכוֹן לְמוֹעֲדֵי רָגֶל. 5

יִשְׁלָיוּ אֹהָלִים לְשֹׁדְדִים וּבַטֻּחוֹת לְמַרְגִּיזֵי אֵל לַאֲשֶׁר הֵבִיא אֱלוֹהַּ בְּיָדוֹ. 6

איוב י"ב 2-6

2   No doubt you are the people, and wisdom will die with you.
3   But I have understanding as well as you; I am not inferior to you. Who does not know such things as these?
4   I am the laughing stock to my friends; I, who called upon God and he answered me, a just and blameless man, I am a laughing stock.
5   Those at ease have contempt for misfortune, but it is ready for those whose feet are unstable.
6   The tents of robbers are at peace, and those who provoke God are secure, who bring their god in their hands. (Job, XII: 2–6)[4]

Job's questioning of the validity of any norms is posed within a sincere claim for justice (although while also satirizing his friends for their naïve belief in divine justice!). The same idea is presented by Voltaire in a far less philosophical (and far more cynical) way, in the following report of the shipwreck that Candide had endured:

Travaillait qui pouvait, personne ne s'entendait, personne ne commandait. L'anabatiste aidait un peu à la manœuvre; il était sur le tillac; un matelot furieux le frappe rudement et l'étend sur les planches; mais du coup qu'il lui donna, il eut lui-même une si violente secousse qu'il tomba hors du vaisseau la tête la première. Il restait suspendu et accroché à une partie de mât rompuë. Le bon Jacques court à son secours, l'aide à remonter, et de l'effort qu'il fit il est précipité dans la mer à la vuë du matelot, qui le laissa périr sans daigner seulement le regarder. Candide approche, voit son bienfaiteur qui reparaît un moment et qui est englouti pour jamais. Il veut se jeter après lui dans la mer, le philosophe Pangloss l'en empêche, en lui prouvant que la rade de Lisbonne avait été formée exprés pour que cet anabatiste s'y noyât. Tandis qu'il le prouvait à priori, le vaisseau s'entr'ouvre, tout périt à la réserve de Pangloss, de

Candide, et de ce brutal matelot qui avait noyé la vertueux anabatiste.
(Voltaire, 1758 [1952]: 100–101).

'Twas in vain to pretend to assist, for no one could give orders or be
heard. The anabaptist gave what assistance he could, and remained upon
the deck, when a brutal sailor knocked him down; but, with the violence
of the blow, the tar himself tumbled head foremost over-board, and fell
upon a piece of the broken mast, which he immediately grasped. Honest
James, forgetting the injury he had so lately received from him, flew to
his assistance, and, with great difficulty, hauled him in again, but, in the
attempt, was, by a sudden jerk of the ship, thrown over-board himself, in
sight of the very fellow whom he had risked his life to save, and who
took not the least notice of him in this distress. Candide, who beheld all
that past, and saw his benefactor one moment rising above water, and
the next swallowed up by the merciless waves, was preparing to jump
after him; but was prevented by the philosopher Pangloss, who demon-
strated to him, that the coast of Lisbon had been made on purpose for
the anabaptist to be drowned there. While he was proving his argument
a priori, the ship foundered, and the whole crew perished, except Pangloss,
Candide, and the ungrateful sailor who had been the means of drowning
the good anabaptist. (Voltaire, [1758] 192?: 50)

According to this view, the very validity of any set of norms and its
relevance is put into question. No predicament, no effort, and certainly no
kind of behaviour or attitude can guarantee either spiritual happiness or
physical well-being. Satire is thus proposed as a partial escape from total
despair, where the last resource for human spiritual strength is the simultaneous retention of norms and the conscious realization of their meaninglessness.
This kind of satire accepts the human existential helplessness but yet, paradoxically, keeps the human right and responsibility to judge according to a
set of norms. The recognition of the consequent logical absurdity is finally
expressed by the satirical laughter. Thus, although its primary structure is
simple, satire can be infinite and thus, as irony, it can reach the borders of
infinite negation.

CHAPTER FOUR

The structure of musical satire

Musical satire must be bound to norms. Therefore, more than any other kind of musical irony, musical satire depends on musical norms, i.e., musical styles and musical topics. Musical satire, thus, is concerned with the assessment of certain phenomena, musical ones or their semantic correlations, against a musical, aesthetic and/or ethical set of norms, and with the implied demand for their rectification.

Since stylistic sets of norms often reflect broader – aesthetic and even ethical – sets of norms of a specific culture, the satirization of a musical set of norms may imply the satirization of other sets of norms within the same culture. Thus, using analogies and correlations, music can also satirize ethical and/or aesthetic sets of norms. For example, tonality, as a preferred value in certain stylistic sets of musical norms, relates to broader cultural values of clarity in rhetoric (Ratner, 1980: 33–37 and 107–108). Accordingly, by mocking tonality and tonal procedures such as harmonic cadences, Prokofiev, in his *Classical Symphony*, is also mocking, even if only by analogy, the broader value of rhetorical clarity. Extramusical values can be reflected in the use of musical topics, too. Hence, within the stylistic context of the eighteenth century, the minuet is a topic correlated with nobility and sophistication (Allanbrook, 1983: 33–34). A failure to perform a stylistically correct minuet may therefore be perceived, by analogy, as a failure to comply with the requirements of nobility and sophistication, thus satirizing simple-mindedness or a 'peasant-like' disposition, as happens in several of Haydn's symphonies. On the other hand, if the minuet is performed correctly, but is incongruent with its own musical context, then the very norm that it represents, i.e. its very topicality and/or the broader social layer of nobility (and its norms), may be the mocked value.

Musical satire that refers to a particular element within a musical set of norms is bound to its specific style. In such cases the satire's target can be either the failure to comply with the musical norms of the specific style or the musical set of norms itself. Examples for the first instance are Mozart's *Musikalische Spass*, which mocks the failure to match the period's stylistic norms, and Bartók's *Concerto for Orchestra*, where he satirizes Shostakovich's apparent failure to comply with Bartók's own norms and definitions of musical banality. The second instance can be illustrated by Mussorgsky's *Rayok*, Shostakovich's *Satirical Cantata*, Prokofiev's *Classical Symphony* or Stravinsky's *Pulcinella*.[1]

Musical correlations of particulars within an aesthetic set of norms characteristically relate to norms that are expressed in both the ethical and the

Fig. 4.1

Related sets of norms in Shostakovich's 'Happiness' (*From Jewish Folk Poetry*, op. 79, No. 11)

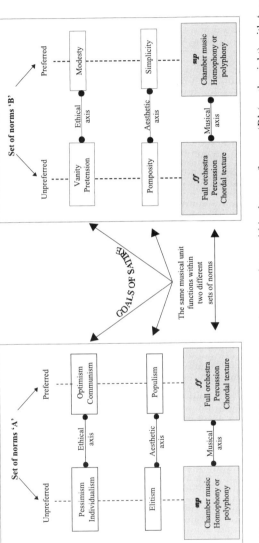

The march, played by a full orchestra with highlighted percussion, correlates within the set of norms 'B' (on the right) with 'pomposity', 'vanity' and 'pretension', all located on the unpreferred poles of its aesthetic and ethical value-axes. Consequently, it is also located on the unpreferred pole of the parallel musical value-axis. It is the exaggeration of dynamics and orchestration that points, in this case and within this set of norms, to the march's incongruity with the preferred poles of 'modesty' on the ethical axis and 'simplicity' on the aesthetic one. A different set of norms, however, may assign to the very same musical unit a completely different value. For example, within the given set of norms 'A'(on the left), it correlates with the preferred unit of 'populism' on the aesthetic axis and the preferred units of 'optimism' and 'communalism' on the ethical axis. Thus an exaggeration, i.e. a stylistic incongruity of the musical unit, within a culture that is familiar with both sets of norms, will point to the satirization of the whole set of norms ('A') within which its correlatives are considered preferred values.

Fig. 4.2

Related sets of norms in Mahler's opening theme of the Fourth Symphony

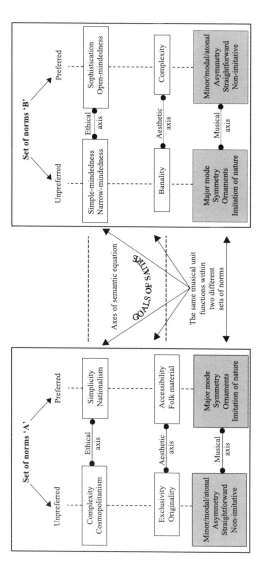

The major, symmetrical and ornamented melody that opens Mahler's Fourth Symphony, with its background sound of sleigh-bells, can be perceived, within one set of norms, as simplistic and banal, while in another set as authentic and charming in its accessibility. The complex network of correlational axes enables Mahler to satirize, directly, banality and narrow-mindedness, by stressing its incongruity with the preferred values of his own set of norms 'B', while at the same time, indirectly and in a more ambiguous way, satirizing the whole value system of another set of norms, 'A'.

aesthetic set of values within a culture. For example, the scene in the newspaper office from Shostakovich's opera *The Nose* satirizes the phenomenon of disconnectedness within a non-musical set of norms, according to which connection, communication and human concern are to be preferred over isolation, miscommunication and indifference. To convey this idea Shostakovich uses the musical correlative of 'disconnectedness': series of disconnected notes in an eight-part *hocketus* texture. The atonal musical context of the scene exaggerates its correlational purport of disconnection, thus creating a double incongruity with norms: one with the musical stylistic norms of the medieval *hocketus* and the other with the non-musical ethical norm of human concern.[2]

Since many musical units correlate with more than one semantic unit, they can be used to connect two different sets of values. Thus, by satirizing a musical characteristic that correlates with an unpreferred value within a certain set of norms, while also correlating with another value that is preferred in another set of norms, a double satirical goal can be achieved: directly, the specific characteristic is satirized as unpreferred within the original set of norms; in addition to that, an entirely different set of norms, within which the semantic correlative of the same musical unit is preferred, is satirized too, albeit indirectly. For example, the heavy, exaggerated major-mode march in Shostakovich's song 'Happiness', which closes his song-cycle *From Jewish Folk Poetry,* directly satirizes its semantic ethical correlative, the vain self-confidence of its narrator. Indirectly, though, it also satirizes communal populism, which is another ethical correlative of the same musical unit, this time functioning within a different set of norms, that of social realism (Fig. 4.1).[3]

Certain of Mahler's symphonic movements can be analysed along these musico-semantic lines, applying the same paradigm of relatedness between musical and ethical norms. The use of exaggeration within these structures will also imply the mockery of yet another set, one of *aesthetic* norms, in which the specific feature that is exaggerated is actually appreciated and preferred: in Mahler's case it is the Austrian urban folk music's set of norms, which prefers simple tuneful melodies with many ornamentations (Fig. 4.2). In this case, though, there is yet another, even more problematic aspect: the semantic units of 'simplicity' and 'naïvety' are associated, within the Christian set of beliefs, with the semantic units of 'innocence' and 'purity' (as they are expressed, for example, in Wagner's *Parsifal*). According to unwritten yet nevertheless very tangible rules, Mahler had converted to Christianity before he became the Vienna Opera House's director. His Second, Third and Fourth Symphonies, written in the years following his conversion, relate to Christian ideals and appear to express a passionate religious belief. For example, the opening theme of the Fourth Symphony was described, using an unmistakably Christian imagery, as 'St. Ursula's smile' (Bauer-Lechner, 1923 [1980]:

152). Regardless of that, Mahler's real spiritual conviction was never completely clear, and his own statements and remarks on this topic are quite ambiguous. In writing this theme he apparently aimed to achieve the utmost expression of a child's simplicity (ibid.). This, however, may imply either childlike innocence or a childish naïvety. Is it possible that in this theme Mahler also mocks, albeit very indirectly, the naïvety and simple-mindedness of Christianity? Moreover, is he pointing to possible axes of semantic equation between Christian naïvety and nationalistic narrow-mindedness? The only hint of that lies in the *stylistic* exaggeration of the musical unit that functions in different roles in each of the above sets of norms.[4]

CHAPTER FIVE

Satirizing techniques

Being always based upon the violation of a set of norms, satire is structurally bound to distort its object, in a way that will make its censure apparent.[1] The distortion can primarily affect its structure, that is the proportions among its components and their essence, and/or one or more of its components, which will be satirized by their exaggeration.

Structural distortion

Structural distortion can be achieved by three main devices: (1) the removal of an essential component from the satirized object; (2) the insertion of a new component, and (3) the replacement of one or more of the object's characteristic components.

Removal of essentials

The removal of an essential component from an object, while keeping all its other components in place, satirizes the tendency to overlook priorities and the inability to separate the wheat from the chaff. The most banal example is the man who walks in the street with no trousers but with his tie on; another example can be seen in Brian Morton's *L'Isle de Gilligan*, a parody on pseudo-educated discourse that originally appeared in *Dissent* under the title 'How not to write for *Dissent*'.

> The hegemonic discourse of postmodernity valorizes modes of expressive and 'aesthetic' praxis which preclude any dialogic articulation (in, of course, the Bakhtinian sense) of the antinomies of consumer capitalism. But some emergent forms of discourse inscribed in popular fictions contain, as a constitutive element, metanarratives wherein the characteristic tropes of consumer capitalism are subverted even as they are apparently affirmed. (Morton, 1990).

The parody presents the reader with a richly adorned flow of words, abundant with characteristic terminology which supplies the 'academic atmosphere' of a pretentious scholarly review. However, when stripped of what is colloquially called 'postmodernist blabber', the subject matter is quite banal, i.e.: 'Postmodernism disapproves of ambiguous expressions concerning consumer culture. Nevertheless, certain popular fictions that apparently encourage this culture, are, in fact, ironic'. The realization that popular fictions are not particularly influenced by postmodernist aesthetic writings enhances the general feel of the absurd. The parody's main satirizing point is, of course, that the richly adorned verbal halo succeeds only in blurring the original meaning, transforming it into a rather vague and confused pile of words, into which the subject matter itself has almost disappeared.

Musical redundancy

Musical applications of this technique highlight music's more redundant components, like conventional accompaniment figures and/or repetitive clichés, which tend to be perceived as background material and therefore do not seem to carry its main purport. However, since music, in itself, does not seem to have 'essential' and 'inessential' components, redundancy in music is not an absolute, and the definition of what is redundant in music is quite complicated. Here again the role of a set of norms, this time one that defines the musically meaningful versus the musically redundant, is apparent. For example, the accepted set of norms at the beginning of the century seemed to regard well-defined melodies and a functional tonality as musical essentials. Thus dozens of invectives on Debussy's music are written in the vein of the following two examples:

> A vacuum has been described as nothing shut up in a box, and the prelude entitled *L'Après-midi d'un faune* may aptly be described as nothing, expressed in musical terms ... The piece begins with a fragment of the chromatic scale played by the flute, manifestly selected with care to express nothing. *(Referee,* London, 21 August 1904, quoted in Slonimsky, 1953: 92)

> It would be impossible to conceive a finer vehicle of expression than that invented by Debussy through the simple yet original process of abolishing rhythm, melody and tonality from music and thus leaving nothing but atmosphere. If we could abolish from the human organization flesh, blood and bones, we should still have membrane. Membranous music is perhaps the fitting expression of *Pelléas et Mélisande.* (James Gibbond Huneker, New York *Sun,* 8 February 1911, quoted in Slonimsky, 1953: 102)

The perception of a musical component as redundant depends, among other things, on cognitive principles of perception, like the *Gestalt* principle of *Prägnanz,* or the 'figure and ground' illusion. This has partly to do with the conscious or unconscious choice that the listener may make to perceive certain musical information as 'foreground' or 'background' material, like the choice to perceive one part of a fugue as 'foreground material', or to prefer the melodic treble of Brahms's Finale of his Fourth Symphony over its chaconne-like bass (Sloboda, 1985: 169–171).[2] Besides such issues of musical cognition there are musical elements which, in suitable contexts, tend to be perceived as 'ground' versus 'figure', for example accompaniment figures, which tend to be patterned and repetitive, versus a melody (ibid.: 172).

Here, of course, stylistic conventions play a major role, with implicit definitions of both 'melody' and 'accompaniment'; an Alberti bass figure is perceived within the eighteenth century's stylistic context as background, and therefore as 'redundant'; but within the twentieth century's minimalist style the very same figure may be in the foreground and perceived as a musical essential.

The most extreme case of the removal of the essential in music, while leaving the redundant in, is apparently John Cage's *4'33"*, which seems to have removed music itself from the musical work. Regardless of the profundity of Cage's own analysis and of explicit programme notes stressing the importance of silence in music, arguing that 'no silence exists that is not pregnant with sound' (Cage, quoted in Revill, 1992: 163), still, in most of the work's performances, the main reactions of the audience are smiles, giggles, and a general feeling of bemusement. The first and strongest impression here is that 'the essential is missing'. Therefore, regardless of any authorial intentions, the reaction is a satirical laughter, that may be directed either at the composer and the audience, or both.

It is quite probable that Cage himself meant the piece, at least originally, as a satire:

> I have, for instance, several new desires (two may seem absurd, but I am
> serious about them): first, to compose a piece of uninterrupted silence
> and to sell it to the Muzak Co. It will be $4\frac{1}{2}$ minutes long – these being
> the standard lengths of 'canned' music, and its title will be 'Silent
> Prayer'. It will open with a single idea which I will attempt to make as
> seductive as the color and shape or fragrance of a flower. The ending
> will approach imperceptibility. (Cage, *A Composer's Confessions* [1948],
> quoted in Pritchett, 1993: 59)

The paramount function of a priori sets of norms regarding music is reflected in our cultural habits and expectations. A semiotic analysis, however, would expose the work's semantic structure of infinite negation, built upon 'the music of silence' as a conceptual basis. The result is an infinite irony which, when measured against various subsets of norms, will render a large amount of probable satires: a satire on the importance of the unimportant, a satire on the public's expectations (and here Gogol's double-edged dagger becomes obvious) or, perhaps, a satire on the unimportance of the important. Such satire would condemn the self-importance of musical content (and perhaps also of music-makers).

Likewise, the implicit aesthetic demand that the audience should come with 'open ears and open minds' could very well be another object of a satire. No audience and no author are free of some set of norms, and therefore the demand to 'come to the work with an open mind' is a demand that has its own structure of infinite irony.

It is not a coincidence that in the same year of composing *4'33"*, Cage was studying the music of Erik Satie. It was Satie (who, again not coincidentally, also happened to be among Debussy's main critics) who suggested the ironical idea of 'furnishing music'. The painter Fernand Léger quoted what Satie had said to him in one of their conversations:

> 'Il y a tout de même à réaliser une musique d'ameublement, c'est-à-dire une musique qui ferait partie des bruits ambiants, qui en tiendrait compte. Je la suppose mélodieuse, elle adoucirait le bruit des couteaux, des fourchettes sans les dominer, sans s'imposer. Elle meublerait les silences pesantes parfois entre les convives. Elle leur épargnerait les banalités courantes. Elle neutraliserait en même temps les bruits de la rue qui entrent dans le jeu sans discrétion'. Ce serait, disait-il, répondre à un besoin. (Léger, 1952: 137)

> 'Even so, there's room for a "musique d'ameublement", that's to say, music which would be part of the noises around it and would take account of them. I think of it as being tuneful, softening the noise of knives and forks without overpowering them or making itself obtrusive. It would fill the silences which can sometimes weigh heavy between table companions. It would banish the need to make banal conversation. At the same time it would neutralise street noises, which can be tactless in their behaviour.' It would, he said, be responding to a need. (Orledge, 1995: 74–75)

It is funny as well as almost pathetic to see the efforts that Satie had invested in his attempts to actualize what he might have perceived as a personal absurd joke, and to create a 'completely redundant' music. His failure to achieve this goal in his *Musique d'ameublement*, 'which was emphatically not to be listened to' (Volta, 1989: 175), is almost telling. Darius Milhaud recounts the original event, a show within an art exhibition, in which Satie's work was played:

> Une notice dans le programme prévenait le public qu'il ne devait pas attacher plus d'importance aux ritournelles qui seraient jouées pendant l'entracte, qu'au lustre ou aux chaises de la galerie. Mais contrairement à nos prévisions, aussitôt que la musique commença, les auditeurs se dirigèrent rapidement vers leurs places. Satie eut beau leur crier: 'Mais parlez donc! Circulez! N'écoutez pas!' Ils écoutaient, ils se taisaient. (Milhaud, 1973: 103)

> A programme note warned the audience that it was not to pay any more attention to the ritornelles that would be played during the intervals than to the candelabra, the seats, or the balcony. Contrary to our expectations however, as soon as the music started up, the audience began to stream back to their seats. It was no use for Satie to shout: 'Go on talking! Walk about! Don't listen!' They listened without speaking. (Milhaud, 1973 [1987]: 100)

Contemporary reactions to the function of 'background music', be it a piece of 'muzak' played at the nearby mall or Mozart's *Jupiter* Symphony played on the radio while we are reading the newspaper, clarify the extent to which the definition of musical purport depends on social conventions and habits. Darius Milhaud lived to see Satie's prophecy become true. In his first autobiography he writes:

> L'avenir donna du reste raison à Satie: aujourd'hui, ménagères et enfants laissent la musique pénétrer chez eux, sans discernement, lisant et travaillant au son de la radio. Et dans tous les lieux publics, dans les grands magasins, les Uniprix, les restaurants, les clients sont sans répit abreuvés de musique. En Amérique, les 'cafeterias' possèdent un assez grand nombre d'appareils pour que chaque client puisse, moyennant la modeste somme de cinq sous, meubler sa solitude ou accompagner la conversation de son convive. N'est-ce pas là de la 'musique d'ameublement', celle qu'on entend, mais qu'on n'écoute pas? (Milhaud, 1973: 104)

> In any case, the future was to prove that Satie was right: nowadays, children and housewives fill their homes with unheeded music, reading and working to the sound of the wireless. And in all public places, large stores and restaurants, the customers are drenched in an unending flood of music. In America, every cafeteria is equipped with a sufficient number of machines for each client to be able, for the modest sum of five cents, to furnish his own solitude with music or supply a background for his conversation with his guest. Is this not 'musique d'ameublement', heard but not listened to? (Milhaud, 1973 [1987]: 101)

Erik Satie was indeed the prophet of Muzak, those 'easy-listening records, string-drenched music specifically intended to linger in the background' (Gifford, 1995). *The New Harvard Dictionary of Music* defines Muzak as 'a trade name for music intended solely for use as background in work or public place', and adds that 'the name has also come to serve as the generic (and sometimes pejorative) term for any bland background music'.[3] Writing about the Muzak Company, Bill Gifford reports that what its musical arrangers mainly do is:

> to take the edges off of songs. Vocals are removed and replaced by a suitably anonymous instrument, usually piano, guitar, woodwinds or vibes. Punchy rhythm parts are deflated a bit; distorted guitars and overly brassy horns are filed down. High, squeaky passages are lowered an octave, and dissonant chords are sweetened … Thus each arrangement is not a single piece of music but a component of a larger whole, a brick in Muzak's wall of sound. The differences between individual bricks are minimal, at best … 'Summertime' is reduced to a collection of pretty riffs, pleasingly arranged but ultimately meaningless. (Gifford, 1995)

A comparison between these musical traits and those specified by Sloboda as musical elements that draw attention sheds some light on the picture. Sloboda lists as musical foreground elements 'high pitch' and 'significant musical events', such as a change against an unchanging background, change of quality or texture of the focal melodic line, and any sudden change in the other parts (Sloboda, 1985: 174). He also mentions the contrary effect, i.e., the lowering of clear perception, that can be achieved by a 'reverberating environment' and the 'masking' of the basses' upper partials or harmonics (ibid.: 172–173), actually meaning that our perception of an independent bass line is lowered by an exclusive use of consonance, resulting in a general 'sound envelope' whose parts cannot be clearly defined.

Muzak's set of norms demands a 'conscious inaudibility' of music. In this context it has various functions: calming down the spirit, stimulating certain types of activity, reducing background noises or filling up embarrassingly silent social space. However, its transfer to another context, governed by a different set of norms, according to which music does have an independent, meaningful purport that should be conveyed and listened to, may create a satire. In such a context, a 'Richard Clayderman concert', for example, can be looked upon as a musical satire, at least in relation to the audience in the concert-hall that listens to it. The satire lies in the incongruity of bringing together an attentive audience and supplying them with musical material that is tailored for another set of norms, according to which redundant musical material should be preferred.

It is quite clear, however, that the audience in such a concert does not perceive any satirical import. This is mainly because its set of norms follows a different definition of musical redundancy, and/or because it is biased towards a preference of visual distracters. On the other hand, the same argument provides the explanation of the fact that such a situation may be perceived as satirical according to another set of norms, biased towards a preference for purely auditory information in the context of a live performance.

Another reason is that the satirical removal of essentials in music cannot be achieved with just the 'simple yet original process of abolishing rhythm, melody and tonality from music', as claimed by the New York *Sun* journalist quoted above, but concurrently must also emphasize the stylistic banality and redundancy of the material. Since we tend to perceive whatever we hear as 'figure', we do have a particular difficulty in discerning redundancy in music. By accumulating musical clichés and repetitions of exclusively 'atmospheric' or 'background' musical material, the satirical import of the present musical inanity is established, while its acceptance as some kind of a new musical style – although the boundaries do sometimes seem quite blurred – is rejected.

Some instances of Satie's attempts to create 'redundant music' are thus easily perceived as satirical, like his 'Españaña' for piano, the third piece of his *Croquis et agaceries d'un gros bonhomme en bois*, written in 1913. Here he accumulates redundancies of the then popular-to-the-point-of-banality 'Spanish musical topic', without actually rendering any musical 'subject matter'(Ex. 5.1).

Within this amalgamated mass of rhythmical and gestural clichés, Satie also quotes from Chabrier's orchestral Rhapsody *España* (1883), which was so popular that Waldteufel wrote on it his series of *España Waltzes* (1886). However,

Ex. 5.1
Satie's Españaña

even without these quotations, and in comparison with works like Albeniz's 'Malagueña' from his own *España* (1890), Granados' first dance from his *10 Danzas Españolas* (1892) and Ravel's 'Malagueña' from his *Rapsodie Espagnole* (1907), Satie's satire becomes apparent. After a series of repetitive banal 'Spanish' musical gestures Satie adds a number of out-of-context chromatic passages, unrelated harmonic progressions and pseudo-modal motifs, making his satire of Ravel almost too realistic and thus far more poignant, since the main point here is not so much the banality as the inanity of the material, which in spite of rendering the general 'Spanish' topic still leaves the listener waiting for 'something to begin' – which it never does.

Banality as redundancy
The musically banal, the musically redundant and background musical material are not synonyms; still, they are related to each other by the paucity of musical information they convey. Therefore positioning the musically banal at the focal point of a musical text can be regarded as a derivative variant of the satirical 'removal of the essential'.

Focusing on inane banality has long been a favourite device of satirists all over the world. In the specific case of the Russian colloquial vocabulary, however, banality is yet further associated with primitivism, bearing the general label 'African Cannibals'. 'Ellochka the Cannibal', for example, is a character from Ilf and Petrov's satirical novel about the New Economic Policy years in Soviet Russia, *The Twelve Chairs*. In the chapter dedicated to the description of Ellochka, a prototype of the ignorant and culturally illiterate New Soviet Woman, the two writers give an almost full account of her thirty-word vocabulary, the most prevalent among which are 'You're being vulgar', 'Ho-ho', 'Great!', 'Ghastly', 'Don't tell me how to live!', 'Ter-r-rific!' and 'Oho!':[4] 'Словарь Вильяма Шекспира по подсчету исследователей составляет двенадцать тысяч слов. Словарь негра из людоедского племени "Мумбо-Юмбо" составляет триста слов. Эллочка Щукина легко и свободно обходилась тридцатью'. (Ильф и Петров, 1928: 213; 'William Shakespeare's vocabulary has been estimated by the experts at twelve thousand words. The vocabulary of a negro from the Mumbo-Jumbo tribe amounts to three hundred words. Ellochka Shukin managed easily and fluently on thirty' [Ilf and Petrov, 1928 (1971): 154]).[5]

Ilf and Petrov were immensely popular in Russia during the 1920s to 1940s, and the characters of their novels became antonomasia.[6] Shostakovich knew their works well and often quoted from their writings. Their approach not only suited his own, but also had an impact on his ethical and aesthetic values. For example, one of his major condemnations of Prokofiev, whose personality he overtly disliked, was what he saw as the composer's superficiality and banal inanity:

> Prokofiev had two favourite words. One was 'amusing' which he used to evaluate everything around him. Everything – people, events, music. He seemed to feel that 'amusing' covered *Wozzeck*. The second was 'Understood?' That's when he wanted to know whether he was making himself clear.
>
> Those two favourite words irritated me. Why the simple-minded cannibal's vocabulary? Ellochka the Cannibal, from Ilf and Petrov's story, had a third word in her arsenal: 'homosexuality'. But Prokofiev managed with just two. (Volkov, 1979: 25)

Primitivism, simple-mindedness and banality are always condemned and satirized in Shostakovich's works. Here, however, satire functions within a complex network of musical imports, and is thus more difficult to decipher. The redundancy in Shostakovich's music does not result from the removal of essentials, but rather from the manifest presence of the 'inessential', that is, the emphatic use of musical banalities, musical clichés and/or musical background material, and in their location in the musical foreground.[7] In these cases the musical set of norms, in relation to which the redundant element is measured and appreciated, is explicitly present, either simultaneously in other elements of the musical texture, or contextually, in relation to other musical sections that appear before and after.

The chorus of servants in the first act of Shostakovich's opera *Lady Macbeth of the Mtsensk District* consists of a banal melodic figure, sung over a hefty parody of a waltz accompaniment pattern, made up of a monotonous drone and open octaves, correlated with the 'folk–peasant' musical topic (Ex. 5.2, mm. 275 ff.).[8] To enhance the simplistic folk effect, the servants sing in unison, and the second phrase begins on the fifth, possibly as a satirical hint to the simple folk's singing, in which the fifth appears, as a sudden new start of the original melody, with no preparation.

This choral portion appears immediately after a section that has no repetitions and no banalities. On the contrary, it incorporates complex harmonic

Ex. 5.2

Shostakovich's *Lady Macbeth of the Mtsensk District*, act 1.

The servants' chorus. After a passage loaded with dissonances comes an emphatically banal, folk-like drone bass-accompaniment to a patterned and repetitive melody.

progressions and consists, almost exclusively, of harsh dissonances. The contextual incongruity of the musically banal and its exaggeration by the hammering drone (thus emphasizing that this banality is neither coincidental nor the result of a compositional miscalculation) make the satire obvious.

A similar analysis may offer a solution to the continuing debate about the meaning of the famous march section in the first movement of Shostakovich's Seventh Symphony, described as 'one of the most notorious and slandered passages in Twentieth-century music' (Blokker and Dearling, 1979: 83). This section was admired as an expression of Soviet courage (Rabinovich, 1959: 73), ridiculed (by Bartók, in his *Concerto for Orchestra*), portrayed as 'the approaching army – from a Leningrader's point of view – happily, almost gaily in anticipation' (Blokker and Dearling, 1979: 84–85) and interpreted as 'surely ... the studied simplicity of totalitarian poster-art' (MacDonald, 1990: 157).

However, a genuinely musical satire cannot distinguish between German and Soviet stupid coarseness, unless by clear musical labels, normally achieved by quotations.[9] Thus, notwithstanding MacDonald's claim, according to which this passage is 'fundamentally a satirical picture of Stalinist society in the thirties' (ibid.: 159), it is more likely that the conductor Yevgeny Mravinsky's alleged remark about its 'universalised image of stupidity and crass tastelessness' (ibid.: 159, no reference given) is the one that should be followed.

The most overwhelming quality of the march in the Seventh Symphony is precisely its blunt banality; its location amidst non-repetitive, non-patterned, and definitely non-banal musical themes, among which it pops up like a sore thumb; and the immediate satirical implications of this contrast (Ex. 5.3). Its *double entendre* is mentioned in almost all of the analyses and descriptions of the work, but only a few of them pay attention to the blunt contrast between this particular theme and its musical context. Even in the cases where this is done, it is normally on a descriptive ground, i.e. the first musical passages are perceived as describing 'the peaceful life in Leningrad before the war', and the march as describing 'the war' (even Blokker and Dearling, who note the ambivalence of all the musical themes, fail to define this obvious contrast between the complex ambiguity of the context and the blatant banality of this specific theme).

Shostakovich is quoted twice – once by Aram Khachaturyan and once by Isaak Glikman – as apologizing for a possible similarity between this passage and Ravel's *Boléro* (Wilson, 1994: 148). This repeated apology, though, could imply quite its contrary: the composer might have been making a statement. This assumption could also be inferred from the following passage, taken from Glikman's memoirs:

Он сказал, что ему захотелось повидать меня и показать начало задуманного им сочинения, которое, быть может, никому не понадобится, раз свирепствует такая небывалая война.

После минутного колебания он сел за рояль и сыграл возвышенно-прекрасную экспозицию Седьмой симфонии и тему вариаций, изображающую фашистское нашествие. Мы оба были очень взволнованы. Надо сказать, что Дмитрий Дмитриевич нередко исполнял свои новые произведения со слезами на глазах.

Мы погрузились в молчание. Он прервал его такими словами (они у меня записаны): 'Я не знаю, как сложится судьба этой вещи, – и после паузы добавил, – досужие критики, наверное,

Ex. 5.3
Themes from Shostakvich's Seventh Symphony, first movement

The last theme, No. 6, is symmetrical, banal, repetitive and predictable.[10] However, it is its incongruity with the context that ascertains its satirical import and its mocking of the musical 'universalized image of stupidity and tastelessness'.

упрекнут меня в том, что я подражаю "Болеро" Равеля. Пусть упрекают, а я так слышу войну'. (Glikman, 1993: 22)

> He said that he would like to see me and let me see the beginning of his planned work, which, possibly, nobody will ever need, once the atrocities of this incredible war are over.
>
> After a minute of hesitation he settled to the grand piano and played the magnificently beautiful exposition of the Seventh Symphony and the Theme and Variations, that represent the fascist invasion. We both were very moved. It should be said that Dmitry Dmitryevich often performed his new works with tears in his eyes.
>
> We sank into silence. He broke the silence with the following words (I have them written): 'I don't know, what will be the fate of these things,' – and after a pause he added, – 'those idle critics, most probably, will reproach me, that I imitate the *Boléro* of Ravel. Let them reproach, but this is how I hear the war.'

This association with Ravel's *Boléro* is not as superficial as it might at first seem. One of Ravel's closest friends reported that the composer, when hearing that during the applause of *Boléro*'s first performance a woman in the public kept shouting 'Rubbish! Rubbish!', replied: 'The old lady got the message' (Hélene Jourdan-Mohange, quoted in Nichols, 1987: 48). The point is that the very music of both *Boléro* and the march of Shostakovich's Seventh Symphony are musical correlations of 'redundancy' (with its colloquial counterpart of 'rubbish'). An analysis of the theme's course of progression shows not only a numerical increase of banal and simplistic musical features that are added to each one of its repetitions, but also that their resilience becomes more and more apparent. A snare drum provides a 'military' ostinato background from the very start of the march section. As an addition, at the beginning of the fourth repetition of the theme, where an exasperatingly consistent echoing of every little melodic fragment transforms banality to imbecility, a short, stupidly simple ostinato bass figure joins in, and lingers through to the march's end (bars 214–250). More than one hundred bars after this bass entrance, at the ninth repetition of the theme, all the high-pitched instruments begin to hammer a fortissimo tonal inversion of this ostinato bass figure (bars 342–360). At this point not only the banal and the cliché, but also the background accompaniment are now located in the musical foreground (Ex. 5.4).

Finally, when all the peaks of musical inanity have been reached, the theme stops its repetitions, and fortissimo, hellish sounds win over, remaining dominant in the scene until almost the end of the movement. Here, where banality culminates in chaos, the aesthetic axis is transformed into an ethical one, and the stupidity of 'crass tastelessness' is correlated with the annihilating stupidity of war. Any further interpretations are bound to more specific, politically related sets of norms, that may be (and may not be) further associated with it.

Ex. 5.4
Shostakovich, Seventh Symphony, first movement

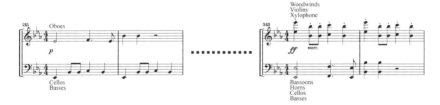

The background ostinato figure becomes a musical foreground.

In a certain sense, Mahler's musical satires are more complicated to analyse, since he never uses musical banality as such, but always distorts it so that it is still recognizable as a cliché (and therefore perceived as a subject of satire) but is never completely redundant. This confusing mixture of the banal and the meaningful is achieved by the incorporation of new musical elements that distort the original cliché, thus abolishing the redundancy of the whole, yet preserving the original, still recognizable redundant element to the extent that it can still function satirically. Such a combination of the banal with the distorted in one integrated musical unit that is located in the musical foreground happens in Mahler's Scherzo from his Fourth Symphony (Ex. 5.5).

Ex. 5.5
Mahler, Scherzo from the Fourth Symphony

Mahler puts together several cliché figures from Viennese waltzes, i.e. from musical material considered by his own cultural set of norms as musically banal. One of these units, which is composed of the rhythmic pattern ♩.♫ and an undulating contour, functions harmonically as a dominant and is located at a structural introductory point. If we compare it with Mahler's melodic figure, which is based on an augmented triad going to a diminished one, with both still functioning as harmonic dominants, we can see the nature of the distortion, which nevertheless still manages to maintain its (undistorted!) harmonic function in the right paradigmatic location, as an introductory figure (Ex. 5.6 and Ex. 5.7).

Ex. 5.6
Introductory figures from Johann Strauss's waltzes

Ex. 5.7
Comparison between three introductory figures

Mahler breaks the banality of the melodic contour, the rhythmic figure, the structural location and the harmonic function by distortion. Integrated and inseparable, both cliché and distortion now feature in the foreground.

Likewise, the Mahlerian turning melodic figures in bars 3–4 of the Scherzo relate to melodic figurations that had become musical clichés (Ex. 5.8).

Ex. 5.8
The Viennese cliché melodic figurations are tonally distorted in Mahler's Scherzo

Another relation, which is still based on stylistic clichés, is to be found in the following section from Strauss's *Frühlingsstimmen* waltz. A paradigmatic comparison shows that Mahler's bars 14–19 from his Scherzo are a distortion of contour, harmony and the melodic patterns of the typical Viennese waltz. A comparison between Strauss's Waltz and Mahler's Scherzo in Ex. 5.9 shows a similarity of harmonic function as well as of melodic contour in the same structural locations. Both start with an augmented chord, but Strauss uses it within the tonal harmonic context (B natural leads through D to C, which is the relative minor, and the B♭ to the tonic E♭), while Mahler's introductory augmented chord G–B–E♭ has no clear leading function: the chord can be interpreted as a distorted inversion of the tonic (B instead of C), a distorted dominant (E♭ instead of D♯, which in its turn is a distortion of D) or a distorted relative major (B instead of B♭). The B natural in the melody also features as part of another distorted dominant chord, the G–B–D–F♯. Unlike the former one, this chord has some leading impetus, but it is very weak: it is precisely the leading F which is distorted into an F♯, changing its downward direction to an upward one. The interesting point is that in spite of the above differences and the apparent non-functionality of Mahler's music, the three last bars of the example do function in exactly the same way in both excerpts. In both cases the subdominant function of E♭ (either IV or II degree) leads to its dominant tone and resolves to its tonic: E♭ (although in Mahler's case it is to an augmented – and thus again functionally distorted – E♭ chord). The difference lies, therefore, not in the functional structure of the musical phrase, but simply in distortion caused by the replacement of certain tones (leading or otherwise harmonically significant) by others.

Ex. 5.9
A paradigmatic comparison between a typical Viennese waltz and Mahler's Scherzo
from his Fourth Symphony

An even more poignant relation is found further on in the same *Frühlingsstimmen* waltz, in the last section of P (this section is often skipped, in accordance with the composer's own indication, thus acknowledging its redundancy). This section seems to be quoted in Mahler's Scherzo of his Second Symphony, in the fortissimo tutti re-entrance to the main theme (bars 147–148), where the similarity is obvious (Ex. 5.10).

Although in both Mahler's Scherzo and Strauss's Waltz banal musical figurations are in the foreground, Strauss's is accepted as 'genuine', i.e. as a one-layered message, while Mahler's is perceived as a double-layered,

Ex. 5.10

The figure appears in Mahler's Scherzo not only as the starting-point of its main theme, but also in the very same structural function, i.e. leading to recapitulation, in which it is used by Strauss

satirical one. The reason for this lies in the different aesthetic sets of norms according to which each of the composers works. The distortions of the stylistic allusions in Mahler's work points to their incongruity with his set of norms. While in Strauss's set of norms the cliché is a preferred characteristic, one that correlates with the preferred ethical value that reassures tradition and continuity, the same cliché is, for Mahler, a sign of cultural stagnation and spiritual death in which his audience is compared with St Anthony's indifferent congregation, allowing the devilish 'Freund Heinz' to freely 'play his fiddle'. Thus Strauss's vi-de mark acknowledges the redundancy of the marked bars on a purely functional level, i.e. the passage can be omitted when it is not needed within the ballroom context. Mahler, on the other hand, highlights the redundancy on its aesthetic level. Not only does he put it in the foreground, but he also gives it to the tutti in fortissimo. To make his point completely clear, he adds a further distortion, moving the metrical location of the figure back one beat, so that the last two semiquavers are left for the sudden pianissimo of the strings, with the special effect of bouncing the bow on the strings ('spring Bogen').

In their mixture of satire and terrifying allusions to spiritual and cultural death, Mahler's hectic scherzos seem more related to the musical grotesque and therefore they cannot be regarded as purely satirical. Similar techniques, though with more emphasis on correlations of violence and horror, occur in the Scherzo of Shostakovich's First Violin Concerto, which uses a banal figuration superimposed with distortions in other musical elements; they also appear in the 'Song of Poverty' from his song cycle *From Jewish Folk Poetry*, where he superimposes a clichéd folk dance accompaniment on a distorted melody, and in the finale of his Second Piano Trio. Although all these works contain satirical elements, they are more related to the grotesque than to satire, and will thus be discussed in the appropriate chapter.[11]

The insertion of a new component

A technique that incorporates a new component that is incongruent with both the satirized object and with its context usually serves to satirize an implicit quality of the object by enhancing it, thus making it explicit. Both the addition of a big pink feather on a top hat of a member of parliament, or a group of bridesmaids carrying the hem of a dean's cloak in a university graduation ceremony will satirize, for example, implicit symbolizations of social distinction: while a top hat makes the wearer 'taller' than he really is, the feather will make him even taller (and definitely more distinct); while the cloak has regal associations, the bridesmaids carrying its hem further enhances the simile to an absurd point. It is important to note that the satirized object here is the social norm requiring an external sign of distinction, and not the distinction in itself.

This technique is particularly effective in the visual arts, since the incongruity of the new component is best apprehended in a simultaneous grasp of the whole message. This can easily be seen in Enzo Apicella's cartoon, showing the cook who is serving a special chicken dish ornamented with a fake tail. 'Proud as a peacock', the cook is satirized by the attachment of a huge peacock tail to his own back, ludicrously echoing the fake tail of the cooked chicken on the dish (Pl. 5.1).

An almost exact musical parallel occurs in the police scene from Shostakovich's *The Nose*, in which the police officer, while participating in a

Pl. 5.1
Enzo Apicella, untitled caricature from *Mouthfool*

A peacock tail, as a new component, incongruent with both the satirized object (the cook) and its context (serving the dish), satirizes the cook's manifested pride.

policemen's choir whose members sing about their miserable life that is 'like a dog's', bursts out in a long howling sound, partly functioning as a 'folklike' drone, but actually highlighting the absurdity of the whole situation.[12]

The march theme in Shostakovich's Seventh Symphony is structured upon the same device, although in a more subtle way. The main part of the theme is twelve bars long (see above, Ex. 5.3, theme 6). However, bars 1–6 seem to be connected to bars 10–12: when played consecutively they convey a simple, symmetrical, predictable and banal melody. Bars 7–11, on the other hand, are motivically alien to this context, providing an almost exact quotation from the second act of Franz Lehár's operetta *The Merry Widow*.[13] Since their removal would render a melody marked by its coherence, symmetry and simplicity, these four bars could be considered an insertion of foreign material (Ex. 5.11). The musico-semantic purport of those bars, however, only enhances the purport of banality that is carried by the surrounding context, thus making these very features of the theme explicitly satirical. The text and dramatic situation in Lehár's assumed source gives further indication and reinforces its meaning of banality and inane lightheartedness.

Ex. 5.11
The insertion of foreign material, most probably a quotation, enhances the satirical purport of the march theme, mocking its inflated banality and stupidity

Failing to understand the satirical function of this insertion, Béla Bartók took it at its face value and condemned this theme as – obviously – banal. His own criticism satirizes Shostakovich by quoting the same theme, exaggerating its simplistic symmetry by the addition of two more sequential repetitions, ornamenting it by banal triplets and inserting new, incongruent elements that enhance his point, actually reaching banality that is tasteless in its own right. An imitation of laughter in the woodwinds, circus-like trombone glissandos and a whirling, aimless and pointless amusement-park music in the background thus transform the whole passage into a circus-like episode, a cheap burlesque commentary on musical banality ('Intermezzo interrotto', bars 69–119).[14]

The question whether Bartók's treatment of the theme is indeed a burlesque highlights the fact that the analysis of satire is a complex and problematic endeavour, and emphasizes the cardinal importance of a definite set of norms. The context of this episode may point to other possible interpretations that could be based, regardless of the source of his quotation, on other incongruities that coexist within Bartók's concerto movement, for example, the fact that this whole passage is located within a larger, earnest unit, which is governed by a calm and expressive motif (which is actually the melodic inversion of Shostakovich's), loaded with modal, harmonic and textural import. Was Bartók expressing his contempt of Shostakovich's music, or was he insinuating here, as he did in other parts of his *Concerto for Orchestra*, that existence should consist of the inane as much as of the significant? Since Bartók was anything but a tasteless composer, nor did he have a cheap sense of humour, as might otherwise be concluded from this passage, the latter could be opted for.[15]

Replacement of a component

The replacement of one characteristic of the satire's subject for another, contextually alien component, which is nevertheless in some respects still compatible and satirically meaningful, usually points to some similarity between the replaced and replacing objects, which in its turn points to the satirized quality. For example, a satirical parody of a Hollywood cliché 'gangsters' meeting', in which one of them sucks a dummy instead of the traditional cigar, thus satirizing the aspects of childish dependency of both smoking and 'organized crime'; or the replacement of Winston Churchill's face with a face of a bulldog, this time keeping in place the eternal cigar, thus satirizing Churchill's stubborn determination, and his bulldog-like 'never letting go' of anything from 'between his teeth'.

The most prevalent musical application of this technique is the replacement of the tonic chord in a cadence by a 'wrong' chord, usually a semitone away from the expected one. Bartók does it in the very same passage quoted above, when he ends the sequence on an E chord instead of the expected E♭ (Ex. 5.12).

This device is common in Prokofiev's music, where harmonic shifts function as a regular index to his tongue-in-cheek parodies of the classical style. The 'Gavotte' from his *Classical Symphony* abounds with such sudden tonal deviations (Ex. 5.13).

Shostakovich used this device mainly in his earlier works. Such cadences appear in his *Three Fantastic Dances* op. 3, and after that, mainly as a light parody. In general it seems that Shostakovich regarded this device as simplistic and suitable for light entertainment only, as in his famous polka from the ballet *The Golden Age* (Ex. 5.14).

Here it could be expected for bars 7–8 to consist only of B♭ major chord notes, and the Bs in bars 10–11 to actually be Cs, as well as the C♯ in bar 13, so that it leads to the dominant F_7 in the following, imperfect cadence.

Ex. 5.12
The 'interruption' from Bartók's *Concerto for Orchestra*

Ex. 5.13
The final cadence of the 'Gavotte' in Prokofiev's *Classical Symphony*

Ex. 5.14
'Polka' from Shostakovich's *The Golden Age*

These techniques are so simplistic that Shostakovich kept them almost exclusively for circus and popular scenes such as the one above, taken from a comic intermezzo of the ballet. Shostakovich used tonal deviations for satirical purposes within rather emphatically simplified textures, in which one sole tonality is overstated, as shown above. However, he further developed this technique, and achieved quite complex results in his manipulation of the tonal system within serious works. In this he chose to follow Rimsky-Korsakov, Skriabin and Stravinsky rather than sharing Prokofiev's frivolous attitude. Thus constant tonal deviations will appear in later works as having tragic connotations (e.g. the opening of his Tenth Symphony or the main motive of the Fourteenth Symphony).[16]

Another way of replacing a characteristic component of a familiar whole with another, to create a satirical effect, is by using parody. In such cases a musical component is trans-contextualized, i.e. taken from one familiar context to another, with which it is stylistically incongruous.[17] This stylistic incongruity with a norm creates a satirical effect. For example, in 'L'Éléphant' from the *Carnaval des animaux* (1886) Camille Saint-Saëns incorporates into his 'elephantine dance' two familiar themes – one from Berlioz's 'Ballet des sylphes' from *La Damnation de Faust*, and the other from Mendelssohn's Scherzo from his incidental music to Shakespeare's *A Midsummer Night's Dream* (Ex. 5.15).

Given the time and place of the *Carnaval des animaux*, it is likely that it refers to the famous contrabass virtuoso Giovanni Bottesini (1821–89), whose technique, according to witnesses, achieved unprecedented heights. A report

Ex. 5.15
Comparison between Saint-Saëns's 'L'Éléphant' and its references

The use of the contrabass as the main melodic instrument in this context is incongruous with its stylistic norms. Therefore, it points at a satire, the subject of which is not the contrabass but stylistically incongruous applications.

of one of his concerts tells 'how he bewildered us by playing all sorts of melodies in flute-like harmonics, as though he had a hundred nightingales caged in his double bass!' (Haweis, 1884: 26–27). Saint-Saëns was a traditionalist who opposed much of the modern music of his times, as well as an irremediable satirist (Harding, 1965: 213–215). Even if Saint-Saëns didn't read Haweis's account (although it is probable that he did), it is quite unlikely that he would overlook the ridiculous aspects of a contrabass doing its best to sound like what it is not, and moreover, that he would resist the temptation to make of it a satirical parody.

The above examples show the close relation that exists between this technique of musical satire and parody, since in order to consider something as 'alien' in a given context it must first be recognized as belonging to another one. In music this is not easy to achieve without such obvious instances as the replacement of the tonic chord with another in cadences. Therefore the majority of the cases in which this satirical device is used are based on quotations and allusions. However, the use of these parodizing techniques requires that the chosen items possess some similar qualities and/or provide a semantic link between their former and new contexts.

Much of Shostakovich's music contains parody and quotations from the classical repertory, popular material and/or his own works. Often these quotations are not satirical and are used just to point to various semantic correlations of the music. Sometimes, though, Shostakovich does use quotation for satirical ends. An example is mentioned by Yury Yelagin, who played violin at the Moscow Vakhtangov Theatre orchestra. In his memoirs he recalls Nikolay Akimov's controversial production of *Hamlet* (1932) to which Shostakovich wrote the musical score. According to his report, in the 'flute scene' (act III, scene 3), Hamlet attached the flute to the bottom of his spine, while the piccolo performed a piercing, distorted version of a popular Soviet march song (Yelagin, 1950 [1988]: 39–40).

When appreciating Akimov's and Shostakovich's contributions, as well as Yelagin's recollections, it is important to be aware of the particular significance that *Hamlet* has in Russian culture. This literary focus is expressed in dozens of translations into Russian, starting from the mid-eighteenth century, and an even larger number of theatrical productions.[18] Its centrality is manifested in that *Hamlet* has found its way into political debates through careful allusions in other literary works. The most famous example of this is Yury Olesha's play, *A List of Assets* (1931). In this play, as well as in Akimov's production of the following year, the flute scene (act III, scene 2) is highlighted, and the idea behind it, according to which 'you cannot play on us as on musical instruments', is particularly emphasized (Rowe, 1976: 139–141).

Yelagin's memory, however, failed him.[19] It is true that the piccolo plays shrill sounds, while the contrabasses play their lowest pitches in a mock march. However, the distorted quotation from this march was not used in the flute scene but in an earlier one, accompanying the conversation between Hamlet and Rosenkrantz in act II scene 2, which refers, in the original Shakespeare text, to the low quality of contemporary theatre, and the fashionable, distasteful use of shrill, loud voices of boys. This scene, in itself, is a private mockery of Shakespeare to the theatre in his own times:

> Rosenkrantz: … But there is, sir, an aerie of children, little eyases, that cry on the top of question and are most tyrannically clapped for't. These are now the fashion and so berattle the common stages (so they call them) that many wearing rapiers are afraid of goose quills and dare scarce come thither. (Act II, scene 2, 362–367)

Akimov, in his turn, largely changed the original text to make it more suitable for his own radical interpretation (Law, 1977: 102). Thus, in a certain accord with the original significance of the scene, but largely changing (and much simplifying!) its text, Akimov gave to Rosenkrantz the following line:

> Roзенкрантз: Когда критики видят героическую пьесу, они говорят, что этого ещё недостаточно, (…)[20] а когда критики видят сатирическую пьесу, они говорят, что это уже чересчур … (Shostakovich, *Collected Works*, Vl. 28: 117)

> When the critics see a heroic work, they say that this is still insufficient … but when the critics see a satirical work, they say that this is by far too much …

The march itself is, indeed, a stereotyped image of the Russian–Soviet militia song. It was written in 1929, and by 1931, when it was quoted by Shostakovich in Akimov's production, it had already gained enormous popularity (Ex. 5.16).[21]

Ex. 5.16

Davidenko's Soviet march 'They wanted to beat us'

The song's text could be the reason for Shostakovich's choice of this particular song for his satirical parody: 'They wanted to beat, to beat us, They tortured us to break us down, (Ekh!) But we did not just remain seated, we were ready, awaiting!'

Ex. 5.17

Shostakovich's satirizing version of Davidenko's song in the incidental music to
Akimov's production of *Hamlet*

Although working with Akimov's version, Shostakovich, who knew Shake-speare's original text only too well, might also have been thinking about the 'little eyases, that cry on the top of question and are most tyrannically clapped for't', as well as about the 'many wearing rapiers are afraid of goose quills and dare scarce come thither'.[22] His dislike of music that 'cries on the top of question' with loud, shrill sounds is obvious, when he engages in his own allusion to criticizing authorities, through his own, reversed criticism, by a distorted quotation of one of the most popular songs at the time (Ex. 5.17). The march that Shostakovich chose had been written by Alexander Davidenko, one of the leaders of the RAPM (the Russian Association of Proletarian Musicians), which ruthlessly ruled over the Soviet musical life between 1923 and 1932 (Volkov, 1979: 84, n.5–6). Shostakovich's mention of this song in his memoirs, although not in direct relation to Akimov's production, strengthens the interpretation of its satirical use.

> These unions had been on everybody's backs. Once the Association came to control music, it seemed that Davidenko's 'They wanted to beat, to beat us' was going to replace all available music. This worthless song was performed by soloists and choirs, violinists and pianists, even string quartets did it. (Volkov, 1979: 84)

It is interesting to compare Shostakovich's satirical parody with Prokofiev's 'Gavotte', shown above. Both composers use parody for satirical purposes, but each satirizes a different set of norms. Prokofiev satirizes the banality of the classical aesthetic ideal of symmetry and its outcomes in the form of easily predicted cadences; Shostakovich, on the other hand, satirizes the attraction this banality has for amateurs, i.e., the coarser, simpler aspects of musical banality. Thus, while Prokofiev highlights cadential points by shifting tonality *on the cadence itself*, Shostakovich emphasizes the musical imbecility of Davidenko's piece by dividing it into its obvious cell-pairs (bars 1–2; 3–4; etc.) and simply writing each cell in a different tonality, not only shifting it by a semitone but also exchanging major for minor mode. The shifts happen not only at *stressed metrical points* but also on melodic skips (e.g. bars 2–3). Unlike Prokofiev's 'Gavotte', where the harmonic shifts happen almost naturally, on continuations of melodic lines, creating the impression of a witty mischief, Shostakovich creates a caricature of a grotesque musical clumsiness. In this respect Shostakovich's parody is closer to Mozart's *Musikalische Spass* than to the work of Prokofiev, his compatriot and contemporary.

While Yelagin's description points to an alleged political satire, Shostakovich's use of Davidenko's march is, in fact, a satire not on the political, but on the aesthetic norms of the Soviet doctrine. Such an interpretation coincides better with his general frame of mind in the years 1931–33, which were a relatively quiet period in his life from a political point of view. His preoccupations were both personal, after he married Nina Varzar and had to face the practical and financial problems as a head of a family, and professional: he was engaged with compositional issues of musical characterization, tonal manipulations and the stylistic use of parody, as can be seen in three of his works written at this time: the opera *Lady Macbeth of the Mtsensk District* (op. 29), his set of 24 Piano Preludes (op. 34) and his First Piano Concerto (op. 35). He was not particularly interested in the music for Akimov's *Hamlet* (op. 32), and his collaboration with him was, among other reasons, induced by the fact he was paid in advance (Volkov, 1979: 64).

Cases in which no text or external allusion serve as a pointer to the significance of an inserted alien component are more complicated. Such is the famous quotation from Rossini's *Overture to William Tell*, inserted in the first movement of Shostakovich's Fifteenth Symphony. As required in such cases, the motif is equally well linked to both contexts. However, this is a particularly difficult case, since it seems to be a double quotation, which alludes equally not only to Rossini but also to many other, earlier works of Shostakovich himself. Moreover, the motif, regardless of any former context in which it might have been present, has strong musical correlations on its own.

Another question that has to be answered is whether the use of the quotation here is satirical at all. MacDonald implies that it is, arguing that the 'toy-shop' imagery that was used by Shostakovich to describe this movement relates to the composer's fascination with 'automata' and 'pseudo-life machinery', and that such thoughts 'underlie most of his satirical passages' (MacDonald, 1990: 242).[23] Likewise, however, he does emphasize the musical purport of the grotesque, as does Roseberry, who speaks about this movement's 'mocking grimace' (Roseberry, 1995: 250). It seems, therefore, that even if using a satirical device, i.e. the replacement of an element by another, alien component, this movement is more related to the grotesque. Moreover, its satirical purport is quite unclear, since the set of norms that he is referring to is far from explicit. Accordingly, this specific instance will be analysed in the last chapter of this study, which deals generally with irony in music, and particularly with grotesque irony.

Exaggeration

Satirical exaggeration is a kind of distortion in which certain characteristics that are to be perceived as deficient, according to a given set of norms, are exaggerated and thus highlighted. For example, Voltaire's *Candide* satirized the idealism of Leibniz by its exaggerated presentation, and the 'Martinus Scriblerus Club' members – Pope, Swift, Gay, Parnell and Arbuthnot – satirized presumptuous erudition in the exaggeratedly inflated *Memoirs of Martinus Scriblerus*.

In music, the extent to which the violation of cultural norms can communicate satirical meanings is perhaps best exemplified in the inappropriate use of a musical topic, due to its more easily definable character. Peter Kivy gives an example for such a violation of a 'topically appropriate' expression in his description of Barbarina's aria from *Le Nozze di Figaro* (Kivy, 1989: 71–73). Here the feeling of exaggeration has a strong connotation of the 'inappropriateness' of a discursive style; obviously, it could equally be related to any other social convention:

> The situation might usefully be compared to one in which, having stepped on someone's foot, instead of saying 'excuse me', or 'I'm sorry', I say 'In God's name forgive me, I beseech you', or 'What agonies of grief and self-mortification I am suffering'. It is not that the wrong sentiment has been expressed. It is customary to ask forgiveness or express contrition if you step on someone's foot. But you must use the accepted formulae: the ones that custom has made suitable to the occasion. (Ibid.: 73)

Exaggeration means, then, transgressing a convention or social agreement about the appropriateness of certain ways to express one's reaction to specific situations and contexts.

The analysis of satirical exaggeration is more complex than the analysis of any of the formerly described satirical techniques, where the mere presence of an incongruent component pointed to the satirical import of the message, making its analysis a relatively simple differentiation between presence vs absence. The ascertainment of satirical exaggeration, on the other hand, is a matter of degree, and even within a specific culture the norms according to which exaggeration is confirmed are often based on indefinable rules. When extremes are not reached, but the presence of an exaggeration is nevertheless felt, it becomes quite difficult to define at what point the satirical varies from the emphatic or from the mere extravagant (not to mention the possible miscalculations, or even more ambiguously, the possibility of bad taste of the author, the analyst, or both).

In his chapter on musical irony, Robert Hatten asks, 'how much is ironic?' (Hatten, 1994a: 185). The scope of this question could, of course, be further extended to the question of 'how much is "too much"?' Where, on the axis ranging between the normal, through the emphasized and eccentric, and finally reaching the abnormal, can we locate satirical exaggeration? Hatten offers the criterion given by 'the governing expressive genre' (ibid.: 184). The importance of the stylistic context in which a musical message is given is stressed by Peter Kivy, too (1989: 71–73). The validity of this criterion, however, is quite limited: in spite of its relation to a standard, the context cannot give any definite measure as to how far from that standard any unit needs to go in order to be perceived as emphatic, exaggerated, insane or simply stylistically incorrect. Likewise, it is extremely hard to draw the line in locating exactly where a portrait becomes a *pièce de caractère*, and moreover, when the exaggerated distortion transforms it into a caricature. Hence the establishment of a portrait as a caricature may become a matter of subtle judgement (Adler, 1995: 89).

As with exaggeration, the definition of caricature is not simple and straightforward. E.H. Gombrich defines it as 'the deliberate distortion of the features of a person for the purpose of mockery' (Kris and Gombrich, 1952: 189), thus seeing it primarily as a satirical device. Philip Thomson is more specific, limiting the kind of distortion needed for a caricature to exaggeration, thus defining it as 'the ludicrous exaggeration of characteristic or peculiar features … [in which] a peculiar feature is exaggerated to the point of abnormality' (Thomson, 1972: 38).

The fact that exaggeration is indispensable for caricature is apparent from the etymology of the word itself, i.e. from the very beginnings of the written theory of caricature. The seventeenth-century Bolognese painters Annibale and Agostino Carracci were the first to coin the term, referring as 'caricature' to their favourite *ritratti carichi*, or 'loaded portraits' (Posner, 1971: 67). The seventeenth-century art theorist Baldinucci defines the verb *caricare* as follows:

> Mettere il carico, aggravare di peso che che sia … E caricare dicesi anche da'Pittori o Scultori, un modo tenuto da essi in far ritratti, quanto si puó somiglianti al tutto della persona ritratta; ma per giuoco, e talora per i scherno, aggravando o crescendo i difetti delle parti imitate sproporzionatamente, talmente che nel tutto appariscano essere essi, e nelle parti sieno variati. (Baldinucci, 1681)

> To load, to add to the weight of something … *Caricare* is also described by painters and sculptors as a method used for making portraits so that they are as similar as possible to the portrayed person; but for the sake of fun, and sometimes for mockery, disproportionally overloading or increasing the defects of the portrayed parts, so that on the whole they look like themselves, while in their components they are different.

A caricature is assessed by a comparison between the portrait and the portrayed subject (Kris and Gombrich, 1952: 189).[24] Thus a caricature requires the choice of at least one characteristic feature of a subject, that will subsequently be satirized by 'disproportionally overloading or increasing' its defects, i.e. by their exaggeration.

Types of exaggeration

A closer inspection reveals Baldinucci's differentiation between two types of exaggeration, defined as *qualitative* and *quantitative*, since a feature can be either *increased* or *overloaded*.

Qualitative exaggeration

A qualitative exaggeration, in which a quality is increased, brings the subject's satirized characteristics to their extreme manifestations (and thus can also be linked with the abnormal and with insanity). The most obvious examples are characters like Cervantes's Don Quixote, or Molière's Argan and Harpagon. The best caricatures in Russian literature were portrayed by Gogol, who managed to exaggerate his protagonists' characteristics to that precise, albeit undefinable point, at which eccentricity and insanity meet, as in the following passage from *The Overcoat*:

> Сколько ни переменялось директоров и всяких начальников, его видели всё на одном и том же месте, в том же положении, в той же самой должности, тем же чиновником для письма, так что потом уверились, что он, видно, так и родился на свет уже совершенно готовым, в вицмундире и лысиной на голове ...
>
> Вряд ли где можно было найти человека, который так жил бы в своей должности. Мало сказать: он служил ревностно, – нет, он служил с любовью. Там, в этом переписываньи, ему виделся какой-то свой разнообразный и приятный мир. Наслаждение выражалось на лице его; некоторые буквы у него были фавориты, до которых если он добирался, то был сам не свой: и подсмеивался, и подмигивал, и помогал губами, так что в лице его, казалось, можно было прочесть всякую букву, которую выводило перо его. (Гоголь, 1842 [1959]: 130–131)

No matter how many directors and principals came and went, he was always to be seen in precisely the same place, sitting in exactly the same position, doing exactly the same work – just routine copying, pure and simple. Subsequently everyone came to believe that he had come into this world already equipped for his job, complete with uniform and bald patch ...

One would be hard put to find a man anywhere who so lived for his work. To say he worked with zeal would be an understatement: no, he worked *with love*. In that copying of his he glimpsed a whole varied and pleasant world of his own. One could see the enjoyment on his face.

> Some letters were his favourites, and whenever he came to write them
> out he would be beside himself with excitement, softly laughing to
> himself and winking, willing his pen on with his lips, so you could tell
> what letter his pen was carefully tracing just by looking at him (Gogol,
> 1842 [1972]: 73–75)

Musical caricatures achieved by qualitative exaggeration are quite easy to
discern when the title and/or the text are of help, as in Mozart's *Musikalische
Spass*, Mussorgsky's *Rayok*, or Shostakovich's *Satirical Cantata*. However,
when there are no such verbal aids, musical satire can rely only on the
stylistic norm, the boundaries of which are not always clear. Another problem
is that of artistic originality, which makes it even more difficult to define
when eccentricity should be related to the aesthetic uniqueness of the work,
to some special stroke of inspiration, or to a satirical exaggeration.[25]

For example, Mahler's opening of his Fourth Symphony sounds quite
banal, with its crushed-notes imitation of sleigh-bells and with the glissando-
like slurs and other ornaments over its simple tune. This music could be
perceived as 'childlike', and/or as a depiction of 'St Ursula's smile' (Bauer-
Lechner, 1923 [1980]: 152), and/or as a caricature of the vulgar folkish style
that was popular at the time of the symphony's writing, as were perceived
similar movements of his in other symphonies (La Grange, 1979: 310).
Biographical data could support any, or all, of the above.

Mahler himself is quoted by Natalie Bauer-Lechner: 'The first movement
begins as if it couldn't count to three … ' (Bauer-Lechner, 1923 [1980]: 154).
The biographer also refers to the 'environmental barbarity' to which Mahler
was exposed while writing the symphony:

> Sometimes the sound of a barrel-organ, or a military band on the oppo-
> site side of the lake, wafts over. The guests at the local hotel sent a band
> of Bohemian musicians to serenade him for an hour at their expense. He
> is all the more exposed to such crude attacks as the people know what
> elaborate arrangements he has made to ensure his undisturbed peace.
> This they find extraordinary, in fact crazy; and so they make him the
> target of their wit.
>   Mahler said: 'We are still surrounded on every side by such barbarity;
> there is no defence against it. Most people have no conception of what it
> means to respect a person's freedom.' (Ibid.: 148)

Such an incident might well arouse someone's desire to take revenge, at
least by ridiculing the source of annoyance. However, a perception of this
movement as a caricature could also be based on theoretical grounds, relating
it not only to the caricature's characteristic exaggeration but also to its ironic
aspects. Deryck Cooke sees the symphony as a reaction against romanticism,
and thus as one of the first attempts at neo-classical writing (Cooke, 1980:
66). Although he does not relate this comment to the detached irony which is
an inseparable part of neo-classicism, but only to the smaller dimensions of
the orchestra that Mahler is using here, the implication can be related to the

general tongue-in-cheek attitude of the neo-classicists. Adorno sees this movement as both written in and opposing sonata form, i.e. as a paragon of irony.[26]
Although he alternates between this main point, which he chooses not to
substantiate by explicit analytical remarks, and his 'technical' argumentation,
still both statements seem to be based on the impressions of incongruity and
of exaggeration – both of them also characteristic traits of caricature:

> Der erste Satz der Vierten freilich ist Sonate, doch archaistisch … das
> zweite Thema wäre für eine eigentliche Sonate ein viel zu selbständiges
> Instrumentallied; auch die Schlußgruppe ist, bei aller Kürze, weniger
> eine solche denn ein drittes Thema, weitab vom Vorhergehenden …
> Trotz alldem jedoch weigert auch diesser Satz sich dem Sonatenwesen,
> nicht nur weil alles in Anführungszeichen komponiert ist; weil die Musik
> spricht: Es war einmal eine Sonate, sondern auch technisch. Die
> expositionskomplexe differieren so sehr, sind auch so energisch getrennt,
> daß sie von vornheirein nicht zu einem Urleilsspruch sich kontrahieren
> lassen. (Adorno, 1971 [1985]: 243)

> The first movement of the Fourth, admittedly, is a sonata, yet archaistically
> … the second theme would be an instrumental song far too self-suffi-
> cient for a sonata as such; in addition, for all its terseness, the closing
> section is more like a third theme, far removed from what preceded it …
> However, this movement also opposes sonata form, not only because
> everything is composed within quotation marks – because the music
> says: once upon a time there was a sonata – but also technically. The
> exposition complexes differ so much, and are so energetically divided,
> that they are incapable from the outset of being contracted into a verdict.
> (Adorno, 1971 [1992]: 95–96)

Thus there seems to be a general agreement that Mahler's Fourth Symphony does have something caricatural about it. Apart from its structural
peculiarities, which relate it to the ironic, the musical content is more explicitly caricatural, and is probably related, among other things, to the composer's
contempt for banality's vulgar aspects. Mahler's sensitivity to dramatic ridicule that is rooted in exaggeration was a well-known fact:

> Mahler observed that all actors and singers move too much, thus weak-
> ening, even destroying the significance and the true expressiveness of a
> gesture … 'Most of them quite unnecessarily emphasize by a gesture
> what is already expressed in the words. If they cry "Du", they point to
> the other person with melodramatic movements of arm and finger; if it
> is a matter of the heart, they put their hands to their heart, and so on. The
> ladies are always fingering their faces till it makes you feel sick!' (Bauer-
> Lechner, 1923 [1980]: 162–163)

The opening of the Fourth Symphony has exactly this characteristic of
doubling information by musical gesticulations, thus conveying the feeling of
'too much'. The musical background, on which the main theme appears, is
already 'putting hands to heart while speaking about the heart', to use Mahler's
own expression: musical allusions to the pastorale topic appear in various

ways, which, instead of enriching, actually weaken one another by creating a picture of exaggerated information: the repeating fifths in the two first flutes are, each and every one of them, ornamented with an acciaccatura. The two remaining flutes play a rhythmic variation on this very idea, receding first into a repetitious octave-fifth figure, and then to an inane repetition of the F♯ alone. Three clarinets elaborate on the idea of ornamentation in a banal triple-graded sequence. Finally, as if the hint of the Tyrolean sleigh-on-snow is not clear enough, we hear on top of all these real sleigh-bells, which add the ultimate unnecessary piece of information to the already pathetically simplistic musical picture (Ex. 5.18).

Ex. 5.18
Mahler, Fourth Symphony, opening theme

Onto this background enters the main theme, which is exaggerated on its own: the accentuation of the first G is further emphasized by the melodic ascending line to it, its location on the first beat, the immediate fall of a major sixth down to the B and its careful shortening. The elements that follow are likewise exaggerated: too many ornamentations are included, and each one of them is highlighted by an accentuation mark and/or a slur and/or a staccato. The abundance of dynamic marks adds yet another ingredient to the general impression of excessive sentimentality. The result is an impression of a 'pure, childlike innocence', that got, so to speak, a bit carried away; it is this feeling of 'too much innocence' that trespasses the thin border of childlike naïvety and reaches the caricatural effect of the simpleton's banality.

While Mahler walks the thin line between the popular, the cliché and the exaggeratedly banal, Shostakovich often takes exaggeration to its abnormal extremes. His musical satires are not a subtle hint that arouses a smile, but a shockingly absurd caricature. *The Nose*, Shostakovich's first opera, is a good example of how a literary work which is, in its own right, a surrealistic picture of a distorted reality, can be further transformed into caricature by taking exaggeration to its furthest extremes. In one episode of the story, the Collegiate Assessor Kovalyev, who has lost his nose, enters the advertising department of a newspaper, and wants to place an advert about his lost nose. The whole situation, of course, is highly absurd. Gogol, however, uses this particular episode for an additional side-satire. His target here is the meaninglessness that rules people's lives, as he described in a letter to his mother, written in 1828:

the people there seem more dead than alive. All the civil servants and officials can talk about is their department or government office; everything seems to have been crushed under a great weight, everyone is drowned by the trivial, meaningless labours at which he spends his useless life. (Quoted by Ronald Wilks in Gogol, 1836 [1972]: 7)

The scene that Gogol describes in the newspaper's advertising department is an exaggerated reflection of this precise meaninglessness that is 'drowning in the trivial', achieved by an accumulative description:

По сторонам стояло множество старух, купеческих сидельцев и дворников с записками. В одной значилось, что отпускается в услужение кучер трезвого поведения; в другой – малоподержанная коляска, вывезенная в 1814 году из Парижа; там отпускалась дворовая девка девятнадцати лет, упражнявшаяся в прачечном деле, годная и для других работ; прочные дрожки без одной рессоры; молодая горячая лошадь в серых яблоках, семнадцати лет от роду; новые, полученные из Лондона, семена репы и редиса; дача со всеми угодьями: двумя стойлами для лошадей и местом, на котором можно развести превосходный березовый или еловый сад; там же находился вызов желающих купить старые подошвы., с приглашением явиться к переторжке каждый день от восьми до трех часов утра. (Гоголь, 1836 [1959]: 54–55)

The room was crowded with old women, shopkeepers, and house-porters, all holding advertisements. In one of these a coachman of 'sober disposition' was seeking employment; in another a carriage, hardly used, and brought from Paris in 1814, was up for sale; in another a nineteen-year-old servant girl, with laundry experience, and prepared to do *other* work, was looking for a job. Other advertisements offered a drozhky for sale – in good condition apart from one missing spring; a 'young' and spirited dapple-grey colt seventeen years old; radish and turnip seeds only just arrived from London; a country house, with every modern convenience, including stabling for two horses and enough land for planting an excellent birch or fir forest. And one invited prospective buyers of old boot soles to attend certain auction rooms between the hours of eight and three daily. (Gogol, 1836 [1972]: 53–54).

While Gogol stresses the meaninglessness of trivia by their accumulation, Shostakovich emphasizes the human *significance* of the scene, presenting the indifference that human beings feel and show for each other as the practical outcome of the disconnectedness between their goals and interests. He does this by using a musical correlation of disconnectedness, embodied in a parody of the imitative texture of *hocketus*, characteristic of a certain type of medieval motet. Each part in this texture has just a few scattered, melodically disconnected notes. The result is a rather dispersed musical information, that in medieval *caccias*, polyphonic 'hunting songs', was often set to meaningless texts, which characteristically consisted of shouts and cries like 'hau', 'hou' or 'houp' (Reaney, 1960: 9–10; 16–17). Shostakovich takes this

Ex. 5.19

The lackeys' mechanical canon in Shostakovich's *The Nose*

Eight lackeys push forward their advertisements in a newspaper's department. The texts are trivial and emphatically disconnected. In spite of being structurally a canon, the music sounds disconnected, too, because of its gasping melodic parts and its *hocketus*-like texture.

technique, which in itself is quite eccentric, one step further: while in the medieval songs the sparse shouts formed together a more musically meaningful picture, created by the planned intercalation of the parts, here, because of the atonal context and the nonsensical melodic line of each part, the disconnection is even more accentuated. Thus, while Gogol paints a picture of discommunication caused by the meaningless, Shostakovich presents musical meaninglessness caused by the non-communicative, manifested in the simultaneous coexistence of superimposed disconnected parts, the joint purport of which is sheer musical nonsense. The fact that this message is really the result of a carefully elaborated canon in eight parts only adds to its ironical purport, while the drumming drone adds to the general mechanistic effect (Ex. 5.19).

More complicated by far is the finale of Shostakovich's Fifth Symphony. In it, so he claimed, he had actually satirized the Soviet demand for 'optimism' in music (Volkov, 1979: 140). Most audiences, however, have accepted the finale's 'optimism' on the face of it, i.e., as a sincere expression of happiness (Wilson, 1994: 126–134; Roseberry, 1981: 88–92; MacDonald, 1990: 134). The symphony ends fortissimo, in a major key, with an 'endlessly repeated A in the violins, like nails being pounded into one's brain' (Vishnevskaya, 1984: 213). Is this a satirical sneer at the demand for optimism, or is it a genuine, even if a bit banal and overstated, expression of happiness? Although an exaggeration might be depicted here, it is not as straightforward as other instances in this chapter: in comparison with other of Shostakovich's works of the same genre, most of the musical elements are not actually exaggerated. On the whole, it seems that the symphony, even if it contains satirical elements, has more of an ironic tendency in it, an expression of despair as well as a resigned acceptance of the inherent ambiguity of reality.

Quantitative exaggeration
The second type of exaggeration is the quantitative. It can take the form either of repetitious appearances of one simple feature, which is thus 'overloaded', or of the accumulation or 'overloading' of as many characteristic features as possible, which are considered deficient within the given set of norms.

Quantitative exaggeration by repetition   'Too many' repetitions of the same element occur in many musical satires. Saint-Saëns's 'Pianistes' from his *Le Carnaval des animaux* are engaged in an arduous drilling in octaves that is relentlessly repeated four times, each time a semitone higher (Ex. 5.20).

This is, in fact, a series of quotations from Czerny's *School of Velocity* piano exercises. The second bar of Saint-Saëns is apparently copied from another Czerny exercise, this time taken from part III of his *School of Velocity*,

Ex. 5.20

Saint-Saëns's 'Pianistes' from *Le Carnaval des animaux*

that is subtitled *On Playing with Expression*. One of the exercises in its first chapter deals with the ability of each finger to emphasize a note independently from the others (Ex. 5.21).

Ex. 5.21

Czerny's *School of Velocity: III. On Playing with Expression*

This is one of the exceptional cases, in which the caricature may be perceived as less exaggerated than its object: letting the 'elephant' play each bar twenty times would transform Saint-Saëns's joke into a burlesque in bad taste, which would eventually sum up to a tedious aural torture. The caricature is thus based not only on the exaggeration, but also on its context, in which material that belongs to 'exercises' is presented within the framework of 'a musical piece', and the emphasis of this difference functions as an additional implicit satirical remark. Actually, it seems that this is, precisely, the main point of Saint-Saëns's caricature: Czerny's exercises may be accepted (albeit with resignation) as long as they are regarded as exercises without any pretension to be regarded as musical pieces. Czerny's 'Exercise for Two Performers' is an example of such a pretension.[27] The exercise is quite long, has many sections, and is structured as having three 'movements': Allegro Moderato, Andante, and a final Coda, Più Allegro. One of the Andante's sections seems to be Saint-Saëns's source for his caricature (Ex. 5.22).

While Saint-Saëns satirizes inane pianistic virtuosity, Mussorgsky satirizes no-less-inane vocal virtuosity in his *Rayok*. His satire, however, is also extended to the blind idolatry that public and critics alike tended to cultivate for vocal virtuosos, aiming his arrows at the popular soprano Adelina Patti, who

Ex. 5.22
Czerny's 'Exercise for Two Performers', *School of Velocity: I*

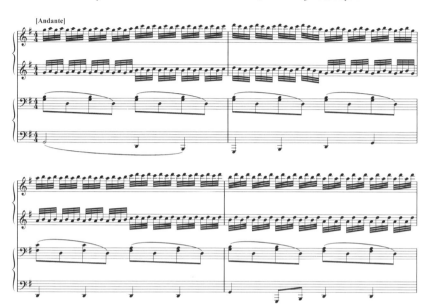

was the object of admiration of his own personal enemy, the music critic Theophil Tolstoy. Repetitions of rhythmic and melodic motifs, parts of words and of phrases are condensed in this caricature, which simultaneously stresses the inanity of the Italian singing style and the boring insistence of its enthusiasts (Ex. 5.23).

Both Saint-Saëns and Mussorgsky, although using repetition as a means to satirize, mollify its effect by allowing the harmonic change that is required by the melodic sequences to fill the aesthetic void caused by the constant repetitions.

Shostakovich, on the other hand, uses the device of repetition to its extreme. Many passages in his first opera, *The Nose*, are such caricatures, based exclusively on endless repetitions of the same, and often a very short, motif. This kind of characteristic minimization of information was noted by Ernst Gombrich in his analyses of caricatures, where he stressed the importance of *simplification*, i.e. the arbitrary emphasis of just a few chosen characteristics of the satirized subject (Gombrich, 1960 [1968]: 281).

In the first scene of *The Nose*, Praskovya Osipovna, Ivan Yakovlevich's wife, throws him out of the house after he has discovered a nose in his morning roll. Beyond the surrealist content of the dramatic situation, two human characters are caricatured: Ivan tries to defend himself and claims he has no idea how the nose got into the bread, while Praskovya Osipovna,

Ex. 5.23
Mussorgsky's *Rayok*

'Patti, Patti, Oh, Patti, Patti, wonderful Patti, divine Patti, Oh, Patti, Patti, Oh, Patti, Patti, wonderful Patti, divine Patti, wonderful, divine, lovely, glorious! Pa-pa, Pa-pa, Pa-pa, Pa-pa, ti-ti, ti-ti, ti-ti, ti-ti, Oh!' – The repetitions in the text coincide with the melodic sequences and join to a satirized manifestation of musical imbecility.

whose dread overcomes her ability to communicate, drives herself into a stream of hysterical, obsessive screams, that culminate in one word: 'Out!'

A comparison with Gogol's original text clarifies the conscious decision to use repetition as a satirical device. In order to convey the overpowering sound with which Praskovya Osipovna attacks Ivan Yakovlevich, Gogol writes 'a stream of words':

> И слушать не хочу! Чтобы я позволила у себя в комнате лежать отрезанному носу? … Сухарь поджаристый! Знай умеет только бритвой возить по ремню, а долга своего скоро совсем не в состоянии будет исполнять, потаскушка, негодяй! Чтобы я стала за тебя отвечать полиции? … Ах ты пачкун, бревно глупое! Вон его! Вон! Неси куда хочешь! чтобы я духу его не слыхала! (Гоголь, 1836 [1952]: 45)

> I don't want to know! Do you think I'm going to let a sawn-off nose lie around in my room … you fathead! All you can do is strop that blasted razor of yours and let everything else go to pot. Layabout! Night-bird!

And you expect me to cover up for you with the police! You filthy pig!
Blockhead! Get that nose out of here, out! Do what you like with it, but
I don't want that thing hanging around here a minute longer! (Gogol,
1836 [1972]: 43)

The musical purport is thus divided into two layers of information: in one
Ivan tries to explain himself on the semantic level, in a non-repetitive, dec-
lamatory style, trying to 'speak sense'. In the other, which is totally
disconnected from the former, semantics is transformed into music: the sole
import is a mechanical, motorical series of repetitive screams in the highest
pitch the voice can achieve, accompanied by similarly hysterical, sudden,
loud and high-pitched 'screams' in the orchestra, in which the shrill sounds of
the piccolo and E♭ clarinet are predominant. This utmost expression of

Ex. 5.24
Shostakovich's *The Nose*, act I, scene 1

PRASKOVYA: Out! Out! Out! Out! Out! Out! Out! Out! Out! Out!
IVAN: The devil knows what happened! I'm not sure if I was or wasn't drunk last
night.

horror, however, is itself transformed, by its sheer repetition, into a piece of sound wallpaper that is transformed into a caricature of itself (Ex. 5.24).

Similar instances are repeated in various scenes of *The Nose*, particularly in the second act. They also appear in the horrifying scene of rape in Shostakovich's second opera, *Lady Macbeth of the Mtsensk District*. These passages, in which the ludicrous caricatures the horrifying, creating blood-freezing instances of the musical grotesque, will be further analysed below in the chapter dealing with the grotesque (Chapter Eleven).

Quantitative exaggeration by accumulation   The second type of exaggera-tion, which is almost exclusively reserved for subjects that represent *types* (a people, a race, a language, a musical or literary style, etc.) is the accumula-tion of as many characteristics of the satirized object as possible. The distortion achieved by this device can be understood as the reversal of the phenomenon noted by Ludwig Wittgenstein in his reference to 'family resemblances'. Wittgenstein pointed out that when we speak of something, what we really have in mind is not any actual manifestation of it but rather an abstract model made up of the accumulated characteristics of its many manifestations. The overlapping of several of the theoretical model's characteristics with several of the particular items is what relates it to the model. Therefore, it might well happen that two items named with the same designation share no common features at all; yet they are regarded as related, due to the fact that several of the particular features of both will appear in the theoretical proto-model.

In order to explain this phenomenon, Wittgenstein chose the example of games. There is not one single feature that is shared by all existing games; nevertheless they are regarded as a 'family' because some of their features belong to the mental model we have of 'games'. Likewise, Wittgenstein noted, no member of a family actually bears all the family characteristics.

> I can think of no better expression to characterize these similarities than 'family resemblances'; for the various resemblances between members of a family: build, features, colour of eyes, gait, temperament, etc. etc. overlap and criss-cross in the same way. (Wittgenstein, 1933–35 [1972]: §67, p. 32e)

If Wittgenstein is right, and no actual realization of any member of a family will include all the family's features, then a manifestation of such a member would be perceived as *overloaded*, and consequently, as a *caricature* of the family. Thus the accumulation of all the features that are considered as characteristic of any group, race, species or type on one sole individual would result in its caricature.

Anti-Semitic caricatures of Jews are based on the accumulation of all the stereotyped 'Jewish' characteristics, which are partly physical and partly the culturally accepted physical correlations of alleged 'Jewish character's' de-fects (Gilman, 1991). Long noses, short and crooked legs, large and protruding

Pl. 5.2
G. Cruikshank, *The Jew Fagin Welcomes Oliver Twist* (Illustration to Dickens's
novel)

Cruikshank's Fagin wears a long caftan that covers his short figure, his back is
crooked, in one hand he holds his hat upside down, almost in a beggar's pose, while
the other exposes long, thin, crooked fingers, ready to grab whatever they find. He is
bald, has protruding ears, a long and crooked nose and a long, black, pointed
(devilish!) beard.

ears, dark hair (and/or bald heads), short-sighted eyes, black beards, long
black coats and long-nailed fingers, always in a greedy pose – all were

accumulated in the caricature's focal object which represented the whole satirized 'Jewish' group. These were combined with the device of *simplification*, according to which the caricaturist focuses exclusively on the characteristics he has chosen to portray (Gombrich, 1960 [1968]: 281).[28]

This kind of accumulation is particularly manifested in the visual arts. Charles Dickens's description of Fagin the Jew in *Oliver Twist* (1837–39) is complex and ambivalent. George Cruikshank's satirical and simplistic illustrations to the story, on the other hand, achieved the caricatural exaggeration of Fagin's figure by the accumulation of all the stereotyped Jewish physical characteristics (Pl. 5.2).[29]

Many caricatures, however, try to overcome their visual limitations by the addition of a caption or by a verbal under-text. The London 'Humorous and Artistic Magazine' *The Butterfly* describes not only the Jewish characteristics that can be seen, but also those that can be heard: its caption uses the 'Jewish language' that reveals the subject's 'Jewish character', regardless of the language he is actually speaking (*The Butterfly*, May–October 1893, reprinted in Gilman, 1995: 103). The physical characteristics are the same as in Cruikshank's caricature, although a bit more developed: crooked legs (giving a hint at the traditional 'devil's limp'), thick lips, a pointed black beard and a darkened figure. To these are added two more informative details: the caricature's title, which points to Throgmorton Street, the famous London business centre, and the distorted language with its emphasis on the characteristic 'Jewish' accent (Pl. 5.3).

The ridiculing of 'Jewish talk' was in no way restricted to late nineteenth-century London journals. The derogatory attitude towards the 'Jewish voice' is deeply rooted in the European consciousness, which is best expressed in its idioms, such as the German *mauscheln*, a popular word the various meanings of which describe the 'Jewish talk' as an unclear, unintelligible, blurred speech, mixed with Yiddish words.

A considerable number of German dictionaries explain this word, as well as its etymology.[30] However, none of the sources specifies exactly how it sounds 'to speak like a Jew'. Luckily, the confused musician is not left in the dark, and the missing substantial information is supplied by Richard Wagner who, as early as 1850, engaged himself in filling this particular gap in European culture. The 'Jewish talk' is thus described in full detail in Wagner's writings, which were enthusiastically read by his followers:

> Im Besonderen widert uns nun aber die rein sinnliche Kundgebung der jüdischen Sprache an. Es hat der Kultur nicht gelingen wollen, die sonderliche Hartnäckigkeit des jüdischen Naturells in Bezug auf Eigenthümlichkeiten der semitischen Aussprechweise durch zweitausendjährigen Verkehr mit europäischen Nationen zu brechen. Als durchaus fremdartig und unangenehm fällt unserem Ohre zunächst ein zischender, schrillender, summsender und murksender Lautausdruck der jüdishcen Sprechweise auf: eine unserer nationalen Sprache gänzlich

Pl. 5.3
Unsigned caricature (The Butterfly, London, 1893): *From Throgmorton Street*

FROM THROGMORTON STREET

FINKELSTEIN (emphatically): "I don'd care vot yer say, yer tief; yer robbed me, I dell yer! yer a liar und a placguard, und a schwindler und a schweinpig: und dot's plain English!"

'I don'd care vot yer say, yer tief; yer robbed me, I dell yer! yer a liar und a placguard, und a schwindler und a schweinpig: und dot's plain English!' Finkelstein's 'emphatical' East European Jewish accent is added to the caricature's accumulation of physical 'Jewish' characteristics.

uneigenthümliche Verwendung und willkürliche Verdrehung der Worte und der Phrasenkonstruktionen giebt diesem Lautausdrucke vollends noch den Charakter eines unerträglich verwirrten Geplappers, bei dessen Anhörung unsere Aufmerksamkeit unwillkürlich mehr bei diesem widerlichen Wie, als bei dem darin enthaltenen Was der jüdischen Rede verweilt. (Wagner, 1852 [1872]: 91)

In particular does the purely physical aspect of the Jewish mode of speech repel us. Throughout an intercourse of two millennia with European nations, Culture has not succeeded in breaking the remarkable stubbornness of the Jewish *naturel* as regards the peculiarities of Semitic pronunciation. The first thing that strikes our ear as quite outlandish and unpleasant, in the Jew's production of the voice-sounds, is the creaking, squeaking, buzzing snuffle: add thereto an employment of words in a sense quite foreign to our nation's tongue, and an arbitrary twisting of the structure of our phrases – and this mode of speaking acquires at once the character of an intolerably jumbled blabber; so that when we hear this Jewish talk, our attention swells involuntarily on its repulsive *how*, rather than on any meaning of its intrinsic what. (Wagner, 1850 [1894]: 85)

Wagner's subtle aesthetic ponderings are in no way characteristic only of himself, of German culture or of the nineteenth century. Similar descriptions of the 'Jewish voice' can be found in French, English and Russian writings from the nineteenth century and the beginnings of the twentieth century (Gilman, 1995: 101–102). For example, Mussorgsky's famous 'Samuel Goldenberg and Schmuÿl' from his *Pictures at an Exhibition* uses this multiple correlation of repugnant traits, painting a musical caricature, almost unique in its cruelty, of the two Jews. Mussorgsky was a known anti-Semite who expressed his dislike of the sound of the Jewish language, as well as of Jews in general (Taruskin, 1993: 379–383). The imitation of the squeaky, gasping, nervous, repetitious, chatter-like voice of the poor Jew is evident in the music that describes him (Ex. 5.25).

Ex. 5.25
Mussorgsky's music imitates Schmuÿl's 'Jewish' voice in his 'Samuel Goldenberg and Schmuÿl', from *Pictures at an Exhibition*

Since this image of the 'Jewish' voice is so obviously based on fiction and prejudice, it could be useful to trace the possible motivations for this cultural correlation, which became an independent cultural unit. And indeed, it just so happens that the sound-qualities of the 'characteristic Jewish voice' are also Western culture's sound-characteristics of the 'evil'.

Throughout the centuries, Western music depicted the Devil, witches and other forces of evil precisely by what Wagner (as many other of his cultural peers) called 'outlandish and unpleasant' sounds. Dissonances and extreme sound-effects appear in musical descriptions of hell, as in the tremolando, fortissimo and sudden outbursts of chords in Gluck's 'Dance of the Furies' from his *Orfeo et Euridice*; this is, too, the way the voices of evil spirits sound, as in the Wolves' Glen scene in Weber's *Der Freischütz*. Witches dance to orchestral 'creaking, squeaking, buzzing snuffles' in Berlioz's 'Witches' Sabbath' scene from his *Symphonie fantastique* and in Mussorgsky's *Night on the Bare Mountain*. Last but not least, the Devil himself is symbolized by the harshest dissonance in Western culture, the *quarta diabolis*. This happens not only in nineteenth-century music, such as Weber's *Der Freischütz* or Saint-Saëns's opening for his *Danse macabre*, but also in a twentieth-century masterpiece like Britten's opening for his *War Requiem*, where the Satanic tritone is used as a blood-freezing ironic remark. This particular symbol of the Devil has been generalized in late nineteenth- and twentieth-century music, and not only tritones, but dissonances and 'harsh sounds' in general often point to the figure of the Devil, as in Mahler's violin solo tune, which is allegedly played by 'Freund Heinz', in the Scherzo of his Fourth Symphony. Other special effects, like *col legno*, sudden changes in articulation or dynamics, etc. add to the general impression of 'outlandish', evil forces. This correlation between the ethically repulsive (the forces of evil) and the aesthetically repugnant ('squeaky, unpleasant noise') is so prevalent in Western music that it has become a cultural unit by itself. As such, it works both ways, and there is no more need for a story line or text in order to perceive the purport of 'evil' when 'unpleasant sounds' are heard.

Musical depictions of Jews thrive on this correlation. Not only are Jews a traditional symbol of satanic evil in Christian culture (the caricatures shown above are just immaterial trifles in the centuries-old manifestations of the Christian demonization of Jews), but also the Jews' very *voice*, apparently, *the way they sound*, correlates with this image of evil.

Such an extreme sound-caricature of Jews, which makes full use of the correlation between 'evil', 'Jewish' and their mutual sound-correlations, is drawn by Richard Strauss in his opera *Salome*. Strauss, who was deeply influenced by Wagner and closely acquainted with his writings, draws a caricature of the five Jews who come to Herod's palace in search of the king's prisoner, Jochanaan (who is, of course, John the Baptist). The Jews' evil intentions as to what should be done with Jochanaan are hardly a secret.[31]

When Herodias suggests to Herod that the prisoner be turned in to the Jews
'that are shouting out there, for months on end', one of them immediately and
abruptly intrudes into the conversation: 'Wahrhaftig, Herr, es wäre besser, ihn
in unser Hände zu geben' ('Indeed, Sir, it would be better if you gave him
into our hands', *Salome*, rehearsal number 188). The five Jews who take part
in the following scene quickly become engaged in an endless, noisy, almost
chaotic blabber, which is contextually contrasted with two other elements:
the deep, serene voice of Jochanaan, and the authoritative demand of Herodias:
'Make them be silent!' The incongruity between the Jews' clearly depraved
intentions and their ludicrous, incoherent 'Pharisee' chatter forms the basis of
their caricature in this scene.

An examination of Wilde's original text for the play shows that Wilde, too,
was in no way sympathetic to Jewish thought and its verbal expressions:

> *Hérodias*: Si, vous avez peur de lui. Si vous n'aviez pas peur de lui,
>   pourquoi ne pas livrer aux Juifs qui depuis six mois vous le demandent?
> *Un Juif*: En effet, Seigneur, il serait mieux de nous le livrer.
> *Hérode*: Assez sur ce point. Je vous ai déjà donné ma réponse. Je ne
>   veux vous le livrer. C'est un homme qui a vu Dieu.
> *Un Juif*: Cela, c'est impossible. Personne n'a vu Dieu depuis le prophète
>   Élie. Lui c'est le dernier qui ait vu Dieu. En ce temps-ci, Dieu ne se
>   montre pas. Il se cache. Et par conséquent il y a de grands malheurs
>   dans le pays.
> *Un autre Juif*: Enfin, on ne sait pas si le prophète Élie a réellement vu
>   Dieu. C'était plutôt l'ombre de Dieu qu'il a vue.
> *Un troisième Juif*: Dieu ne se cache jamais. Il se montre toujours et dans
>   toute chose. Dieu est dans le mal comme dans le bien.
> *Un quatrième Juif*: Il ne faut pas dire cela. C'est une idée très dangereuse.
>   C'est une idée qui vient des écoles d'Alexandrie où on enseigne la
>   philosophie grecque. Et les Grecs sont des gentils. Ils ne sont pas
>   même circoncis.
> *Un cinquième Juif*: On ne peut pas savoir comment Dieu agit, ses voies
>   sont très mystérieuses. Peut-être ce que nous appelons le mal est le
>   bien, et ce que nous appelons le bien est le mal. On ne peut rien
>   savoir. Le nécessaire c'est de se soumettre à tout. Dieu est très fort. Il
>   brise au même temps les faibles et les forts. Il n'a aucun souci de
>   personne.
> *Le premier Juif*: C'est vrai cela. Dieu est terrible. Il brise les faibles et
>   les forts comme on brise le blé dans un mortier. Mais cet homme n'a
>   jamais vu Dieu. Personne n'a vu Dieu depuis le prophète Élie.
> *Hérodias*: Faites-les taire. Ils m'ennuient.
> (Wilde, 1893: 42–44).

> *Herodias*: I tell you, you are afraid of him. If you are not afraid of him
>   why you not deliver him to the Jews, who for six months past have
>   been clamouring for him?
> *1st Jew*: Truly, my lord, it were better to deliver him into our hands.
> *Herod*: Enough of this subject. I have already given you my answer. I
>   will not deliver him into your hands. He is a holy man. He is a man
>   who has seen God.

1st Jew: This cannot be. There is no man who hath seen God since the prophet Elias. He is the last man who saw God. In these days God doth not show Himself. He hideth Himself. Therefore great evils have come upon the land.

2nd Jew: Verily, no man knoweth if Elias the prophet did indeed see God. Peradventure it was but the shadow of God that he saw.

3rd Jew: God is at no time hidden. He showeth Himself at all times and in everything. God is in what is evil even as He is what is good.

4th Jew: That must not be said. It is a very dangerous doctrine. It is a doctrine that cometh from the schools of Alexandria, where men teach the philosophy of the Greeks. And the Greeks are Gentiles. They are not even circumcised.

5th Jew: No one can tell how God worketh. His ways are very mysterious. It may be that the things which we call evil are good, and that the things which we call good are evil. There is no knowledge of any thing. We must needs submit to everything, for God is very strong. He breaketh in pieces the strong together with the weak, for He regardeth not any man.

1st Jew: Thou speakest truly. God is terrible; He breaketh the strong and the weak as a man brays corn in a mortar. But this man hath never seen God. No man hath seen God since the prophet Elias.

Herodias: Make them be silent. They weary me.

(Wilde, 1893 [1954]: 332–333)

Wilde's text of the Jews' sequence in his *Salomé* is satirical. His description is fact-like, it exposes the Pharisees' discussions as irrelevant and their conclusions, which are based on Jewish canons, as illogical. Thus he intentionally builds his satirical text as a discussion which is more irrelevant than meaningless, a quality that becomes particularly evident when compared with the high dramatic tension of the scene within which it takes place: Herod's wooing of Salomé, who is infatuated with Jokanaan, and Jokanaan's voice heard from his prison-cell, announcing his prophecies of doom.

Strauss, however, is not satisfied with Wilde's mere satire. For him a discussion among Jews should be materialized in the Wagnerian *Geplapper*: a meaningless blabber. Obediently following Wagner's prescription concerning 'its repulsive *how*, rather than … any meaning of its intrinsic *what*', he creates in this episode a grotesque caricature, in which the semantic content is nearly lost among all the other accumulated characteristics of 'Jewish blabber': the 'creaking, squeaking, buzzing snuffle' that is conveyed in 'an intolerably jumbled blabber'. In order to make the text sound like 'a blabber', Strauss (unlike Wilde) uses repetitions. However, in order to create the necessary 'jumble', the Jews' parts, after being presented homophonically, so that their irrelevant content will be duly and clearly conveyed, grow into a chaotic contrapuntal web of noisy 'Jewish blabber', to which the instruments contribute their own share, to make the general impression even more chaotic. In order to achieve the required Wagnerian effect of 'creaking, squeaking, buzzing snuffle' Strauss chose the uncharacteristic and unbalanced combination of four tenors and one baritone (to be compared, for example, with a more balanced male-voice quintet in Puccini's *La Bohème*, which is made of one bass, two baritones, one tenor, and the landlord's voice, which has no specification). The impression achieved by this distribution of voices, which emphasizes the upper, more 'squeaky' register of the male voice, is even further highlighted by the large amount of 'a', 'ä', 'e' and 'i' vowels in the text, to which, although originally translated by Hedwig Lachmann, Strauss himself contributed significantly:

> *Herodias*: Ich sage dir, du hast Angst vor ihm. Warum liefest du ihn nicht den Juden aus, die seit Monaten nach ihm schreien?
> *1er Jude*: Wahrhaftig, Herr, es wäre besser, ihn in unsere Hände zu geben.
> *Herodes*: Genug davon! Ich werde ihn nicht in eure Hände geben. Er ist ein Hil'ger Mann. Er ist ein Mann, der Gott geschaut hat.
> *1er Jude*: Das kann nicht sein. Seit dem Propheten Elias hat niemand Gott gesehn. Er war der letzte, der Gott von Angesicht geschaut. In unseren Tagen zeigt sich Gott nicht. Gott verbirgt sich. Darum ist grosses Übel über das Land gekommen, grosses Übel.
> *2er Jude*: In Wahrheit weiss niemand, ob Elias in der Tat Gott gesehen hat. Möglicherweise war es nur der Schatten Gottes, was er sah.
> *3er Jude*: Gott ist zu keiner Zeit verborgen. Er zeigt sich zu allen Zeiten und an allen Orten. Gott ist in schlimmen ebenso wie im Guten.
> *4er Jude*: Du sollest das nicht sagen, es ist eine sehr gefährliche Lehre aus Alexandria. Und die Griechen sind Heiden.
> *5er Jude*: Niemand kann sagen, wie Gott wirkt. Seine Wege sind sehr dunkel. Wie können nur unser Haupt unter seinen Willen beugen, denn Gott ist sehr stark.
> *1er Jude*: Du sagst die Wahrheit. Fürwahr, Gott ist furchtbar. Aber was diesen Menschen angeht, der hat Gott nie gesehn. Seit dem Propheten Elias hat niemand Gott gesehn. Er war der letzte ... *usw.*
> *2er Jude*: In Wahrheit weiss nieman, *usw.* Gott ist furchtbar, er bricht den Starken in Stücke, den Starken wie den Schwachen, den jeder gilt ihm gleich. Möglicherweise ... *usw.*
> *3er Jude*: Gott ist zu keiner Zeit verbogen ... *usw.*
> *4er Jude*: Du solltest das nicht sagen ... *usw.* Sie sind nicht einmal beschnitten. Niemand kann sagen, wie Gott wirkt, denn Gott ist sehr stark. Er bricht den Starken wie den Schwachen in Stücke. Gott ist stark.
> *5er Jude*: Niemand kann sagen, wie Gott wirkt, ... *usw.* Es kann sein, dass die Dinge, die wir gut nennen, sehr schlimm sind, und die Dinge, die wir schlimm nennen, sehr gut sind. Wie wissen von nichts etwas.
> *Herodias*: (zu Herodes) Heiss sie schweigen, sie langweilen mich.

This cumulative quintet is to be performed 'Sehr schnell', very fast. It is written in 6/8; the metronome mark is 120 for every dotted crotchet, while the rhythm is mostly based on shorter note-values, mainly quavers. The orchestra, which up to this point has played long-held chords, becomes a chaotic, dissonant chatter of chromatic semiquavers. The use of instruments is likewise telling, being based on brass and double-reed woodwinds, with their nasal sounds: two oboes, one English horn and the rare loud heckelphone provide the required sound-quality for the 'snuffle' effect, while one piccolo and three flutes pierce ears with shrieking sounds. The general orchestral sound tends toward the higher pitch-range, so that the first entrance of the Jew, with his high-pitched tenor and jagged melodic leaps, only heightens the caricatural effect of 'The Jewish Voice'. (See Ex. 5.26 and Fig. 5.1, which describe the passage between one bar before rehearsal number 196 and three bars after rehearsal number 204.)

Shostakovich uses a similar device of accumulation in his caricatures of the Russian people. He chooses a series of musical characteristics of Russian folk music, such as unified choral singing, rich harmony, slow march rhythms, chordal texture and high-pitched held notes.

It should be noted, though, that since not only the former Soviet Union, but also the smaller territory considered as Russia proper, is such a vast geographical unit, including many traditions and many cultures, the very term 'Russian folk song' is, to a large extent, misleading.[32] Russian folk music, as a generic term, is an indeterminate entity which since the eighteenth century has been charged with various political connotations. In genuine Russian folk song the aforementioned musical characteristics would appear only in a diffused way, and it is unlikely that more than one of them would feature in any one song (Warner and Kustovskii, 1990: 9; Lineff, 1905: iii–iv; Zemtsovsky, 1980: 388).

It was politics that interfered with the natural boundaries of Russian musical traditions. One of the outcomes of nineteenth-century Russian nationalism was the collection and research of Russian folk songs, which began as early as the eighteenth century (Warner and Kustovskii, 1990: 4; Zemtsovsky, 1980: 388), and continued throughout the nineteenth and well into the twentieth century.[33] It is important to emphasize that these collections not only stemmed from a pure scholarly enterprise but were also an expression of a political approach searching for a unified all-Russian culture. Within this context, the existence of a 'genuine Russian folk song' was perceived to be proof of the political unit of Russian nationality. Moreover, Russian composers since the nineteenth century were expected to write in a 'Russian folk musical idiom'. During this time, as a result, hundreds of new songs, written 'in the manner of folk songs', i.e. according to musical characteristics compiled from various anthologies, were published. Such 'folk songs' were written by Glinka, Borodin, Balakirev, Mussorgsky, Rimsky-Korsakov and even Tchaikovsky. Some of these songs were so popular that they were absorbed back into the real folk culture, and became 'genuine folk songs', whose non-folk roots were forgotten (Warner and Kustovskii, 1990: 2–3). Unlike the genuine material, much of this newly written folk music, which was intentionally written to be 'characteristic',

Ex. 5.26

Voices, dissonances, fast tempo, triple meter and shorter rhythmic values all contribute to the sound chaos of 'the Jewish blabber'. The bass motif, after the entrance of the 2nd Jew, resembles the figure that accompanies Wagner's Alberich (in the first scene of *Das Rheingold*): Strauss describes Jews by the musical correlative of his cultural unit of evil

included several of the following features: a melody leaping in fourths, fifths and minor sixths; plagal cadences; polyphonic part-writing in parallel thirds; minor modes that would invariantly modulate into their major relative through the flattened seventh, used as the relative's dominant, high-pitched held notes, 'whooping' of vocal parts; changing meters and asymmetrical phrases, reflecting the peculiarly Russian way of stressing words within songs, and the changing number of syllables in each line of the typical poems (Lineff, 1905: xvi; Zemtsovsky, 1980: 394).

Thus, as happened with Wittgenstein's games and the 'Jewish character' in anti-Semitic works, Russian folk songs evolved, from a family in which none of the members bears all its characteristic features, into one artificial entity that was to be regarded as 'characteristically Russian'. Consequently a *cultural unit* was created, whose relation to its origins can only be traced by following each one of its features separately.

Fig. 5.1
A graphic representation of the accumulation process in the Jews' quintet from
Salomé

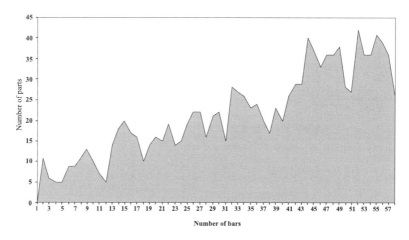

Strauss draws a caricature of Jews based on a literal musical accumulation and the
correlational accumulation of their alleged vocal characteristics. While the voices of
the Jews accumulate, the orchestra accumulates, too, and grows from 4 instruments
to 43.

The Soviet approach to folk music had continued this trend. This resulted
in Soviet songs, modelled to be 'characteristically Russian'. A famous example is Lev Knipper's 'Red Army' song *Stepnaya Kavaleriiskaya* ('The Steppes'
Cavalry', 1938), which has gained popularity far beyond the Soviet Union. A
closer inspection of its musical elements clearly shows their various folk
sources: this is a characteristic 'Soviet folk song', tailored to suit a political
unity which was never actually realized in the genuine folk material (Ex.
5.27). In this new cultural unit the 'whooping' acoustic effect, a very high-
pitched note on which the singers dwell after reaching it with an acute
glissando at the end of each stanza, characteristic of the 'summoning songs'
of the western regions of Smolensk, Bryansk and Kaluga (Warner and
Kustovskii, 1990: 67) was mated with the *Protyazhnaya*, a slow lyrical song,
traditionally performed by a male choir, and popular among the Ukrainian
Don Cossacks, and traditionally performed by cavalry soldiers on the march.
In it 'one characteristic feature is the solo voice part known as the *dishkant*
… A single tenor voice, weaving a complex melodic ornament at the top end
of the singer's range, would rise above and dominate the other voices in the
squadron' (Warner and Kustovskii, 1990: 13; see also Hoshovsky, 1980:
394). To the resulting hybrid are added the Armenian, Byelorussian and
Latvian traditions of long-held notes (At'ayan, 1980: 339, 347; Tsitovich,

Ex. 5.27

Lev Knipper's *Stepnaya Kavaleriiskaya* (1938)

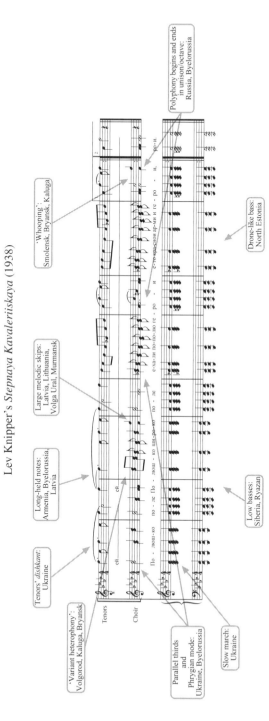

The song was tailored to fit the synthetic cultural unit of 'a Russian folk song', by incorporating in it characteristic features of folk songs from different regions of Russia and the Soviet Union.

1980: 355; Vitolinš, 1980: 371); the North Estonian drone effect (Tampere, 1980: 358); the semi-Phrygian minor modality and the parallel thirds, taken from Byelorussian and Ukrainian traditions (Tsitovich, 1980: 356; Warner and Kustovskii, 1990: 11 and 107–109; Hoshovsky, 1980: 411); the 'variant heterophony' characteristic of the regions of Belgorod, Kaluga and Bryansk (Warner and Kustovskii, 1990: 10, Lineff, 1905: xxiii); the large melodic skips prevalent in Latvian, Lithuanian, Volga–Ural and the northern Murmansk songs (Vitolinš, 1980: 370, 374; Slobin, 1980: 405; Warner and Kustovskii, 1990: 12); polyphony that begins and ends with a unison or an octave (and begins with a soloist), which features in West Russian and Byelorussian music (Zemtsovsky, 1980: 394; Lineff, 1905: xv; Tsitovich, 1980: 356), and the low bass notes, prevalent in the music of Siberia and Ryazan (Tanimoto, 1980: 399; Zemtsovsky, 1980: 394).

This, however, is still not a satire, since it is not incongruent with any norm of the culture that produced it, and therefore it lacks the intentional mockery which must be made apparent by the insertion of an implicit norm within the message itself.

In order to transform such a unit into a satire, the normatively positive value that is attached to either the process of feigned unification and/or the 'simple folk' must be questioned. Shostakovich not only hated the simple-mindedness and vulgarity of song and dance ensembles like the Red Army chorus, which he claimed did 'drive him mad', and which he would totally abolish, if only he could (Volkov, 1979: 16); he was also sensitive to both the distortion of folk music by its artificial 'unification' and to human faults in general, and his music satirizes all of these.[34] In his memoirs he differentiates between authentic folk songs and the Soviet materials that were written and sold to the Soviet public as 'genuine' during the 1930s:

> There was a crying need for triumphant songs and dances for festivities in Moscow, and for musical accusations of the past and musical praise for the new. They needed 'folk' music that retained one or two reminiscent melodies from authentic folk art, something like the Georgian *Suliko*, the leader and teacher's favourite song.
>
>   The real folk musicians had been almost completely eradicated, only individuals here and there were left alive. And even if they had been spared, they wouldn't have been able to do it. The ability to switch over instantaneously is a quality of the professional of the new era. It's a quality of our *intelligentsia* … It called for an 'extraordinary nimbleness of thought', to use Gogol's phrase, and a similar attitude toward the local national culture. The composers I'm talking about were strangers and professionals. And they were also very very scared. Thus all the necessary prerequisites for a 'lush burgeoning' (as they began calling it) – of national art – a completely new socialist national art – were there. (Volkov, 1979: 166)

In the third act of Shostakovich's opera, *The Nose*, a group of Russian policemen are trying to cheer themselves up in a sing-along session, while waiting for a carriage to leave the station. Shostakovich draws their musical caricature by writing an exaggerated 'New Soviet Folk Song' in which he accumulates various features from diverse Russian folk traditions, and inserts his implicit set of norms by highlighting musical features that correlate with the defects he is trying to point to: the Gogolian 'extraordinary nimbleness of thought' of both the new degenerate musical form and of the policemen who are performing it. In order to achieve this goal, Shostakovich makes use of the characteristic device of *condensation*, in which one exaggerated feature serves to satirize more than one feature – physical, behavioural, mental and/ or psychological – of the satirized subject (Gombrich, 1968 [1960]: 281).[35] The satirical text, which describes the Russian policeman's life, is sung to a ridiculous amalgam of exaggerated characteristics of Russian music: a disorganized series of octave, fifth and sixth melodic leaps is compatible with the Latvian, Lithuanian and Volga–Ural traditions while also correlating with the lack of direction, meaninglessness and futility of the policemen's role; the characteristic Volgorod, Kaluga and Bryansk 'variant heterophony' is distorted to a nonsensical series of dissonances, the purpose of which is totally unclear, and which, in its own turn, correlates with the senselessness of the plot in general, the dramatic situation, and the satirized figure of the Russian policeman.[36] To all these is added a repetitious background with the violas' 'North Estonian' drone, accompanied by a dull 'Siberian' bass drum and even deeper violoncellos and contrabasses, also correlating with the Russian policemen's dullness of thought as well as with their '*de profundis*' misery. The result is a composed musical caricature that alludes to the dull, monotonous cliché images of 'the endless Russian steppes', of 'a typical Russian folk song' and, on top of everything, of the no less clichéd misery and stupidity of the Russian policeman (Ex. 5.28).

Moreover, and as if all the above were not enough, after a while, in which this long, monotonous singing continues, and in which, a few bars later, a series of 'Byelorussian' parallel thirds is incorporated, the policemen's captain becomes a 'heroic tenor leader' and, while the same endless, repetitious background continues in the choir, he breaks into a Ukrainian-like *dishkant* salient solo part, albeit with a long, falsetto-voiced 'Smolensk-rooted whooping' high-pitched note which is held for a long while, in the Armenian tradition. The caricatural condensation, however, goes far beyond the mockery of folklore anthologies: the result directly (and more tangibly!) also correlates with the resilience of a long 'dog's howl' sound, ridiculously suitable to the text's description of the policeman's life, which is 'like a dog's' (Ex. 5.29).

Thus, by using the double, triple and quadruple correlations of each one of his musical elements, Shostakovich creates a multiple satire, bringing his caricatural description to the boundaries of the comic musical metaphor.

Ex. 5.28

Shostakovich, *The Nose*, act 3, scene 7: the policemen's choir describes the typical
Russian policeman, in a self-encouraging sing-along session: 'His tail is sagging like
a dog's, like Cain he is shaking all over, and tobacco is dribbling from his nose.'

Ex. 5.29

The folk-like 'whooping' is doubly satirized: once as a dog's howl, and once as a
Russian policeman's emotive expression

Repetition and accumulation as the objects of satire
Everything, including sets of norms and satirizing processes, can become a target for satire. Therefore, processes that were regarded hitherto as mere techniques can also become objects for satirical treatment. Thus accumulation in itself can be, too, a subject of a satirical utterance. In the aforementioned excerpt from Strauss, a long process of accumulation is put into action, highlighting the congested character of the Jews' quintet. By this Strauss satirizes not only the 'noisy Jewish blabber', but also the act of crowding in itself. Crowdedness, particularly in Shostakovich's works, has strong connotations of the violent, threatening and even of the terrifying, which tend to diminish its pure satirization, and bring it much closer to the hybrid domain of the grotesque. Therefore, repetition and accumulation as objects for satirical treatment will be further dealt with in the chapter on the grotesque (Chapter Eleven).

PART IV
PARODY

CHAPTER SIX

Definitions of parody

A parody is an ironic utterance, the layers of which are embedded in two or more incongruent encoded texts.[1] In its reference to pre-existing texts (works of art, styles, etc.) that implicitly present a critical and/or polemical commentary, parody is simultaneously a text and a meta-text (Rose, 1979: 22). This particular feautre is the source of the extra role assigned to it by the Russian formalists, who regarded parody as the catalysing agent of artistic innovation (Shklovsky, 1917; Tinyanov, 1921 and 1927; Bakhtin, 1929 and 1934–5). Given its ironic structure, and using the terminology suggested at the beginning of this study, parody can serve either as *a stimulus* or as *a terminus*. In the former case it functions as a satirical device; in the latter it either indicates romantic irony, i.e. an artistic parabasis, or makes a statement of existential irony.[2]

Parody is characteristically based on elements of imitation, which it modifies by the insertion of incongruous critical and/or polemical components (Tinyanov, 1921 [1979]: 101; Bakhtin (1929, 1963 [1984]: 193); Karrer, 1977: 88; Hutcheon, 1984: 6). The degree of incongruity between its layers, which functions as a clue to the existence of a parodical attitude, provides the difference between imitation, stylization and parody (Tinyanov, 1921 [1979]: 104; Bakhtin, (1929, 1963 [1984]: 186ff.) Rose, 1979: 22). The perception and understanding of parody require some degree of acquaintance with the parodied object (Karrer, 1977: 21; Hamm, 1984: 107; Hutcheon, 1984: 19). Hutcheon applies Umberto Eco's term 'overcoded discourses' to describe parodies that pose a problematic challenge for analysis because of the multiplicity of their sources, which often also parody each other, such as the works of James Joyce, Thomas Mann and Umberto Eco in literature or of Gustav Mahler, Luciano Berio and Peter Maxwell Davies in music (Hutcheon, 1984: 16 and 1985: 12, 15, 29, 42).

There is a historical and etymological link between parody and the comic, which has affected modern parodies and theoretical writings on the subject (Dane, 1988 and Rose, 1993). Consequently, considerable argumentation for and against the inclusion of the comic in the definition of parody has developed.[3] Moreover, the principles presented in some theoretical writings seemingly contradict the very literary material that they present as a support: Bakhtin, for example, regards parody as exclusively comic, although his analyses of it show the contrary (193?: 51–52). At the other extreme stand the works of Shklovsky and Tinyanov, who write about parody without even mentioning its relation to the comic, but choose works that are predominantly comic as their examples, like *Don Quixote*, *Tristram Shandy*, Gogol's works and Dostoevsky's satirical parodies of these.[4] The structuralist term 'inter-textuality', suggested by Julia Kristeva, seemed to solve the problem by clearly distinguishing between the satirical reference to other texts, which continued to be called 'parody', and the non-satirical type, which was generally labelled 'intertextual' (Kristeva, 1966).[5] It is undeniable that many parodies are, indeed, satirical, and therefore relate directly to the comic; on the other hand, there are many parodies that at least overtly are not comic (Hutcheon, 1985). It is important to remember, though, that the very presence of structural incongruity does associate parody (and irony) with the absurd, and therefore, although indirectly, with the comic, too (Hinchliffe, 1969: 1).

Taking these reservations into account, this study avoids the label 'comic' and prefers the use of 'satirical' versus 'non-satirical' parody. The definition offered above, which perceives parody as structurally ironic, allows it both satirical and non-satirical instances, resulting, respectively, in satirical and non-satirical parodies.

Satirical parody

Satirical parody, like satire, is based on a normative approach that points to one of its layers as the one that should be preferred. Debussy satirizes Wagner's 'Tristan chord' by parodying it in 'Golliwogg's Cakewalk', from his *Children's Corner* (1906–8). The pitch-combination that creates the famous

Ex. 6.1
The pitch-set of Wagner's 'Tristan chord' is enharmonically transformed and becomes a motif in Debussy's 'Golliwogg's Cakewalk'

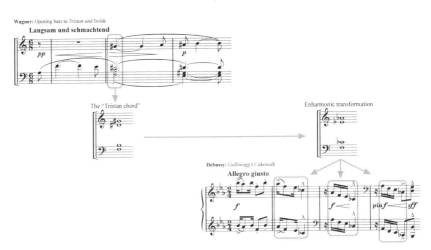

'yearning' leitmotif in Wagner's opera is transferred here into the new context of a Black American minstrels' cakewalk, which stylistically relates to light entertainment or even to burlesque, creating a stylistic incongruity and thus a parody (Ex. 6.1).

Like a ragtime, a cakewalk is based on melodic syncopations over a regular rhythmic accompaniment. However, being itself a parody, it is a rather slow, perhaps clumsier version of ragtime.[6] Scott Joplin's *Original Rags* (1895) provides a good example of a cakewalk, in that it lacks the typical ragtime semiquaver runs, and its syncopations are simpler and more repetitive. Joplin's ragtimes were very popular at the turn of the century, and his *Original Rags* probably provided the model for Debussy's cakewalk, as show the similarities of texture, rhythmic patterns, accompaniment figuration and even of the first melodic idea, based on a neighbouring tone (Ex. 6.2a and 6.2b).

There is, however, a further complication to this structure, since the new context is in itself parodied: Debussy's piece is not simply a 'cakewalk' but

Ex. 6.2a and 6.2b

Debussy's 'Golliwogg's Cakewalk' relates stylistically to Joplin's *Original Rags* in its rhythmic patterns, texture, accompaniment figure and the neighbouring-tone head-motif

'Golliwogg's Cakewalk', Golliwogg being a black, grotesque rag-doll that was very popular at the turn of the century.[7] When Debussy chooses the pathetic, grotesque and clumsy Golliwogg as his main protagonist for the dance, he is creating a satirical grotesque parody that borders on the pathetic, and all this before the work's further allusion to Wagner's motif.

The result is a parodical combination of *ludus* and *pathos*. Like a Pierrot, Golliwogg moves between a mockingly clumsy dance to a distorted 'Tristan motif' melody and an over-emotional, pathetic quotation of the original Wagnerian 'yearning leitmotif' (Ex. 6.3).

Ex. 6.3
Debussy's parodied quotation of Wagner's 'yearning' leitmotif from *Tristan und Isolde*

Debussy's subtle sophistication is particularly apparent in this central part of the dance, since none of its expressions is unambiguously mocking. It sounds almost as if a healing potion lubricates each poisoned satirical arrow: there is always some musical counter-remark, some softening notes that convey an aesthetic distance, a double outlook which is, simultaneously, satirizing and self-satirizing, always examining and re-examining one's own aesthetic values, too.

The note-combination of the 'yearning' motif (the tension of which is mockingly exaggerated by a full bar rest) is satirized right at the beginning by the simple cadential solution. The simplicity of the answer itself, however, is parodied on its own account, by the insertion of unexpected, asymmetrical semiquaver 'outbursts' into the otherwise conventional introductory rhythmic pattern (Ex. 6.4).

These 'outbursts' function on two different levels of signification. Ostensibly, they mockingly imitate the clumsy, disorganized movement of Golliwogg, the rag-doll. On a deeper aesthetic level, however, they satirize the banality of the repetitive ragtime accompaniment precisely by breaking it. Thus, Debussy satirizes not only the over-complication of Wagner's harmony, but also the

Ex. 6.4

Debussy's satirizes the Wagnerian harmonic tension by a simple cadential resolution, and ragtime's banality by the introduction of asymmetry into the introductory accompaniment figure

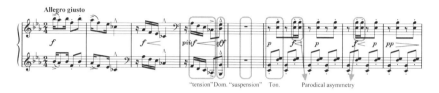

over-simplicity of popular music. It is this complex picture of a double satire, a parody and an almost burlesque-like description of a grotesque, that defines this parody as a masterpiece of multi-layered discourse.

The original motif's expression marks in the middle section, *avec une grande émotion*, are exaggerated, but only in relation to the new context, and not the Wagnerian one (it is very hard, if not impossible, to create a musical expression that would outreach the over-emotional strain of *Tristan*'s opening). It is the prevalence of the new context and its incongruity with the *Tristan* motif that should point here to the preferred aesthetic norm of ironic distance. This norm, however, remains questionable. Although the mocking repeating quavers, played immediately after the quotation, and its unexpectedly straightforward harmonic resolution in the second phrase seem to highlight the norm of 'ironic distance', these 'critical comments' are somehow too short and too soft. They are very different, for example, from the kind of burlesque that Bartók uses in his 'Intermezzo' from the *Concerto for Orchestra,* where he mocks Shostakovich's Seventh Symphony (Ex. 6.5).[8]

Bartók's joke in these bars is a farce. The quotation from Shostakovich's symphony is twice distorted (bars 75–84 and 96–103), the second time with an added exaggeration to the distortion itself.[9] After the first quotation there is an accumulation of four different mocking figures over the space of eight bars. It starts with a forte 'wrong' cadential chord (B major instead of E♭ major), a long fortissimo trill on the interval of a major second, a series of 'laughing' staccato quavers, on the same interval, repeating in the flutes and descending in the clarinets, and two forte glissandi in the bass brasses.[10] These figures, all aping mocking gestures, are followed by a merry-go-round introduction figure that prepares the repetition of the quotation which is again followed by jeering figures similar to the previous ones. Here there is neither irony nor double-layered discourse: Bartók's laughter is straightforward; Debussy's, on the other hand, is ironic. His pianissimo 'mocking commentary' creates balance, and functions rather as a distancing device of aesthetic criticism than a clownish thumb-on-the-nose gesture. It is satirical, since it puts into perspective and places a question mark on Wagner's aesthetic values.

On the other hand, it also admits its beauty: the following bars, with their tenderly falling harmonies that pour out of the satirized chord, are far from satirical (Ex. 6.6).

Ex. 6.5
The mocking musical figures in Bartók's *Concerto for Orchestra*

Ex. 6.6
Debussy's ironical *dédoublement*: is he satirizing Wagner's music or actually enraptured by the beauty of his satire's subject? Or is he perhaps ironically contemplating his own fascination with that old-fashioned, over-emotional outpouring?

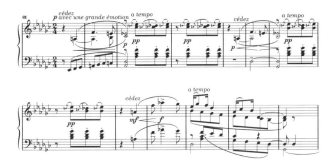

Here, Debussy the artist cannot but succumb to the beauty of the Tristan chord and melodic gesture, nor contain his own creative response to it. On the other hand, Debussy the ironist satirizes not only Wagner's but also his own sentimentality, his own aesthetic pleasure in the 'yearning' chord he intended to criticize. His Baudelairean *dédoublement* can almost be seen as his two *personae* – the ironist and the sentimentalist – look at each other with both pleasure and contempt.

A satirical parody can end in a simple burlesque. However, it can also combine satirical devices with the more specific qualities of parody's 'infinite mirroring', and therefore can evolve to a more complex, subtler satire.

Non-satirical parody

A non-satirical parody presents two or more stylistic layers without necessarily exaggerating or distorting any of them. The parody will be made apparent by the very stylistic clash that will result from its structure. Its purport, therefore, will be ironic, but not necessarily satirical.

Debussy's 'The Little Shepherd', again from the *Children's Corner*, is such a parody. Here the context is not given within the work but is only implied: it is the more general stylistic context of Debussy's own 'pastorale genre' as expressed in his 1895 *Prélude à l'après-midi d'un faune* (Ex. 6.7).

Ex. 6.7
Debussy's 'The Little Shepherd' relates to his earlier *Prélude à l'après-midi d'un faune* in the monodic, non-rhythmical opening, the falling melodic line and the outstanding ambitus of the tritone

The *Prélude* is a relatively long work with a heavily loaded atmosphere. Melodic shreds meander without any clear rhythmic pattern and hover over pending chords that seem to have no tonal function. The musical aporia builds to an almost unbearable tension which evolves into luscious eruptions of dynamic tone colour that achieve no apparent solution, but only function as temporary releases, almost physical in their non-premeditated nature.

The parody in 'The Little Shepherd' is extremely subtle: the ephemeral music of the *Prélude* is transferred from its former context, which is so abundant with sexual insinuations, into a 31-bar-long naïve, childlike piano miniature.

The same type of motif, which evoked the faun's sexual yearning and served as basis for the the *Prélude*'s tense atmosphere is here treated topically, as a simple sign for a 'pastorale'. After hovering shortly, it simply 'resolves' into an incongruent perfect cadence that is not its direct outcome, but is simply located after it (Ex. 6.8).

Ex. 6.8

A stylistically incongruent simple cadence closes the 'pastorale' musical phrase in Debussy's 'The Little Shepherd'

This clumsy little incongruity, together with a small figure of dotted dance-steps, is repeated three times during the work. The original deep erotic signification of the aimless melody is lost, and 'The Little Shepherd' ends up as a parody of the way a child perceives a pastorale and its significance. This parody is not satirical, though, but a subtle and loving psychological portrait of puerile innocent perception.

In spite of the ambiguity that might arise due to the historical association of parody with the satirical, I choose to retain the term and not use the indifferent 'intertextuality'. The reason for this decision is the cultural context that is explored in this study: Dmitri Shostakovich's music is influenced, as I show below, by the Russian formalists' theories of parody, cast within the ambiguous framework described above. This ambiguity, then, is also an integral part of Shostakovich's musical parodies, and thus an essential part of his conception of the artistic function of parody.

CHAPTER SEVEN

The structure of parody

Like all ironic structures, parody is composed of two incongruent layers. In the specific case of parody both layers are taken from pre-existing cultural contexts, such as specific works of art, personal artistic styles, stylistic genres, topics or stylistic periods.

Most theories of parody, including those of the Russian formalists, regard it as a device for satirization or for alienation rather than as a structure. Even when parody's double-layered structure is pointed out, or when the requirement for incongruity is mentioned, it is brought up in regard to parody's functions and contents and not as an independent subject of enquiry. Thus Tinyanov speaks about the necessary 'struggle' between those levels, which acts as a catalyst for artistic innovations, and Bakhtin uses this structure as a bedrock for his theory of heteroglossia or plurivocality (Tinyanov, 1921 [1979]: 104; (Bakhtin, 1929, 1963 [1984]: 185). Other theoreticians are engrossed in the philosophical aspects that are raised by both art works and analytical studies, and reflect on parody's multi-layered commentary as an instance of infinite ironic parabasis (Rose, 1979: 65–69; Deguy, 1984: 2; Golopentia-Eretescu, 1984: 130; Dane, 1988: 149). However, in spite of their thorough descriptions and insightful analyses, none of those studies explicitly offers a comprehensive structural scheme into which all parodies can fit.[1]

This ostensible oversight is probably rooted in the variety of ways in which the two levels of parody seem to relate to each other and the confusion that this causes. Other obstacles are the numerous techniques used for parodic modification and parody's tendency, inherent in its nature as a meta-text, to develop its two primary layers into an open and multi-layered structure.

The neglect of structural questions concerning parody is also due to historical circumstances, since the classical writings on parody are more prescriptive than descriptive. Subsequently, practically all the theories of parody tend to examine its techniques rather than its structure.[2] Another reason for the medley of techniques, types of relation between parody's various levels, and its philosophical implications, is the widespread correlation between parody's double-layered structure and the semantic opposition 'authority versus transgression' or 'tradition versus innovation' (Hutcheon, 1985: 69).[3] This opposition, which was regarded by some writers as structural (Shlonsky, 1966; Rose, 1979), has mistakenly been correlated with the various techniques that modify the parodied object: imitation, quotation, and stylization were correlated with 'tradition' and 'authority', and variation, distortion and collage with 'innovation' and 'transgression'. Obviously, even a superficial inspection of a random selection of existing parodies will show that there is no such necessary correlation. The resulting fallacious equation between techniques and structural components impeded a straightforward description of parody (Fig. 7.1).

Fig. 7.1
Fallacious correlations lead to a fallacious equation

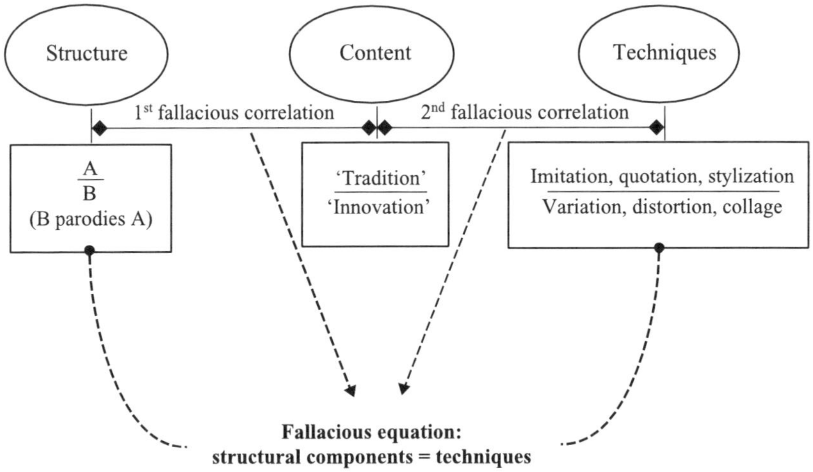

When the multi-layered structure of infinite irony is combined with the above confusing scheme, the fallacy becomes more encumbering, since in such cases both layers contain the two *content* components of 'tradition' and 'innovation'. Since these components are so strongly correlated with parody's structure, the scheme tends fallaciously to cancel the *structural* differentiation among these *layers of content* (Fig. 7.2).

This multi-layered structure can continue endlessly in both directions, at one end to the very historical beginnings of artistic creation, and at the other to an infinite series of interpretations, commentaries and self-commentaries. Such a scheme, therefore, is not only a source of confusion between structure and content, but also of the fallacious equation between the *structural functions* of the parodying and the parodied layers.[4] The combination of these fallacious equations renders a muddled picture in which all the techniques can also be regarded as structural components that operate in all the structural layers.[5]

All the above is not meant to deny or overlook the infinite nature of the parodic process, which had a major influence not only on the development of aesthetics but also on the very process of artistic creation (Eco, 1967 and 1979b; Berio, 1985: 102–103). However, due to the philosophical (rather

Fig. 7.2
Fallacious equation between content and structure

'Tradition'   *etc.*
'Tradition' = 'Innovation'
'Tradition' = 'Innovation'
'Tradition' = 'Innovation'
'Innovation'

than analytical) character of certain studies, they are unclear with regard to a pragmatic but cardinal point: one of the two primary structural layers must be *the cultural or artistic context of the commentator that each specific analysis chooses to be its starting-point.* This layer is often, though not always, the writer's explicit or implicit personal style and cultural context. The parodied objects, on the other hand, may split into secondary substructures of parodying and parodied layers, all of which must be explicitly present. In such cases two or more incongruent objects are joined in the layer of the parodied object; their incongruity is thus secondary, and acts as a modifier of the parodied object, while the parodying layer functions as a structural ironic commentary. This point was stated by Bakhtin:

> Там, где есть в авторском контексте прямая речь, допустим, одного героя, то перед нами в пределах одного контекста два речевых центра и два речевых единства: единство авторского высказывания и единство высказывания героя. Но второе единство не самостоятельно, подчинено первому и включено в него, как один из его моментов. (Бахтин, 1929: 107–108)

> Whenever we have within the author's context the direct speech of, say, a certain character, we have within the limits of a single context two speech centres and two speech unities: the unity of the author's utterance and the unity of the character's utterance. But the second unity is not self-sufficient; it is subordinated to the first and incorporated into it as one of its components. (Bakhtin, 1929, 1963 [1984]: 187)[6]

Ignoring the hierarchy between the primary and secondary types of layers leads to Bakhtin's later concept of heteroglossia, which crushes all the parodic substructures into one single layer, creating a 'reversed', chaotic world.[7] Interpreted in this way, all works could be regarded as 'endlessly open', as all words have 'loopholes', are therefore 'plurivocal', and consequently none is susceptible to a finite analysis (Bakhtin, 1929: 181; 1963 [1984]: 233).[8] Following such a theoretical path, according to which 'the word with a loophole ... is only the penultimate word and places after itself only a conditional, not a final, period', leads to a point at which a comprehensive structural analysis must be declared an impossibility. A pragmatic approach, that will enable *any* structural analysis to be performed, must therefore explicitly confine itself to defined boundaries within this infinite 'loophole' process.

Karrer (1977) and Hutcheon (1985) attempted a systematic approach to the structure of parody as a distinct topic. Karrer partly clarified the picture by distinguishing between parody's syntactic and semantic components, but then added to the general disarray his mixture of structural and syntactic traits: the 'forms' of parody he lists are, in fact, not parody's structural components but various kinds of reciprocity between the various levels and techniques for the manipulation of the parodied object (Karrer, 1977: 60).

Hutcheon's work comes closest to a useful suggestion of a structure, mainly due to the structuralist tendency of her definitions of parody. Her most important contribution in this respect is the term 'trans-contextualization', which describes not only the transfer of a subject from its original context to a new one, but also the incongruity, or the 'ironic confrontation', within the new entity (Hutcheon, 1985: 11). Its semantic aspects are portrayed in the description of parody as 'a form of imitation, but imitation characterized by ironic inversion, not always at the expense of the parodied text', and as a 'repetition with critical distance, which marks difference rather than similarity' (Hutcheon, 1985: 6).[9] This description can be expressed in a schematic way (Fig 7.3).

Fig. 7.3
The structure of parody

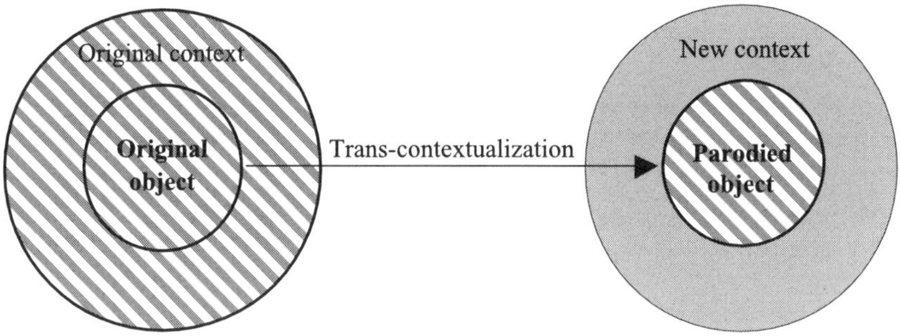

The parodied object is trans-contextualized from its original context to a new one, with which it is incongruous.

While 'trans-contextualization' provides the scheme with its structural form, 'relation' and 'incongruity' (respectively shown in the scheme by the trans-contextualized object in its original and new context) provide it with parody's semantic structural components. This scheme presents, thus, a clear-cut ironic structure, based on pre-existing texts, which this study accepts as the starting-point for the examination of parody.

CHAPTER EIGHT

Historical background

The sources of parody can be traced back at least to Aristophanes' parodies of Euripides, if not earlier than that (Dane, 1988; Rose, 1993). The following lines, however, will focus particularly on the theories that are the most relevant for understanding the musical parodies in the works of Dmitri Shostakovich: the Russian formalists' theories of parody, which were conceived in St Petersburg in the years 1915–30.

A basic premise of this study is that Shostakovich's techniques of composition were influenced to no less a degree by his literary, theatrical and artistic environment than by his musical background. The influence of literature and literary ideas on Shostakovich is remarkable. All his biographers agree that besides being a tireless student of music, he was also a fervent reader. This is apparent in his musical works, too. In spite of being generally regarded a symphonist, Shostakovich seems to be rather a 'literary' composer. A considerable amount of his music is related to extra-musical ideas; far fewer than half of his works (59 of his 147 opus numbers) are purely instrumental music, and even a considerable portion of this part is programmatic or bears some referential features, such as suggestive titles, significant dedications or telling inscriptions. For example, his opus 13, a series of short piano pieces, is called *Aphorisms*; his Eighth String Quartet bears the inscription 'In Memory of the Victims of Fascism and War', and his Fifth Symphony op. 47 is subtitled 'A Soviet Artist's practical creative reply to justified criticism' (Hulme, 1991: 32, 270, 118). The rest of his works consist of two operas, song cycles, ballets and incidental music for the theatre and for films. Even his symphonies bear the hallmark of referential music: four of them (almost a third of the fifteen he wrote) have texts; the Thirteenth ('Babi-Yar') and Fourteenth Symphonies could be regarded as song cycles; the Second and Third Symphonies use texts, and the Eleventh and Twelfth Symphonies, although without texts, are programmatic. The use of literary devices in music seems to be, therefore, characteristic of Shostakovich's music.

A possible explanation for this phenomenon, besides his natural disposition towards literature, could be the kind of influences he was exposed to, particularly during his formative years as a composer at the conservatory of St Petersburg. An overview of the circle of Shostakovich's friends is enlightening in this respect.[1] His best friends were not musicians, but writers and men of letters: Mikhail Zoshchenko, the writer, Yury Tinyanov, the literary critic and formalist theoretician, Vsevolod Meyerhold, the theatre director (with whom Shostakovich had not only worked but also stayed, while working at his theatre in Moscow); his closest friend, Ivan Sollertinsky, in spite of being a musicologist (mainly due to his acquaintance with Shostakovich), began his academic career as a philologist and specialized in the history and criticism of literature, theatre, film and ballet. These acquaintances not only enhanced Shostakovich's love for theatre and literature in general, introducing him to Shakespeare, Byron and Heine, but particularly encouraged him to focus more intensively on the writings of Gogol and Dostoevsky, his favourite writers (Seroff, 1943: 89); these writers were also subjects of many of the formalists' critical analyses in the years 1917–30.

The significance of the Russian formalists in developing the theory of parody is fundamental (Karrer, 1977; Rose, 1979 and 1993; Hutcheon, 1985; Dane, 1988). An examination of their cultural background and literary output may also explain their substantial role in the development of Shostakovich's compositional techniques. Therefore, before launching into an analytical description of parody's goals and techniques, and their relevance and manifestation in the works of Dmitri Shostakovich, a brief survey of the Russian cultural milieu in the first years of the Revolution and the main ideas that flourished there is necessary.

In the first three decades of the century St Petersburg, which became Petrograd (1914) and then Leningrad (1924), was a centre of hectic cultural activity. There were dozens of literary, poetical and artistic groups, each with its own slogan – revolutionary art, anti-symbolist poetry, constructivist ideas, etc. – forming a confused complex of agitated cultural life.[2] In a rather oversimplified scheme, however, made for the sake of clarification, these groups could be divided into two main trends: the 'revolutionaries' who stood for the idea of total innovation and destruction of the old and decadent world, and those who advocated at least some amount of conservation and continuation of former cultural traditions. The poet Vladimir Mayakovsky (1894–1930), for whose play *The Bedbug* (1929) Shostakovich had written the incidental music, belonged to the 'revolutionary' groups Oktyabr and Lef. Shostakovich's closest friends, however, were generally closer to the other trend, those who were derogatorily called the Fellow Travellers, a general term that described all those who were reluctant to join the Party but who did not overtly object to it, thus keeping a certain degree of intellectual independence without too much personal risk. To this category belonged the writer Yevgeny Zamyatin (1884–1937), who was acquainted with Shostakovich and made contributions to the libretto of *The Nose* (Volkov, 1979: 205).

During the same period many artists left Russia and emigrated to West European cultural centres: Berlin, Vienna, Paris and Prague. Thus was formed the Blaue Reiter group in Vienna, which included Kandinsky and Kokoschka as well as Schönberg, the Russian *émigré* circle of musicians, poets and ballet artists in Paris, and the semiotic circle of Prague under Roman Jakobson, who emigrated from Moscow. Other artists, writers and theoreticians remained in the Soviet Union: the painter Malevich and the architect Rodchenko enhanced their futurist–constructivist ideas in art; the theatre directors Tairov, Vakhtangov and Meyerhold, who worked with contemporary playwrights Vladimir Mayakovsky and Yevgeny Zamyatin, and the film directors Pudovkin and Sergey Eisenstein broke new ground in theatre and film aesthetics. The Russian musical world was divided as well: many musicians escaped from revolutionary Russia, most famous among them Stravinsky and Prokofiev (who later, in 1936, returned to Russia), while others, like Dmitri Shostakovich, remained. It is not a coincidence that the *émigrés'* society included more musicians and painters than writers: the linguistic barrier was too great to be overcome, so that most of the Russian writers chose to stay in their home-land. This may be one of the reasons for the evident dominance of poetry and literature in Russian cultural life from the 1920s on, although it must be remembered that literature in all its manifestations, regardless of the circum-stances, was always located at the centre of Russia's cultural life.

These facts obviously do not provide sufficient proof of an ideological influence of the formalists on Shostakovich; among the writers dealt with by the formalists were also Akhmatova, Blok, Bryusov, Beliy, Byron, Cervantes, Heine, Khlebnikov, Küchelbecker, Lermontov, Mayakovsky, Nekrasov, Pushkin, Sterne, Tolstoy and Tyutchev. While Shostakovich's interest in Gogol, Dostoevsky and Pushkin as a proof of his connection with the formalists could have easily been dismissed, since these writers were admired by virtu-ally all of the Russian intelligentsia, his interest and knowledge of the poems of Heine, and particularly of a lesser poet like Küchelbecker, make his acquaintance with the many writings of Yury Tinyanov on the latter far more plausible, especially when his personal friendship with Tinyanov is taken into account (Tinyanov, 1924 [1981]: 140–144; Volkov, 1979: 162). In this light, Shostakovich's interest in particular aspects of Gogol and Dostoevsky becomes clearer: these two writers were a main subject in the writings of the formalists, but particularly of Tinyanov, whose article 'Dostoevsky and Gogol: towards a theory of parody' (1921) is considered a milestone in this field.

Moreover, Shostakovich had close contacts with members of another group, The Serapion Brothers, who, although being considered by the authorities as 'Fellow Travellers', were formally organized and declared as their common ideal 'not to be on the side of anybody', as Lev Lunz, one of the group's founding members, wrote: 'Whose side are we, Serapion Brethren? We are the side of the hermit Serapion.'[3] The Serapion Brothers had regular meet-ings, a publication, and even a formalized greeting: 'Zdravstvuy, brat! Ochen' trudno pisat'!' – meaning, in a free translation – 'Greetings, brother! Writing is a bother!' (Kasack, 1988: 354).[4] One of the founding members of the group was Mikhail Zoshchenko, Shostakovich's close friend, who used to visit and stay with the Shostakovich family in Petrograd, and who is much quoted in the composer's memoirs (Sollertinsky, 1979: 295; Volkov, 1979: 8–11, 87–

89, 207–211).[5] All the members of this group were students of the leading formalist writers: Boris Eikhenbaum (1886–1959), Viktor Shklovsky (1894–1984) and Yury Tïnyanov (1896–1943), and were strongly influenced by their ideas. Shostakovich was acquainted with several members of the group: besides Mikhail Zoshchenko he certainly knew Shklovsky, who was an influential figure in the group, and, of course, Yury Tïnyanov, who also participated in some of the group meetings (Erlich, 1955: 151). The year of their formation as a group, 1921, was also the year of important formalist publications such as Shklovsky's 'Sterne's *Tristram Shandy* and the Theory of The Novel' (later reprinted as 'A Parodying Novel: Sterne's *Tristram Shandy*'), Tïnyanov's 'Dostoevsky and Gogol: Towards a Theory of Parody' and Eikhenbaum's *The Melodics of Verse*.[6] It is more than likely that these works were read and discussed in the Serapion Brothers' meetings, at some of which Shostakovich was present.[7] Given the fact that the New Economic Policy, which permitted the renewal of cultural connections with the West, including concerts of contemporary music, was still one year ahead, it is likely that these literary meetings were Shostakovich's first impressions of contemporary culture, the impact of which should not be under-estimated. Shostakovich continued his connection with members of the group during the 1920s, and thus it is feasible that their ideas combined with the first impressions of the new music he heard in those years.

There were more than coincidental theoretical and ideological connections between the Serapion Brothers and the formalists: like the formalists, they emphasized the freedom of the individual artistic creativity and 'the poet's right to dream and fancy' (Slonim, 1977: 295); like the formalists, they supported the Revolution's causes and aims while nevertheless believing in the importance of carrying on pre-revolutionary aesthetic trends. These two features can be clearly seen in Shostakovich's life and work, too (Volkov, 1979: 61, 131). Thus, unlike other contemporary artistic trends such as the futurists, the confrontational combination of tradition and innovation (a combination which the formalists saw embodied in parody) was part of their artistic as well as political ideology. This, however, was only in the background: the main concerns were the formal and technical aspects of art. This professional focusing again characterizes the Serapion Brothers' and the formalists' ideas; in their articles, discussions and literary works, they stressed the importance of literary craftsmanship: writing technique and literary devices were more substantial for them than any 'psychological and dramatic context' (Shklovsky, 1917 [1965]: 6; Slonim, 1977: 296). Shostakovich's own expressions on the subject show the applications of these ideas to music (Volkov, 1979: 181).

Another connecting point with the formalists was the Serapion Brothers' interest in the effects of literary incongruities. They dealt with 'contrapuntal composition' and made extensive use of the grotesque and the fantastic.

Furthermore, they shared the formalists' interest in parodic devices, therefore working with neologisms, twists of syntax and grammatical structure, and intersection of colloquial and vernacular speech in an otherwise literary style. Some of them, like Yury Olesha, Yevgeny Zamyatin and Mikhail Zoshchenko, who were closer to Shostakovich, specialized in satirical writing. It is thus feasible that formalist ideas did influence Shostakovich's composing traits: at first it is apparent in his tendency toward satirical parody; later, however, and to a greater extent, it influenced the general ambiguous character of his music.

My main argument in this chapter is that Shostakovich's literary bias is not only expressed in the relatively superficial 'literary tendencies' of his music, but that the literary theories of the time affected the very structure and basis of his compositional techniques, and influenced his development as a composer. In order to understand this process, it is necessary to have a closer look at some of the formalists' ideas and theories.

The basic concepts of Russian formalism

Russian formalism was influenced by Husserl's phenomenology, particularly in its Russian interpretation, presented in the works of Gustav Shpet (1879–1937).[8] These ideas offered new positivist approaches, which partly agreed with Marxist materialistic ideas and were partly a reaction to the growing subjectivity in art and literature at the turn of the century. Decidedly anti-metaphysical and anti-religious in his ideology, Shpet saw philosophy as a 'rigorous science' and presented it as a study of data provided exclusively by consciousness-phenomena and of the 'meanings' which phenomenological reduction discloses. Shpet emphasized in his writings the social character of consciousness, and referred to language as the bearer of meanings in social intercourse (Erlich, 1955: 62). Thus Russian phenomenology is focused on the factual in language, rejecting any 'historicism' or 'psychologism' in literary criticism. This attitude proved to be of major significance for further development in Russian thought about literature, because it supported not only a new 'materialistic' approach to literature, but also recognized the importance of a dialogic intercourse with existing phenomena; this philosophical approach became the theoretical basis of the formalists' subsequent theories of parody.

Eikhenbaum, Shklovsky and Tinyanov, the leaders of the formalistic circle in Leningrad, saw in literature an art that uses language as its material. Their main claim was that the use of language for everyday needs eroded its effect as an artistic device; words are so familiar to us that we are numb to their artistic (i.e. non-practical) potential and usage, and let them pass unnoticed. Shklovsky presented the problem in his first article, 'Art as technique':

... У ШИ берутся счетом и пространством, они не видятся нами, а узнаются по первым чертам. Вещь проходит мимо нас как бы запакованной, мы знаем, что она есть, по месту, которое она занимает, но видим только её поверхность. Под влиянием такого восприятия вещь сохнет, сперва как восприятие, а потом это сказывается и на её делании ...

    Так пропадает, в ничто вменяясь, жизнь. Автоматизация сбедает вещи, платье, мебель, жену и страх войны.

    'Если целая сложная жизнь многих проходит бессознательно, то эта жизнь как бы не была.' (Шкловский, 1917 [1929]: 12–13)

... we apprehend objects only as shapes with imprecise extension; we do not see them in their entirety but rather recognize them by their main characteristics. We see the object as though it were enveloped in a sack. We know what it is by its configuration, but we see only its silhouette. The object, perceived thus in the manner of prose perception, fades ... And so life is reckoned as nothing. Habitualization devours works, clothes, furniture, one's wife, and the fear of war. 'If the whole complex lives of many people go on unconsciously, then such lives are as if they had never been.' (Shklovsky, 1929 [1965]: 11–12.

Therefore, according to Shklovsky and the formalists, the goal of the art of literature is to draw attention to the words as artistic devices: *to lay bare the device*. This can be achieved by *ostranenye*, the 'estrangement', alienation, defamiliarization of the word from its everyday practical context, so that its artificiality and function as an artistic device (rather than as a practical means to transmit information) is made apparent.[9] Consequently, the formalists' task was to examine literature as 'a set of literary artistic devices' (Tinyanov, 1924 [1981]: 9). It is interesting to see the connection that Shklovsky makes between the phenomenological assertion that opens his statement, 'the purpose of art is to impart the sensation of things as they are perceived and not as they are known', and his conclusion, that such a perception as required here needs the device of defamiliarization:

Целью искусства является дать ощущение вещи, как видение, а не как узнавание; приёмом искусства является приём 'остранения' вещей и приём затрудённой формы, увеличивающий трудность и долготу восприятия, так как воспринимательный процесс в искусстве самоцелен и должен быть продлен; *искусство есть способ пережить деланье вещи, а сделанное в искусстве не важно.* (Шкловский, 1917 [1929]: 13)

The purpose of art is to impart the sensation of things as they are perceived and not as they are known. The technique of art is to make objects 'unfamiliar', to make forms difficult, to increase the difficulty and length of perception because the process of perception is an aesthetic end in itself and must be prolonged. *Art is a way of experiencing the artfulness of an object; the object is not important.* (Shklovsky, 1917 [1965]: 12)

Parody in the writings of the formalists

Parody only gradually became part of this network of ideas. In 'Art as technique', for example, Shklovsky used the word *ostranenye*, while parody was not mentioned at all. His article about Sterne's *Tristram Shandy*, which first appeared in 1921 as a monograph, was titled on the cover as '*Tristram Shandy* and the Theory of the Novel', while the title given on its first page was 'Sterne's *Tristram Shandy*: Stylistic Commentary' (Lemon and Reis, 1965: 25). The very same essay is reprinted in the 1929 anthology *O teorii prozï*; here, however, it has the title 'A Parodying Novel: Sterne's *Tristram Shandy*'. Since the change of title was not accompanied by any change in the text, it is apparent that the definition of its content has changed in the eyes of the writer. Indeed, in the glossary at the end of *O teorii prozï* appears the word *parodirovaniye*, defined as *priyom ostraneniya*: a technique of defamiliarization.

When reading their writings, it is important to remember that the series of articles that the formalists published during the early 1920s are not conclusions of their scholarly work, but essays describing the process of their research, during which their ideas gained final shape. In the twelve years that passed from the first publication of 'Art as technique' until its appearance in the 1929 edition, the formalist theory was transformed from a series of avant-garde controversial pamphlets into a serious theory of literary criticism. The years preceding the 1929 edition saw hundreds of meetings and discussions in which participants not only read each other's works, but actually discussed and crystallized their ideas in a long process of mutual work. The modification and coming into life of their theory is thus a result of continual manipulation and dialogic working and re-working of concepts and terms. Shklovsky's adoption of Tinyanov and Eikhenbaum's terminology made parody into a device for defamiliarization, as can be seen in the above change of title (although the article itself does not deal with parody but with the manipulation of narrative) and in the way he refers to it in the glossary of his book; the terminology was, during these years, in a process of becoming, and terms were used inconsistently (Erlich, 1955: 178). The fact that translation of the formalists' writings was rather sporadic and unsystematic did not help to build a useful parallel terminology in English that would be clear and consistent.[10]

To partly solve this problem, in order to discuss the formalists' ideas, I have chosen certain terms that are explained in the scheme below (Fig. 8.1). According to this scheme, when discussing the Russian formalists' views of art I shall use for the literary word (or, for the sake of this study, the musical work or part of work) the term *artifice*; defamiliarization (which I prefer to 'alienation' and 'estrangement' in this specific context, since it seems to point most accurately to the formalists' use of it) is a *device* that serves to bare the

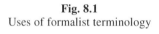

Fig. 8.1
Uses of formalist terminology

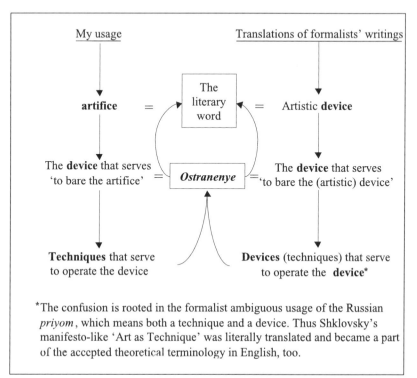

*The confusion is rooted in the formalist ambiguous usage of the Russian *priyom*, which means both a technique and a device. Thus Shklovsky's manifesto-like 'Art as Technique' was literally translated and became a part of the accepted theoretical terminology in English, too.

artificiality of the artistic artifice. There are several *techniques* that serve to operate this device.[11] All formalists agree upon the necessity of defamiliarization. Not all of them, though, pointed to the same techniques that would serve to operate this device.

The techniques for achieving defamiliarization

According to Shklovsky, parody is one of the techniques that could be used to achieve defamiliarization. As noted above, in the glossary of his 1929 edition of *O teorii prozï* the word *parodirovaniye*, i.e. parodying, is explained as *priyom ostraneniya* – a device for defamiliarization (Shklovsky, 1929: 259).[12] However, in the article itself Shklovsky mentions parody only in passing, merely hinting at the way in which parody bares the device by defamiliarizing it, relying on an implicit premise according to which the reader is aware that the plot of a story is a mere artistic device, and thus a mere conventionality:

Стерн пользовался другими способами или, пользуясь старыми, не скрыл их условность, а выпячивал её, играл с нею ... (он) 'пародировал' развертывание новеллы и вторжение нового матириала в неё. (Íklovskey, 1929: 180–181)

Sterne makes use of new devices or, when using old ones, he does not conceal their conventionality. Rather, he plays with them by thrusting them to the fore ... he parodies the deployment of the plot line and the intrusion of new material into it. (Shklovsky, 1921 [1965]: 150)

The connection is made clear when 'conventionality' is apprehended as *the reason for our perceiving things without becoming aware of them*. Things can be defamiliarized if our attention is attracted to their conventionality, an end that can be achieved by *distorting the convention*. The awareness of conventionality is achieved by its parodying: its replication with a distortion. Thus parody became the main technique for defamiliarization. In 1921, Yury Tinyanov, who worked side by side with Shklovsky, wrote the article that is regarded as a milestone in the history of the theory of parody: 'Dostoevsky and Gogol: towards a theory of parody' (Tinyanov, 1921 [1979] and 1921 [1975]). Tinyanov gives a more accurate explanation about the process of defamiliarizing conventionality through parody when he writes about the way in which Dostoevsky parodied Gogol's style. As in the case of Shklovsky, in Tinyanov's writings, too, the fact that they are a reflection of a continuous discussion rather than the result of scholarly research is apparent from the order in which he deals with his materials. This early article of his starts with examples from Dostoevsky and Gogol, while the main theoretical question is posed only in passing, although the title of the article relates directly to it. It seems as if the theory of parody was such an obvious issue for the Russian formalists that it went without saying that this lay behind all the analyses and examples. Tinyanov deals with the concepts of stylization and parody, too, without explicitly relating them to the device of defamiliarization. Only in his later article 'On Literary Evolution', published in 1927, does he explain the connection between the 'effacement' of a literary device and its 'automatization'. The need for parody to point to the 'automatized' literary element, however, is taken for granted, and the word 'parody' is used immediately thereafter, as if it is an evident outcome which needs no justification, again pointing to the fact that the article reflects an ongoing discussion (Tinyanov, 1927 [1971]: 69–70). However, an important point must be made here: since 'automatization' has been perceived by Tinyanov as an anti-artistic phenomenon that should be rejected, then parody, which is the device for its unveiling, is necessarily related to the satirical. Yet this is never stated explicitly. On the contrary, the function of parody is stressed almost as a learning tool, by which an artist, a writer or a composer 'plays' with the style of a former artist; it is by the continuous manipulation, or 'stylization' of the older style, that a 'struggle' emerges in the form of 'parody', which enables the new personal style of the younger artist to take shape:

Когда говорят о 'литературной традиции' или 'преемственности',
обычно представляют некоторую прямую линию, соединяющую
младшего представителя известной литературной ветви со
старшим. Между тем дело много сложнее. Нет продолжения
прямой линии, есть скорее отправление, отталкивание от
известной точки, – борьба. (Тынянов, 1921 [1929]: 412)

When speaking about 'literary tradition' or 'succession', you usually
imagine a definite straight line which unites a younger representative of
a well-known literary branch with an elder. However, the matter is much
more complicated. There is no continuation of a straight line, there is
rather a departure, a repulsion from a known point, – in short, a struggle.
(Tïnyanov, 1921 [1979]: 101)

The influence of Tïnyanov's and Shklovsky's ideas on parody are reflected
in Shostakovich's own words: 'Parody and stylisation are one and the same,
after all' (Volkov, 1979: 13). This is a genuinely 'formalist' declaration, most
probably recalled from some old memory of the formalist circle of friends.
Testimony is presented as a series of recollections mainly linked by the
composer's personal associations. This sentence appears in connection with
the names of Zoshchenko, one of the members of the Serapion Brothers, and
Zamyatin, one of their patrons (it should also be remembered that the alma-
nac notes of the Serapion Brothers' meetings were taken by Tïnyanov).
Shostakovich's immediate association with this group of formalists' students,
Zoshchenko, Tïnyanov and Zamyatin, points to the central place that the
concepts of parody and stylization had in their conversations and professional
interrelationship.

On the other hand, the rather confused thoughts of Tïnyanov, who mixes
up parody as a critical tool and as a comic genre, also show up in the works of
Shostakovich. For example, they are reflected in his explanation of his opera
The Nose as 'not funny at all', or in the opera *Lady Macbeth of the Mtsensk
District*, in which Leskov's tragic story is sprinkled with many newly written
comic instances, either satirical or macabre. The most important point of
Tïnyanov's article for the understanding of Shostakovich's parody, however,
lies in the explicit and detailed description of the techniques of parody. A list
and examination of these techniques and their comparison with some of
Shostakovich's works shed a new light on several of the composer's hereto-
fore unexplained techniques. The close relation between the techniques of
parody, as described and analysed by Tïnyanov, and the parodic techniques of
Shostakovich may point to a direct influence, and it seems apparent that
Shostakovich is applying, in his music, literary techniques of parody.[13]

It is indeed a fact that Shostakovich had a 'natural disposition' toward
parody. It is enough to have a look at 'The Ass and the Nightingale' from his
Two Krylov Songs op. 4, which parody the style of Rimsky-Korsakov, or at
his *Three Fantastic Dances* op. 5, with their stylizations of Dvořák, of Ravel,
and of the harmonies of Mussorgsky. In these early works, however, this is a

mere tendency: it is difficult to judge whether these stylizations are a result of sincere efforts of the teenager who is genuinely influenced by those composers, or first attempts at a parody. In any case, this tendency was undoubtedly reinforced by Shostakovich's work as a café pianist and as an accompanist to silent movies – two jobs that must have required all his abilities of 'playing in the style of' whatever was shown on the screen, and of providing an array of light, popular background music.

Influences of literary criticism appear in the works of Shostakovich only later, and in two main ways that respectively reflect two different modes of theoretical thought. One is immediate, and is usually manifested in the rather superficial aspects of a musical work: its title, subject or immediate content. An example of this is Shostakovich's decision, in 1927, to write an opera based on a Gogol story, most probably influenced by the formalists' frequent analyses of Gogol. The interest that Tïnyanov had in music (more than any other of the formalists) could only help the professional kinship between him and the composer. Gogol and Dostoevsky were not his only field of interest, and perhaps not even the main one; in 1924 he published an article entitled 'Film–Poetry–Music' and his book *The Problem of Verse Language*, which deals mainly with quasi-musical questions of sound and rhythm in poetry. Two years later, in 1926, he wrote a film script based on Gogol's *The Overcoat*, also incorporating material from *Nevsky Prospekt* (from which he draws several of Gogol's quoted examples in the earlier article from 1921). In 1927 Shostakovich started working on his opera *The Nose*, based on Gogol's story, to the libretto for which Yevgeny Zamyatin, one of the Serapion Brothers' patrons (among whom was also Tïnyanov), is mentioned as one of the contributors.[14]

Tïnyanov sees 'the portrayal of people as masks' as Gogol's basic device (Tïnyanov, 1921 [1979]: 105). A mask can be based on anything from inanimate objects, through verbal sound-imagery and types of motion, to geometric concepts, etc. Almost half of Tïnyanov's article deals with a detailed description of Gogol's techniques of 'the creation of masks'. Actually, he claims, any exaggerated appearance may serve as a mask (Tïnyanov, 1921 [1979]: 106).

Such 'exaggerated appearances' emerge in the music of every single scene of *The Nose*. The hysterical musical portrayal of Praskovya Osipovna is immediately followed in the next scene by another exaggerated 'mask' – that of the policeman, who sings in an incredibly high pitch, a mode of performance that puts a substantial stress on the singer's vocal cords.[15] Besides the comic effect that results from the sheer abruptness of the high tessitura, this immense vocal effort adds a further, physical feature to the caricature. The scene opens with the barber Ivan Yakovlevich, who, after he has found a nose in his morning bread-roll, tries to get rid of it by throwing it into the river. He finds the right moment and throws the nose into the water. Unfortunately, at that very moment a police constable shows up, and begins a tortuous enquiry, while constantly getting closer and closer to Ivan Yakovlevich (Ex. 8.1). Besides being a caricatural 'exaggerated mask', the whole scene is also a parody on the first scene of *Wozzeck*:[16] Shostakovich uses here, when he 'plays' with Berg's stylistic traits, exactly the same techniques that Tĭnyanov describes as parodical stylization:

> Стиль Достоевского так явно повторяет, варйируeт, комбинируeт стиль Гоголя, что это сразу бросилось в глаза современникам ...
> Эти письма переполнены гоголевскими словцами, именами, фразами ...
> Здесь стилизация; здесь нет следования за стилем, а скорее игра им. И если вспомнить, как охотно подчеркивает Достоевский Гоголя ... как слишком явно идёт от него, не скрываясь, станет ясно, что следует говорить скорее о стилизации, нежели о 'подражании', 'влиянии' и т.д. (Тынянов, 1921: 414–416)

> Dostoevsky's style so obviously repeats, varies, combines the style of Gogol that his contemporaries were immediately struck by it ...
> Dostoevsky's letters are crammed with Gogolian *bon mots*, names and phrases ...
> What we have here is stylization; it is not a question of following a style but rather of playing with it. And if one recollects how readily Dostoevsky underlines Gogol ... how he so obviously proceeds from Gogol without concealing the fact, it becomes clear that it is more

Ex. 8.1

'The scene by the river' from act I, scene 2 of *The Nose*

Constable: Come here, please.
Yakovlevich: My best wishes to your excellency.
Constable: No, No, "Brother", not "Excellency"; tell, what were you doing there, standing by the river?
Yakovlevich: By God, Mister, I wanted to see that I'm shaved, so I figured I'd pop to the river.
Constable: You're lying, you're lying, if so, you would not be throwing anything. Will you please answer?
Yakovlevich: I will shave your excellency twice, even thrice a week, with no argument at all!
Constable: No, my friend, this is a trifle! I have three barbers that shave me, and they regard it as a great honour. Please tell me, what have you been doing there.

appropriate to speak about stylization than about 'imitation', 'influence', and so on. (Tinyanov, 1921 [1979]: 102–103)

The constable's incredibly high pitch parodies the hysterical high register of the captain's voice in *Wozzeck*, and the similar rhythmic figure within which the highest note resides further supports the parodying effect (Ex. 8.2a). Yakovlevich's spoken answers not only highlight by contrast the exaggerated caricature, but also echo Wozzeck's brief monotone replies. Concurrently, the captain's laughter and large melodic descent are echoed in the constable's part (Ex. 8.2b).

Ex. 8.2a and Ex. 8.2b
Similarities between the 'officers'' parts in *Wozzeck* and *The Nose*

Shostakovich's 'Kvartïlniy' and Berg's 'Hauptmann' sing in a high falsetto voice, have abrupt leaps to high pitches, and share similar motivic melodic musical gestures.

The parody is not only of the musical performance, but also of the text, since Ivan Yakovlevich exaggerates even more Wozzeck's meek replies with his 'I wish your Highness the best.' Concurrently, the constable role parodies the captain's not only in the similar melodic and rhythmical contours, but also in the sound of the vowels: the captain's laughter is usually performed as 'he, he', using the vowel 'e' that is echoed in the constable's 'Nyet! Nyet!'. Shostakovich exaggerates both characters, transforming Berg's characters into 'masks': Yakovlevich is shifted to a completely speaking role and the constable's high pitch is higher than that of the captain. Moreover, he inverts the tragic situation into a comic one, thus echoing here, too, Tinyanov's association of parody with the comic:[17]

Стилизация близка к пародии. И та и другая живут двойною
жизнью: за планом произведения стоит другой план, стилизуемый
или пародируемый. Но в пародии обязательна невязка обоих
планов, смешение их; пародией трагедии будет комедия (все
равно, через подчеркивание ли трагичности, или через
соответствующую подстановку комического), пародией комедии
может быть трагедия. При стилизации этой невязки нет, есть,
напротив, соответствие друг другу обоих планов: стилизующего
и сквозящего в нем стилизуемого. Но все же от стилизации к
пародии – один шаг; стилизация, комически мотивированная
или подчеркнутая, становится пародией. (Тынянов, 1921 [1929]:
416)

Stylization is close to parody. Both live a double life: behind the apparent structure of a work, its first level, lies a second level, that of the
work which it stylizes or parodies. But in parody it is obligatory to have
a disjunction of both levels, a dislocation of intent; the parody of a
tragedy will be a comedy (it matters little whether this is done through
an exaggeration of the tragic intent or through a corresponding substitu-
tion of comic elements), and a parody of a comedy could be a tragedy.
In stylization there is no such disjunction. There is, on the contrary, a
correspondence of the two levels – the stylizing level and the stylized
level showing through it – one to another. Nevertheless, it is but a single
step from stylization to parody; stylization that is comically motivated
or emphasized becomes parody. (Tinyanov, 1921 [1979]: 104)

This change of tragic moments into comic ones is expressed in *The Nose* in
even more peculiar ways than those seen above. Unlike the captain in *Wozzeck*,
this constable is not particularly mean nor insane: he is a caricature of a
characteristic constable, and thus it is satirical and not grotesque, as is the
case in *Wozzeck*.[18]

While the figure of the captain in *Wozzeck* could somehow be perceived as
a comic character, albeit in quite a grotesque way, the last act in *Wozzeck* can
hardly be regarded as a subject for a comedy. Following the idea according to
which a parody transforms the tragic into comic, in this scene in which the
nose is thrown into the water there are some parodying instances of the tragic
drowning of *Wozzeck*. The whole scene in which Ivan Yakovlevich approaches
the river, looks for the right place, shows clear signs of fear, and finally
throws the 'evidence of his crime' into the water is a comic distorted mirroring of the scene in which Wozzeck, scared and frantic, seeks the evidence of
his real crime and then throws it into the water. Shostakovich plays with the
'mask' of the nose, both as an inanimate object and as a living being, as it
will appear during the rest of the opera. The drowning scene in *Wozzeck*
involves several moments of ascending and descending motion that are expressed in ascending and descending lines in the orchestra. The rising of the
moon is accompanied by an ascending line; the sinking of the knife by a
descending line in Wozzeck's vocal line, and his own drowning by a chromatic ascent in the orchestra, alluding to his perception of the water's ascent

around him (Jarman, 1989: 56). The nose is thrown into the water in the same vein as the knife in *Wozzeck*. However, since the nose is also a 'being', it really 'drowns', accompanied by an *ascending* glissando. The similarity is enhanced by the musical introduction to both scenes: in *Wozzeck* it is the polka in the tavern; in *The Nose* it is a galop that accompanies Ivan Yakovlevich on his way to the river, meeting strangers and acquaintances who innocently greet and wave at him. Besides the syntactical position, 'before the scene of throwing the object to the water', there are also musical and motivic correspondences (Ex. 8.3).

Ex. 8.3

Motivic correspondences between the 'polka in the tavern' in *Wozzeck* and the 'galop on the quay' in *The Nose*

In the bars that follow, further similarities, such as the repetition of the theme at a higher pitch (as in bar 4 of the above excerpt from *Wozzeck*) can be seen in *The Nose*, too.

Another Gogolian device mentioned by Tïnyanov is his use of 'the enumeration, one after the other, in the same intonation, of objects which have no connection with one another' (Tïnyanov, 1921 [1979]: 105), when these objects are inconsistently taken from the domain of the animate and the inanimate. Tïnyanov gives an example from Gogol's *Nevsky Prospekt* (a story by Gogol that later served him as additional material for his film script *The Overcoat*), in which pedestrians who are walking in the avenue are described:

> Один показывает щегольской сюртук с лучшим бобром, другой – греческий прекрасный нос ... четвертая (несет) пару хорошеньких глазок и удивительную шляпку ... (Гоголь, *Невски Проспект*, в Тынянов, 1921 [1929]: 418)

> One displays a foppish frockcoat with the finest beaver, another – a lovely Grecian nose ... the fourth – a pair of pretty eyes and a marvellous hat ... (Gogol, *Nevsky Prospekt*, quoted in Tïnyanov, 1921 [1979]: 105)

The description of a human being as an inanimate object was an appealing idea in the first decades of the century, when the 'mechanization' of human nature was the focus of interest, looked upon with both admiration and horror. In this scene as well as in other scenes, further on in this opera, musical echoes of this quotation can be heard, in which incongruent musical materials are superimposed and juxtaposed. Likewise, the 'inanimate masks' are meticulously applied by Shostakovich in a mechanized, impersonal way of singing, particularly in the scenes of crowds, where the number of people involved in a scene deprives them of any personality and they become 'one collective mask': the mask of the mob. Such mechanized descriptions abound in the opera: at the end of the ninth scene, where eight lackeys engage in a surreal, disconnected canon, Kovalyev's introductory outburst, first in de-spairing shouts and then in tears, only emphasizes the horrible caricature of his fellow-men's totally indifferent, completely mechanized reaction to his personal tragedy. This transformation of a crowd into an inanimate mask repeats itself until it practically dominates the whole fourteenth scene. A particularly interesting instance is the twelfth scene, in which Shostakovich engages in a process in which living people, characters each with a personal means of expression, gradually merge with each other into a mass spectacle of mechanized musical motion.[19]

Another influence on Shostakovich's parodic writing came, probably, from the writings of Mikhail Bakhtin. There is no evidence that the men were acquainted. Bakhtin was a central figure in Petrograd's intelligentsia circles during the years 1924–29. These are the years in which Shostakovich was a student at the Petrograd Conservatory, graduated, and became ac-quainted with many members of these circles. However, the strongest point that relates him to Bakhtin is his closest friend, Ivan Sollertinsky, who had been an active participant in Bakhtin's circles since 1919, when Bakhtin was still in Nevel. Sollertinsky followed Bakhtin from Nevel' to Vitebsk, where he lived from 1920 to 1921, and then joined his groups when Bakhtin arrived in Petrograd (Clark and Holquist, 1984: 49, 97). A glance at Sollertinsky's diary from 1920 to 1921 shows that in seven months, be-tween September 1920 and April 1921, he heard at least thirteen lectures by Bakhtin, two or more of which were given in Bakhtin's flat in Vitebsk, on subjects such as 'Conscientious Moments in Culture', 'On Words', 'New Russian Poetry', 'The Poetry of Vyacheslav Ivanov', 'The Philosophy of Nietzsche', 'The Moral Ideas of Tolstoy', 'Symbolism in the New Russian Literature', 'The History of New Philosophy', 'Aesthetics', 'Medieval Lit-erature' and 'French Literature in the Eighteenth century'. Two other lectures at least (not given by Bakhtin) are marked as given in Bakhtin's flat, apparently as part of the meetings of Bakhtin's circle. These titles appear in a much longer list of lectures which he attended at the same period, all of which were given by participants of the Bakhtin circle: mainly Bakhtin himself, Medvedev and Pumpyansky (Mikheyeva-Sollertinskaya, 1988: 28ff.; Clark and Holquist, 1984: 97–98).

Sollertinsky also participated in Bakhtin circles in Petrograd from 1924 to 1929. In April 1927 he met Shostakovich and from then on, until his death in 1944, they had a very close relationship, which was manifested in daily talks, either face to face or on the phone, and, when one of them was away, by correspondence (Sollertinsky, 1979: 44–45; Mikheyeva Sollerintskaya, 1988: 74–75). Sollertinsky's ideas about music and aesthetics are often reflected in the composer's work (Mikheyeva Sollerintskaya, 1988: 70ff.): it seems that whatever interested Sollertinsky was immediately reflected in Shostakovich's musical output, which seems to have developed in an amazingly parallel path to Sollertinsky's articles (Figs 8.2a and 8.2b). Although most sources mention a mutual influence, it seems that the influence of Sollertinsky on Shostakovich played the main role in their relationship, the former being not only Shostakovich's senior by four years, but also far more erudite in general subjects such as literature, philosophy, history of art and languages. Sollertinsky certainly knew the formalists and their ideas, since he attended Viktor Zhirmunsky's lectures and took at least one course, on Dostoevsky, with Viktor Shklovsky. However, the main influence on him was that of Bakhtin, especially since Bakhtin himself arrived in Petrograd by 1924, and formed his circles again, in which Sollertinsky (again, with Maria Yudina, Pumpyansky and Medvedev) took an active part.

A further connection of Bakhtin's ideas and personality with Shostakovich might have been through Maria Yudina, the concert pianist who was a fellow-student of Shostakovich, and who is often mentioned in his memoirs. Like Sollertinsky, she too was an enthusiastic participant in Bakhtin's circle meetings in Nevel, in Vitebsk and in Leningrad. She was also one of the foremost activists in the campaign for Bakhtin's release when he was arrested in 1930 (Clark and Holquist, 1984: 142–143); Shostakovich mentions several times, in his memoirs, his disapproval of Yudina's taking unnecessary pains for other people's sake (Volkov, 1979: 40). Another figure mentioned in association with Sollertinsky and the Bakhtin circles is the conductor Nikolay Malko, who conducted the première of Shostakovich's First Symphony and introduced him to Sollertinsky (Mikheyeva-Sollertinskaya, 1988: 22). It is therefore highly unlikely that Shostakovich himself was unacquainted with Bakhtin's writings or opinions, at least as early as 1927–28. Moreover, a clear parallelism of ideas can be traced between Bakhtin's aesthetics, concepts of dialogue and heteroglossia and certain of Shostakovich's compositional techniques in the early 1930s. Even if he was unacquainted with Bakhtin through Sollertinsky, it is unlikely that Shostakovich had not read his works. During the 1930s and 1940s Bakhtin's writings, although unprinted, were known to Soviet scholars (Morson and Emerson, 1990: 458). Shostakovich, who moved in intelligentsia circles throughout his life, could have had access to Bakhtin's later writings even in those years. Moreover, after 1963 Bakhtin was rehabilitated and became a known and admired scholar in the USSR, and by the early 1970s he

Fig. 8.2a and 8.2b
Connections between Russian intellectuals and Shostakovich

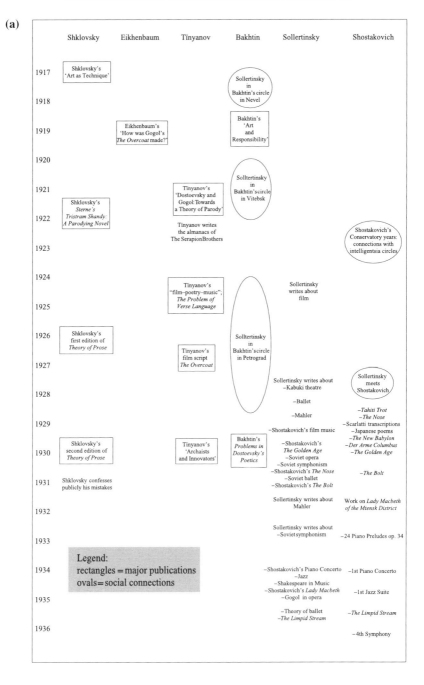

(b)

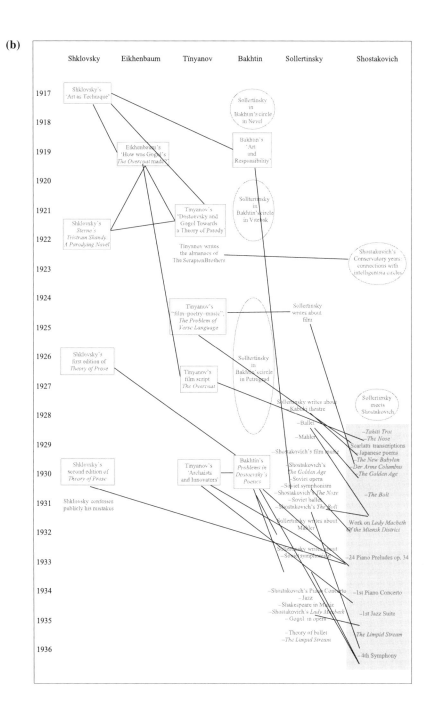

became 'something of a cult figure in the Post-Stalinist Soviet Union' (ibid.: 67). On the other hand, Bakhtin is not mentioned in Shostakovich's memoirs nor in any biographical books about him, and people who were acquainted with him are ambiguous when answering questions on this subject.[20]

Bakhtin knew the formalists' theories, and often argued with their main ideas. Although he disagreed with their main premise of 'art for art's sake', in his 1929 book about Dostoevsky he quotes Eikhenbaum's article on Gogol's *Overcoat* with much respect for his work.

One of the main concepts that Bakhtin contributed to the literary research of the twentieth century is the concept of multi-voicedness, or heteroglossia. The term appears in many forms: polyphony, heteroglossia, double-voiced discourse, multi-voicedness, plurivocality. The idea is the same: many voices speaking through one utterance. In this interpretation parody belongs to the more general phenomenon of many-voicedness. Following a similar methodological approach to Shklovsky and Tinyanov, Bakhtin wrote a great deal about double-voicedness and made many analyses that included this concept. Yet he never defined it and, even more confusing, he used it inconsistently (Morson and Emerson, 1990: 231–232).

Bakhtin wrote his first major publication twice: the first edition, of 1929, was revised, the difference consisting mainly in some clarifying sections that were added. Conceptually, however, this does not help to understand his ideas in 1929, since in the additions he uses the term 'multi-voicedness' freely, again without really explaining what he means. This use is probably due to the fact that in the 34 years that passed until the new edition of 1963 he had not only worked and re-worked the concept, but had also written other works, the echoes of which reverberate in the new edition.

As complicated as the concept of heteroglossia might be, its sources can be traced to Bakhtin's grouping of many phenomena that share a common trait: a discourse that simultaneously refers to two referential objects. His 1929 version begins thus:

> Sушествует группа художественно-речевых явлений, которая в настоящее время начинает привлекать к себе особое внимание исследователей. Это – явления стилизации, пародии, сказа и диалога.
>
> Всем этим явлениям, несмотря на существенные различия между ними, присуща одна общая черта: слово здесь имеет двоякое направление – и на предмет речи, как обычное слово, и на другое слово, на чужую речь.
>
> ... Указанные явления имеют глубокое принципиальное значение. Они требуют совершенно нового подхода к речи, не укладывающегося в пределы обычного стилистического и лексикологического рассмотрения. (Бахтин, 1929: 105–106)

There exists a group of artistic-speech phenomena that has long attracted the attention of both literary scholars and linguists ... These

> phenomena are: stylisation, parody, *skaz*, and dialogue ... All these phenomena, despite very real differences among them, share one common trait: discourse in them has a twofold direction – it is directed both toward the referential object of speech, as in ordinary discourse, and toward *another's discourse*, toward *someone else's speech*.
>
> ... These phenomena are of far-reaching and fundamental significance. They require a completely new approach to speech, one that does not fit within the limits of ordinary stylistic and linguistic purview. For the usual approach treats discourse within the limits of a *single monologic context* ... (Bakhtin, 1963 [1984]: 185)[21]

Most of the chapter on 'Discourse in Dostoevsky' is a meticulous analysis of all the varieties of this particular phenomenon of 'double-voiced speech'. Bakhtin describes and analyses stylization, parody, the technique of *skaz* (a folk-like story-telling) and what he calls 'dialogue': two or more contradictory purports, contained within one utterance (Bakhtin, 1963 [1984]: 189–199). The order of appearance of these four 'phenomena' follows their gradual independence from former utterances: stylization is completely dependent on another discourse; it stems from it and relates to it. Parody, although still dependent, argues with its source and negates it (thus becoming part of another group – that of ironic utterances). *Skaz* uses a presupposed style or a defined narrator while creating a new discourse, and dialogue is the phenomenon in which two or more new and *unfinalizable* utterances are pronounced.[22]

A link to Shostakovich that supports the assumption of Bakhtin's possible influence on him through Sollertinsky can be found in Sollertinsky's article 'Historical Types of Symphonic Dramaturgy' (1941):

> Бетховен был великим симфонистом и создал один из основных типов мирового симфонизма. В свою историческую эпоху этот тип оказался самым плодотворным и значительным. Этому типу, надо думать, принадлежит большое будущее и в советском симфонизме ... Этот тип симфонизма прежде всего можно определить как симфонизм, построенный на обЪективном и обобщенном отражении действительности и совершающихся в этой действительности процессов борьбы; как симфонизм драматический, ибо драма есть процесс, действие, где наличествует не одно, а несколько человеческих сознаний и воль, вступающих друг с другом в борьбу; следовательно – как симфонизм полиперсоналистический (прошу извинения у читателя за несколько 'гелертерский' термин, но не могу подобрать другого, более точного и более легкого), 'многоличный'. Словом, симфонизм бетховенского типа исходит не из монологического, а из диалогического принципа, из принципа множественности сознаний, множественности противоборствующих идей и воль, из утверждения – в противоположность монологическому началу – принципа 'чужого я'. (Soll r tenskey, 1941: 338)

Beethoven was a very great symphonist and created one of the basic types of symphonies. In his historical epoch this was considered the most fruitful and significant type. It is in this type, one is made to think, that a great future for the Soviet symphony lies ...

   This type of symphony can, first and foremost, be defined as a symphony constructed on objective and generalised reflections about the realities of the process of conflict; as a dramatic symphony, for the drama is a process, a movement, where the consciousness of not one but several human beings is given expression as they struggle against one another. Consequently, it can be seen as a 'polypersonality' symphony (excuse the rather strange terminology), as a 'many-faceted' symphony. In short, the symphony of the Beethovenian type does not stem from a principle of monologue but from the principle of dialogue, from the principle of the multiplicity of consciousness, the multiplicity of ideas and wills struggling with one another, from the assertion of the principle of the 'other I'. (Sollertinsky, 1941 [in Roseberry, 1989]: 525–526)

Here, apparently, Sollertinsky uses Bakhtinian terminology. In 1941, the year in which this article was written, Bakhtin managed, finally, to defend his doctoral thesis on Rabelais, after it had been postponed and rejected several times.[23] It is important to remember the historical and cultural context of this book, which praises the joyful expression of the corporeal: since 1932 Stalinist puritanism had been imposed in the Soviet Union, and works that had sexual elements were condemned as 'naturalist' and even 'zoologist'.[24] Mentioning Bakhtin's name, in those years, was simply dangerous. Sollertinsky, however, does refer to Bakhtin's 'strange terminology', ironically hinting at the terminology of the exiled scholar. His apology for the '*gelerterskiy termin*', an awkward Russified German word which he himself puts in inverted commas, and which mockingly means 'a scholarly term', strengthens even more the hint towards Bakhtin and their mutual background in German philosophy. The concept of 'pluripersonality' is a clear derivative of Bakhtin's 'plurivocality'. The inserted 'several human beings in struggle' is, too, taken from the formalist vocabulary.

Even more interesting is the fact that Shostakovich, in his article about Sollertinsky to commemorate the second year from his death, chooses to use, from all possible terms and ideas, the very same concept of 'polypersonality':

Вообще, в отношении установления связей молодой советской музыкальной культуры с музыкальным наследием прошлого, Соллертинский сделал чрезвычайно много. При этом им были установлены связи в пределах самого наследия. Так, например, очень тонко его наблюдение о том, что у Мусоргского господствует шекспировско-бетховенский принцип изощренной психологической характеристики разных типов (полиперсонализм) ... (Шостакович, 1946: 94)

Sollertinsky did a tremendous amount of work in connection with establishing connections between the young Soviet musical culture and the musical heritage of the past. He also established connections with the works of immediate predecessors. Thus, he makes the accurate observation that Mussorgsky has a good command of the Shakespearian–

Beethovenian principles of refined psychological characteristics of different types ('polypersonalism') ... (Shostakovich, 1946 [in Roseberry, 1989]: 552)

Indeed, Bakhtin did explain his ideas about the unfinalizability of the artistic work, which stems from its dialogic multi-voicedness, with examples from Shakespeare (Morson and Emerson, 1990: 287). The reason why Sollertinsky (and after him Shostakovich) stressed the relevance of these ideas for Soviet music in particular can be found in Bakhtin's ideas about 'the word', which we could easily exchange for the concept of 'the cultural unit'. The quotation is, indeed, very long, but it is necessary to understand the development of Bakhtin's ideas, the connections between unfinalizability, plurivocality and parody, and their relevance to Sollertinsky and, subsequently, to Shostakovich:

Проблема ориентации речи на чужое слово имеет первостепенное социологическое значение. Слово по природе социально. Слово не вещь, а вечно подвижная, вечно изменчивая среда социального общения. Оно никогда не довлеет одному сознанию, одному голосу. Жизнь слова – в переходе из уст в уста, из одного контекста в другой контекст, от одного социального коллектива к другому, от одного поколения к другому поколению. При этом слово не забывает своего пути и не может до конца освободиться от власти тех конкретных контекстов, в которые оно входило. Каждый член говорящего коллектива преднаходит слово вовсе не как нейтральное слово языка, свободное от интенций, не населенное чужими голосами. Нет, слово он получает с чужого голоса и наполненное чужим голосом.
   ... Каждой социальной группе в каждую эпоху свойственно свое ощущение слова и свой диапазон словесных возможностей. Далеко не при всякой социальной ситуации последняя смысловая инстанция творящего может непосредственно выразить себя в прямом, непреломленном, безусловном авторском слове. Когда нет своего собственного 'последнего' слова, всякая творческая интенция, всякая мысль, чувство, переживание должны преломляться сквозь среду чужого слова, чужого стиля, чужой манеры, с которыми нельзя непосредственно слиться без оговорки, без дистанции, без преломления. Если есть в распоряжении данной социальной группы сколько-нибудь авторитетный и отстоявшийся мидыум преломления, то будет господствовать условное слово в той или иной его разновидности, с тою или иною степенью условности. Если ж такого medium'а нет, то будет господствовать разнонаправленное двуголосое слово, т.е. пародийное слово во всех его разновидностях, или особый тип полууусловного, полуиронического слова (слово позднего классицизма). (Бахтин, 1929: 131–132)

The question of the orientation of discourse toward someone else's words is paramount in the social sciences. The word is by nature a social entity. For the word is not a material thing but rather the eternally mobile, eternally fickle medium of dialogic interaction. It never gravitates toward a single consciousness or a single voice. The life of the word is contained in its transfer from one mouth to another, from one context to another context, from one social collective to another, from one generation to another generation. In this process the word does not forget its own path and cannot completely free itself from the power of these concrete contexts into which it has entered. When a member of a speaking collective comes upon a word, it is not as a neutral word of language, not as a word free from the aspirations and evaluations of other, uninhabited by other's voices. No, he receives the word from another's voice and filled with that other voice … Every social trend in every epoch has its own special sense of discourse and its own range of discursive possibilities. By no means all historical situations permit the ultimate semantic authority of the creator to be expressed without mediation in direct, unrefracted, unconditional authorial discourse. When there is no access to one's own personal 'ultimate' word, then every thought, feeling, experience, must be refracted through the medium of someone else's discourse, someone else's style, someone else's manner, with which it cannot immediately be merged without reservation, without distance, without refraction. If there is at the disposal of a given epoch some authoritative and stabilized medium of refraction, then conventionalized discourse in one or another of its varieties will dominate, with a greater or lesser degree of conventionality. If there is no such medium, then vari-directional double-voiced discourse will dominate, that is, parodistic discourse in all its varieties, or a special type of semiconventionalized, semi-ironic discourse … (Bakhtin, 1963 [1984]: 202)[25]

A plurivocal parody: Shostakovich's Piano Prelude op. 34 No. 2

In Shostakovich's works of the early 1930s appear similar techniques, applied to music for the first time; the music seems to be constructed in several layers, each one related to some other stylistic trait. Such a structure leads to a double, and sometimes even to triple, functioning of certain musical instances. The Second Prelude of his 24 Preludes op. 34, written in 1932–33, is such a case. On the face of it, the piece is a satirical parody of the very popular 'Spanish' style. However, a closer inspection shows neither exaggeration nor clear distortion of any of the so-called 'Spanish' traits – the rhythmic arpeggio figure in the left hand or the use of the Phrygian mode, traditionally associated in Western culture with Spanish music. On the contrary; their use seems to be subtle and restrained in a way that excludes any satirical interpretation. Moreover, other stylistic traits are apparent, too, but none of them seems either to dominate the others or to be satirically exaggerated. In fact, this prelude is a musical 'plurivocal discourse'.

The structure of the work is almost ridiculously symmetrical: it consists of three main sections – an opening, a middle, and a closing section, which is followed by a final cadence. Each of the sections has 12 bars, subdivided as follows:

Fig. 8.3

Structure of Shostakovich's Piano Prelude op. 34 No. 2

Opening section 12 bars		Middle section 12 bars		Closing section 12 bars		Final cadence
4 bars of introduction	8 bars of the main theme	6 bars of the theme's development	6 bars of free development	3 bars of the main cadence	9 bars of coda	2 bars

The modal and harmonic structure of the work constitutes four superimposed layers, each one obeying different restrictions. This juxtaposition is the source of the impression, characteristic of Shostakovich's works, of many 'tonal deviations' with no seeming consistency, but that none the less never break to atonality. These modal layers are distributed in different structural levels of the work, although not necessarily restricting any specific mode to any one level. Consequently, it often happens that one note, or one chord, functions simultaneously in more than one tonal layer, thus acquiring the quality of a Bakhtinian heteroglossic expression.

The first layer, which I call the *tonal*, is expressed in the structural bass line, in leading-note functions, and in other, secondary tonal functions, mainly manifested in harmonic prolongations. The second layer is focused on *relations of thirds*, turning up either as various manifestations of the mediant or in chord series based on leaps of thirds. Eventually, the relation of thirds is also associated with a whole-tone scale. The third layer highlights *relations of seconds*, expressed either by emphasizing various manifestations of the supertonic or by chord series based on consecutive notes. The last layer is the closest to the musical surface, and includes various manifestations of the Phrygian mode, either by in stylistic gestures, mainly in the melody, or by the emphasis of a lowered 'Phrygian' or 'Neapolitan' chord that may function both as a supertonic and/or as pure harmonic colouring.

Each one of the four layers parodies a musical style that may be associated with a musical period: the tonal layer is built, very much as a classical work, over the structural harmonic scheme of I–II–I$^6_4$–V–I; the harmonic relations of thirds allude to early nineteenth-century harmony in the style of Schubert and Chopin (whose preludes were a source of inspiration for the present set of preludes); the layer of the relations of seconds includes parallel progressions of consecutive chords, which recall some of Mussorgsky's characteristic harmonic progressions, and whole-tone scales that recall Debussy's style, thus alluding to the late Romantic 'Russian' and/or the French impressionistic style; the last layer seems to parody Rimsky-Korsakov's 'Spanish' style, which is manifested not only in the use of the Phrygian mode, but also in more particular melodic gestures that are evoked in the prelude.

In order to see how Shostakovich uses parody to create a 'Bakhtinian plurivocality' in music, each one of the layers is analysed here separately, after which the mutual interrelationship of the four layers is examined.

Examples 8.4 and 8.5 are intended to clarify what follows. In Ex. 8.4 the prelude is reproduced four times, each of which highlights one layer by a colour: red is used to show the parts that participate in the tonal layer, blue shows the relations of thirds, yellow the relations of seconds, and green points to the various uses of the Phrygian mode. In Ex. 8.5 the colour indications of the four layers are superimposed, pointing at the 'musically plurivocal' points at which the same element simultaneously takes part in more than one musical 'voice'.

The tonal level

This level relates to A minor as its tonic. It is manifested mainly in the bass line, and at particular structural points of the work. Thus it can easily be described in a scheme which will include the basic tonal motions, but also point to weaker, but still within the tonal functioning, more surface motions (Ex. 8.6).[26]

Ex. 8.6
Basic tonal relations in Shostakovich's Piano Prelude, op. 34 No. 2

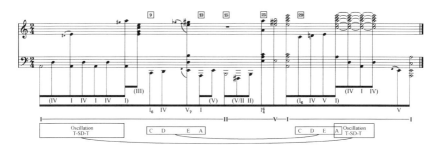

The straight line near the bottom of the scheme, connecting I–II–V–I, indicates the basic harmonic progression. The slurs below this line point to symmetrical connections, showing the importance of lesser harmonic progressions in relation to the main structural scheme.

Additional tonal relations, similar to those found in the above scheme, also appear (in various gradations of clarity) closer to the surface of the composition. For example, bars 9–10 give the impression of a progression I–V in C minor (in spite of the B♭ in bar 10); bars 16–17 render a I₇–VII₇–I cadence in C major, and in bars 23–24 there is a short digression, by a I–V₂–I harmonic gesture, to E♭ major.

Tonal functional ambiguities   Besides these functional straightforward moments, there are also some functional harmonic ambiguities. Unlike the syntagmatic ambiguity of a modulatory axis chord, which can be unambiguously resolved in terms of 'before' and 'after' the musical event, these tonally ambiguous chord-functions are paradigmatic, in the sense that their ambiguity is built upon their appearance and functioning in more than one simultaneous event.[27]

Generally speaking, there are two kinds of functional ambiguity. One often occurs in eighteenth- and nineteenth-century tonal music, when a chord can be interpreted in two alternative functions. The oscillatory bass A–D in bars 1–7 and 30–33 can quite easily be interpreted as a tonic–subdominant prolongation. However, both the F, which is the necessary third of the subdominant, and A, its fifth, are missing. Instead, B and D$^\sharp$ appear. The B could be interpreted as the root of a B–D–F diminished chord, i.e. as the degree of II$_6$, which retains the subdominant character of the chord and allows the interpretation of the D$^\sharp$ as a heightened fourth leading to the dominant. On the other hand, the very same chord has certain qualities which, although not strong, are still powerful enough to indicate a convincing dominant meaning. The D and B could be part of a V$_2$ chord, and the D$^\sharp$ would thus be perceived as a lower auxiliary between the two structural 'tenor' Es (bars 1 and 3). A 'compressed' version of the same relation occurs in the final cadence, where it is unclear whether the E$^\flat$m$_{13}$ is a raised IV or a lowered V, and therefore, whether the dominant functions as early as the second beat of bar 37 or only at its very end. A simpler case occurs in bar 23, where the third beat is a superimposition of both subdominant and dominant of E$^\flat$ major, in the shortest tonal digressions of the piece.[28] The other, more subtle type of tonal ambiguity occurs in bars 13–25. Here two simultaneous processes take place, functioning not only on two different layers, but also related to the tonal layer, in a way that makes their hierarchical prioritization impossible: one is built upon the progression I–III–I, and the other on I–II–I (Fig. 8.4).

Fig. 8.4
Ambiguous structure of tonal functions in Shostakovich's Piano Prelude op. 34
No. 2

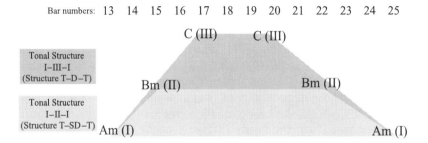

Bar numbers: 13   14   15   16   17   18   19   20   21   22   23   24   25

C (III)   C (III)

Tonal Structure
I–III–I
(Structure T–D–T)   Bm (II)   Bm (II)

Tonal Structure
I–II–I
(Structure T–SD–T) Am (I)   Am (I)

Relations of thirds

The relations of thirds in this prelude have two facets. The first is related to the nineteenth-century use of tonal mediants, which function within the traditional context either as an agent of the tonic function, within a harmonic prolongation, or as an agent of the dominant function, in a weak cadence (Harrison, 1994: 61–64). In a minor mode, without special alterations, the former is a major chord (i.e. it relates to the natural minor) and the latter an augmented triad (only in harmonic minor) which here, however, never appears. Shostakovich, who writes within the Russian tradition of the late nineteenth and early twentieth centuries, is following the footsteps of Mussorgsky, Rimsky-Korsakov and Stravinsky, who worked within a cultural framework that mixed traditional Russian and Eastern sonorities with Western *Harmonielehre*. This tradition created a variety of theoretical systems that have as their common denominator the potential alteration not only of any degree, but also of any note within a triad built on any degree (Carpenter, 1995). The peculiarity of this system (which is actually a 'system of systems'), when used in Russian music, is that in spite of the alteration the seven degrees of the tonal system nevertheless fulfil the same basic tonal functions of tonic, dominant and subdominant, and keep the traditional agent-functions of the secondary degrees (Harrison, 1994: 60). Moreover, since the alterations were often used to strengthen the effect of leading notes, they do not blur the feeling of tonal gravitation, but actually enhance it. These constant alternations between tonality and modality, and between free alteration and strong commitment to tonal functional tradition, are characteristic of Russian music in general. However, their strongest manifestations are particularly apparent in the music of Rimsky-Korsakov and Shostakovich.

The use of relations of thirds in this prelude is characteristic of this approach. To one of the traditional mediant chords, C major, Shostakovich adds an altered version, with a lowered third, resulting in a chord of C minor; the other traditional mediant, an augmented chord of C, never appears; in its stead appears the altered-root version in the shape of C♯ minor. The result is three different mediant chords, two of which function as agents of the tonic, and the third, C♯ minor, as an agent of the dominant. As an agent of the tonic, C major appears in several formal structural points (bars 8, 17 and 19–20), while C minor appears only once, as a prolongation of the C major (bar 9); C♯ minor sounds as a dominant in bars 12 and 28 (in the right hand).

However, these three alternatives of the mediant also relate to each other as colouristic shades, as in bars 17–20, where the swift passage in the right hand, in bar 18, gives to the C major environment a sharpened, minorized shade. Another colouristic instance of mediants occurs in bar 28, where a C♯ minor arpeggio is superimposed on a C major melodic descent.

Stylistically, this may be connected to the mediant relations prevalent in early Romantic music, particularly Chopin's, whose set of piano preludes

Picasso (1927). Discussed on p.268. Copyright © Succession Picasso /DACS 2000.

Example 8-4. Shostakovich, Piano Prelude op. 34 No. 2

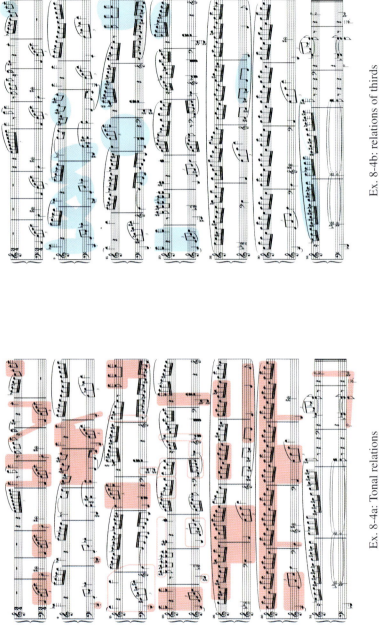

Ex. 8-4a: Tonal relations

Ex. 8-4b: relations of thirds

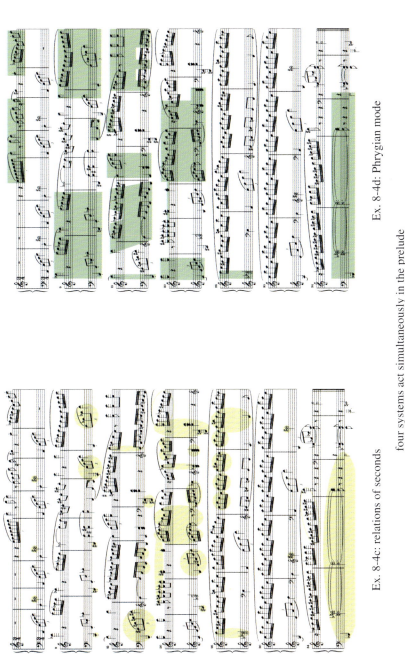

Ex. 8-4c: relations of seconds

Ex. 8-4d: Phrygian mode

four systems act simultaneously in the prelude

Example 8-5: "Structural plurivocality" in Shostakovich's Piano Prelude op. 34 No. 2.

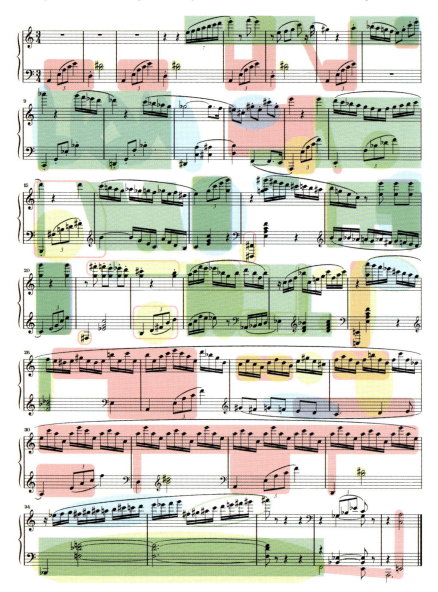

Four tonal and modal layers are superimposed, creating a complex musical
correlation of ironical ambiguity.

was the inspiration for Shostakovich's ordering of keys in op. 34. The relative importance of the mediant may also be rooted in Russian music, where modulations to the III degree of a minor mode are particularly characteristic. Finally, its sources can be traced to the classical cliché modulation of a minor theme to its relative major. In all these cases the result is a parody.

The other facet of relations of thirds that Shostakovich uses in this prelude are series of consecutive thirds. This technique is used here in two different ways. The first, in bars 9–10, consists of a series of triads that are built on the consecutive series A♭–Cm–E♭–Gm–B♭–Ddim–Fm. Although not appearing as harmonic triads, nor as clear arpeggios, their presence is strongly felt as a result of the motivic note-combinations between the two hands. Indeed, the whole 'circle of thirds' can be read from bar 9 to bar 11, where the D♯ functions, in regard to the motifs in the right hand, as E♭. The second time is at the end, bars 34–35, where a series of ascending melodic motifs consist, each one, of a major third, while one starts a minor third above its former, completes the 'circle' on the first beat of bar 35, and continues the ascending line in a whole-tone scale (Ex. 8.7).

Ex. 8.7
Tertial relations in Shostakovich's Piano Prelude op. 34 No. 2

This melodic ascent of thirds, each of which, by itself, consists of two major seconds, could also be perceived as 'many starts of a whole-tone scale, apprehended by triadic connection', from which the whole-tone scale, starting on F# on the second beat of bar 35, is felt almost like a physical outburst .

Relations of seconds
Relations of seconds, when separated from tonal functions, can be mainly expressed in parallel motions, either as scalar progressions of different types, both traditional and newly defined ones, or in progressions of parallel consecutive chords. In both cases the relations of seconds can develop towards two extremes. One is the gradual enlargement of the seconds to the extreme of a whole-tone scale, thus relating it to impressionistic style; the second, conversely, gradually diminishes the seconds to the extreme of the chromatic scale.

Shostakovich manipulates both ways, thus simultaneously alluding to more than one style. By this he 'defamiliarizes' them and highlights their functioning as an artistic device that has a pure stylistic signification rather than a specific content. There are some instances that hint to a whole-tone scale (bar 25) and to chromaticism (bars 16, 19 and 21). For example, in the series of chords in the left hand, Am–B♭m–Bm–C7+–Bdim7 (Dm?) in bars 13–16, Am functions also as tonic; B♭m also as a Neapolitan;[29] B minor as a II (melodic) degree; C as agent of the tonic that is then tonally strengthened by Bdim7 which is its VII_7, resulting in a cadence-like motion in bar 17.[30] Another series of consecutive chords starts on the last beat of bar 27 and continues until the first beat of bar 29, in the right hand: Gm–Am–Bdim–C♯m–Dm. Again, each chord, except for the Gm, can be also interpreted in tonal harmonic terms, although they don't necessarily function in this way (for example, unlike in bar 12, the C♯m does not really function here as a dominant since it leads to Dm, which is the subdominant).

The most interesting use of consecutive chords happens in bars 23–24, where several layers are superimposed. In these two bars Shostakovich manages to compress two series of consecutive chords. The first series starts on the last beat of bar 22, and consists of the chords of G–F–E♭. On the last beat of bar 23 another series starts: A♭–B♭–C–D(–F–Am). In this second series, however, a compression occurs and the consecutive chords overlap, creating a *stretto*-like feeling that is even enhanced by the last three chords that leap in consecutive *thirds* to the A minor chord, on the main structural cadential point of I_4^6, in bar 25. These two series, the one starting on G and the other on A♭, in a I–IV–V–I subsidiary cadence on E♭, from the second beat of bar 23 to the first beat of bar 24, have overlapping subdominant and dominant that cause in a similar vein to bar 2, a mixed impression of IV and V_2. This blurring of the harmonic function is also expressed in two climactic points by a whole-tone scale – the maximal expression of a non-functional motion of seconds: on the aforementioned I_4^6 in bar 25, and at the end, as the last part of the scalar process in bars 34–36.

As can be seen from this analysis, Shostakovich's work with consecutive chords is often also related to the chords' simultaneous function in the different layers rather than to any particular structure of the series of seconds themselves. In other words, Shostakovich puts into practice the whole 'plurivocal' potential that lies within the relations of seconds.

Relations of seconds that belong to the tonal context are thus brought into play, mainly in stepwise progressions of harmonic degrees, like I–II–I, I–VII–VI–V etc. This type of relations is stylistically associated with the music of Mussorgsky and Debussy (whose style is also linked with the whole-tone scale). Within this frame of reference, Shostakovich's use of the II degree is particularly evident, creating a new kind of 'stylistic plurivocality', or, to use the Bakhtinian term, of stylization.

Like the mediant, the II degree appears in two alterations, neither of which is the 'tonal' II degree, which should be a diminished triad on B. In its stead, considerable importance is given to the chord of B minor (the II degree with an altered fifth), and to B♭ minor, which functions as an altered 'Neapolitan' lowered II degree. This 'Neapolitan' flavour suits the fourth layer, which is built around the Phrygian mode.[31] This lowered 'Neapolitan' appears several times: in bar 14, 26 and, most important, in a relatively long anticipation of the final cadence (bars 34–36).

Although two 'non-altered' II degree chords do appear in the prelude, they are not fulfilling their traditional subdominant function, but rather participate as subsidiary degrees in secondary cadences. For example, the diminished triad on B acts as VII/III (bar 16), and as one in a series of consecutive parallel chords (bar 28). The only instance when it appears to have a sub-dominant function is a fleeting moment, where it functions rather as a passing note (bar 29). The B♭ major chord, that would function as a more traditional Neapolitan chord, appears like the diminished chord on B, in a secondary cadential gesture (bars 23–24) and as a part of a chord sequence (bar 10). This 'inverted use of a cliché' points to the further function of parody in Shostakovich's music: the function of a catalyst for artistic innovation.[32]

The Phrygian mode
Several instances in the prelude follow stylistic traits of the 'Spanish' style that was popular at the end of the nineteenth and beginning of the twentieth century.[33] His main focus is on Rimsky-Korsakov's *Capriccio espagnol*, and through it he incorporates some other characteristic traits of the composer, mainly from *The Golden Cockerel*. Shostakovich parodies in the Russian formalistic sense: he makes a stylization of the parodied object, 'playing' with and manipulating its various characteristic elements, which are manifested in the harmony, modality, rhythm and the melodic gestures of the prelude (Ex. 8.8).

Shostakovich parodies the harmonic ambiguity that Rimsky-Korsakov plays with in the ostinato accompaniment of his *Capriccio*. The modal V_7 (the second half of each beat) used by Rimsky-Korsakov, which purports, to a tonally tuned perception, a superimposition of the dominant and subdominant functions, is parodied by the harmonic ambiguity in the accompaniment of the second beat in Shostakovich's prelude. Here Shostakovich almost literally applies two of the techniques mentioned by Tinyanov as parodying techniques: exaggeration and inversion (Tinyanov, 1921 [1979]: 106). The harmonic ambiguity is exaggerated, by actually changing the bass line into a clear I–IV motion, and the *Capriccio*'s V_{-5}^{7} diminished chord is 'inverted' into an apparent presence of an augmented V_{7+}.

The *Capriccio* is written in A Phrygian, which explains the B♭ in the key signature while the 'tonic' is on A. Consistent with his parodying musical hyperbolism, Shostakovich uses in his prelude five forms of the Phrygian mode, unsystematically, as if by chance, distributing them throughout the piece:

Ex. 8.8
Rimsky-Korsakov's harmony, modality, rhythm and melodic gestures parodied in
Shostakovich's Piano Prelude, op. 34 No. 2

he starts with the Phrygian on E (bars 4–6, 16–17, 19–20), continues with a
Phrygian on A (bars 7–8, 13–15), with patches in the Phrygian on G (bars 9–
10), on C♯ (bar 18) and on D (bar 23).[34] These transpositions are, in some
respects, incongruent: they do not necessarily relate to other musical elements
in the same context. The Phrygian mode is mainly used in the melodic level;
however, on several occasions chordal occurrences and/or progressions are
influenced by it. For example, in bars 13–17 there is a 'modulation' from A
minor to C major (in the tonal layer), which is an ascent of a minor third. On
the melodic level, however, Shostakovich performs a 'melodic modulation'
from Phrygian on A to Phrygian on E, an ascent of a fifth (Ex. 8.9).

Ex. 8.9
A modal 'modulation' in the melody, a tonal one in the harmony

Within the same harmonic context, the use of the Neapolitan lowered II
degree can be related to this modal frame, too, although it is also connected
to the various tonal uses of the supertonic.

The accompaniment rhythmic arpeggiato figure (e.g. bar 1) traditionally
consists of notes that all belong to one chord. Shostakovich, however, 'plays'

with the possibilities of an arpeggio; he often gives an unexpected chord progression (for example, in bar 9, where he gives a Cm$_7$ instead of C chord) or changes an existing relation in the middle of the arpeggio (as he does, for example, in bar 14, where the bass moves from I to V, while the arpeggio moves from I to lowered II).

Inter-function between the layers

As can be seen in Ex. 8.5, most musical instances in the prelude function simultaneously in more than one layer. All the chords that relate to the mediant, for example, also function in one of the Phrygian modes – C major in the Phrygian on E (bars 8, 17 and 19–20); C minor – in the Phrygian on G (bars 9–10), and C$^\sharp$ minor – in the Phrygian on C$^\sharp$ (bars 12, 18 and 28). C major also functions as the tonal mediant, that is, the major parallel of the tonic. Besides, the C major chord in bar 16 and the C$^\sharp$ minor in bar 28 also function as one chord within a series of parallel chords moving in seconds. Another instance of clear double functioning are the supertonic chords, which function in the tonal level, where they appear as B minor (bars 15 and 22), or as B$^\flat$ minor (bars 14, 26 and 34–36). B$^\flat$ minor, though, also functions in the Phrygian level, being the Phrygian supertonic of A. Other instances are more sporadic and more subtle, like the D$^\sharp$ in bar 11, which functions as a leading note to the dominant in the next bar (where both D$^\sharp$ and F lead to E), in the tonal layer, but also, if interpreted as E$^\flat$, participates in the series chords built on consecutive thirds in bars 9–11.

There is a further point: if we consider Rimsky-Korsakov's style as an added, fifth stylistic layer, other instances could be added, such as the parallel sixths in bars 10–11, which echo the bassoon parallel sixths in *The Golden Cockerel*; or the peculiar scalar ascent within thirds, in bars 34–36 of Shostakovich's prelude. A similar technique creates a series of major thirds, alluding to a whole-tone scale (with which Shostakovich ends this ascending line) in *The Golden Cockerel*. These allusions, however, seem to be more stylistic additions than instances which influence the structural aspects of the musical parody here (Exs 8.10a and 8.10b).

Exs 8.10a and 8.10b
Interfunctioning of the Phrygian, the tonal and the stylistic layers

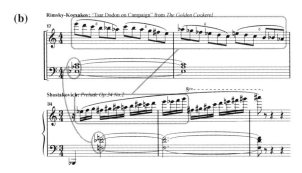

CHAPTER NINE

Techniques of parody

All the techniques of parody can be traced back to parody's two basic semantic components of imitation and incongruity (Karrer, 1977: 88).

Parody can refer to a variety of subjects and topics, ranging from a specific work of art to general principles such as stylistic characteristics of a person, a period or a culture (Bakhtin, 1963 [1984]: 194). Therefore, the imitative operations that reflect the parodied object – replication, quotation, allusion and stylization – differ from each other mainly in the elements that are chosen to be imitated: a whole specific object, a part of an object, a characteristic aspect, a typical component or general stylistic principles. However, while the difference between the various techniques of imitation is more a matter of size and specificity than a question of essence, the more consequential issue is the modification exercised upon the parodied object, i.e. the kind and amount of incongruities inserted into its imitation (Rose, 1979: 22). This greater significance assigned here to the mechanisms of incongruity is also due to the fact that its presence within or between the layers reveals the operation of more than one meaning in the work, and thus acts as the sole indicator of parody.

Imitation and incongruity seem to contradict each other. Nevertheless, they are not contraries, and consequently they cannot be considered as two opposing poles of one semantic axis. Imitational forms can be located on the semantic axis of similarity/dissimilarity; incongruity, on the other hand, purports not just a 'dissimilarity' but also requires a derisive relation with its context (Bakhtin, 1963 [1984]: 193–195; Rose, 1979: 13–14; Houdebine, 1984; Dane, 1988: 135). Such criticism can range between 'hostility' and 'battle' (Tinyanov, 1921 [1979]: 101; Bakhtin, 1963 [1984]: 193–194) to self-reflection without any negative undertones (Rose, 1979: 45–53; Hutcheon, 1985: 103ff.). The semantic axis of incongruity extends, thus, along the opposition of agreement/disagreement (Fig. 9.1).

The importance of a clear differentiation between similarity and agreement is cardinal: stylization, for example, uses dissimilar elements but does not rely on incongruity (Bakhtin, 1963 [1984]: 193). Thus, when speaking about the techniques of parody, the two axes must be regarded separately. The examination of the axis of imitation will deal with the different degrees of particularity and distance between the parody and the parodied object: replication, quotation, allusion and stylization. The description of the incongruity axis will specify techniques of variation, distortion and parodic collage.

Fig. 9.1
Semantic axes of imitation and incongruity

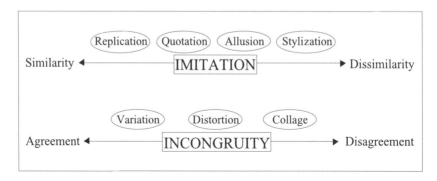

   This scheme, however, is not unequivocal: none of the specified techniques
can function without a certain measure of both imitation and incongruity. For
example, 'stylization' needs a considerable amount of incongruity; 'variation', on the other hand, must be based on some kind of imitation, although it
is regarded here as a technique of incongruity. Thus variation, distortion and
collage cannot create incongruities without some imitation, while stylization,
allusion and quotation need some incongruity in order to function. Even in
exact replication there is never a complete identity, since when something is
said twice, the fact that it has already been said signifies not only its identity
but also its separation from the original, and even more so if it is repeated by
someone else (Bakhtin, 1963 [1984]: 194–195; Riffaterre, 1984). The above
techniques and their application to music described here should be understood, therefore, within these restrictions.

Imitation

Imitation lies at the etymological basis of parody; its use in classical rhetorics
follows this line (Markiewicz, 1967: 1265; Rose, 1993: 7).[1] However, references to parodic imitation are always restrained: the eighteenth century's
description of parody as parasitic refers, eventually, to its basically imitative
nature, but concurrently regards it as 'polemic and critical' (Dane, 1988:
135). In a similar vein, definitions of parody include 'imitation with a difference' and 'imitation with a distance' (Hutcheon, 1985: 6).
   Parodic imitation was associated with genres and forms like travesty, pastiche, burlesque and caricature and with the techniques of quotation, allusion
and stylization (Bakhtin, 1963 [1984]; Karrer, 1977; Hutcheon, 1985). In
spite of the amount of material written on it and its theoretical cardinality, the
term 'imitation' itself is never clearly specified. Its problematics seem to be

due to the various degrees and areas of similarity and particularity (Karrer, 1977: 68). Consequently, although all writings about parody acknowledge the primary importance of imitation, the meaning of imitation varies considerably and its use is inconsistent even within the work of one writer.[2] In fact, in a considerable number of analyses the term is used to clarify the ways in which parody *differs* from imitation, up to the point of regarding imitation as the reason for parody's self-destructive nature (Deguy, 1984: 7). These various outlooks on imitation affect, of course, the appreciation of its function within parody, from defining parody as an 'imitation of a literary work' (Shlonsky, 1966: 797) to seeing imitation as just one among many other mechanisms of parody (Karrer, 1977: 60). Some critics use parallel terms, which range from the rather vague 'reflection or reflexion' (Rose, 1979), through 'commented quotation' (Karrer, 1977: 98) and 'resemblance' (Tinyanov, 1921 [1979]: 102; Bakhtin [1929, 1963 (1984): 185]), up to the apparently synonymous 'repetition' (Hutcheon, 1985: 37 and 101). This last term, however, is controversial, since it appears in various writings as a technique for creating incongruity no less than as an imitational device. Hutcheon's equation is wrong because it ignores the difference between 'repetition' and 'replication'. While 'replication' relates to the degree of similarity of an imitation to its original, 'repetition' is a *quantitative* term that, by changing the number of times a phenomenon appears, actually introduces incongruity. It is characteristic of the paradoxical nature of parody that the concept of repetition, allegedly most related to imitation, is actually regarded as a device of incongruity, created by a quantitatively exaggerated imitation. Consequently, when discussing the axis of imitation, I prefer to use the term 'replication', while the term 'repetition' will appear later, as one of the distortion techniques, on the axis of incongruity.

Replication

Apparently, an exact reproduction of the parodied object is the closest imitation possible. However, a replica can never trespass the boundaries of its object and become completely identical with it. Its very existence negates its being the original, so that replication is an ironical object by definition. Thus every replication bears an alienating purport that may serve either of two purposes: the first is to create an aesthetic distance, as happens, for example, in musical replication signalled by repetition marks, such as at the end of a theme in a theme-and-variations form, or at the end of an exposition in a sonata form. This kind of replication serves to define the musical object as an aesthetic entity. The second purpose is to create an ironic distance, negating the purport of the repeated entity. Bakhtin bases his explanation of this device, which he calls 'the use of someone else's words', on Leo Spitzer's commentary:

> Mit der Übernahme eines Stückes der Partnerrede vollzieht sich schon
> an und für sich durch den Wechsel der sprechenden Individuen eine
> Transposition der Tonart: *die Worte 'des anderen' klingen in unserem*
> *Mund immer fremd, ja sehr leicht höhnisch, karikiert, fratzenhaft ...*
> (Leo Spitzer, *Italienische Umgangssprache*, Leipzig, 1922: 175–176,
> quoted in Bakhtin [1929: 120]. Bakhtin's italics)

> When we reproduce in our own speech a portion of our partner's utter-
> ance, then by virtue of the very change in speakers a change in tone
> inevitably occurs: *the words of 'the other person' always sound on our*
> *lips something alien to us, and often have an intonation of ridicule,*
> *exaggeration, or mockery.* (Bakhtin, 1963 [1984]: 194)[3]

Thus every imitation bears a trace of ironic negation. Bakhtin distinguishes
between 'the use of someone else's words' and citations that occur, for
example, in scholarly articles, where the source of the quotation is explicitly
presented (ibid.: 188). While these are 'monologic', and confronted with
other 'monologic' utterances of the article's writer, the use of a quotation
without an explicit citation bears a double purport, or in Bakhtin's words, an
'ironic, or any other double-voiced, use of someone else's words':

> Пародийному слову аналогично ироническое и всякое
> двусмысленно употребленное чужое слово, ибо и в этих
> случаях чужим словом пользуются для передачи враждебных
> ему интенций. В жизненно-практической речи такое пользование
> чужим словом чрезвычайно распространено, особенно в диалоге,
> где собеседник очень часто буквально повторяет утверждение
> другого собеседника, влагая в него новую интенцию и
> акцентируя его по-своему: с выражением сомнения, возмущения,
> иронии, насмешки, издевательства и т.п. ...
>   Чужие слова, введенные в нашу речь, неизбежно принимают
> в себя новую, нашу, интенцию, т.е. становятся двуголосыми.
> (Бахтин, 1929: 119–120)

> Ironic, or any other ambiguous use of someone else's words, is analo-
> gous to parodistic discourse, because in these cases too the other's word
> is used for conveying purports that are hostile to its intentions.[4] In the
> ordinary speech of our everyday life such a use of another's words is
> extremely widespread, especially in dialogue, where one speaker very
> often literally repeats the statement of the other speaker, investing it
> with new value and accenting it in his own way – with expressions of
> doubt, indignation, irony, mockery, ridicule, and the like ...
>   Someone else's words introduced into our own speech inevitably
> assume a new (our own) interpretation and become subject to our evalu-
> ation of them; that is, they become double-voiced. (Bakhtin, 1963 [1984]:
> 194–195)

In music such instances happen quite often, too. One of the most obvious
cases is Haydn's divertimento for piano four hands *Il maestro e lo scolare*, in
which the 'pupil' replicates the 'teacher's' playing in a series of variations on
a theme. The result of these insistent replications is utterly comic, particularly

Ex. 9.1
Haydn's *Il maestro e lo scolare*

since they are repeated, in the same vein, through the whole work (Ex. 9.1).[5]

Another instance of ironical replication is the letter-writing duet in the second act of *Le Nozze di Figaro*. The countess dictates to Susanna a letter that is allegedly addressed by her to the count. Susanna repeats after her, creating a double ambiguity: although both women join in the deception of the count, Susanna has her own further reservations. In the duet she echoes but does not replicate the countess, except in one instance when the countess asserts: 'and as to all the rest – he will understand'. Here Susanna replicates the countess's music, saying 'indeed, indeed, he will understand' (Ex. 9.2).

Ex. 9.2
Ambiguous replication in Mozart's *Le Nozze di Figaro*

It is precisely Susanna's replication that adds the necessary tone of scepticism, and perhaps even of antagonism to the role ascribed to her, with which she does not wholeheartedly agree.[6]

Shostakovich uses parodic replication mainly in his vocal music. Signs of it already appear in his earliest vocal piece, *The Dragonfly and the Ant* op. 4, written in 1922, when he was sixteen, on one of Krylov's fables. In Krylov's text the ant asks the dragonfly what he has been doing all the summer, given the fact that now, in winter, he is cold and starving. The dragonfly explains that he has been singing, and the ant sarcastically replicates his words:

Ex. 9.3
Ironic replication in Shostakovich's *The Dragonfly and the Ant*

'(Я) - - - - лето целое все пела'/ 'Ты все пела? Это дело!'[7] ('The whole summer I have been singing'/ 'The whole (summer) you have been singing? That's nice!'

While this early example presents a fairly simple correlation between text and music, i.e. the musical repetition echoes the textual replication, 'A Warning', the fifth in the song cycle *From Jewish Folk Poetry* op. 79, shows a far more subtle approach. The mother's warning is heard as a part of a whining, repetitive, circular motif of the instrumental introduction. The listener realizes the replication only when the voice enters with the same motif; at this stage the voice is actually replicating the instruments. However, the voice replication is cut off by the instruments, which continue the same phrase, replicating themselves. The result is a double purport: a saying is replicated, but the first notes we hear are already a replication of an earlier original, which is hinted at by the first words of the mother: 'Listen, Khasya!' – continued by the instruments (Ex. 9.4).

Ex. 9.4
'Warning', in Shostakovich's *From Jewish Folk Poetry*

The impression is of a phrase that is endlessly repeated, so that the instruments already 'know' how to continue it, and are repeating it in a circular fashion in a cycle into which the listener enters at some middle point. The instruments thus anticipate the mother's words before they are uttered. At a certain instant the dialogic situation, hinted at by the text, becomes obvious in the music: the daughter, although verbally silent, is not only present but is also reacting; her reaction and her opinion of the mother's nagging are articulated by the instrumental commentary. The mocking clarinet replication knows the original so well that it can anticipate, 'sing along' and even replace it. The comic effect is enhanced six bars later by the closure and repetition of the ending motif, echoing the repeating word 'beware', parodying her words (Ex. 9.5).

Ex. 9.5
'Beware!' – mother's warning and the clarinet's parody in Shostakovich's *From Jewish Folk Poetry*

Quotation, allusion and stylization

Quotation, allusion and stylization belong to a larger group of phenomena which use formerly existing art works, a practice that is particularly prevalent in music (Burkholder, 1994). Unlike replication, these techniques are not necessarily ironic, and therefore not always parodic (Hutcheon, 1985: 33).[8] Their importance for literary innovation has been stressed particularly by the Russian formalists (Shklovsky, 1929 [1991]: 145; Tinyanov, 1921 [1979]: 103–104; Hutcheon, 1985: 35–36 and 84–85). While their centrality to musical composition is a long-acknowledged fact, it seems that, besides medieval examples that are mainly based on pre-existing *cantus firmus* melodies, these techniques are particularly characteristic of the music written in the twentieth century (Burkholder, 1994: 863; Hutcheon, 1985: 40–42).[9]

While some writers regard any quotation as an alienating element, others see every borrowing as potentially indifferent.[10] Bakhtin differentiates between parodic and non-parodic quotation when he distinguishes between 'monologic' and various kinds of 'double-voiced' discourses according to the resulting congruence or incongruity between the various utterances that are brought together. He describes the transition from a 'monologic' quotation to parody in a meticulous analysis of each and every stage:

> В научной статье, где приводятся чужие высказывания по данному вопросу различных авторов ... перед нами случай диалогического взаимо-отношения между непосредственно интенциональными словами в пределах одного контекста ...

Это не столкновение двух последних смысловых инстанций, а обЪектное (сюжетное) столкновение двух изображенных позиций, всецело подчиненное высшей, последней инстанции автора. Монологический контекст при этом не размыкается и не ослабляется ...

Но автор может использовать чужое слово для своих целей и тем путем, что он вкладывает новую интенцию в слово, уже имеющее свою собственную предметную интенцию и сохраняющее ее. При этом такое слово, по заданию, должно ощущаться как чужое. в одном слове оказываются две интенции, два голоса. Таково пародийное слово, такова стилизация, таков стилизованный сказ ...

Условное слово – всегда двуголосое слово. Условным может стать лишь то, что когда-то было неусловным, серьёзным. Это первоначальное прямое и безусловное значение служит теперь новым целям, которые овладевают им изнутри и делают его условным ...

Иначе обстоит дело в пародии. Здесь автор, как и в стилизации, говорит чужим словом, но, в отличие от стилизации, он вводит в это слово интенцию, которая прямо противоположна чужой интенции. (Бахтин, 1929: 110, 111, 112, 118)

The scholarly article – where various authors' utterances on a given question are cited ... is one instance of a dialogic interrelationship among directly signifying discourses within the limits of a single context ... This is not a clash of two ultimate semantic authorities, but rather an objectified (plotted) clash of two represented positions, subordinated wholly to the higher, ultimate authority of the author. The monologic context, under these circumstances, is neither broken nor weakened ...

But the author may also make use of someone else's discourse for his own purposes, by inserting a new semantic intention into a discourse which already has, and which retains, an intention of its own. Such a discourse, in keeping with its task, must be perceived as belonging to someone else. In one discourse, two semantic intentions appear, two voices. Parodying discourse is of this type, as are stylization and stylized *skaz* ...

Conditional discourse is always double-voiced discourse. Only that which was at one time unconditional, in earnest, can become conditional. The original direct and unconditional meaning now serves new purposes, which take possession of it from within and render it conditional ...

Stylisation stylizes another's style in the direction of that style's own particular tasks ... The author's thought, once having penetrated someone else's discourse and made its home in it, does not collide with the other's thought, but rather follows after it in the same direction, merely making that direction conventional.

The situation is different with parody, Here, as in stylisation, the author again speaks in someone else's discourse, but in contrast to stylisation parody introduces into that discourse a semantic intention that is directly opposed to the original one. (Bakhtin, 1963 [1984]: 188, 189, 190, 193)

It is difficult to draw a clear line between parodic stylistic allusion and a 'monologic', non-polemical use of formerly existing styles, genres and musical topics. This is particularly hard when the object of enquiry is the work of a young student, who writes within the context of a paradoxical cultural environment as Shostakovich did. On one hand, the Petrograd Conservatory strongly relied on and encouraged traditional writing, which should be based on a thorough knowledge and absorption of the musical heritage, a task with which Shostakovich complied with great success (Wilson, 1994: 24–25). In Bakhtin's terminology it could be formalized as the encouragement of musical utterances which, while indeed referring to 'someone else's words' (this 'someone' being normally their forerunners), still keep their monologic character; that is, they do not struggle with those former styles. On the other hand, the Romantic approach, which enhanced original individuality, and much more than that, the *fin-de-siècle* ironical approach to literature, art and music, promoted double-voiced, tongue-in-cheek parodies.

Following Tinyanov's and Bakhtin's definitions of parody, the element that exists in parody and is not present in stylizations is an 'inversion', a polemical opposition, or in other words an incongruity inserted between the object of reference and the referring work. Thus, if an incongruity is to be found in a work between the referring and the referred-to objects, at least the possibility of a parody must be taken into account.

Shostakovich's earliest works have elements of allusion, but it is unclear whether they are parodic or not. For example, the song 'The Ass and the Nightingale' from his op. 4 (1922) does evoke the style of Rimsky-Korsakov, but it seems to do so in a monologic, non-conditional way, since no incongruity appears in the music. On the other hand, stylistic incongruities are inserted in each one of the *Three Fantastic Dances* op. 5 (1920), thus transforming them into parodic utterances: the first sounds like a parody of Dvořák's *Humoresque*, the second of a lyrical Viennese waltz and the third of a folk-like polka. However, these pieces were composed before Shostakovich became involved with the Serapion Brothers and acquainted with the formalists' ideas (although there is no clear-cut evidence for this, since from 1919 he was a student at the Petrograd Conservatory). Thus it seems feasible to regard such manifestations of double-voiced musical utterances as a natural tendency of Shostakovich, which was later fused and enhanced by his early absorption of the contemporary approach to art.[11]

In the First Symphony op. 10 (1926) an apparent 'double voice' appears in the waltz melody inserted as its second subject. Unlike former stylizations, here the parodic use of existent forms is clear: it is not only that the first and second theme are contrasted in their musical purport (as would be the case with a classical sonata form); the semantic and cultural connotations of the stylistic layers that each of these themes is alluding to – the first to a Straussian

Till Eulenspiegel style, and the second a Viennese waltz – are incongruent with each other, too.

The inspiration for such an incongruity may have been Mahler, with whose works Shostakovich could have been acquainted even at this early stage. This apparent influence, however, can be described in terms of general sonority rather than in the musical content. In this symphony Shostakovich may be alluding to Mahler's plurivocal utterance, but his own musical commentary is still an univocal, monologic one. This case, though, should be regarded as an exception. Even his Fourth Symphony op. 43 (1934–36), which is clearly influenced by Mahler, sounds more like a series of internally congruent utterances, and is not directly related to the fundamental incongruity of Mahler's musical purport.[12]

Throughout his early and middle periods, approximately between 1930 and 1960, Shostakovich normally parodies single-voiced utterances, as in his Preludes and Fugues op. 87 (1952), thus creating a 'single-levelled parody'. The early and mid-1930s see a whole array of Shostakovich's works built around quotations and stylistic allusions. This period followed not only his readings (or re-readings) of Tinyanov's 1929 edition of his articles, but also discussions with Sollertinsky about Mahler, most probably influenced by Bakhtin's ideas of plurivocality as expressed in his book on Dostoevsky.

The most popular example of this early type of musical plurivocality is, of course, the Piano Concerto op. 35 (1934); however, the stylistic allusions in the set of piano preludes op. 34, written in the same year, are more subtle and far more interesting. Other examples can easily be found in the music for the stage production of *Hamlet* op. 32 (1932), the film scores of this period, and the Jazz Suite No. 1 (1934). This trend continued into the late 1930s, as shown in his Jazz Suite No. 2 and the transcriptions of Johann Strauss's *Pleasure Train Polka* and the operetta *Wiener Blut*, all from 1938.

Stylistic allusions to dance topics are particularly prevalent. Baroque dances such as the gigue (in *Hamlet* op. 32), the gavotte (in *The Golden Age* op. 22 [1930]) and the sarabande (in *The Golden Age* and the second movement of the Piano Concerto No. 2 op. 102, [1957]) occupy a special place in his series of stylistic allusions. Modern dance forms appear too: the foxtrot seems to be a particular favourite of Shostakovich, since it appears in his two Jazz Suites as well as in his ballet *The Golden Age* and in his incidental music for *The Bedbug* op. 19 (1929). Even tap dance appears in a scene of *The Golden Age*.

It is the nineteenth-century dance forms, however, that occupy a prominent place in his work, probably written under a mixture of influences ranging from the ball descriptions in the writings of Gogol and Dostoevsky to Mahler's overtly banal waltzes and folk-like tunes. These stylistic allusions tend to bear particularly strong satirical repercussions. The most obvious among them is the galop, which appears both in Shostakovich's stage music and in his symphonic works. From the very start the galop is perceived as a grotesque mixture between a lowly, vulgar expression of mirth and a terrifying accumulation of mass energy. As such it appears in the Second Symphony op. 14 (1927) and the Third Symphony op. 20 (1929), in the operas *The Nose* op. 15 (1928) and *Lady Macbeth of the Mtsensk District* op. 29 (1932), in the stage productions *The Bedbug, Allegedly Murdered* op. 31 (1931) and *Hamlet*, and in the film music to *Alone* op. 26 (1931). The galop can be connected with the polka, another vivacious nineteenth-century dance form which appears with similar connotations, although not with the same purport of intrinsic violence. The polka first appears in Shostakovich's works as the third of the *Three Fantastic Dances* op. 5. Further allusions to it can be found in the ballets *The Golden Age* and *The Bolt* op. 27 (1931) and in the incidental music for *Allegedly Murdered* and *Hamlet*. Other nineteenth-century dance forms that Shostakovich alludes to include the Polonaise (in the opening of the second act of *Lady Macbeth of the Mtsensk District*, echoing Mussorgsky's satirical polonaise in *Boris Godunov*), the can-can (in *The Bolt, The Golden Age* and *Hamlet*), and obviously, the waltz, which is a musical topic that appears in Shostakovich's music throughout all his life, and is used by him to convey various purports, from straightforward satire (as in the Servants' Waltz from *Lady Macbeth*) to the sweetest melancholic romance (as in the second movement of his First Piano Concerto).[13]

Likewise prevalent in Shostakovich's music are other musical topics: Baroque forms such as canon (in *Aphorisms*, op. 13 and twice in *The Nose*), passacaglia (in the organ entr'acte in *Lady Macbeth*), and the fugue, which first appears in his Second Symphony op. 14 (1927), and from then on functions as an integral part of his musical language – the most obvious example being his 24 Preludes and Fugues op. 87 (1952). Through many other instances, such as the first movement of his Eighth String Quartet op. 110 (1960), the fugue is brought to the point that it becomes a symbol of his musical profession, in 'Career', the fifth movement, in the Thirteenth Symphony 'Babi-Yar' (1962).

Allusions to Mahler's style occupy a special place in Shostakovich's musical output. Shostakovich transformed Mahler's interpretations of musical topics, such as the waltz, the scherzo and the march, into allusion-topics in themselves. Thus, while Shostakovich's first allusions from the early 1930s are mostly satirical stylizations, they gradually become more profound and subtle. Yet a real parodic approach to Mahler's double-voiced discourse, and perhaps also to the phenomenon of double-voiced discourse as a whole, appears only in Shostakovich's late string quartets and symphonies. This process is accompanied by a growing tendency of the composer towards self-quotation, in a way that seems to create from certain motifs and themes almost 'musical characters', which develop like literary characters in a novel. Indeed, in his later works Shostakovich uses a kind of 'musical plurivocality', which might be the result of an attempt to apply Bakhtin's ideas about literary plurivocality to music. His late works often include double-voiced musical parodies about double-voiced musical utterances; far from mere parody, they become musical versions of the Bakhtinian unfinalizable dialogue.

Quotations, allusions and stylization in the Fifteenth Symphony

The particularly rich musical patchwork of motifs and parts of motifs in the Fifteenth Symphony, which relate not only to other musical works but also to various cultural units, has often been noted.[14] Here the boundaries between a parodic borrowing from a specific work and replications of a motif which has cultural, gestural and projectional connotations become blurred. The final result is a disturbing, multi-layered message, of which only one level may be related to parody.

The Symphony includes quotations from the overture to Rossini's *William Tell*, the 'death' or 'fate' motif from Wagner's *Der Ring des Nibelungen* and from several of Shostakovich's own works. Seemingly, there are no significant connections among all these various quotations.[15] This variety creates a musical collage that functions through a network of associations and correlations of cultural units rather than creating a one-way parody.

It is particularly the quotation from Rossini's overture to *William Tell* that appears to be completely incongruous with the remaining sombre material, both in its tonality and in its cultural connotations as a popular, lighthearted musical work (see Ex. 9.11). However, a comparison of this motif, which repeats the rhythmic pattern of a quaver and two semiquavers, which is arguably also the most characteristic motif in the music of Shostakovich, points to the obvious musical association. This motif appears in so many of Shostakovich's works that an exhaustive list of its various manifestations and their manifold derivatives would be an enormous enterprise (some manifestations appear in Exs 9.6–9.11). However, the more interesting question concerns the possible meanings that Shostakovich did ascribe to this motif, and the chain of associations that connect this meaning with its appearance in Rossini's overture.

Intrinsically, the motif has an energetic gestural potential that could be modified to convey either gaiety and liveliness (a euphoric expression of energy), or violence and obsessive compulsion (a dysphoric expression of energy). Even a superficial browsing over its various appearances in Shostakovich's works discloses that it is used to convey not only euphoric or dysphoric musical purports, but also compound messages, in which these two contradictory purports function simultaneously. Concurrently, a general trend can be detected, according to which in his early works the motif appears more in euphoric contexts, and sometime in the 1930s, particularly in his Fifth Symphony op. 47 from 1937, its use becomes more and more dysphoric (see Ex. 9.7).

The change of the musical purport is achieved by the modification of other musical parameters, such as pitch, tonality, tempo and dynamics. Thus, when bearing a euphoric purport, the motif normally includes various pitches, and also tends to be in a tempo allegretto, reside in the bright, but not extremely high, register, and remain within a piano or a mezzo-piano dynamics.

The main musical element that conveys the dysphoric aspect of the motif is its performance on one repeating note versus on different pitches; likewise, it is in a very fast tempo, resides in an extreme register – usually a very high one, but it can also be a very low one – and tends towards a fortissimo or even fortississimo dynamics.

The first time that Shostakovich uses this motif systematically is in his first opera, *The Nose* op. 15 (1928). Here it is connected exclusively with scenes of the police, always with a satirical connotation that also can be associated with the grotesque; thus from the very start the motif is perceived by Shostakovich as conveying both the ludicrous and the terrifying, that is, it has both extreme euphoric and extreme dysphoric expressive potentials.

The motif appears in *The Nose* five times (Ex. 9.6): in the scene on the bridge, before Ivan Yakovlevich meets the policeman;[16] in the scene in the police station, before the policemen begin singing their 'Song of the Dog';[17] in the repetitious cries of the pretzel vendor, before the policemen begin to harass her; in the scene where the policeman returns the lost nose to Kovalyev, and in the last scene, in which Kovalyev, amused, continues chasing women in the street, as if nothing has happened at all. All the scenes, except the last one, have connotations of the police, that is – in Shostakovich's vocabulary (and in the associations arising from the plot itself) – with violence that is looked upon satirically. The last scene is connected with Kovalyev's own laxity, which in the opera is looked upon derisively, too. This double purport of both amusement and threat of violence continues throughout the whole of Shostakovich's musical output.

In the earlier works in which this motif can be found, mainly the Third Symphony op. 20 and *The Golden Age* op. 22 (both written in 1929) the motif is correlated with amusement and joy. The tempo is not too fast, the pitch bright, but not extremely high, and the whole texture is balanced. Similar moments appear in the three courting scenes in *Lady Macbeth*, the first when Sergey challenges Katerina to a mock contest, the second when he enters her bedroom, and the last, where he woos Sonyetka.

It is in the Fifth Symphony that Shostakovich begins to exploit the dysphoric potential in an intensive way. Here it is also the first time in which he fully develops this impact of the motif through its use as an ostinato figure, on a single repeating pitch, for considerable lengths of time (Ex. 9.7).

This use is further exploited in the burlesque of the Violin Concerto op. 77 (1948), where the violins in the third octave and the violas in the second scream the motif in shrill, repetitive harmonic minor seconds. This use of open octaves

Ex. 9.6(1)–9.6(5)

Excerpts from *The Nose*. The characteristic quaver–two-semiquavers motif is associated with accumulation of energy – both euphoric and dysphoric

1. *The Nose* act 1: Ivan Yakovlevich approaches the river in order to get rid of the nose. As his tension grows, particularly when he sees the police constable, the rhythmic motif's pitch ascends, the dynamic grows, and its repetitions become more and more condensed (2 bars before rehearsal fig. 58):

2. *The Nose* act 2: In the police quarters. The tension that is connected with the police force is slowly built up.

3. *The Nose* act 2: The pretzels-seller. Her insistent cries, on one pitch and in the high register, arouse the anger of the policemen, who will eventually attack her.

4. *The Nose* act 2, scene 7: The police constable returns the lost nose to Kovalyev, whose exhilaration does not find enough channels for its outburst, as is pointed out by the tense motif in the accompaniment.

5. *The Nose* last scene: This example is too long to be quoted here. On the background of scherzando figures of the motif, Kovalyev appreciates the Petersburg beauties who stroll along the Nevsky Prospekt, ready for new adventures. The music is cheerful, in a piano dynamics, with a clear tendency towards a major tonality. The general register covers the first and the beginning of the second octave. The motif itself, although repeating the same note, functions as the background for a lighthearted tune.

Ex. 9.7

The gradual growth in tension in the first movement of the Fifth Symphony owes much to the insistent use of the rhythmic motif that appears stronger each time, and in a wider range (the motif in the last excerpt is actually heard in the first, the second and the third octaves)

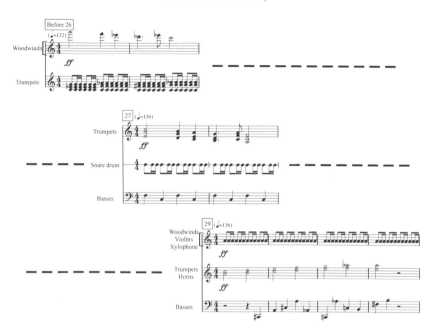

between the instruments that perform the motif, always in a fortissimo, also occurs when the pitch does not repeat itself, as in figure 97 of the second movement of the Tenth Symphony op. 93 (1953). Here, however, the repetitive, compulsive element is provided by the strings, which play an ostinato of two oscillating thirds. The tempo is very fast: $\downarrow$ = 176. Later in the same movement (rehearsal figure 199), the trumpets and timpani join in a hectic repetition of the motif, reduced here to its rhythmic element alone, while the strings play another, but also repetitive, motif. The climax arrives in the last movement, where, at rehearsal figure 202, the horns and trumpets scream the DSCH motif while the trumpets provide the background, with the ostinato motif, played in their middle, shrill register. Similar instances happen in the first and second movements of the Thirteenth Symphony, 'Babi-Yar' (1962), and in the second movement of the Tenth String Quartet op. 118 (1964). As mentioned above, this list is far from exhaustive, but in all the pieces the impression is the same. It is the repetitive, obsessive nature of the motif that lends to its alleged lighthearted nature the shade of uncontrollable, violent compulsion and looming insanity.

Concurrently, the double meaning of the motif continues to appear in Shostakovich's works: in his Third String Quartet, op. 73 (1946) the motif has both purports. This also happens in his Seventh String Quartet op. 108 (1960). A combination of correlatives of contradictory significations is at work here: the dynamic marking is indeed piano, the tempo is moderato, and the violin solo plays in the middle register; however, the tonality is far from clear and the meter keeps changing, conveying a peculiar feeling of sickly amusement (Ex. 9.8).

Ex. 9.8
Contradictory correlatives in Shostakovich's Seventh String Quartet

In the third movement of the quartet the violent potential of the motif is fully exploited: the instruments are required to play fortissimo on the strings, which are muffled with sordini (in itself a self-contradictory way of playing), and the hectic ascending motion is a clear echo of the violent outburst in the Scherzo of the Tenth Symphony (Ex. 9.9).

Ex. 9.9
Contradictory correlations in the third movement of Shostakovich's Seventh String Quartet

The effect of combined dysphoric–euphoric purport is achieved by the combination of musical elements that correlate, each one separately, with another aspect of the energetic gestural correlative. An extreme case of double meaning is the fourth song of the song cycle *From Jewish Folk Poetry*, 'Before a Long Separation'. For instance, the bitter-sweet accompaniment in the song uses one of the versions of this motif in low, piano sounds, but with its inner threatening energy enhanced by the repeating E in the bass. This happens in the musical setting of the text where the lover remembers, in the moments before his departure to exile and imprisonment, the sweet moments he shared with his beloved, to whom he is saying his farewell: 'Do you remember, as we stood in the doorway, what you told me in secret then?' (Ex. 9.10).

In spite of his great popularity and generally buoyant reputation, Rossini was, for Shostakovich, a sad figure: in one of his letters he refers to the

Ex. 9.10

Contradictory correlations evoke a mixture of fear, anguish and sweet memories

composer's compositional crisis, at the age of forty, when speaking about his own crisis (Wilson, 1994: 267). It is thus quite probable that Rossini is used here as a musical exegesis of this motif, the double contradictory purport of which seems to have evaded the eyes of his analysts. Its closest prior description was as an '*idée fixé*' (Roseberry, 1989: 107). The use of the Rossini motif is, then, doubly and perhaps even triply motivated. It is interesting, in this respect, to observe the slight distortions that Shostakovich incorporated into Rossini's theme (Ex. 9.11).

Ex. 9.11

Comparison between Rossini's theme in his *William Tell* overture and Shostakovich's quotation in his Fifteenth Symphony

Some of the distortions are rather satirical, such as the fact that the first bar of the theme, in Shostakovich's symphony, is actually in 3/4 time, thus breaking the former flow of 2/4, to enter the new one, of the quotation, with a slight 'hiccup'. Similarly satirical is the entry of the trumpet in forte, immediately 'correcting' it back to the original piano. Here, however, there is another distortion: Shostakovich seems to 'mellow' Rossini's extreme parameters: the original 'Allegro vivace' becomes a mere 'Allegretto'; the dynamic marking is 'piano' and not 'pianissimo' as in the original. On the other hand, the brass instruments, instead of the original strings, sound clownish, almost grotesque, in their attempt to play piano and staccato. It seems that Shostakovich is 'playing' here with the parameters, in accordance with the formalist conception of stylization. However, his melodic change, which emphasizes the obsessive character of the motif (and its connection to his own characteristic motif), distorts the feeling of parody. It seems that the amusement is not complete. The eerie context of the quotation strengthens this impression and leads the interpretation of the excerpt towards the infinite irony of a rather terrifying nature – that of the grotesque.

PART V
THE GROTESQUE

CHAPTER TEN

Definition, structure and content of the grotesque

The grotesque is an unresolvable ironic utterance, a hybrid that combines the ludicrous with the horrifying.[1] As such, it appears frequently in Romantic literature as well as in art and music at the beginning of the century, and seems to hold a special interest for Russian writers and artists in the first thirty years of the twentieth century. Therefore it has a special importance for the present study.

Irony is founded upon intellectual, discursive processes (Muecke, 1969: 220; Thomson, 1972: 47). Its interpretation as a problematic phenomenon is based on specific thought-principles that regard the components of semantic contraries, such as euphoric/dysphoric, life/death, tragic/comic or beautiful/ugly, as mutually exclusive. According to this thinking, 'euphoric' would equal 'not dysphoric' and 'tragic' would equal 'not comic'; when this is applied to logical deductive thinking, 'beauty' cannot coexist with 'ugliness', 'loyalty' cannot coexist with 'betrayal', nor 'life' with 'death'.

This mode of thought was applied to aesthetics by Aristotle, in his *Poetics*, and afterwards by all the schools that derived from and followed his thought. Consequently, juxtapositions of aesthetic units that form contradictory semantic pairs such as tragic/comic, terrifying/ludicrous or ugly/beautiful are interpreted, according to the Aristotelian aesthetic doctrine, as unresolvable hybrids, or grotesques.

Wolfgang Kayser, whose work on the grotesque is considered a classic source, regards the grotesque as a structure in which the perception of the ludicrous resides on its ostensible level, while the terrifying is its hidden import. For Kayser the grotesque's structure is its very purport, and his definition of it includes both form and content:

> Das Groteske ist eine Struktur ... das Groteske ist die entfremdete Welt. ... Aber sie ist keine entfremdete Welt. Dazu gehört, daß was uns vertraut und heimisch war, sich plötzlich als fremd und unheimlich enthüllt ... Das Grauen überfällt uns so stark, weil es eben unsere Welt ist, deren Verläßlichkeit sich als Schein erweist. (Kayser, 1957: 198–199)

> The grotesque is a structure ... The grotesque is the estranged world ... Yet the world is not estranged, that is to say, the elements in it which are familiar and natural to us do not suddenly turn out to be strange and ominous ... We are so strongly affected and terrified because it is our world which ceases to be reliable. (Kayser, 1957 [1981]: 184)

This structure is apparently not simply the juxtaposition of the two components of form and content, but rather their admixture. This confusion of form and content is not accidental, since here they are particularly interdependent. As an unresolvable hybrid, the grotesque can be regarded as a particular case of existential irony. Both have two layers of contradictory meanings, neither of which is to be preferred: both regard doubt and disorientation as the basic condition of human existence, finally, the main purport of the grotesque, as well as that of existential irony, is its unresolvability.

Yet not all messages of existential irony are grotesques. Specific imports in various such messages may vary, and unresolvable situations, caused by a compulsory choice between two equally valid and positive alternatives, are, at least according to Aristotelian aesthetic principles, the core of tragedy. Such choices, which abound in life situations as well as in dramatic ones, stimulate such extreme propositions as Thomas Mann's, who presented the question of irony as '*das Leben oder der Geist*': the human being has no escape from choosing between his moral values and life's realities (Mann, 1918: 423).

This intrinsic irony of the human condition can take two opposing directions: on the one hand, it can continue with its contradictory meanings in a process of infinite negation, resulting in Kierkegaard's concept of irony, which eventually is a nihilistic despair (Kierkegaard, 1841 [1989]: 261). On the other hand, it can start a similarly infinite line of affirmations, that will eventually accumulate to form the Bakhtinian concept of the grotesque, in which all possible meanings of a phenomenon are clustered and accepted as an experienced reality. This 'excess of meanings', resulting from the very same contradictory state of human existence that generated the infinite negation of irony, is triumphantly celebrated by Mikhail Bakhtin when he explores the literary techniques of excess and ambivalence: for Bakhtin the grotesque is the result of an additive process, i.e. the *acceptance* (instead of negation) of all the imagery with which a subject is presented. The outcome of such a process is one of the grotesque's main traits: an unresolvable, inevitable ambiguity. In his chapter on 'The Grotesque Image of the Body', Bakhtin analyses Rabelais's imagery of a monastery belfry fertilizing a woman. All the possible meanings, connotations and associations – satirical, joyous, repugnant and even mythological – are enumerated and accepted as part of the whole and compound grotesque import (Bakhtin, 1941 [1984]: 310–312). This idea is related to Bakhtin's concept of the *unfinalizability of reality* which, according to him, is reflected in the imagery of the grotesque body, which he describes as 'cosmic and universal', a body that 'can fill the entire universe'. It is:

> a body in the act of becoming. It is never finished, never completed; it is continually built, created, and builds and creates another body. Moreover, the body swallows the world and itself is swallowed by the world ... The grotesque ignores the impenetrable surface that closes and limits

the body as a separate and completed phenomenon. The grotesque image displays not only the outward but the inner features of the body: blood, bowels, heart and other organs. The outward and inward features are often merged into one. (Bakhtin, 1941 [1984]: 317–318)

Therefore, rather than being 'an attempt to invoke and subdue the demonic aspects of the world', as Wolfgang Kayser describes it, the grotesque is perceived by Bakhtin as a victorious assertion of all life's infinite 'buds and sprouts' (Kayser, 1957 [1981]: 188; Bakhtin, 1941 [1984]: 318).

Infinite irony is the result of a subtractive process, in which meanings are constantly negated and rejected.[2] Contrary to that, the grotesque is the result of an additive process, in which all meanings are accepted and accumulated. Thus, while irony rejects everything, the grotesque accepts everything; irony nullifies everything, while the grotesque is all-affirming. The grotesque rejects the very principles of logical deduction: while irony systematically rejects contradictions (and therefore results in the Kierkegaardian 'infinite negation', the grotesque is the result of a systematic admission of contradictions. Viewed in this context, although irony and the grotesque share the same structure, they are located at two opposing poles: the one of eternal negation versus the one of eternal affirmation.

This model points to a problematic aspect of infinite irony: since the same structure can accommodate both the grotesque and the infinite negation, it seems that the classical definition of infinite irony *qua* infinite negation is incomplete, and must be re-phrased to include the possibility of an infinite affirmation. This tentative model, which accepts both infinite negation and affirmation as substructures of infinite irony, is regarded here as the model of existential irony.[3] The grotesque, then, is a particular case of existential irony that accepts all contradictions and is based on the hybrid of the ridiculous and the horrifying.

Contrary to irony's requirement of analytical, intellectual mental processes, the grotesque stimulates rather sensual reactions.[4] While irony respects logical heuristic procedures, regarding apparent contraries that are left in their unresolved state as unresolved puzzles, the grotesque rebels against these very same rules of logic, embraces the phenomenological approach and, refusing to see any phenomenon as excluding another, admits and accepts the existence of whatever is, regardless of any reasoning procedures. The grotesque is therefore the result of the irrational and impulsive reaction to the same paradoxical reality that, when stimulating rational reaction, was the source of general irony.

The grotesque is connected with the Aristotelian comic: in its arousal of dysphoric reactions it parallels the imitation of lowly human traits, while ironic thought, which is devoted to systematic negation, parallels the Aristotelian tragic, which is considered the 'loftier', aesthetically preferred mode of artistic expression (Aristotle, [1963]: 10–11).

Although infinite irony, in its traditional interpretation, is based on a 'negative' process, which systematically eliminates any possible meaning of a message, the import of each subject of its unresolvable intellectual dichotomies is mostly euphoric values, such as 'life', 'honour' or 'loyalty'. On the other hand, the grotesque, based on a 'positive' process of accumulation that regards all imports as equally valid, presents not only a statement which is logically problematic, but also one that leads to sensual and emotional disorientation. The grotesque not only presents, but actually embraces, dysphoric human values: the despised, the ridiculous and the horrifying. This is normally expressed by two contradictory emotional reactions to the grotesque: the impulse to laugh and the feeling of dread. Thus the grotesque always seems to bear just one contradictory import of the same two negative value-laden elements: the unresolvable reaction to the hybrid of the fearsome and the ludicrous. Consequently, while the basic reaction to negative infinite irony is intellectual despair, the primary reaction to the grotesque is emotional despair.

The structure of the grotesque is never as clear as that of the ironic message, nor are its two contradictory constituents – the ludicrous and the horrifying – as differentiated from each other as are the contradictory levels in an ironic message. The grotesque's structural clash is an outcome of the particular meanings of the double reaction it evokes: laughter and horror. These, on the other hand, acquire much of their semantic import from their formal, syntactic position, since the very meaning of laughter is transformed when juxtaposed with the horrifying, and vice versa. The grotesque, then, is not just a structure, as general irony is, but is also defined by its specific content.

Hyperbole in the grotesque

Being based on accumulation, the grotesque's imports are always exaggerated. The grotesque therefore conveys a distorted reality of a hyperbolic nature. A grotesque object is thus never 'comic', but rather 'ludicrous'; never just 'unpleasant', but rather 'repellent' or 'horrifying'.

This prerequisite of hyperbolic distortion implies, as in satire, the existence of a norm from which the exaggerated element deviates. However, unlike satire, the norms of the grotesque are not based on stylistic conventions, but seem to refer to what is perceived as a 'normal' human body and face:

> We can see at once what the standard form is that undergoes change; it
> is that of the human body and face. A distorted house or other structure
> may be called grotesque, but the usage is somewhat less than convinc-
> ing, and probably no one would think of applying the term to a distorted

square or triangle. Even the most outlandish demon is human in its general appearance, however inhuman its individual features may be. Where combinations of man and beast occur, the most grotesque are undoubtedly those in which man predominates ... The peculiar effect of the human skeleton, too, is based on its resemblance to an absurdly thin and bony living person ... The impression of humanness must not be too strong, the distortion not too great that it obliterates all traces of the human figure; but, on the other hand, it must show a drastic departure from the elements of human appearance and personality that we commonly experience. This is shown in the case of the deformed person; the deformity must be sufficiently pronounced that we momentarily forget that we have an actual person before us ... The grotesque object is a figure imagined in terms of human form but devoid of real humanity. (Jennings, 1963: 8–9)

In the musical grotesque, then, the exaggerations are often applied to anthropomorphic sound-analogies, in accordance with a possible conceptual projection of the human body on the soundscape (Sheinberg, 1996a). In such a projection, what is musically comfortable for the human body or voice – in terms of pitch, speed and density of sound – will be considered as its 'projection' on a soundscape, the potential of which is, obviously, larger. Therefore, a choice of a comfortable tempo, like andante or moderato, a register that accommodates the natural speaking voice and tempered dynamics of sound would most probably render a 'normal', comfortable kind of music. The opposite would convey a musically distorted, perhaps exaggerated and, if many such musical parameters are accumulated, grotesque purport. A good example of this can be seen in Bartók's *Two Portraits* op. 5, of which one is called 'Ideal' and the other 'Grotesque'. The 'Ideal Portrait' begins with a violin solo, in tempo andante, piano, in the middle register, with the instruction 'semplice' (Ex. 10.1).

Ex. 10.1
Bartók's theme for the 'Ideal Portrait'

The 'Grotesque Portrait', on the other hand, uses the very same musical theme, but in tempo presto, at a very high pitch, fortissimo, and with a clear exaggeration of the rhythmic values: the quavers become semiquavers, while the long, dotted and tied C# has more than doubled its length. This changes the time proportion between the short notes and the long one from 1:4 into the musical hyperbolic proportion of 1:33! The syncopated entrances of the trumpet highlight still more the awkward feeling (Ex. 10.2a).

Even when he writes in a very high register, Bartók keeps in the 'Ideal Portrait' the balance between the musical parameters. The extremely high

pitch of the solo violin, although perceived as 'out of the human scope', is balanced by the comfortable andante, the pianissimo, and the moderate rhythmic proportions, as well as by a general harmonic support that fills in the musical space. The melodic theme is conveyed by the woodwind, whose timbre closely resembles the human voice (oboe, English horn, bass clarinet and bassoon), and is written in the register and range of the 'speaking voice' (Ex. 10.2b).

Ex. 10.2a
Bartók's 'Grotesque Portrait'

Ex. 10.2b
Bartók's 'Ideal Portrait'

Even when, two bars later, the solo violin touches the fortissimo dynamics, still the other instruments are limited to a poco forte level – and that for less than a bar. Contrarily, all the musical parameters accumulated in the main theme in the 'Grotesque Portrait' – high pitch, tempo presto, fortissimo and extreme rhythmic proportions – point to the violence and abruptness that characterize the grotesque. To these he then adds the special effects of shrilling trills in the high woodwind and an instruction for the first trumpet to play fortissimo con sordino and for the cymbals to play col legno. These exaggerations draw the grotesque object away from the 'normally' human by emphasizing the uncomfortable, unnatural and foreign to whatever feels 'normal' in music (Ex. 10.3).

Ex. 10.3
Exaggerated musical expression in Bartók's 'Grotesque Portrait'

While the 'violent' musical traits of the theme are here exaggerated and drawn out of balance, so is the dance-like accompaniment. Although hinting at the scherzo topic, the dynamics, the heaviness and density of the chords and their orchestration all point to much heavier, more violent motion than is needed for a dance. The exaggeration leads to extremes: the amusing becomes ludicrous, thus functioning as a part of the whole grotesque picture. Bartók's 'Grotesque Portrait' obeys what seems to be a basic law of the grotesque structure: neither of its elements should overcome or obscure the other, transforming it either into a burlesque or into a forthright horror story. In order to keep the required balance, then, it seems that both the grotesque's ludicrous as well as its horrifying aspects, theoretically at least, should be endlessly exaggerated. This would result in the grotesque's systematic use of both incongruities and exaggeration *ad absurdum* – with no aesthetic restrictions whatsoever. The fact that breaking all feasible rules of aesthetic norms creates an aesthetic entity is just one more paradox in the long series of paradoxes that characterize the grotesque.

In order to emphasize the importance of the grotesque as an independent genre, Bakhtin takes great pains to differentiate it from satire (Bakhtin, 1941 [1984]: 303–311). The main goals of exaggeration in the grotesque are totally different from those of satire. While satire values abstract systems of hierarchical norms (and thus rejects all exaggeration), the grotesque celebrates the endless cycle of physical existence that encompasses life and death, thus embracing abundance of any kind. The fact that some of life's values contradict our standards of ethical behaviour is just an unfortunate coincidence, says Bakhtin, but from the grotesque's point of view it is a mere maladjustment. Sexual activity and the metabolic system are actually what our physical life is about, and thus they are admired and enhanced by the grotesque, regardless of the fact that lust and gluttony are pejorative traits in our behavioural codes of ethics.

Bakhtin stresses the differences between satire and the grotesque in order to explain the joy and pleasure we draw from grotesque descriptions that exaggerate whatever is connected with ingestion and sexual activity. This pleasure, argues Bakhtin, is not based on our sense of righteousness, looking from above at a satirized subject, but rather from a sense of participation in a carnivalesque feast. There is not necessarily a connection between the fact that some of the grotesque's subjects are also satirized and the pleasure we draw from them. Thus, while satire is based on alienation, the grotesque functions only within an empathizing context. Questioning Schneegans's interpretation of the grotesque as a kind of satire, Bakhtin writes:

> The interpretation of the grotesque image as purely satirical, that is, negative, is widespread … [it is] typical but radically erroneous. It is founded on the complete neglect of a series of essential aspects of the grotesque and first of all neglect of its ambivalence … even with considerable effort it is impossible to find the satirical orientation in all of Rabelais' exaggeration … the author of the grotesque is carried away, is 'drunk' with hyperbole, at times forgetting the true role of exaggeration and losing his grasp on satire … A grotesque world in which only the inapproriate is exaggerated is only quantitatively large … Satire alone would not suffice to explain even the positive pathos of the quantitative exaggeration, not to speak of the qualitative wealth … [Schneegans] could not understand the possibility of combining in one image both the positive and negative poles. Even less was he able to understand that an object can transgress not only its quantitative but also its qualitative limits, that it can outgrow itself and be fused with other objects. (Bakhtin, 1941 [1984]: 306–308)

The exaggeration of the grotesque serves, then, to trespass the objects' own boundaries, to participate in the infinite process of becoming. The exaggeration is what enables the grotesque object to be simultaneously itself and not itself. In this it not only differs from satire, which is based on the stability of its subjects, but actually contradicts it. A subject becomes grotesque when the exaggerated trait does not seem 'exaggerated', but when it causes the object to become something else; it happens when 'the human nose is transformed into a snout or a beak', and when the monastery's belfry becomes a phallus, the shadow of which can fertilize women. Bakhtin writes about this Rabelaisian imagery, rejecting any satirical interpretation of it:

> This is no mere exaggeration of monastic 'depravity'. The object transgresses its own confines, ceases to be itself. The limits between the body

and the world are erased, leading to the fusion of the one with the other
and with surrounding objects. (Bakhtin, 1941 [1984]: 310)

Our primary, sensual reaction to the grotesque is a feeling of pleasure
drawn out from its life-enhancing traits: we celebrate with Rabelais's excessive descriptions of food, drink, copulation and excretion regardless of any
norms or logic, and we enjoy the exaggerated image of a monastery belfry's
shadow impregnating women far beyond its satirical implications: what we
really enjoy, according to Bakhtin, is the triumph of life over life-suffocating
asceticism and celibacy.

Our participation in the grotesque is primarily sensual and physical. In this
respect it coincides with one of the most important sources of musical pleasure: the almost automatic physical empathy with the lively rhythmic pulse of
a scherzo or a march. The fact that this is a purely sensual reaction, and that it
happens regardless of the subject or connotations of the performed piece, is
the source of many musical grotesques, such as the various versions of a
danse macabre, military marches and even propaganda music: music used in
advertising relies highly on this phenomenon. This might also be the source
of the grotesque atmosphere that is created in many of Shostakovich's symphonic movements, for example, the march in the first movement of his
Seventh Symphony or the finale of his Fifth Symphony. The use of this effect
as a device for the grotesque achieves chilling results in the scene of the
group rape of Aksynia, in *Lady Macbeth of the Mtsensk District*, and in the
pogrom scene in the first movement of the Thirteenth Symphony, 'Babi-Yar'.
In all these instances the motoric impetus draws even the most reluctant
listener into an automatic whirlpool of sensual and physical empathy, regardless of any of its contradictory emotional and intellectual purports.[5]

Not just in its structure, but also in its numerous functions, the grotesque is
a multi-faceted phenomenon, a hybrid. Since it aims toward various ends,
ranging from mere ridicule to the expression of profound existential beliefs,
it can appear as an element in satire and parody as well as in expressionist
and surrealist works of art. Historically, it plays a considerable part in traditional folk art-forms as well as in the over-refined *fin-de-siècle* European
culture. Therefore, in order to understand the grotesque and its position in
modern Russian culture, it is imperative to discriminate between the grotesque's various aims and functions in general, as well as within the more
limited scope of Russia in the first three decades of the century, and deal with
each one of them separately.

The emotional and physical appeal of the grotesque

While irony and satire communicate through concepts, the grotesque uses
visual images and physical empathy. Any comic statement can be made either

in an ironical and satirical manner or by a grotesque image, depending on the nature of the devices used: a conceptual discourse or a vibrating sensual image. This double potential can be examined by a comparison of two descriptions of balls, one by Anton Chekhov and the other by Nikolay Gogol.

The ball in Chekhov's *The Cherry Orchard* is an example of irony: lingering on the verge of financial catastrophe, the Russian noble family is compelled to sell its estate, the symbol of its past. In an escapist, despaired outburst, the mother of the family organizes a ball that is held in the house, while in the nearby town the estate is actually being sold at an auction. Under the ostensible layer of merry dancing exists a hidden layer of desolation and disaster. Chekhov ironizes this family ball by hinting at their slow social and cultural degradation:

> *Слышно, как в передней играет еврейский оркестр ... В зала танцуют гранд-ронд.*
>
> ...
>
> *Варя тихо плачет и, танцуя, утирает слезы.*
>
> ...
>
> *Пищик*: Ницше ... философ ... велишайший, знаменитейший ... громадного ума человек, говорит в своих сочинениях, будто фальшивые бумажки делать можно.
> *Трофимов*: А вы читали Ницше?
> *Пищик*: Ну ... Мне Дашенька говорила.
>
> ...
>
> Любовь Андреевна напевает лезгинку (Чехов, 1904 [1978]: 229–230)

> From an ante-room comes the sound of the Jewish orchestra ... In the ballroom they are dancing the 'grand-rond'.
>
> ...
>
> Varya is quietly weeping, and wiping her eyes as she dances.
>
> ...
>
> *Pishchik*: Nietzsche – the philosopher – very great philosopher, very famous one – man of enormous intelligence – he claims in his books that it's all right to forge banknotes.
> *Trofimov*: You've read Nietzsche, have you?
> *Pishchik*: Well ... my daughter Dashenka was telling me about him.
>
> ...
>
> *Ranyevskaya hums a Caucasian dance, the Lezghinka.* (Chekhov, 1904 [1978]: 324–325)

The blurring of boundaries between noble and peasant, the educated and the uneducated, happens at the intellectual level; it relies on conventional cultural signs that are conceptually perceived and decoded.

Apparently, nothing is really exaggerated: the irony is transmitted through slight incongruities, such as the presence of a Jewish folk band in the Russian nobles' house–estate, or the lady of the house humming the *Lezghinka*. Seemingly, there is nothing wrong with any of these details; actually, inviting

Jewish bands to play at Russian balls was quite a common custom. However, in this particular context, where the real issue is the degradation of status of Russian noble families by the end of the nineteenth century, this detail adds a tinge of irony to the general atmosphere: Jewish people, although highly regarded in their professional circles, were always looked upon as of a status lower than that of gentiles, and suffered from fewer civil rights. The *Lezghinka* is just a popular folk tune, with no particular value-judgement attached to it. However, in modern Russian culture it was accepted as an indication of simplicity, banality and even vulgarity. This semiotic function continued to be valid throughout the twentieth century.[6]

A more general cultural sign is the expression 'dancing with tears', which here ceases to be a metaphorical expression and gains a concrete meaning: Varya, Ranyevskaya's adopted daughter, actually weeps while dancing. The replacement of a conventional metaphor with its actual concretization is itself ironic, and in a way also points to a cultural degradation, which is constantly insinuated here, concurrently with the family's social degradation.

Further knowledge of Russian cultural background is needed to grasp the irony in calling the postmaster and the stationmaster, who are guests at the ball, by their titles (Chekhov, 1904 [1978]: act 3). This is part of an older Russian literary tradition that already appears in Gogol's descriptions of balls, always signalling a provincial society that pretends to be more than it is. In *The Government Inspector* we meet the postmaster, who is one of the main characters throughout the play. However, he has a special role in the ball, which is the climax of Gogol's satire on that society's naïve pretentiousness and provincialism: the postmaster is the first to receive the news from the big city, and therefore a personage of major importance in a provincial society. It is also the postmaster who, at the ball, announces the fraud: it is he who finds Khlestakov's letter to his friend, in which he laughs at all the protagonists of the play, describing in detail each one's faults (Gogol, 1836 [1926]: act 5, scene 3). In this play the personages that occupy the highest social positions are actually provincial philistines of the low middle class: the school inspector, the judge, the charity commissioner, the postmaster and the district doctor.

This crooked mirror of a pretentious middle-class society is taken to extremes in the description of the ball in *Dead Souls*, where the real star is not the postmaster, but his wife. The satire on provinciality is more than obvious in the long and ridiculous list of the galop dancers: the postmaster's wife, the police captain, a lady with a pale blue feather, a lady with a white feather, the Georgian prince, Chipkhaykhilidzev, an official from Petersburg, an official from Moscow, a Frenchman called Coucou, Perkhunovsky and Berebendovsky (Gogol, 1842 [1961]: 174).[7]

When the postmaster's wife waltzed, she 'put her head on one side so languorously that she really gave the impression of something not of this earth', while another lady danced in spite of 'a slight *incommodité* in the shape of a corn on her right foot', just 'to make sure that the postmaster's wife did not take it into her head to think too much of herself' (ibid.: 178). 'The celebrity's wife' is a character that became a 'cultural unit' in the Russian consciousness. Shostakovich makes use of it when he tells of Zinaida Raikh, Meyerhold's wife, and quotes from a satirical poem by Sasha Chërnyi: 'While a celebrity, Chërnyi says, may casually give you his hand, his wife at best will offer two fingers' (Volkov, 1979: 59).

The cultural ostentation of the stationmaster, as a representative of what Meyerhold, in his later analysis of the play, called 'Philistines', is laughed at when he quotes some lines of a poem by Aleksey Tolstoy (Braun, 1969: 28). These cultural associations are made explicit when, almost immediately after the stationmaster is hushed by the sound of a waltz coming from the next room, the old servant of the house says:

> Нездоровится. Прежде у нас на балах танцевали генералы, бароны, адмиралы, а теперь посылаем за почтовым чиновником и начальником станции, да и те не в охотку идут. (Чехов, 1904 [1978]: 235)

> I'm not right in myself. When we gave a ball in the old days we used to have generals dancing here, we had barons, we had admirals. Now we send for the postmaster and the stationmaster, and even they're none too eager. (Chekhov, 1904 [1978]: 332)

Chekhov is ironic in his descriptions. These, however, need a familiarity with cultural signs and their intellectual interpretation in order to conceive their ironic import. The reader (or spectator) contemplates the scene, reads the signs, and conceives their ironic meaning.

A totally different case is the ball scene of Gogol's *Dead Souls*. Here, too, a description is given of a corrupted society on the edge of its own downfall during an ostensibly merry dance. However, Gogol makes very little use of our knowledge of or acquaintance with conventionalized cultural signs: the incongruities are grasped by the reader through physical empathy and exaggerated gestural imagery, achieving a purely grotesque representation of a ball. Gogol's dancers are not 'dancing' but 'whirling madly'; they 'dash off', 'their heels crashing down'; they 'execute steps' and 'work hard'. The coarse cheerfulness reaches madness.[8]

Motion and the grotesque

The ball scene is a *locus classicus* of the grotesque, most probably due to the fact that grotesque images seem to gain more prominence when in motion (Jennings, 1963: 19–20). In Russian culture this association has a particular importance, which is expressed not only in the literature, but also in the theatre, with which Shostakovich had a continuous connection.

The most significant grotesque dance in the modern Russian theatre was the beggars' wedding-dance from Yevgeny Vakhtangov's 1922 production of An-sky's play *Haddybuk*, in Moscow. This is one of the most powerful scenes in the play, which tells of the ghost of Leah's dead betrothed which returns to haunt her on the night of her wedding to another man. A traditional custom at Jewish weddings is the 'open table', a festive meal to which all the beggars of the town are invited as the first act of charity of the newly wed. Out of happiness and gratitude, and in order to cheer up the miserable-looking bride, the beggars embark on a dance. Leah, however, is terrified of their contorted motions, and faints. The distorted human figures of the beggars, hopping in a spirited wedding-dance, shocked the Russian audience, as related by Russian theatre historian Konstantin Rudnitsky:

> The most turbulent and frenzied group was a grotesque crowd of beg-
> gars who danced at the wedding. Vakhtangov transformed the crowd of
> beggars into a crowd of monsters and freaks: hunchbacks, the blind,
> lame and cross-eyed. The critic Georgy Kryzhitsky wrote that in
> Haddibbuk all these 'beggars, the blind and deformed, with their writh-
> ing arms and crippled torsos, consumptive and crazy hunchbacks, straight
> out of an engraving by Goya, these terrifyingly grey clumps of con-
> torted bodies, this swarming mass of half-beasts resembling delirious,
> nightmarish apparitions, were moved about and grouped by Vakhtangov
> in endless diversity, imparting a monstrous, sinister awfulness to their
> grimaces.' (Kryzhitsky, in *Muzïka i teater*, 25.vi.1923; quoted in
> Rudnitsky, 1988: 54)

This kind of dance, in which the sickly cripples skip, leap, hop and bounce around the scared bride, comes very close to classical images of a *danse macabre*. By using fearsome make-up, masks and sharp-angled motion it not only combined, as does the typical Dance of Death, the skeleton's fearsome traits with an incongruously amused dance, but also presented one of the main imports of the grotesque: the blurring of the boundaries between life and death, the animate and inanimate. Through this link the grotesque is also related to puppet-shows like the Russian *balagan*, animate dolls such as Hoffmann's Coppelia and Olympia, and mechanized human beings like the one made by Dr Frankenstein, all popular throughout the nineteenth century's literature and culture. The skeletons dancing a *danse macabre*, in spite of their human semblance, are freakish, awkward, and also funny and puppet-like. In this respect the Dance of Death may be regarded as the most characteristic instance of the grotesque (Sheinberg, forthcoming).

Many musical instances of the Dance of Death use the scherzo musical topic, mainly conveyed by a quick, triple metre (Samuels, 1995: 123–131; Sheinberg, forthcoming). Examples of this range from Mendelssohn's 'Tar-antella' in his *Italian Symphony*, through Berlioz's 'The Dream of a Witches' Sabbath' in his *Symphonie fantastique*, Liszt's *Totentanz* and Saint-Saëns's *Danse macabre*, to modern versions of it, where the import of a Dance of

Death becomes the Mahlerian inane, futile Dance of Life of his scherzos, in Alban Berg's *Wozzeck*, Berio's *Folk Songs*, Penderecki's *The Devils of Loudon* and Shostakovich's *Lady Macbeth of the Mtsensk District*, not to mention the numerous scherzos in his symphonies and chamber works.

The cyclical, perpetual motion can also be connected to yet another blurred fringe that is often purported by the grotesque: the boundary between sanity and insanity. The music points to a fast, perpetual, uncontrolled motion that evokes associations of ecstatic rituals and possessed dances, while the repetitive character of the dancing, often supplemented by repetitive rhythmical patterns as well, can point to obsessive behaviour. All these belong to the realms of insanity, possession and uncontrolled behaviour rather than to merely innocent amusement.

The fantastic and the grotesque

Wolfgang Kayser quotes Friedrich Schlegel, who interchanged, in some of his writings, the terms 'grotesque' and 'arabesque'. In this context, the grotesque is a 'pleasant confusion' of incongruous elements; thus the bizarre mixture which Schlegel refers to is an unthreatening one, and lacks, according to Kayser, 'the abysmal quality, the insecurity, the terror inspired by the disintegration of the world' (Kayser, 1957 [1981]: 52). This kind of grotesque stresses its relation to the fantastic. Indeed, it does retain a certain measure of the frightful, but this is not dominant. Hoffmann's Kleinzach, Dr Coppelius and even his wax dolls are horrifying, in a sense, but to a far lesser extent than, for instance, the Captain and the Doctor in Büchner's *Woyzeck*. All these figures are grotesque, but the latter are more threatening, because they stand closer to actuality; they are more familiar and their real existence is more likely.

Kayser points to the important role of the transformation process from the familiar to the bizarre, and refers to it as a major component of the feeling of terror evoked by the grotesque (Kayser, 1957 [1981]: 67). The more familiar the vantage-point, the greater the horror in seeing its transformation into the bizarre. The frame of reference of the Romantic grotesque, as it appears in Hoffmann's tales, belongs to the fantasy-world. Although sometimes chilling, the unreal is not as frightful as a more plausible horror: as the subject becomes more and more fantastic and remote from any familiar actuality, so its terrifying power lessens and its ludicrous potential grows. From the very beginning the grotesque subject tends to be located in a fantastic realm of witchcraft, romance and exoticism that ostensibly, at least, has no connection with actuality, bringing out its more ludicrous aspects.

Such programmatic musical pieces as the movement 'In the Hall of the Mountain King' from Grieg's music to *Peer Gynt*, 'The Dream of a Witches'

Sabbath' from Berlioz's *Symphonie fantastique* and Mussorgsky's 'Baba Yaga' from *Pictures at an Exhibition*, as well as his *Night on the Bare Mountain*, exhibit ludicrous traits. In all of them the three elements of the ludicrous, the fantastic and the horrifying are combined so that their fairy-tale side over-rules any real fear they might evoke.

However, there are musical pieces called simply 'grotesques', without having any specific subject, which share the same musical traits. Such are Stravinsky's second movement from *Trois Pièces pour Quatuor à Cordes* (1914) or Bartók's 'Grotesque Portrait' from his *Two Portraits* op. 5 (1911).

The musical elements that are common to all these musical pieces are a tendency to triple metre, which enhances the feeling of whirling, uncontrollable motion, sudden unexpected outbursts, loud dynamics, extreme pitches, marked rhythmical stresses, dissonances or distortions of expected harmonic progressions, and many repetitions of simple and short patterns. These traits not only contribute to the sweeping atmosphere, but also enhance a feeling of compulsive obsession that relates to the insane, bizarre side of the grotesque and to its unreal, unnatural aspects.

The lack of boundaries

The particularity of the fantastic in the grotesque lies in its being part of a hybrid: that is, the boundaries between fantasy and reality are not only blurred, but seem to be non-existent. Moreover, it is not only these kinds of boundaries that seem to be missing from the grotesque, but all boundaries, too, seems to be blurred. Thus the difference between human, animal and vegetable is often unclear, as is the difference between the animate and inanimate. Doors sing, horses run backwards and pieces of furniture move by themselves in Gogol's *Evenings near Dikanka*, a wax doll comes to life in Hoffmann's Dr Coppelius episode, cockerels play the guitar and the violin in Chagall's pictures, and Gregor Samsa, in Kafka's *Metamorphosis*, wakes up in the morning only to realize that during the night he has become a huge insect.

The lack of boundaries between the familiar and the unfamiliar evokes a feeling of horror when we realize that such a transformation has occurred (Kayser, 1957 [1981]: 61). What is appalling is not the aberration in itself, but the natural, almost imperceptible way in which the transformation often takes place. Therefore, the more gradual the process of transformation, the more the grotesque phenomenon loses its ludicrous aspects and becomes a source of anxiety. Perhaps this is why gradual musical processes that involve crescendo, accelerando and a gradual pitch ascent are so effective in creating the impression of a grotesque, particularly when combined with obsessive repetitions.

Technically, the lack of boundaries means a distortion of something familiar in that the boundary between 'being itself' and 'not being itself' is blurred. This implies not only the knowledge of the familiar entity in question, but also a feeling of what is a distortion, and how it can be differentiated from a mere change that does not cause a trespassing of the entity's defining boundaries to the extent that it ceases to be itself. Not every distortion will result in a grotesque; thus, in order to understand the grotesque it is important to examine the concept of 'distortion' and the ways in which processes of transformation take place:

> Things may be distorted (i.e. changed for the worse) in many ways, and not all of these ways are grotesque. We must ask what has been distorted, how, and to what end. If everything exaggerated or eccentric is to be considered grotesque, the concept becomes so broad as to be virtually meaningless. (Jennings, 1963: 5)

Jennings's questions necessarily relate to a familiar norm, from which a deviation (in this case, a distortion) can occur (ibid.). The norm Jennings is referring to is the human body, the human face, human natural rhythms and measures (ibid.: 6). According to this approach, when an entity does not fit comfortably into these norms, it is perceived as 'the norm being distorted': 'There seems to be a basic grotesqueness ... in the figures often seen in any irregular shapes, such as ink-blots, gnarled branches and roots, clouds, rock formations' (ibid.: 7–8).[9] Thus the degree of grotesqueness is related to the distance by which an entity is separated from a physical human norm, on which it is projected. This is true of an entity's forms as well as its motion: a too fast tempo, too high pitch, too heavy, or irregular, steps, etc. – each and every one of these may point towards a purport of the grotesque.

Consequently, a grotesque distortion is a gradual transformation of a physical human norm towards whatever is non-human, either in its shape or in its motion. However, while in pictorial art the very superimposition of two incongruent entities may result in a grotesque (as long as at least one of them can be related to some human physical norm), literature and music need the presentation of a norm first, thus requiring time for the process of distortion. Thus the element of time, which allows transformation to occur as a process, is of utmost importance for the musical grotesque.

Such transformation through time particularly affects the blurring of boundaries between different, often contradictory emotions. Thus Verdi's Rigoletto evokes laughter, in the first scene of the opera, then fear, and, finally, a boundless mixture of compassion and disgust, as do similar figures, like Hugo's Quasimodo, in *The Hunchback of Notre-Dame*, and Umberto Eco's Salvatore from *The Name of the Rose*. Almost dehumanized when presented as ludicrous (particularly by his heteroglossial speech) and physically repelling as a monster, Salvatore is transformed, after the inquisition-session, into a miserable, tortured, martyrized human being.

In music we find such a figure in Verdi's Rigoletto. His grotesqueness is most markedly described in two dramatic turning-points of the opera: in his first meeting with Sparafucile and in his search for his daughter. Rigoletto's unexpected meeting with Sparafucile, the mercenary assassin, is loaded with dramatic tension. However, in contrast to the prevailing feelings of humiliation, anger, hatred and revenge, the music is in a major key, almost hopping lightheartedly (Ex. 10.4).

Ex. 10.4
The 'background music' to Rigoletto's conversation with the murderer Sparafucile is incongruently (*and* ambiguously!) lighthearted

Yet the very same musical excerpt also correlates with Rigoletto's limping. The continuously eerie impression is achieved by the incongruities between the chilling scene, which contains the seeds of a murder, and Rigoletto's farcical, clownish movement, which simultaneously reminds us of his physical disability, shame and suffering.

The boundaries between merriment and frenzy are also often blurred in the grotesque. This happens particularly when the element of horror takes the lead: the grotesque deformities in the beggars' supper in Luis Buñuel's film *Viridiana* (1961) are terrifying rather than ludicrous.[10] Merriment also turns into frenzy in the beggars' wedding-dance from *Haddybuk*.[11] This opposition between sane gaiety and insane frenzy was particularly developed in expressionistic works of literature, art and music.

The grotesque, in this case, will be achieved by a gradual distortion of 'normal' behaviour. However, since a clear definition of insanity is practically non-existent, there is no clear-cut boundary between eccentric behaviour (what some people would even call 'genial') and insanity. When an eccentric behaviour, with all the revulsion it usually arouses, provokes laughter, it becomes grotesque.

The figure of the captain in Berg's *Wozzeck* is such a grotesque: although there is more than a tinge of insanity in his generally buffoon-like presentation, he is perceived at the beginning of the opera as ludicrous. This changes gradually during the work, at the end of which his power to abuse Wozzeck is horrifying, while the ludicrous is diminished to the slightest hint. It is rather hard to take seriously the grotesque figure that keeps parroting philosophical clichés in an awkward parody of bel-canto melodic lines (Ex. 10.5).

Ex. 10.5

An exaggerated parody of bel-canto starts as a ludicrous grotesque

However, as the scene develops, the captain's apparently mischievous remarks, quickly ascending to the high-pitched falsetto trill and then skipping aimlessly in large intervals, give more than a hint of insanity (Ex. 10.6).

Ex. 10.6

The grotesque becomes more and more ominous, bordering on insanity

Finally, as his emotional abuse of Wozzeck becomes evident, the ludicrous figure acquires an ominous overtone. The sudden falsetto outbursts are transformed from a farcical expression of madness into a threatening signal of danger. The same thing happens with the doctor, who appears in the fourth scene. At first his figure seems an object for satire, but gradually his ominous and megalomanic cruelty becomes apparent, and the ridicule of his obsession with his scientific theory becomes a chilling awareness of its horrible results.

In the second act of *Wozzeck* there is a genuine satirical scene that could put into the shade many *commedia dell'arte* stage-situations. The doctor and the captain meet. The doctor, obssessed by his professional aspirations, promptly examines the captain's complexion, concluding with the unshakable diagnosis of a lethal illness: the captain is obviously suffering from *apoplexia cerebri*, and is soon going to die a terrible death, after being paralysed for a while, as the doctor takes pains to describe in thorough detail.

Berg indicated that the following phrase, taken from this grotesque scene, should be performed as 'a swinging waltz':

Ex. 10.7
A horrifying instance of insanity is expressed in a waltzing grotesquerie

A totally different dramatic situation in which cruel frenzy is mixed with merriment happens in Shostakovich's opera *Lady Macbeth of the Mtsensk District*, where Aksinya, the servant-girl, is brutally attacked by a group of servant-men, as a part of their leisure-games. The shrieks of Aksyinia, who is screaming hysterically for help, are rhythmically intertwined with the men's laughter and obvious enjoyment, so that all the different pieces of information – horror, amusement and cruelty – become one amalgam, the rhythmical, dance-like sound of a frenzied grotesque.

Following German Expressionism, which emphasized the lack of boundaries between sanity and insanity, the Russian engagement with this particular aspect of the grotesque grew, too. However, it seems that it was mostly related to a growing interest in Dostoevsky's writings, particularly in those that dug into the depth of the human split personality. Dostoevsky's shorter novels that deal with these questions, like *Notes from the Underground* and *The Double*, became a focus of interest for Dostoevsky scholars. The analysis of and enquiry into the compound personalities of Dostoevsky's characters, who did not seem to differentiate between reality and hallucination, were the source of Bakhtin's ideas of heteroglossia and unfinalizability. These ideas clearly present the connection between his two main subjects of research – Dostoevsky's 'plurivocality' and the Rabelaisean carnival – as centred on the grotesque.

The grotesque as a folk-art form

The grotesque appears in primitive art and in folklore in various forms: myths, masks, dances, rites, extravagant poetic imagery, dramatic representation and literary descriptions, ranging from folk tales to dramatic improvisations such as the *commedia dell'arte*.

By the turn of the nineteenth century the Western world seemed to be fascinated by primitive art; this almost obsessive occupation with the 'primitive', taken in its broadest sense, covers almost every subject that is rooted in the aboriginal cultures of pre-Christian Europe.

Vast folklore research was done all over Europe: the first modern research on myths and folk-tales was performed by the Russian Vladimir Propp, who followed less meticulously analysed anthologies like those of the Grimm brothers in Germany and Alexander Afanasyev in Russia. In music, large ethnomusicological collections were compiled by Bartók and Kodály in Hungary, the Balkans and North Africa, by Vaughan Williams in Britain, by Yoel Engel in Russia, and by Zvi Idelsohn in Russia, Germany and Palestine.

Myths and folk-tales appeared not only in literature, poetry and drama, but also in art, ballet and music: Stravinsky's ballets *The Firebird* and *The Rite of Spring*, Prokofiev's *Scythian Suite*, Sibelius's *Kullervo*, Ravel's *Daphnis and Chloe* and Stravinsky's *Oedipus Rex* are the most obvious examples of the late nineteenth and early twentieth century's use of those themes. Other expressions of this yearning after the ancient and authentic are expressed in the renewed scholarly interest in medieval times and in the Renaissance. Studies of Boccaccio, Rabelais and Cervantes expressed this trend as much as the artistic tendency to popular folk-like forms of entertainment, such as the circus and the *commedia dell'arte*. Clowns and *commedia dell'arte* masks became a favourite subject in the arts as well as in poetry, like Albert Giraud's *Pierrot Lunaire* and Aleksander Blok's *Balaganchik*. This trend was also apparent in symbolistic, expressionistic and modern dramatic plays and in music, regardless of its style: *commedia dell'arte* characters abide in Schönberg's expressionistic setting of the *Pierrot Lunaire* song-cycle as well as Stravinsky's neo-classical *Pulcinella* suite and the collage-like *Petrouchka* ballet, and Prokofiev's *The Love of Three Oranges*, which was suggested to him as a subject for an opera by Meyerhold (Braun, 1969: 116).

Russian playwrights and theatre directors displayed a clear preference for the *commedia dell'arte*, particularly in the years immediately preceding and after the Revolution (Worrall, 1989: 1–3). Blok's *Balaganchik* (1906), Meyerhold's production of *Columbine's Scarf* (1916) and Vakhtangov's production of Gozzi's *Turandot* (1922) were just the tip of an iceberg that included productions and works that were related to the *commedia dell'arte* in all the fields of art. After the Revolution, the great importance that was given to theatre, going far beyond its relative share among the arts, further encouraged this trend. The theatre as a mass-education tool was quickly put to use by the Soviet authorities. The reason for this was a new political and social situation in which a vast audience, most of which was illiterate, practically flooded the theatre halls: factory workers, soldiers and peasants were given free access to theatre productions that soon became their sole cultural source (Clark, 1995: 75–79). According to the new instructions, the theatre should appeal to all the people, and therefore it should be 'as simple as ABC' (Rudnitsky, 1988: 41).

Theatre was expected to be based on popular folk materials and techniques of entertainment. This request for an appeal based on popular entertainment had two main outcomes: the first was manifested in the almost constant use of the most popular forms of entertainment, such as circus-like shows that involved clowns and acrobats; these were to be not only the basic material for new plays, but were also intertwined in existing plays (Clark, 1995: 110); the second outcome was the agitprop plays, the text of which was based on slogans and shouts in the style of newspaper headlines. The theatre became practically a part of life, and mass spectacles, in which a large part of the citizens of a city took part, became the rule rather than the exception (ibid.: 128–129). A famous example, based almost entirely on slogans, mass action and circus shows of clowns, acrobats and even tamed animals, was Vladimir Mayakovsky's play *Mystery-Bouffe* (1918), which was planned for the celebration of the first anniversary of the Revolution. The extent to which artless simplicity was interchanged with folklore is manifested in Rudnitsky's report of the play as based on 'old folkloric tradition' (Rudnitsky, 1988: 42).

The lowly comic, the farce and the burlesque, and their Russian counterpart, the *balagan*, were popular among the Soviet directors and artists, who were encouraged to use the grotesque as a genuine expression of the people's spirit and reflect it in the form of mass entertainment. However, not all the productions that allegedly appealed to the popular taste did so: for instance, Alexander Blok's play *Balaganchik* (*The Puppet-Show*, 1906) is a sophisticated work of symbolistic poetry that uses the grotesque to express a far from popular existential standpoint. The play, which was the first milestone in the presentation of the grotesque as an independent subject in the Russian theatre, was staged in 1907 by Meyerhold, who also played in it the role of Pierrot.[12]

In many cases it seems indeed that Soviet artists used the folk element of the grotesque as a pretext to continue with their artistic work as undisturbed as possible.[13] Characters from the *commedia dell'arte* and circus clowns, which could be perceived as folk-grotesquerie, often served in the Soviet theatre in a double role expressing other, less authorized, artistic purports, such as the Bakhtinian idea of the infinite freedom and unfinalizability of a subject. The formal reason for the use of these characters in theatre performances, given as an interest in the revival of Russian folklore and popular ways of entertainment, was not necessarily the real, or at least not the sole, reason for the Russian artists' fascination with the grotesque that seemed to saturate Russian art in the first three decades of the century. Folk idioms, allegedly serving the cause of enhancing popular culture but actually dealing with the more ominous purports of the grotesque, were used by Vakhtangov in his *Haddybuk* production, and, many years later, by Shostakovich in his Piano Quintet, Second Piano Trio, Eighth String Quartet and the song-cycle *From Jewish Folk Poetry*. These works, hiding behind the mask of interest in the people's genuine spirit, go far beyond popular taste and focus on other problems.

Theatre directors like Meyerhold and Vakhtangov developed 'theories of the Grotesque': Vakhtangov, in a discussion with the actors of his studio in

1922, spoke about 'imaginative realism', which was his own term for the grotesque (Vakhtangov, 1982: 155–158) and Meyerhold, in his article 'The Fairground Booth' ('Balaganchik'), spoke about the grotesque as the basis of his theatrical technique (Braun, 1969: 119–142). After he has quoted the definition of the grotesque from the Russian *Bolshaya Entsiklopedia*, he exclaims: 'This is the style which reveals the most wonderful horizons to the creative artist' (ibid.: 137).

It is possible that Blok's choice of *commedia dell'arte*'s masks and a puppet-show context for his play is rooted in the split personality, the double, the unfinalizability that is more related to Bakhtin's ideas about the carnivalesque than to any interest in folk culture (Westphalen, 1992 and 1993). However, it should be remembered that Bakhtin's theories about unfinalizability were formalized much later, during the 1930s (Emerson and Morson, 1990: 66). Therefore, it seems more plausible that it is the grotesque character of the *commedia dell'arte* protagonists, and particularly their asso-ciation, in Russian folk-theatre tradition, with puppets that has made the *commedia dell'arte* a favourite subject for Russian grotesque. The puppets' lack of boundaries between life and death, the animate and inanimate, the human and the mechanized had thus a particular appeal for the Russian theatre, which regarded the grotesque as its aesthetic ideal.

CHAPTER ELEVEN

The satirical grotesque

While the grotesque deals with the unresolvable, satire has corrective ends. The grotesque presents defects that are beyond control, such as physical deformities. While satire arouses laughter that is rooted in contempt, the grotesque provokes feelings of horror and disgust, mixed with a helpless despair.

However, there is a kind of satire that makes use of the grotesque. In this kind the apparently incorrigible physical deformities function as reflections of some other spiritual and behavioural deformities, which are the actual object of the derisive comment.

Two layers of expression are created as a result: the grotesque is the first, immediately visible, ostensible one: a mechanically moving person (as was Tackleton in Vakhtangov's production of Dickens's *The Cricket on the Hearth*); an unnaturally ugly old man, each feature of whom seems to be grabbing or concealing something (as is Plyushkin in Gogol's *Dead Souls*), or a beautiful ballerina that is a cardboard figure (as was Columbine in Meyerhold's production of Blok's *Balaganchik*). Nevertheless, there is a second, satirical layer, in which the behavioural faults that are insinuated by the physical grotesque characteristics require correction: Tackleton's stiffness, Plyushkin's avarice and Columbine's insensitivity. The women at the governor's ball in Gogol's *Dead Souls* are fat, and apparently this is the main vehicle for describing their grotesqueness:

> Длинные перчатки были надеты не вплоть до рукавов, но обдуманно оставляли обнаженными возбудительные части рук повыше локтя, которые у многих дышали завидною полнотою; у иных даже полнули лайковые перчатки, побужденные надвинуться далее … (Гоголь, 1842 [1953]: 169)

> The long gloves were not drawn up as far as the sleeves, but purposely left bare those alluring parts of the arm above the elbow that in many of the ladies were of an enviable plumpness; some ladies had even split their kid gloves in the effort to pull them up as far as possible … (Gogol, 1842 [1961]: 173)

However, the satire is not on the fat, but on the women's coquettish presumption that it is the way of dressing that tempts men:

> Эти 'скромности' скрывали напереди и сзади то, что уже не могло нанести гибели человеку, а между тем заставляли подозревать, что там-то именно и была самая погибель. (Гоголь, 1842 [1953]: 169)

These 'modesties' concealed in front and in the back what could not possibly bring about a man's ruin and yet made one suspect that it was there that final disaster lay. (Gogol, 1842 [1961]: 173)

The other satirized trait is the aspiration 'not to look provincial':

Словом, кажется, как будто на всём было написано: нет, это не губерния, это столица, это сам Париж! Только местами вдруг высовывался какой-нибудь невиданный землею чепец или даже какое-то чуть не павлиное перо в противность всем модам, по собственному вкусу. (Гоголь, 1842 [1953]: 169–170)

In short, it was as if everything had been inscribed with the legend: 'No, this is not a provincial town! This is the capital city! This is Paris itself!' Only here and there a bonnet of a shape never seen on earth before, or some feather that might have been a peacock's, was thrust out in defiance of all fashion and in accordance with individual taste. (Gogol, 1842 [1961]: 173)

The description of the landowners from whom Chichikov purchases the dead souls renders a series in which the grotesque is used for satirizing purposes. One of the most effective of these is the description of Plyushkin, whose avarice has made him a name among all his fellow-landowners. After a long and detailed description of the dirty sitting-room of his house, in the centre of which an incredible amount of rubbish, collected by the owner, is piled up, there is a description of Plyushkin himself:

Лицо его не представляло ничего особенного; оно было почти такое же, как у многих худощавых стариков, один подбородок только выступал очень далеко вперёд, так что он должен был всякий раз закрывать его платком, чтобы не заплевать; маленькие глазки ещё не потухнули и бегали из-под высоко выросших бровей, как мыши, когда, высунувши из тёмных нор остренькие морды, насторожа уши и моргая усом, они высматривают, не затаился ли где кот или шалун мальчишка, и нюхают подозрительно самый воздух. (Гоголь, 1842 [1953]: 120)

His face was not anything out of the ordinary; indeed, it was practically like that of the faces of many gaunt old men, except that his chin jutted out rather a lot, so that he had always to cover it with his handkerchief to avoid spitting on it; his tiny eyes had not yet gone dim with age and kept darting about under his beetling brows like mice when, poking their sharp noses out of their dark holes, pricking up their ears and twitching their whiskers, they look around carefully to see whether a cat or a mischievous boy is lying in wait for them, and suspiciously sniff the air. (Gogol, 1842 [1961]: 125)

This lengthy description of Plyushkin's face, and especially of his eyes, mixes their human nature with that of mice, to the point that the reader begins to forget that the description is related to a human being. This mixture between the human and the animal is quite characteristic of the grotesque. However, this is not yet a satire, because nothing in it can be changed. It is only in the following lines that the satirical aim of the grotesque is slowly but persistently revealed:

Я давненько не вижу гостей, – сказал он, – да, – признаться сказать, в них мало вижу проку. Завели пренеприличный обычай ездить друг к другу, а в хозяйстве-то упущения ... да и лошадей их корми сеном! Я давно уж отобедал, а кухня у меня низкая, прескверная, и труба-то совсём развалилась: начнёшь топить, ещё пожару наделаешь. (Гоголь, 1842 [1953]: 126)

'I haven't had visitors for a long time,' he said, 'and, to tell the truth, I don't see much use in them. We've introduced a most unseemly custom of visiting one another and as a consequence there's a terrible neglect in the management of our estates and – er – besides, they expect you to provide hay for their horses, too. I had my dinner a long time ago and my kitchen is, anyway, rather mean and in a very bad state, the chimney, too, has practically fallen to pieces: light the stove and you will burn the place down.' (Gogol, 1842 [1961]: 130)

Satirical grotesque in music would be, then, a musical correlative of a behaviour or an attitude that can be described in physical terms, and that is to be regarded in a derisive way. This exclusive limitation to musical correlatives of physical manifestations necessarily leads towards musical correlatives of motion: dances, marches, chases, etc. In Western culture, the preferred mode of motion is one of moderate and consistent pace and range, generally quiet, restrained and refined. Thus an extremely fast pace, or a pace that suddenly and inconsistently changes, extremely large gestures, and a generally unrestrained mood will be correlated not only with ridiculous clumsiness, but also with vulgarity and coarseness.

The description of the ball at the governor's house in Gogol's *Dead Souls* is a complex construction of a sweeping crescendo, which begins with slight irony and arrives at a nightmarish whirlpool of crowded motion, achieved by carefully calculated shifts from one mode to another. The description itself, which moves from the crowd as a whole, to a small group, to Chichikov himself, and back, without any apparent order, creates a general impression of chaotic motion. The grotesque is transmitted by little hints, here and there, gradually transforming an apparently satirical passage into an overcrowded, hellish grotesquerie. The first hints of the grotesque are already given in the description of Chichikov's preparations for the ball, although it is satirical irony that is mainly emphasized here:

Целый час был посвящён только на одно рассматривание лица в зеркале. Пробовалось сообщить ему множество разных выражений: то важное и степенное, то почтительное, но с некоторою улыбкою, то просто почтительное без улыбки; отпущено было в зеркало несколько поклонов в сопровождении неясных звуков, отчасти похожих на французские, хотя по-французски

Чичиков не знал вовсе. Он сделал даже самому себе множество
приятных сюрпризов, подмигнул бровью и губами и сделал кое-
что даже языком; ... надевая подтяжки или повязывая галстук,
он расшаркивался и кланялся с особенною ловкостию и хотя
никогда не танцовал, но сделал антраша. Это антраша произвело
маленькое невинное следствие: задрожал комод, и упала со
стола щетка. (Гоголь, 1842 [1953]: 167)

A whole hour was devoted solely to the examination of his face in the
looking-glass. He tried to assume a multitude of various expressions:
one moment he tried to look grave and important, another moment
respectful but with the ghost of a smile, then simply respectful without a
smile; a number of bows were made to the looking-glass, accompanied
by inarticulate sounds remotely resembling French, though Chichikov
did not know French at all. He even gave himself a number of pleasant
surprises, winking an eye and twitching a lip, and even did something
with his tongue ... he bowed and scraped with particular adroitness, and
though he had never danced in his life, he executed an *entrechat*. This
entrechat produced a small and harmless effect: the chest of drawers
shook and the brush fell from the table. (Gogol, 1842 [1961]: 171–172)

This mildly benevolent satirical description immediately gives way to an
overwhelming, ever-increasing grotesque tumult:

Появление его на бале произвело необыкновенное действие. Всё,
что ни было, обратилось к нему навстречу ... 'Павел Иванович!
Ах боже мой, Павел Иванович! Любезный Павел Иванович!
Почтеннейший Павел Иванович! Душа моя Павел Иванович! Вот
вы где, Павел Иванович! Вот он, наш Павел Иванович! Позвольте
прижать вас, Павел Иванович! Давайте-ка его сюда, вот я его
поцелую покрепче, моего дорогого Павла Ивановича!' Чичиков
разом почувствовал себя в нескольких объятиях. Не успел совершенно
выкарабкаться из объятий председателя, как очутился уже в
объятиях полицеймейстера; полицеймейстер сдал его инспектору
врачебной управы; инспектору врачебной управы – откупшику,
откупшик – архитектору ... (Gogolw, 1842 [1953]: 167–168)

His arrival at the ball created an extraordinary sensation. Everyone there
turned round to look at him ... 'Mr Chichikov! Good Heavens, Mr
Chichikov! Dear Mr Chichikov! Most honourable Mr Chichikov! My
dear Mr Chichikov! So here you are at last, Mr Chichikov! There he is,
our dear Mr Chichikov! Bring him here and let me give him a big kiss,
my dear, dear Mr Chichikov!' Chichikov felt himself embraced by several people all at once. He had barely time to extricate himself from the
president's embrace, when he found himself in the arms of the chief of
police; the chief of police handed him over to the inspector of public
health, the inspector of public health to the government contractor, the
government contractor to the architect ... (Gogol, 1842 [1961]: 172)[1]

From this description of disordered accumulation, which just touches the
abnormal (the mechanical exulted repetition of his name and the ludicrous
details that follow, which recall frantic descriptions of football-games), Gogol

continues with the dance itself. Gradually, and as if casually, he inserts expressions (such as 'whirling madly', 'steps such as no one had ever executed in his wildest dreams' and, again, 'something not of this earth') which transform the ball from a simple satire to a grotesque picture, bordering on insanity:

Галопад летел во всю пропалую: почтмейстерша, капитан-исправник, дама с голубым пером, дама с белым пером, грузинский князь Чипхайхилидзев, чиновник из Петербурга, чиновник из Москвы, француз Куку, Перхуновский, Беребендовский – всё поднялось и понеслось ...

Почтмейстерша, вальсируя, с такой томностию опустила набок голову, что слышалось в самом деле что-то неземное. Одна очень любезная дама, – которая приехала вовсе не с тем, чтобы танцовать, по причине приключившегося, как сама выразилась, небольшого инкомодите в виде горошинки на правой ноге, вследствие чего должна была даже надеть плисовые сапоги, – не вытерпела, однако же, и сделала несколько кругов в плисовых сапогах, для того именно, чтобы почтмейстерша не забрала в самом деле слишком много себе в голову ...

Четыре пары откалывали мазурку; каблуки ломали пол, и армейский штабс-капитан работал и душою и телом, и руками и ногами, отвертывая такие па, какие и во сне никому не случалось отвертывать. (Гоголь 1842 [1953]: 170–175)

The galop was at its height: the postmaster's wife, the police captain, a lady with a pale blue feather, a lady with a white feather, the Georgian prince, Chipkhaykhilidzev, an official from Petersburg, an official from Moscow, a Frenchman called Coucou, Perkhunovsky, Berebendovsky, all were whirling madly in the dance ...

When she waltzed, the postmaster's wife put her head on one side so languorously that she really gave the impression of something not of this earth. One very amiable lady who had come with no idea of dancing at all because, as she herself expressed it, of a slight *incommodité* in the shape of a corn on her right foot as a result of which she was even obliged to put on plush boots, could not, however, resist joining in the dance and taking a few turns in her plush boots to make sure that the postmaster's wife did not take it into her head to think too much of herself ...

And already four couples were dashing off a mazurka, their heels crashing down on the floor, and an army major was working so hard with arms and legs, body and soul, executing steps such as no one had ever executed even in his wildest dreams. (Gogol, 1842 [1961]: 171–178)

Dance, in Western culture, is associated with lightness and grace. Whatever clashes with this basic assumption will be perceived as a grotesque. A grotesque dance, then, is the antonym of a refined dance. As such it is heavy, clumsy and exaggerated.

It is not a coincidence, then, that Gogol chose for his ball in *Dead Souls* the galop, the mazurka and the waltz. The galop is known as a fast, rather hectic dance, which is historically and socially connected with the quadrille and later with the can-can (Lamb, 1980: 133). As such, it is perhaps the most apt for grotesque descriptions of a jumbled, chaotic dance. The mazurka is not necessarily hectic, but its changing metrical stress and its rather fast tempo allow some associations of heaviness with it, too, that again point to disorderly confusion. It is not a coincidence that the waltz itself is not described in the text, apart from the 'languid' way in which the ladies danced it, which is more satirical than grotesque.

Popular social dances are often used, sometimes distorted, in musical compositions the purport of which is the satirical grotesque. The can-can appears in Offenbach's *Orpheus in the Underworld* as a satire in itself, and is further satirized by Saint-Saëns in his grotesque 'Elephants' Dance', from his *Carnaval des animaux*; it is not a coincidence that the can-can appears in fine art with grotesque connotations, such as in the pictures by Toulouse-Lautrec. Coarse, almost violent dances also appear in Haydn's and Beethoven's third movements, in Weber's *Der Freischütz*, and later in Alban Berg's *Wozzeck*, where the waltz, danced in the tavern, signals the starting-point of a violent attack that will end only in another hellish dance – the polka danced in the same tavern, after Maria's murder. Shostakovich has countless grotesque distortions of social dances, not only in his ballets, operas and music for films; heavy galops, polkas and waltzes abound in his instrumental works, too, where the influence of Mahler's grotesque waltzes and marches on his music is evident.

For Shostakovich, these dances are always connected with high tension and even with a certain amount of violence: an escape, a chase or a frantic motion that was caused by some horrible, even if undefinable, threat. A comparison between his galop at the sixth scene of *The Nose* and three samples of Johann Strauss's galops immediately displays the difference in approach (Ex. 11.1).

Strauss writes light, amusing galops: the tempo is 'a tempo of galop': about $\downarrow$ = 120. The dynamics are piano. The pitch-range never exceeds the middle of the third octave, and mostly resides within the first and second octaves. The accompaniment figures tend to change, in pitch as well as in their pattern, every few bars, so the ostinato background, which is a necessary element for the dance, does not become a source of tension. On the other hand, Shostakovich's galop accompanying Kovalyev to the police-station where he reports the loss of his nose is one of the earliest examples of the composer's characteristic musical correlative of violence: a duple meter, fast tempo, always in fortissimo, and almost always accompanied by a heavy, stamping accompaniment of quavers; the first of each beat stays always in the bass, while the second is in a higher register, like the characteristic accompaniment pattern of a galop. However, Shostakovich is not satisfied with the

Ex. 11.1
A comparison between Strauss's galops and Shostakovich's galop in *The Nose*

The comparison shows the difference in approach: while Strauss aims at a light and swift impression, Shostakovich repeats bass note, writes a fortissimo dynamics, asks for an extremely fast tempo and an extreme pitch-range. All these distort and exaggerate the characteristic traits of the galop and, using the musical correlatives of violence, create a heavy, frenzied grotesque caricature.

mere change of elements like dynamics and tessitura in order to shift his galop to the grotesque–violent side. His four bars of introduction, mockingly imitating the topical galop introductions, caricature the element of tension and 'fall to the start' evoked in the originals by giving a very tense note – an A♭ in the fourth octave, fortissimo, which literally 'falls', in a huge glissando, to his heavy galop accompaniment. This is distorted, too: the bass notes are not only lower than Strauss's, but also repeat themselves at the very same pitch throughout the whole galop, evoking the heavy, violent and almost insanely compulsive Gogolian impression of 'heels crashing down on the floor … as no one had ever executed even in his wildest dreams'.

Ex. 11.2
The characteristic galop accompaniment as a musical correlative of violence

A. In Vocal Works

The Chase: end of the 8th scene from *The Nose*

The crowd, furiously chasing after the nose, screams on the second quaver of each beat the word 'Где?' ('Where?').

The rape of Aksynia from *Lady Macbeth from the Mtsensk District*

Aksinya is raped by the workers of the farm. Her scream is replied by their laughter, in quavers coinciding
with the orchestral accompaniment.

The Servants bidding farewell in *Lady Macbeth from the Mtsensk District*

The servants burst in a mocking-sorrowful exclamation: 'Why are you leaving us, master?' The bass drum
and timpani join the basses, in the first beat of each bar, creating a particularly heavy mock-waltz.

The pogrom scene, 1st movement of the 13th Symphony

'Blood is spattered over the floor,' sing the choir, on a melody which reminds a characteristic folk Russian
song. Here, too, the bass drum joins the heavy beats of the bar.

B. In Instrumental Works

Burlesque from the **1st Violin Concerto**

The violin solo supplies the first quaver of each beat, and then leaves it for the melody. The accompaniment, unchanged, sticks to the second quaver of each beat.

Finale from the **2nd Piano Trio**

While the piano performs the melodic line, the violoncello and violin create the typical accompaniment, each in large chords on all four strings, creating a particularly heavy effect.

3rd Movement from the **9th String Quartet**

The music gains impetus by the use of the accompaniment; the 1st violin begins on a *piano* dynamic, but grows into *forte* while the other instruments, in a similar way to the violin concerto, continue stamping the unstressed beats of each bar.

2nd Movement from the **10th Symphony**

Not only the violence of the chords, on the unstressed beats each, creates here the momentum, but also the sudden doubling of rhythmic values, both in the accompaniment and in the theme itself.

Such instances in the music of Shostakovich are always related to a purport of violence which, in his case, are almost as a rule connected with pictures of a racing, attacking mob. Thus many of his waltzes, polkas and galops are not only heavy, clumsy, and thus grotesque; the element of violence in them often exceeds that necessary for the grotesque and approaches a stage of frenzied insanity. The scenes of the crowd chasing the nose belong to this kind. Such are also the 'waltz of the servants', where the servants bid farewell to Zinoviy Borisovich Izmaylov, and the scene of the workers raping Aksinya, both in *Lady Macbeth of the Mtsensk District*. A similar instance is when the drunken mob performs a pogrom in the first movement of the Thirteenth Symphony. Even purely instrumental pieces, like the second movement of the Tenth Symphony, the scherzo of the Fifth String Quartet, the burlesque of the First Violin Concerto and the finale of the Second Piano Trio, provide many instances in which the violent purport of the music does not need any explicit, extra-musical explanation (Ex. 11.2).

Since the grotesque is the unresolvable hybrid of the ludicrous and the horrifying, emotional responses play a considerable part in its perception. Consequently, certain grotesque units can have two satirical layers: one on the subject of the grotesque, and the other on our own involuntary reaction which may fail to comply with our own norms. Laughter caused by repulsion from a stumbling drunkard, for example, is an instance of the first layer: the subject, whose appearance is both ludicrous and frightening, fails to comply with a certain norm, and is thus laughed at. The second layer is more complex, and involves an ironical self-contemplation and awareness of the nature of the reaction itself. If this reaction does not comply with a certain norm, for example the norm of compassion for the wretched drunkard, whose drunkenness is possibly the result of much suffering, then our very laughter, in itself, exposes a deficiency and thus can be satirized. In a satirical grotesque, the shift, in which the accusing finger, which first pointed to some element in the work, turns around to point at the reader, listener or spectator, happens suddenly, at the point at which we not only become aware of our own reaction, but also realize its normative inadequacy.

The grotesque object as the target of satire

The last song in Shostakovich's song-cycle *From Jewish Folk Poetry* is titled 'Schast'ye' ('Happiness'). However, nowhere in the text of the song does this word appear: the title is an ironic remark about the picture illustrated in the text, in the first person, by the Jewish cobbler's wife (which in itself is an ironic reversal of the Gogolian 'governor's wife' and 'postmaster's wife') who, so it seems, achieved the peak of happiness.[2]

Счастье	*Happiness*
Я мужа смело под руку взяла	I boldly took my husband's arm,
Пусть я стара, и стар мой кавалер	though I am old, and old is my beau.
Его с собой в театр повела	I took him to the theatre with me,
И взяли два билета мы в партер.	And we got two tickets for the stalls.
До поздней ночи с мужем сидя там,	Till late at night I sat there with my man,
Все предавались радостным местам,	All carried away with joyful dreams.
Какими благами окружена	What blessings surround
Еврейского сапожника жена.	a Jewish cobbler's wife!
Ой, Какими благами окружена	Oy, what blessings surround
Еврейского сапожника жена.	a Jewish cobbler's wife!
И всей стране хочу поведать я (Ой!)	And what I want to tell the whole land (Oy!)
Про радостный и светлый жребий мой: (Ой!)	About the joy and the light which is now my lot: (Oy!)
Врачами, врачами, наши стали сыновья (Ой!)	Doctors, doctors are what our sons have become, (Oy!)
Звезда горит над нашей головой! (Ой!)	A star shines over our heads.
Ой, ой, ой, ой,	Oy, oy, oy, oy,
Звезда горит, звезда горит	A star shines, a star shines
Звезда горит над нашей головой!	A star shines over our heads.
Врачами, врачами, наши стали сыновья	Doctors, doctors are what our sons have become.
Звезда горит над нашей головой!	A star shines over our heads.
Ой!	Oy!
	(Translation by Z. Weaver, Decca, 425069–2 1987)

According to the report of the cobbler's wife, a star is shining above her head, her sons became doctors (the traditional dream of the Jewish mother as it appears in characteristic Jewish jokes), and she is sitting with her husband in the theatre stalls, where everybody can see her. Indeed, who could ask for more?[3]

The full impact of the horror that is hidden beneath these entranced commentaries is revealed only gradually. The ordering of the lines is carefully calculated: first appears the satirical description of the empty pride and self-centredness of the cobbler's wife who 'boldly' drags her husband to the most expensive seats in the theatre, so she can fulfil her joyful daydreams. The statement about the sons who became doctors disturbs this mild satirical picture. In fact, this statement, uttered here with joyful assurance, had horrifying implications for the Jewish population in Russia in the years 1948–52. The original Yiddish text of the song speaks of 'engineers', but this was replaced by 'doctors', hinting perhaps at the Doctors' Plot of 1952, when more than four hundred Jewish intellectuals – doctors, artists and scholars – were arrested and executed on Stalin's orders.[4] The double meaning of this phrase, said with great pride and self-confidence, is especially chilling since the feeling of horror is embedded precisely in the sons' professional success, which was also the source of their misfortune (Braun, 1986). At this point of the text the satirical grin begins to fade, and a sense of horror creeps in. Allegedly, the star that 'shines over our heads' is a continuation of the protagonist's happy daydreaming. On a deeper layer, however, it bears ominous undertones as well as self-satirical double meanings: the first allusion is to the Jewish star, which was attached to the Jews' clothes in Nazi-ruled areas; the second allusion is to the symbol of the Soviet state, an idea that in itself bears satirizing (and self-satirizing) double meanings, since it also alludes to the 'blessing' of a star 'that shone in the East'. It is significant that the original Yiddish words are 'the sun shines over our heads'.[5] The ludicrous Jewish cobbler's wife becomes tragic in her unawareness of the real situation, of which the listener is fully aware.

Shostakovich enhances this feeling of the grotesque by a parody of a ceremonial march, stressing the inappropriateness of the woman's positive feelings as well as caricaturing the heaviness of her self-assured motion (Ex. 11.3).

Ex. 11.3
A heavy, self-confident accompaniment caricatures the self-assuredness of the poem's protagonist

In a middle section, as well as in the last verse, Shostakovich incorporated the Jewish 'Oy' in a musical contrast with the ceremonious heavy march.[6] A series of haunting harmonies of parallel chords is sung to this 'Oy', moving then to 'The star shines on our head', while the victorious exclamations, 'Doctors, doctors are what our sons have become!' are satirically accompanied by inane, 'optimistic' B♭ major chords (Ex. 11.4).

Satire on our reaction to the grotesque

The incongruity generated between laughter and horror, the two structural elements of the grotesque, and its dependence on emotional impact, often causes aesthetic responses to the grotesque to be ethically problematic. This incongruity between the two value-laden norm systems, the ethical and the aesthetic, may result in a satirical grotesque the object of which is the aesthetic approval it receives. Thus a subject who is aesthetically enjoying the grotesque may find that, simultaneously, a poignant satire is being made at his own expense.

Mikhail Bulgakov, with whom Shostakovich had a long-lasting friendship, wrote a short novel, titled *A Heart of a Dog* (1925), which presents a black

Ex. 11.4
The musical grotesque hovers between the ludicrous and the horrifying

satire about the ideals of the Soviet Revolution. Again, we witness the gradual transformation of what seems a mild satire on the poor physical conditions of the Soviet people in a blood-freezing scene in which a description of the Frankenstein-like scientist who, intending to prove his theory, transplants human testicles and pituitary gland into a dog, transforming it into what Bulgakov sees as the materialization of the ideal Soviet citizen: an illiterate drunkard and thief who makes progress up the Soviet's party ladder by cheating, stealing, blackmailing and lying while parroting phrases from Karl Marx's writings – in short, a creature with a human brain and a heart of a dog.

Two layers of satire are present here: the simpler one, which is direct and has very few grotesque implications, likens the Russian people to a dog that is willing to endure whatever humiliation or mistreatment for a little food:

Что такое? Кол-ба-су. Господин, если бы вы видели, из чего эту колбасу делают вы бы близко не подошли к магазину. Отдайте её мне!

Пес собрал остаток сил и в безумии пополз из подворотни на тротуар ... запах, победивший больницу, райский запах рубленой кобылы с чесноком и перцем ... О, мой властитель! Глянь на меня. Я умираю. Рабская наша душа, подлая доля! ... Y-Y-Y-Y ... Что ж это делается на белом свете? Видно, помирать-то ещё рано, а отчаяние, и подлинно, грех? Руки ему лизать, больше ничего не остается.

Загадочный господин ... отломил кусок колбасы, называемой 'Особенная Краковская'. И псу этот кусок! О, бескорыстная личность. Y-Y-Y-Y! ... Бери! Шарик, Шарик!

Опять 'Шарик'! Окрестили! Да называйте как хотите. За такой исключительный ваш поступок ... с всхлипыванием вгрызся в краковскую и сождал её в два счета ... Ещё, ещё лижу вам руку. Целую штаны, мой благодетель! ... Бок болел нестерпимо, но Шарик временами забывал о нем, поглощенный одною мыслью, как бы не утратить в сутолоке чудесного видения в шубе и чем-нибудь выразить ему любовь и преданность. И раз семь на протяжении Пречистенки до Обухова переулка он её выразил. Поцеловал в ботик, у Мертвого переулка, расчищая дорогу ... (Bulgakov, 1925 [1989]: 121–124)

What's that he's holding? Sausage. Look sir, if you knew what they put into that sausage you'd never go near that store. Better give it to me.

The dog gathered the last of his strength and crawled fainting out of the doorway on to the pavement ... The smell that overpowered the hospital smell was the heavenly aroma of minced horsemeat with garlic and pepper ... Oh, master! Look at me. I'm dying. I'm so wretched, I'll be your slave for ever! ... Oowow-owow ... What can I do? I'm too young to die yet and despair's a sin. There's nothing for it, I shall have to lick his hand. The mysterious gentleman ... broke off a piece of the sausage, which was labelled 'Special Cracower'. And gave it to the dog. Oh, immaculate personage! Oowow-oowow! ... 'Come on! Take it, Sharik!'

He's christened me Sharik too. Call me what you like. For this you can do anything you like to me ... Mouth watering, he bit into the Cracower and gobbled it down in two swallows. Tears started to his eyes ... Let me lick your hand again, I'll kiss your boots – you've saved my life ... His flank hurt unbearably, but for the moment Sharik forgot about it, absorbed by a single thought: how to avoid losing sight of this miraculous fur-coated vision in the hurly-burly of the storm and how to show him his love and devotion. Seven times along the whole length of Prechistenka Street as far as the cross-roads at Obukhov Street he showed it. At Myortvy Street he kissed his boot. (Bulgakov, 1925 [1968]: 10–11)

The other one is a chilling grotesque presentation of the creators of the Revolution, who with the best intentions tried to turn theories into human reality. Here the real grotesquerie of evil human nature comes into play, condemning all realizations of ideologies as monstrous scientific experiments. The grotesque of the operation scene is enhanced by the exaggeration and caricaturing of the doctors, while in the background are heard the sounds of 'Celeste Aïda', the scientist's favourite aria. There is nothing amusing in this gross description, although our reaction to it may well be nervous outbursts of laughter:

Зубы Филиппа Филипповича сжались, глазки приобрели остренький колючий блеск, и, взмахнув ножичком, он метко и длинно протянул по животу Шарика рану. Кожа тотчас разошлась, и из неё брызнула кровь в разные стороны. Борменталь набросился хищно, стал комьями марли давить Шарикову рану, затем маленькими, как бы сахарными, шипчиками зажал её края, и она высохла. На лбу у Борменталя пузырьками выступил пот. Филипп Филиппович полоснул второй раз, и тело Шарика вдвоем начали разрывать крючьями, ножницами, какими-то скобками. Выскочили розовые и жёлтые, плачущие кровавой росою ткани. Филипп Филиппович вертел ножом в теле, потом крикнул:

– Ножницы! ...

Один раз ударил тонкий фонтан крови, чуть не попал в глаза профессору и окропил его колпак. Борменталь с торзионным пинцетом, как тигр, бросился зажимать и зажал. Пот с Борменталя полз потоками, и лицо его стало мясистым и разноцветным. Глаза его метались от рук Филиппа Филипповича к тарелке на столе. Филипп же Филиппович стал положительно страшен. Сипение вырывалось из его носа, зубы открылись до десен. (Булгаков, 1925 [1989]: 155–157)

Philip Philipovich clenched his teeth, his eyes took on a sharp, piercing glint and with a flourish of his scalpel he made a long, neat incision down the length of Sharik's belly. The skin parted instantly, spurting blood in several directions. Bormenthal swooped like a vulture, began dabbing Sharik's wound with swabs of gauze, then gripped its edges with a row of little clamps like sugar-tongs, and the bleeding stopped. Droplets of sweat oozed from Bormenthal's forehead. Philip Philipovich made a second incision and again Sharik's body was pulled apart by hooks, scissors and little clamps. Pink and yellow tissues emerged, oozing with blood. Philip Philipovich turned the scalpel in the wound, then barked: 'Scissors!' ... Once a thin stream of blood spurted up, almost hitting the professor in the eye and spattering his white cap. Like a tiger Bormenthal pounced in with a tourniquet and squeezed. Sweat streamed down his face, which was growing puffy and mottled. His eyes flicked to and fro from the professor's hand to the instrument-table. Philip Philipovich was positively awe-inspiring. A hoarse snoring noise came from his nose, his teeth were bared to the gums. (Bulgakov, 1925 [1968]: 54–56)

Ex. 11.5
'Interlude' is the title of the scene that presents the rape of Aksinya in
Shostakovich's *Lady Macbeth of the Mtsensk District*

Bars 1-7: Aksinya: Ay! Ay! • Workers: What a voice!
(The repeated quavers in the orchestra purport a static tension; the repetition of Aksinya's voice, though, purports something ludicrous, almost amusing in its musicality.

Bars 36-44: Aksinya: Ay! Ay! • Workers: Ha, ha, ha, ha, ha! • Sergeii: Beautiful! Beautiful! • Workers: Go on! Go on!
(The repeated laughter becomes an amalgam of sound, almost a rythmic cluster. In this context, Sergeii's exclamation is almost a musical relief.)

Bars 69-74: Aksinya: Help! Help! • Workers: Ha, ha, ha, ha, ha!
(The tempo becomes *presto*, the orchestra conveys a melody that is in the register of screams.
The tune, however, is comfortably rhythmical and patterned. The accompaniment becomes galop-like.)

Bars 101-104: Workers: Go on, Aksinya! Go on, Seryozhka!
(The melody in the orchestra becomes more patterned, symmetrical, and comfortable in its circus-like character.)

Bars 161–184: Aksinya: Oy! • Workers: Ha, ha, ha, ha, ha! He is killing us with laughter, killing, killing! • Sergeii: Stand still! • Aksinya: Devil!
Workers: He had killed us with laughter! Ha, ha, ha, ha, ha!
(The crotchets' melody of the workers is built on a pattern similar to Russian folk songs, with its harmonic thirds and its skips of fourth and fifth.
Its clear pattern and symmetry, built on a folk-like A-A' pattern and based on sequence, adds to the comfort it purports.
After the former chaotic sounds this part sounds relaxing and almost inviting to join in with the singing.)

There certainly is satire here: satire on the Soviet environment, seen through the eyes of the dog, an allegorical satire on the Russian people seen as a dog, satire on the scientific zeal of experiment, regardless of ethical considerations. Yet an additional level is functioning here, one that satirizes our very aesthetic appreciation of this description (which is largely enhanced by the detailed report of visual elements, colours, motions and expressions) as a target for satire. The very experience of reading this passage satirizes our shocked enjoyment of the horrors.

The journalistic sources quoted in Lee Byron Jennings's study of the grotesque contain similar, inherently grotesque descriptions. Quite overtly, these make use of the term 'grotesque' as related to 'dead, dying or injured persons. Thus, a body struck by a car spins grotesquely, the feet of a dead man protrude grotesquely, a shooting victim collapses in a grotesque sitting position, and war dead lie in grotesque postures' (Jennings, 1963: 7). To this genre belong wartime 'casualty-jokes' and other manifestations of black humour, such as the graphic descriptions of physical mutilation in Joseph Heller's *Catch 22*. However, ludicrous representations of death and suffering also exist in more sophisticated works of art, such as the paintings of Hieronymus Bosch or the engravings of William Hogarth. The macabre grotesque appears in music as well, covering various degrees of complexity. Tom Lehrer sings to a waltz-melody tune an ostensible love-song: 'I hold your hand in mine, dear'. Only gradually does the listener understand that the hand, at its other end, is not attached to a body. A parody on love-songs, which seemed at the beginning to mock and satirize musical popular banalities, is gradually transformed into a grotesque scene of macabre humour. As a reaction we laugh, and then are embarrassed by this laughter, which *ethically* is inappropriate. Still, laughter at the macabre seems to be a necessary psychological device that helps us to confront and deal with the horrifying aspects of human life. In our laughter at the macabre, though, there is also an aspect of joining in, of a certain kind of delight (Clark, 1991: 2). Here music seems to play a major role, since it can sweep the listener into an empathetic participation in the ethically despicable. The rape scene in Shostakovich's *Lady Macbeth of the Mtsensk District* begins with the hysterical, almost ridiculous screams of Aksinya, the servant girl who is being attacked (Ex. 11.5).

The rhythmicity of the screams combined with the rhythmical accompaniment induces the listener into a paradoxical mood of disgust mingled with complacency. The real horror, however, lies in the fact that no feelings of contempt are aroused in the listener: due to the comfortable rhythm, the rising melody of the men's voices, in a folk-like tune, the listener is unconsciously tempted to empathize with the rapists rather than to the raped, whose insane, hysterical screams are, however, aesthetically repellent.

A similar scene takes place in the first movement of Shostakovich's Thirteenth Symphony, when a pogrom is described with no purport of the grotesque, but just with the bare, horrifying realization of complacency, of joining in a despicable event. The power of music to ignore moral considerations, and its potential to manipulate our feelings by our unconscious reactions of projection and empathy, is horrifying in itself.[7] The horror is not generated by the grotesque, but stems from the fact that we, by the contradictory reactions that are *evoked* by the grotesque, become aware of our own share, our psychological participation in the grotesque:

> Die groteske Welt ist unsere Welt – und ist es nicht. Das mit dem Lächeln gemischte Grauen hat seinen Grund eben in der Erfahrung, daß unsere vertraute und scheinbar in fester Ordnung ruhende Welt sich unter dem Einbruch abgründiger Mächte verfremdet, aus den Fugen und Formen gerät und sich in ihren Ordnungen auflöst. (Kayser, 1957: 38)

The grotesque world is – and is not – our own world. The ambiguous way in which we are affected by it results from our awareness that the familiar and apparently harmonious world is alienated under the impact of abysmal forces, which break it up and shatter its coherence. (Kayser, 1957 [1981]: 37)

CHAPTER TWELVE

The grotesque at the beginning of the twentieth century

In the first decades of the twentieth century art seems to be saturated with the grotesque. This trend originated mainly in Germany, where it was closely related to the expressionistic stream in literature and the arts. Plays written by Georg Büchner (1813–37), Frank Wedekind (1864–1918) and August Strindberg (1849–1912) were widely performed, particularly by the German theatre director Max Reinhardt (1873–1944). Interrelationship and mutual influence between the arts were particularly in vogue: Strauss's *Salome* (1903–5) and *Elektra* (1906–8) were influenced by Reinhardt's 1902 and 1903 productions of Wilde's and von Hofmannsthal's plays; Arnold Schönberg wrote his *Pelleas und Melisande* (1902–3) at the same period as Reinhardt's work on his 1904 production of Maeterlinck's play. Similarly, Alban Berg's *Wozzeck* (1917–22) was created when Reinhardt engaged in his own 1921 production of Büchner's *Woyzeck*. Berg's second opera, *Lulu* (1929–35), was also an adaptation of an expressionistic play – this time Wedekind's, which was directed by Reinhardt as well. The artists Oskar Kokoschka (1886–1980) and Wassily Kandinsky (1866–1944) both engaged in theatrical productions, and Edvard Munch (1863–1944) made the stage-setting for Reinhardt's 1906 Berlin production of Ibsen's *Ghosts*. Arnold Schönberg painted and was a member of the Blaue Reiter group of artists, and the painter Paul Klee (1879–1940) engaged in theatrical productions. This was also the time of the first expressionistic German films, the most outstanding of which was Carl Mayer's (1894–1944) *Das Kabinett des Dr Caligari* (1919), a macabre horror-story combining psychological and supernatural elements. Other expressionistic films in the same vein were Paul Wegener's *The Golem* (1920) and F.W. Murnau's *Nosferatu* (1922).

The paintings of George Grosz (1893–1959), Max Ernst (1891–1976) and Egon Schiele (1890–1918) reflect this trend as well. New philosophical ideas and aesthetic theories are intertwined, and extreme emotional expressions are overlapped and mixed with the Berlin alienated culture of the cabaret, as is described in Franz Werfel's (1890–1945) ironic lines:

Eucharistisch und tomistisch,	Eucharistic and Thomistic,
Doch daneben auch marxistisch,	And besides a bit Marxistic,
Teosophisch, kommunistisch,	Theosophistic, Communistic,
Gotisch leinstadt-dombau-mystisch,	Gothic-cathedral-religionistic,
Aktivistisch, erzbuddhistisch,	Activistic, Arch-buddhistic,

Überöstlich taoistisch,	Super-eastern-Taoistic,
Rettung aus der Zeit-Schlamatik	Saving-all-from-the-mess-we're-nistic,
Suchend in der Negerplastik,	Seeking truth in negro aesthetic,
Wort- und Barrikaden wälzend,	Constructing barricades and phrases,
Gott und Foxtrott fesch verschmelzend, –	Combining God with foxtrot paces …
Dazu kommt (wenn's oft auch Last ist),	And, though it bores us half the time
Dass man heute Päderast ist …	Pederasty's not a crime …
Also lautet spät und früh	Night and day, it's bidding fair
Unser seelisches Menu.	To be our mental bill-of-fare.

(Werfel, 'Spiegelmensch', 1920, quoted in Patterson, 1981: 48)[1]

To a certain extent, all the manifestations of Expressionism had in them something of the grotesque, and most of them made conscious use of it, both as their subject and in their stylistic devices: Jack Ellis speaks about the 'tall, thin, grotesquely made up and costumed' *Nosferatu*, who 'moves in a trance' (Ellis, 1979: 68); the captain in Woyzeck, looking at the doctor and Woyzeck running down the road, says:

> Mir wird ganz schwindlich vor den Menschen, wie schnell, der lange Schlingel greift aus, es läuft der Schatten von einem Spinnbein, und der Kurze, – das zuckelt. Der Lange ist der Blitz und der Kleine der Donner. Haha, hinterdrein. Grotesk! Grotesk! (Büchner, 1836–37 [1967]: 100)

> People, they make me dizzy – Look at them. One sparking and veering while the other reaches after him like a spider's shadow. The long one is the lightning and the shorter is the thunder. Haha, one follows the other – Grotesque! Grotesque![2]

Besides the emphasis on the grotesque, this wealth of artistic output is characterized by its concern with the unknown depths of the human soul and with the existential chaos of the human condition 'Der Mensch ist ein Abgrund, es schwindelt Einen, wenn man hinunterschaut … mich schwindelt,' says Wozzeck in Alban Berg's opera.[3] Insanity, the symbol of the internal chaos of the human soul, is a favourite subject; the world is frequently shown distorted, as it is perceived by the madman's eyes. The settings of *Das Kabinett des Dr Caligari* are described as 'a maze of crooked streets … houses like clusters of strange geometrical blocks balanced precariously' (Ellis, 1979: 66); the protagonist of the film is a fairground exhibitor who is also a director of a mental asylum. The external chaos is often symbolized by the motif of the fairground, and as such it is opposed in this film to the mental asylum, which is presented as its sole alternative. The only choice mankind can make is between these two regimes: anarchy, which is the regime of the fairground, and dictatorship, materialized in the image of the mental asylum (Kracauer, 1947: 73–74).

The grotesque in twentieth-century Russian culture

Perhaps due to the number of Russian *émigrés* among the expressionist artists, like Kandinsky, Bakst (1866–1924), Goncharova (1881–1902) and Chagall (1887–1985), all of whom emigrated between 1900 and 1922 to Germany or to Paris, and perhaps also due to the historical influence or even affiliation between the French and German Western cultures and the Russian one, these trends found fertile ground in Russia. In the first three decades of the century the grotesque was apparent in all fields of Russian literature and art. However, here it seemed to be disconnected from its dependence on expressionism and to be associated rather with satire and macabre humour than with plain horror. Russian art in those years rendered a wealth of art works that in no way could be described as expressionistic, although they made ample use of the grotesque, which in its various manifestations always tended toward the ludicrous and the satirical. However, and in spite of its apparently lighter character, there is one aspect of the Russian grotesque that seems particularly affiliated with German expressionism: one of its main purports is chaos: the chaos of human existence at the personal as well as at the social level. It is this motif of chaos, in the guise of the fantastic, the folkloric, the unexpected or the bizarre, that was materialized in one way or another in the typically Russian presentations of the circus and the fairground ('*Balagan*'), with its inevitable fairground theatre-booth that presented *commedia dell'arte* kind of shows, either with real actors ('*Balagan*', as well) or with puppets ('*Balaganchik*'): it is significant that, besides meaning 'fairground', *Balagan* also means, in colloquial Russian, 'a mess', 'disorder' or 'chaos'.

Here, too, there was a tight interrelation between the arts: the poet David Burlyuk (1882–1967) was also a painter, and the painter Marc Chagall wrote poetry. Vladimir Mayakovsky (1894–1930) was a poet, a playwright, a painter and a set-designer – he made some of the stage designs and costumes for his own *Mystery-Bouffe* (1918), and the stage director Nikolay Akimov (1901–68) planned many of the stage designs and costumes for his own productions, and was also known as a painter.

It is obvious that Russian culture emphasizes aspects of the grotesque different from those of its German and French counterparts. Thus it is necessary to examine further instances of the grotesque in its specifically Russian manifestations, which, in spite of the composer's familiarity with twentieth-century West European music, are far more likely to be a source for Shostakovich's ideas about the grotesque.

The grotesque occupies such a dominant place in Russian culture that it seems to be a fundamental part of its very nature. It appears in Russian art, poetry, literature, theatre and music. Thus Shostakovich's natural predisposition toward ironic modes found a fertile ground for some of the most poignant musical grotesqueries of the twentieth century.

From his early childhood he was fond not only of the literary grotesqueries of Gogol and Dostoevsky, but also of the art works of Boris Kustodiev, the music that Mikhail Gnesin wrote for Meyerhold's theatre productions, and these very productions, which were probably most influential through Meyerhold's 'Theory of the Grotesque' in the theatre.

Thus a survey of the grotesque in Russian art, poetry, literature and theatre seems to be necessary for the understanding of Shostakovich's musical grotesques. As was the case with parody, many of his works that purport to be grotesque seem to be generated no less by literary, poetical, pictorial and theatrical elements no less – and perhaps even more – than by music.

The grotesque in Russian painting

The first Russian artist whose paintings can be related to the grotesque is Boris Kustodiev (1878–1927). True, his characteristic paintings of broad and sensual women are not grotesque, at least not in the common sense of the word, yet they nevertheless seem to reside on some border between the fascinating and the satirized. His women are beautiful and of hedonistically extravagant sizes, like *A Merchant's Wife with a Mirror* (1920), who seems to have fallen in love with her own reflection (Pl. 12.1), or *A Merchant's Wife at Tea Time* (1918), immersed in an abandoned rapture amongst the fondling cat, the tea, and the fruits and sweets on the table (Pl. 12.2).[4] Their luxurious sensuality, with all its apparent potential for bodily pleasures, yet seems still, stiff and inane; it touches on one hand the bizarre and on the other the satirized. A comparison of *A Merchant's Wife at Tea Time* with the ostensibly identical subject portrayed in *A Cabman in the Tavern* (1920) could clarify this point: this figure is almost ludicrous, with his dumb face and empty eyes, unaware of his own shallowness; he is not even bored, but looking vaguely out of the window, conscientiously drinking while holding tightly the half-eaten *boublik* in his other hand (Pl. 12.3). The merchant's wife, on the contrary, seems to conceal, under her apparent, almost intentional stillness, a vibrating inner life that is focused on her own sensual perceptions. While he is obvious, blunt and simple, she, in an identical situation and position, is an enigma.

The almost ridiculous self-indulgence of Kustodiev's women (see also Plates 12.4 and 12.5: *The Bather-Girl* from 1921 and *The Russian Venus* from 1925–26) is fascinating precisely because of the unexplained charm of their devotion to their own sensuality. In the simultaneous transmission of the ridiculous and the astonishingly beautiful, Kustodiev's ambiguity borders on the grotesque.

Kustodiev was one of the first artistic influences on Shostakovich, who, as a child, was a frequent guest of the painter, played the piano and posed for him (Volkov, 1979: 12). Kustodiev's characteristic paintings of broad, sensual

Pl. 12.1
Kustodiev, *A Merchant's Wife with a Mirror* (1920)

Pl. 12.2
Kustodiev, *A Merchant's Wife at Tea Time* (1918)

kupchikhas (merchant-women, or merchants' wives) seem to be reflected in the figure of Katerina Izmaylova, Shostakovich's heroine of his second opera, who happens to be, coincidentally or not, a *kupchikha*: a merchant's wife.[5] In his memoirs, the composer mentioned the influence that the painter's works had on his music: 'I was deeply impressed by Kustodiev's passion for voluptuous women. Kustodiev's painting is thoroughly erotic … If you dig deeper into my operas, *The Nose* or *Lady Macbeth*, you can find the Kustodiev influence – in that sense' (Volkov, 1979: 12). The magic magnetism of the Kustodiev woman, which is intangibly hued with the grotesque, is apparent in the fifth scene of the second act of *Lady Macbeth of the Mtsensk District*, which opens with a series of static, mysterious pianissimo harmonies, leading to a love-song that Katerina sings to Sergey (Ex. 12.1). The musical line is chromatic, slow and sensual. The harmonies creep from one major chord to its closest neighbour; although the melodic character of the singing is evident, there is no apparent tonal direction or functionality. A feeling of tension is imported also through the position of the sounds in the texture: a large space lies open between the high

Pl. 12.3
Kustodiev, *A Cabman in the Tavern* (1920)

Pl. 12.4
Kustodiev, *The Bather-Girl* (1921)

notes and the bass ones. The prevailing pianissimo dynamics add to the sensual
tension that is sustained until the emotional outburst in bar 40, where the whole
harmony becomes fuller and the dynamics change to fortissimo, sung on the
highest note of this aria. This love-song is introduced by a series of chords of
the same kind of enigmatic harmonies, over which Katerina softly calls Sergey.
However, this magic musical veil is abruptly torn by Sergey's brief and practical comment: 'What will happen to us?' Katerina, immersed in her own love,
continues rapturously: 'You are mine' – to which Sergey answers with an
insipid and laconic 'Da!', which is incongruous with the rest both in its harmony and in its metrical stress (Ex. 12.2).

The resulting incongruity is similar to the incongruity between Kustodiev's
Merchant's Wife (Pl. 12.2) and his *Cabman* (Pl. 12.3). Shostakovich, however, superimposes the two characteristic traits – the sensual enigmatic and
the inane simpleton – in one scene, exposing both the ridiculous as well as
the tragic in Katerina's situation, and throws over Katerina's love-song a
shade of the grotesque: it lies not only in Sergey's inability to match even

Pl. 12.5
Kustodiev, *The Russian Venus* (1925–26)

approximately her capacity for love, which Shostakovich referred to as 'genial' (Volkov, 1979: 81), but also in the fact that her love, as unique as it is, is
yet totally inappropriate to its context. The grotesque stems not just from this
incongruity but also from Katerina's total unawareness of her situation. When
balanced against the murders she commits for the sake of this love, the
mixture of compassion, repulsion, mockery and admiration we feel for her is
transformed into a chilling macabre grotesquerie, a purport which is wholly
grasped precisely when the sounds of the love-song are drifting around in this
magical, daydreaming atmosphere.

Shostakovich's insistence on a grotesque impression of this song is much
more evident in the continuous, almost ostinato-like rhythmic motif, played
alternately by the clarinet, viola and violins, that 'creeps' in the midst of the
open sound space between the two extreme registers.[6] The incongruity, then,
is constantly present throughout the entire love-song. The dotted rhythmic
pattern is structured in upward melodic motions, with harmonies that are
completely incongruent both with Katerina's singing and with Sergey's remarks. It bears a further ominously sensual purport, which is conveyed by the
minor mode, the dotted rhythm, and the slightly flat tone of the violas (Ex.
12.3).

Ex. 12.1
Katerina's love-song is congruently accompanied by slow, drifting chords

Ex. 12.2
Sergey's laconic remarks are highly incongruent with Katerina's romantic mood

This dotted motif made its first appearance in the *entr'acte* between this scene and the former one, which ended with the death of Boris Timofeyevich. The motif creeps in a cat-like motion, bearing an ambiguous import: in a way, because of the middle register, the timbre of the clarinet, and the peculiar rhythmic progression, it is perceived as sensual; however, it also has a

Ex. 12.3
Katerina's love-song and viola accompaniment

This example shows the same aria, with the added dotted counter-melody of the
violas. The result is a triple purport of incongruent elements, very similar to the
purport that can be found in Kustodiev's pictures: Katerina's romantic daydreaming
– a cloud of enchanted, sensual beauty; Sergey's simple, down-to-earth, inane
remarks; finally, underlying the former two, a continuous dotted melodic figure,
creeping like an ominous serpent, hinting at something basically wrong with the
idyllic picture that is allegedly present.

vile flavour, which is rather cunning and even threatening in its 'limping' and
in the dissonant clashes it has with the song's harmonies.

This very same motif has some satirical connotations as well. This is not
only due to its sharply accentuated motion, special timbre and upward-creep-
ing melodic line, but also because of its contextual position in the general
narrative of the scene, following a brilliant burlesque on the priest who
arrived for the confession of the dying Boris Timofeyevich. After the death,
when Katerina, the new rich owner of the estate, clearly states that 'these
things happen quite often, when you eat mushrooms at night', and while the
orchestra is playfully performing scherzando figures, the priest is abruptly
transformed from a respectful representative of the church, mumbling prayers
in ecclesiastic intonations, into a merry Russian peasant, much resembling
some Russian-life pictures of Kustodiev, who joyously quotes Gogol: 'Oh,
these mushrooms and cold soups are too much, as said Nikolay Vasilich
Gogol, the illustrious writer of the Russian nation!' The orchestra seals this

Ex. 12.4

The priest's 'Da' will be echoed by Sergey's, pointing at their parallel callousness

last pious declaration with a parodic final flourish, characteristic of an operetta's ending, and with a rustic, peasant-like 'Da!' at its end (Ex. 12.4).[7]

The scene with the priest does not appear in Leskov's story; it was added by Alexander Preis, who worked with Shostakovich on the libretto. Macabre humour also appears in the works of Kustodiev, who tended to link the macabre and the satirical. His two drawings from 1905, both ironically called *An Introduction to the Revolution*, present a huge grinning Death skeleton. In the first, Death is shown running with blood-dripping hands over the city, the tiny inhabitants of which are crushed under his feet (Pl. 12.6). In the second drawing Death is standing over the city, contemplating with obvious delight the result of his deeds (Pl. 12.7). The satirical message is much further enhanced when compared with *The Bolshevik* (1920). Here the triumphant Bolshevik, this time with a fierce, righteous look in his eyes, and waving a huge red banner, walks over the city; its tiny inhabitants are crawling at his feet in a frame, proportions and scenery almost identical to those in the two former drawings, in which the main protagonist is Death (Pl. 12.8).

It is typical of Soviet art that the satire is apparent only to those who know Kustodiev's art well enough to remember the two earlier, quite untypical drawings in relation to which the Bolsheviks are correlated with Death. It is also typical that *The Bolshevik* was much acclaimed and admired in the Soviet Union, a reaction that allowed yet another, concealed mockery of the artistic illiteracy of the authorities. The same technique of inner references to earlier works in order to convey a satirizing message was probably applied by Shostakovich in later years, in works like his Fifth, Seventh, Thirteenth, Fourteenth, and Fifteenth Symphonies.

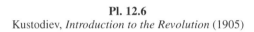

Pl. 12.6
Kustodiev, *Introduction to the Revolution* (1905)

This piece of musical burlesque follows a parody of a traditional Russian dirge, sung by Katerina over the body of her father-in-law, whom she has just poisoned, and a stern passacaglia for organ, which functions as the *entr'acte* between this scene and the next, in which Katerina, in her bedroom with Sergey, sings the beautiful love aria quoted above. The dramatic and stylistic inconguity between the consecutive events – Sergey's violent lashing, the poisoning scene, Katerina's mocking dirge, the joing priest and the emotionally charged, almost ecstatic love scene – results in a general impression of unease caused by the mixture of the depraved and the sublime, the horrifying and the ludicrous. In short – it results in the grotesque.

Shostakovich evidently differentiated between several levels of the grotesque: while the juxtapositions of horror, burlesque, parody and satire make this scene an obvious example of the grotesque of the simplest kind, in the very next scene the grotesque takes a subtler, more Kustodievan shape. Here the macabre is intertwined not only with the ludicrous and the satiric, but with the grace granted by the magically beautiful and the feelings of human compassion: without the rhythmic-pattern background, what remains would be a completely congruous, beautiful love-song. It is the presence of the 'other', alien musical element, which is a reminder not only of the horrific

Pl. 12.7
Kustodiev, *Introduction to the Revolution* (variant) (1905)

character of the murder, but also of its parodic, satiric and ludicrous aspects; and it is the unresolvable clash between these two incongruent elements that makes this scene a musical grotesque.

While Kustodiev's influence on *Lady Macbeth of the Mtsensk District* can clearly be seen, *The Nose* seems less directly inspired by him. Viewed in a wider sense, however, a general inclination toward the corporeal in all its revelations can easily be discerned (an approach which is in perfect accord with Gogol's and Leskov's tendencies, as well as with Bakhtin's).[8]

For instance, the third scene of *The Nose*, which opens with Kovalyev's snoring, is performed in a hyper-realistic, exaggerated grotesque manner. As in most of his depictions of the grotesque, Shostakovich uses here the extremes of the orchestral compass: the contrabassoon and the trombone, in their darkest, almost indecipherable sounds, in a series of moans and groans, echo Kovalyev's snores, while a solo violin, in high-pitched squeaks of glissandos, flageolets, trills and out-of-tune sounds, mockingly imitates the wealth of whistles, sighs, and shrill sounds of sleep (Ex. 12.5).

Another characteristic of Kustodiev is the colourful agglomerations of people that are also typical of *The Nose*: the crowd on the bridge before Ivan Yakovlevich throws the nose into the river, the curious series of mask-characters in the descriptions of the passengers in their wait for the carriage, and the

Pl. 12.8
Kustodiev, *The Bolshevik* (1920)

Ex. 12.5

The Nose: a grotesque, hyper-realistic sound-description of sleep

frenzied chase of the mob after the nose, towards the end of the work: all these are, dramatically and musically, based on Russian motifs that are parallel to Kustodiev's depictions of fairgrounds and market-places.[9]

The grotesque, which is insinuated in Kustodiev's pictures, becomes more tangible in the works of the Jewish Russian artist Marc Chagall, whose fascination with chaos is manifested in his systematical distortion of features,

Pl. 12.9

Chagall, *Start of the Show* (1911)
Copyright © ADAGP, Paris and DACS, London 2000

Pl. 12.10
Chagall, *Clown with Violin* (1956)
Copyright © ADAGP, Paris and DACS, London 2000

Pl. 12.12
Chagall, *Man with Marionettes* (1916)

Pl. 12.13
Chagall, *Dedicated to my Fiancée* (1911)

Pl. 12.14
Chagall, *Homage to Charlot* (1929)

postures and proportions, constant incongruities, improbable juxtapositions, fantastic sceneries and classical symbols of chaos: the circus, the fairground and the fairground-theatre, with their clowns, acrobats and puppets (Pl. 12.9).

In sharp contrast to Picasso's pensive clowns and acrobats, for example, those of Chagall are blatantly grotesque (Pls 12.10 and 12.11, pl 12.11 can be found on the first page of the colour plate section in this book). Especially revealing is his use of puppets as an allegory of Man as a puppet in the hands of a stronger force, as depicted in his *Man with Marionettes* (1916), in which the marionettes seem to have a more human appearance in their helplessness than their manipulator, who is granted a devilish face characterized by the sharp angularity of all its features (Pl. 12.12).

In Chagall's paintings animal and human features are mixed almost as a rule: *Dedicated to my Fiancée* (1911) shows a human figure leaning its cow-head on one hand (Pl. 12.13), and *Homage to Charlot* (1929) presents Chaplin as a hybrid of a human and a bird (Pl. 12.14). Other favourite mixtures are the animate with the inanimate, as in the 1922 *The Musician* and the 1939 *The Cellist* (Pls 12.15 and 12.16).

Satirical, surrealist, expressionist and cubist trends are intertwined in these paintings, creating a chaotic stylistic impression on the one hand, and on the

Pl. 12.15
Chagall, *The Musician* (1922)
Copyright © ADAGP, Paris and DACS, London 2000

other, grotesque scenes that stem from the juxtapositions of unrelated items, remarkably similar to the way unrelated dramatic and musical units are put together in both of Shostakovich's operas.

There is no proof that Shostakovich was influenced by Chagall, who left Russia for good in 1922. However, some quite convincing links can be drawn. Chagall, who was interested in and influenced by literature and poetry, was particularly engaged with literary works that reflected the satirical grotesque: in 1919 he planned stage-settings for Gogol's *The Government Inspector*, *The Wedding* and *The Gamblers* (though none of these productions eventually materialized), as well as making a series of illustrations for *Dead Souls* (1923–27; for example, Pl. 12.17). He worked in the theatre with Nikolay Yevreinov (1879–1953), a friend of Meyerhold and his follower, who shared many of his ideas about the theatre and the arts. For a stage production of three satirical stories by Sholem Aleikhem in the Kamerny State Jewish Theatre in Moscow he not only made the stage-settings and costumes, but also had almost total control of the *mise-en-scène*. This production, in which he worked with the Jewish actor Solomon Mikhoels (1890–1948), had an impact not only in this theatre, but also in the parallel Moscow Jewish Theatre, Habimah, which worked under the directorship of Yevgeny Vakhtangov. Actually, Vakhtangov

Pl. 12.16
Chagall, *The Cellist* (1939)
Copyright © ADAGP, Paris and DACS, London 2000

wanted Chagall to make the stage-settings for his 1922 production of *Haddybuk*. This did not materialize, but Nathan Altman (1889–1970), the artist who eventually was responsible for the design, was requested by Vakhtangov to make them '*à la Chagall*' (Meyer, 1963: 294).

Chagall was a famous artist, and, what is perhaps more important, he was admired by the 'reactionary' artistic circles, generally close to Bakhtin (and as a consequence, to Sollertinsky), both of whom lived in Vitebsk, as Chagall did. Although there is no proof of their actual meeting, since Bakhtin arrived in Vitebsk in 1919 and Sollertinsky in 1920, the very same year in which Chagall left Vitebsk, it is still improbable that such a central artistic figure as Chagall, even regardless of the fact that he served there as the Commissar of Arts and as the foremost art teacher in the town, his pictures and designs actually covering the walls of Vitebsk, could have passed unnoticed by Bakhtin and Sollertinsky.

Later on, in 1920, Chagall worked with the Jewish Theatre in Moscow, in a close relationship with the Jewish artist Solomon Mikhoels who, with his family, later became close friends of Shostakovich.[10] Jewish grotesque figures are perhaps the most characteristic trait of Chagall's art. In the *Introduction to the Jewish Theatre* (1920–21) traditional Jewish figures are mixed with the

Pl. 12.17
Chagall, *The Police Arrive*, from the illustrations to *Dead Souls* (1923–27)
Copyright © ADAGP, Paris and DACS, London 2000

Pl. 12.18
Chagall, *Introduction to the Jewish Theatre* (1920–21)
Copyright © ADAGP, Paris and DACS, London 2000

Pl. 12.19
Chagall, *The Acrobat* (1918)
Copyright © ADAGP, Paris and DACS, London 2000

realms of art and the circus, providing a whole picture of the chaotic and the irrational. Juxtapositions of totally incongruent motifs, such as the bearded, half-naked circus acrobat standing on his hands while wearing his philactery on his arm and forehead, coexist in strange affiliation with the upside-down flying cow and the weird contortions of the dancing Jewish musicians (Pl. 12.18); his *Acrobat*, from 1918, emphasizes the purport of the grotesque, which is achieved by its chaotic mixture of the animal with the human and of religious symbols with the life of the circus (Pl. 12.19).

These awkward, simultaneously horrifying and ludicrous dance movements of a maimed nation were apprehended by Shostakovich, who incorporated their correlatives in his music.[11] In the 'Song of Poverty', the seventh in the song-cycle *From Jewish Folk Poetry*, the protagonist celebrates his miserable life in a hopping dance, holding in his arms his starving baby. Grotesque incongruities are already present in the original text, a strange mixture of a traditional Jewish lullaby, self-satirical exclamations, an existential outlook on life and a sincere, heartbreaking expression of misery. The expression 'Vïshe! Vïshe!' ('Higher! Higher!'), that is repeated in the song's refrain as part of the dance's exclamations, was the main slogan of the official Stalinist rhetorics during the 1930s and 1940s, where it pointed at 'a higher order of reality', to which 'ordinary citizens do not have access' (Clark and Holquist, 1984: 311).

The music enhances the grotesque by juxtaposing a hopping dance rhythm, a very high-pitched whirling, repetitive motif, and a minor, Dorian mode, with an emphasized augmented second, that stands in a strong musico-semantic incongruity with the otherwise lighthearted musical import (Ex. 12.6).

A similar phenomenon appears in the Finale of the Second Piano Trio, op. 67. Here the grotesque incongruities of the hopping dance are taken further, reaching the domain of insanity: obsessive repetitions with cumulative grotesque traits. The movement apparently begins without any grotesque (nor any characteristically Jewish) musical traits.[12] The piano plays repetitive chords while the violin presents the dance-like theme, tinged with strangeness due to its minor seconds and its melodic skips of major sevenths and minor ninths (Ex. 12.7).

The theme repeats itself; this time the accompaniment acquires the banal 'oom-pah' accompaniment figure, still in pizzicato articulation. The meaning that this figure conveys, though, is far from banal. The accompaniment figure is shared by the cello, which marks the beats, and the piano, which is bound to constant syncopation. This necessarily renders an aggressive and abrupt attack on the metrically light quaver of each beat. Thus the mere orchestration of a simplistic accompaniment figure results in an ambivalent, incongruent import, and the dance becomes a limping, weird, crippled hopping (Ex. 12.8).

More violence awaits, with the rhythmically identical accompaniment figure now divided between the cello and the violin, in full four-note chords, pizzicato and fortissimo. Over this background the piano bursts with a pierc-

Ex. 12.6

Shostakovich's 'Song of Poverty': a mixture of misery and dance

Песня о нужде	A Song of Poverty
Крыша спит на чердаке	The roof sleeps over the garret
под соломой сладким сном.	dreaming sweetly under its thatch.
В колыбелике спит дитя	In a cradle sleeps the baby
без пеленок, нагишом.	without swaddling, all bare.
Гоп, гоп, выше, выше!	Hop, hop, higher, higher!
Ест коза солому скрыши.	The nanny-goat's nibbling the thatch.
Гоп, гоп, выше, выше!	Hop, hop, higher, higher!
Ест коза солому скрыши, ой!	The nanny-goat's nibbling the thatch, oy!
Колыбель на чердаке,	There's a cradle in the garret,
паучок в ней ткет беду.	and a spider there spinning trouble.
радость он мою сосет,	He's sucking out all my joy,
мне оставив лишь нужду.	leaving me just poverty,
Гоп, гоп, выше, выше …	Hop, hop, higher, higher …
Петушок на чердаке,	There's a cockerel in the garret,
яркокрасный гребешок.	with a bright red comb.
Ой, жена, займы для деток	Hey, wife, borrow for the children
хлеба черствого кусок.	a little crust of dry bread.
Гоп, гоп, выше, выше …	Hop, hop, higher, higher …

(Translation by Z. Weaver, Decca 425069-2)

Ex. 12.7

Shostakovich's Finale from the Second Piano Trio, bars 5–11

Ex. 12.8

Finale from the Second Piano Trio, bars 17–24: the dancing motion becomes a limp

Ex. 12.9

'The Jewish motif' in the Finale of the Second Piano Trio: obsessive repetitions, violent articulation, extreme pitches and loud dynamics create a grotesque image of despairing insanity

ing plea, in a characteristic Jewish East European mode, which achieves its
peak by obsessive repetitions in a growing rhythmical density (Ex. 12.9). The
continuous alternation between the terrifying insanity of such emotional peaks
and the apparently folk-dance idiom, which returns as abruptly as it left (bars
59ff.), enhances the grotesque purport of the whole movement.

A similar amalgam of an allegedly cheerful dance with the dread of a
compulsive obsession is presented without any preparatory stage in the First
Violin Concerto, op. 77 (1947–48). The whirling movement of the Scherzo
becomes a maze of contrapuntal confrontations between the violin, which is
bursting in insane, shrieking glissandos, and the instruments of the orchestra.
The hopping accompaniment of the dance in the final Burlesque becomes a
series of jerked syncopations, the heavy beat supplied only by the hectic
melodic line of the violin, into which is woven Shostakovich's musical acronym, D–S–C–H, to which later is added a contrapuntal line of the bassoon.
The violent chords of the accompaniment create an overwhelming wave of an
accumulated mass of sound, as also happens in the mob scenes in
Shostakovich's music: the chase in *The Nose*, the rape of Aksinya in *Lady
Macbeth of The Mtsensk District* and the pogrom scene from the Thirteenth
Symphony. In the concerto this process is enriched by the combination of the
characteristic 'Jewish' mode with the DSCH motif.[13] This combination results in a new system of signs, according to which Shostakovich is not only
likened to, but actually becomes identified with, the figure of the persecuted
Jew. Indeed, in the violent Scherzo of his Eighth String Quartet, which he
claimed was autobiographical, appears a large quote of the 'Jewish motif'
from the Second Piano Trio.

This potential of the grotesque to oppose the Jewish humorous characteristics with the characteristic of a violent mob is developed in Chagall's work,
too. In *The Revolution* (1937), as in other manifestations of the grotesque in
Russian poetry and literature, the grotesque is intertwined with the dread of a
massive crowd: the mob features again. In the middle ground between a
proletarian mob which is waving red banners as well as deadly weapons, and
a surrealistic scene of the Jewish little town, which ironically is not devoid of
a red banner of its own, Jewish acrobats appear around and on top of a table,
in all kinds of acrobatic positions, together with a seated, pensive Rabbi (Pl.
12.20).

Another undated caricature of a revolutionary crowd is, in a sense, even
more satirical because of its apparent reference to the famous *Ecce Homo*
picture of Hieronymus Bosch:[14] the mass of coarse, almost savage, people is
presented as a caricatured and yet terrifying entity (Pls 12.21 and 12.22).[15]
Thus the mob becomes an embodiment of the grotesque, very much as it does
in the music of Shostakovich's *The Nose*.

As Chagall did in painting, so Shostakovich satirized the faceless crowd in
his music. His musical descriptions of mobs purport unrestrained violence,

Pl. 12.20
Chagall, *The Revolution* (1937)

Pl. 12.21
Chagall, *The Revolution* (illustration for a poetry book)

and thus have very little of the ludicrous, dwelling rather in the domain of the horrifying. Such are the policemen that attack the pretzel-seller in *The Nose*, the mob in the pogrom scene from the Thirteenth Symphony and the group of workers in the rape scene from *Lady Macbeth of the Mtsensk District*.[16] All these are characterized by, besides the fast tempo and loud dynamics, their homogeneity, which is achieved by a tendency towards repetitive short patterns and a completely homorhythmic texture.

There is, however, another kind of musical description which, despite eventually achieving the same result, involves a narrative process of development where a number of individuals become a 'group'. The fascinating trait of this process is that each one of the individuals never loses his/her own 'voice'. Even when a chaotic multitude of accumulated voices mingles into an indecipherable noise of a horrifying and dangerous mob, the individual voice still keeps his/her own specific musical characteristics.[17] This technique is closer to the grotesque, since it provides many opportunities for the presentation of ludicrous individuals and their gradual transformation into a faceless and terrifying mob. While this type of 'crowd-texture' usually conveys a grotesque musical picture, the second type, contrarily, is a picture of a mechanized mob, which transcends the limits of the grotesque and moves

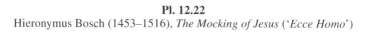

Pl. 12.22
Hieronymus Bosch (1453–1516), *The Mocking of Jesus* (*'Ecce Homo'*)

toward a purely horrifying rendering of unrestrained violence (Exs 12.9 and 12.10).[18]

Sometimes the transition from the first to the second type creates a chilling report of a mob's dehumanization process. The score of *The Nose*, which lists about seventy *secondary* roles in the opera, presents such an instance in the scene in which passengers gradually gather in a queue waiting for the carriage. Shostakovich uses this gradual gathering for a musical study not only of a crowd's accumulation, but also of the alchemical process in which an individual becomes part of a crowd. Among the people who gather in the queue are, for example, 'two passengers', each one with his own typical voice and intonation. Then arrive 'a mother, two children, and their father'. Shortly afterwards appears 'an old baroness' who, in the middle of the cheerful hubbub, suddenly breaks into a long, slow soliloquy in which she declares that she is going to die and that she is preparing herself for death. Two other characters stand beside her, without knowing how to respond, and mumble in a kind of embarrassed cheerfulness, in a desperate attempt to ignore this tangible knowledge of death: 'Only God knows what you are talking about.' These characterized, individualized passengers turn gradually into a mob that will eventually participate in 'the great chase' of the nose. This gradual transformation of a human, pathetic and ludicrous group of individuals into a homogeneous mob, rhythmi-

Ex. 12.10

The Nose: the crowd of individuals begins to accumulate

cally shouting in unison the same repeated word, is one of the most powerful satirical peaks of the grotesque: pitiful, harmless individuals who uncontrollably accumulate into a terrifying social chaos.

At the beginning of the process (rehearsal number 463, shown in Ex. 12.10) the various parts are individualized: the tempo moderato allows a comfortable pace of speech, and the piano dynamics enable each one of the voices to be clearly discerned. Indeed, these strengthen the impression of speech. The impression is that people are talking, each one expressing their own thoughts, although all of them are enquiring about the nose and its whereabouts. The melodic lines are different and the entrance point of each part seems disconnected from the others. In this coincidental group of individuals each retains their characteristic figures of speech. However, after six bars, more and more people utter the same word: 'Gde?' ('Where?'). This similarity is the starting-point not only of the musical process of accumulation, but also of the psychological process in which the individuals become a crowd. At rehearsal number 479 (Ex. 12.11) the tempo has become presto, and the dynamics fortissimo. Still, some individual voices remain distinct: the pretzel-seller who is crying at the top of her voice, the man who has a speaking (and not singing) role, and the colonel, who shows personal initiative when he stands on a bench to see the scene better. One of them begins to cry on a monotone pitch, a feature belonging to Shostakovich's characteristic homorhythmic type of crowd-music, and the rest gradually join in. The most impressive change, however, is the fact that instead of individuals, the eight remaining parts in this excerpt are divided between 'two choirs', possibly a metaphor for the individuals' musical loss of identity for the sake of a unified, homogenized group sound. These two choirs, seemingly dispersed but only for a very short time (the two bars after 479), unite their voices in an obstinate, repetitive note, crying all at once, fortissimo, homorhythmically: 'Smotrite! Smotrite!' ('Look! Look!'), forming a huge, simultaneously dissonant and resonant chord, built on minor seconds, fifths and octaves (Ex. 12.11).

Ex. 12.11
The Nose: the crowd becomes a faceless mob

The grotesque in Russian literature and poetry

The mixture of the macabre, sensual and satirical that makes up the grotesque is so characteristic of Russian literature that it is almost hard to think about a Russian literary work that is devoid of this trait. The grotesque is a main device in Gogol's *The Government Inspector* (1836) and in his *Dead Souls* (1835–52); it is a dominant factor in Dostoevsky's works, starting from *Poor*

Folk and *The Double*, both written in 1846, through *The Village of Stepanchikovo* (1859) and *The Idiot* (1868–69), up to *The Possessed* (1872) and *The Brothers Karamazov* (1879–90). It appears in Leskov's *Lady Macbeth of the Mtsensk District* (1865); it plays a major role in the stories of Saltikov-Shchedrin, for instance, *The Golovlyov Family* (1876); in Aleksandr Blok's *Balaganchik* (1906), in Shklovsky's *A Sentimental Journey* (1922), in Isaac Babel's *Stories from the Civil War* (1920–22), in Mikhail Bulgakov's *A Heart of a Dog* (1925) and in his *Master and Margarita* (1940).

Literary research in Russia since the end of the nineteenth century seems to have focused on the grotesque; moreover, many writers who emphasized the grotesque in their works were also engaged in literary criticism. Therefore, it is not surprising that most of the subjects of their research were works related to the grotesque. The attitude of Russian literary criticism toward the grotesque can thus be approached from two vantage-points. One views the literary works that were written at this period; the other examines the subjects of literary research and literary criticism undertaken at the same time.

One of the most influential Russian scholars by the end of the nineteenth century was Alexander Veselovsky (1836–1906). He wrote on a wide range of literary subjects: *The Iliad*, *The Eddas*, *The Kalevale*, *Beowulf*, *The Nibelungenlied*, medieval Provençal and French *Chansons de Geste*, Boccaccio, Petrarch, Montaigne, Rabelais and Shakespeare; however, his monographs are analyses of Rabelais and Cervantes, both known for the grotesque character of their works (Veselovsky, 1939 and 1940). Veselovsky was much admired by the young literary scholars in St Petersburg (Shklovsky, 1940: 111). In spite of the formalistic avoidance of questions regarding literary content, and the formalists' allegedly exclusive interest in technical and formal issues, they nevertheless have often chosen, from the list of Veselovsky's scholarly undertakings, to pursue the analyses of writers and works the purport of which is mainly the grotesque. For example, Shklovsky wrote about Lawrence Sterne's *Tristram Shandy* and Cervantes's *Don Quixote*, while Eikhenbaum and Tīnyanov focused on Dostoevsky and Gogol (Shklovsky, 1929: 177–205, 91–124; Eikhenbaum, 1918 [1974]: 266–291; Tīnyanov, 1929: 412–455). On the other side of the theoretical fence, fervently objecting to formalist ideas (but nevertheless following Veselovsky's footsteps as he did so), Mikhail Bakhtin wrote, in his book about Dostoevsky, ideas which later developed, in his study on Rabelais, into a whole theory about the literary, social, ethical and existential aspects of the grotesque (Bakhtin, 1929 [1963] and 1941 [1975]).

Although it is hard to draw a sharp line between symbolist, psychologist and grotesque utterances, there are certain kinds of Russian poetry, like Mayakovsky's 'futuristic' poems, for instance, that undoubtedly draw their symbolist and psychologist imagery from the grotesque:

Вашу мысль	Your thought
мечтающую на размягченной	Musing on a sodden brain
как выжиревший лакей на засаленной кушетке	like a bloated lackey on a greasy couch
буду дразнить об окровавленной сердца лоскут,	I'll taunt with a bloody morsel of heart;
...	...
А себя, как я, вывернуть не можете,	But you cannot turn yourselves inside out,
чтобы были они сплошные губы	like me, and be just bare lips!
...	...
В стеклах дождинки серые	On the windowpanes, grey raindrops
свылись,	howled together,
гримасу громадили,	piling on a grimace
как будто воют химеры	as though the gargoyles
Собора Парижской Богоматери.	of Notre Dame were howling.
(Маяаковский, 1913 [1985–87]: Vl.1)	(Mayakovsky, 'The Cloud in Trousers', 1913 [1960]: 60–109)

His poem 'The Backbone Flute' (1914–15) seems closely related to a characteristic carnival–grotesque feeling:

За всех вас,	For all of you,
которые нравились или нравятся,	who once pleased or still may please,
хранимых иконами у души в пещере,	guarded by icons in the catacomb of the soul,
как чашу вина в застольной здравице,	I shall raise, like a goblet of wine
подемлю стихами наполненный череп.	at a festive board, a skull brimful of verse.
...	...
Смех из глаз в глаза лей	Pour laughter from eye to eye
Былыми свадьбами ночь ряди.	Festoon the night with weddings past.
Из тела в тело веселье лейте.	Pour out joy from body to body.
Пусть не забудется ночь никем.	Let no one forget this night.
Я сегодня буду играть на флейте.	On this occasion I shall play the flute.
На собственном позвоночнике.	Play on my own backbone.
...	...
Мысли, крови сгустки,	Thoughts, sick and coagulated
Больные и запекшиеся, лезут из черепа.	clots of blood, crawled from my skull.
(Маяаковский, 1914–15 [1985–87]: Vl.1)	(Mayakovsky 1914–15 [1960]: 110–131)

These two poems were among Shostakovich's favourites (Volkov, 1979: 190). 'The Backbone Flute' might have influenced Shostakovich's musical interpretation of the flute scene in Akimov's controversial production of *Hamlet* (1932), when the actor playing Hamlet, after saying 'Call me what instrument you will, though you can fret me, you cannot play upon me' (*Hamlet*, act III, scene 3), 'pressed a flute to the lower end of his spine, while in the orchestra a piccolo accompanied by a bass and a drum played shrill, false notes of the famous Soviet song "They tried to vanquish us" in a parody of Davidenko's proletarian song' (Yelagin, 1950 [1988]: 39–40).[19]

The shrill timbre introduces a grotesque import to the scene, which in the original text could be perceived as nothing more than a mildly mocking remark (Ex.12.12). The choice of instrumental timbre is significant: Shostakovich never wrote first at the keyboard, but had in mind the instrumental sound-image as an organic part of the musical work, writing straight into the score (Volkov, 1979: 177). His association with 'The Backbone Flute' might be, then, more than coincidental. Shostakovich's choice of the

Ex. 12.12

Shostakovich's music for the 'flute scene' in Akimov's production of *Hamlet*

tuba, by the end of this musical passage, is not accidental either; often it seems that he preferred the lower registers in his musical depictions of grotesqueries.

This can also be seen in his musical setting of the *Four Verses of Captain Lebyadkin* op. 146, the texts for which were taken from Dostoevsky's *The Possessed*. The figure of Captain Lebyadkin can be regarded as a classical example of the Russian grotesque, in which both characteristics of illiteracy and drunkenness are regarded with a mixture of amusement and dread. These marks of the grotesque are intermingled in the following lines from *The Possessed*, in which the first meeting with Lebyadkin is described:

> Только что я занес ногу за высокий порог калитки, вдруг чья-то сильная рука схватила меня за грудь.
>   – Кто сей? – взревел чей-то голос, – друг или недруг? Кайся!
>   – Это наш, наш! – завизжал подле голосок Липутина, – это господин Г-в, классического воспитания и в связях с самым высшим обществом молодой человек.
>   – Люблю, коли с обществом, кла-сси-чес ... значит, о-бра-зо-о-ваннейший ... отставной капитан Игнат Лебядкин, к услугам мира и друзей ... если верны, если верны, подлецы!
>   Капитан Лебядкин, вершков десяти росту, толстый, мясистый, курчавый, красный и чрезвычайно пьяный, едва стоял предо мной и с трудом выговаривал слова. (Достоевский, 1872 [1974]: 95)

> No sooner did I lift my foot over the high beam at the bottom of the gate than I was suddenly seized by the chest by a strong hand.
>   'Who's that?' roared a voice. 'Friend or foe? Own up!'
>   'He's one of us, one of us!' Liputin squeaked in his thin voice nearby. 'It's Mr G—v, a young gentleman of classical education and in close touch with the highest society'.
>   'I like a chap who belongs to society, classi- – that means high-ly educ-cated. Retired Captain Ignatius Lebyatkin, sir, at the service of the world and friends – if they're true friends, if they're true friends, the scoundrels!'

> Captain Lebyatkin, a stout and fleshy man over six feet in height, with curly hair and a red face, stood before me. He was so drunk that he could scarcely stand on his feet and he articulated his words with difficulty. (Dostoevsky, 1872 [1953]: 127–128)

Dostoevsky allotted Lebyadkin a considerable part of his notes to *The Possessed*. In these literary diaries he described the captain and wrote whole tentative dialogues in which he featured and composed his crude verses. These already appear in the first drafts for the novel, implying that they are organic constituents of the author's basic conception of this protagonist (Dostoevsky, 1968: 44–45, 82, 163). Lebyadkin is a grotesque. He is terrifying, drunk, violent, unpredictable: 'Kartuzov is always abrupt (though softspoken and polite) as on the occasion when he reads his poem about the cockroach' (Dostoyevsky, 1968: 42).[20] He is also ridiculous, almost a buffoon:

> ... товарищам он становится хоть и забавен, но и ненавистен. ... *Комичнее*, загадочнее и интереснее поставить с 1-го разу фигуру Картузова перед читателем. Все хищные и романтические моменты, при всей своей правде и действительности, должны быть *уловлены из природы* с комическим оттенком. (Dostoevskey, 1974: 44)

> ... his comrades find him amusing, but hateful as well ... Present the figure of Kartuzov to the reader in a more comic, more mysterious, and more interesting light, right from the beginning. All of the savage and romantic moments, their truthfulness and realism notwithstanding, should be *drawn from nature* with a comical tinge. (Dostoevsky, 1968: 41)

Wasiolek writes in the introduction to his translation of Dostoevsky's *Notebooks for The Possessed*:

> In his notes, Kartuzov is ambiguously foolish and pure, dignified and comic, a defender of the Amazon's (Horsewoman's) honor and something of a pest in his defense of her. The portrait degenerates by the time it reaches the final version, where Lebiadkin is a drunk, a mistreater of his sister, only a pest to Lisa, and the pawn of people like Liputin. The love and defense of his lady, and the dignity, are still there, but both are distorted, eccentric, unpredictable. Lebiadkin is a comic buffoon, foolishly clutching shreds of dignity. (Dostoevsky, 1968: 36)

Unaware of (or just ignoring) some facts of life, Lebyadkin falls in love with Lisa, the beautiful heroine of the novel. He courts her with love-letters and love-songs, alternately begging and threatening her. His hopeless love is pitifully laughable, as is his particular style, a grotesque mixture of lofty eloquence with quasi-illiterate, clumsy and simplistic rhyming. 'I had a terrible time trying to find out what he knew and what he didn't know,' writes Dostoevsky in his *Notebooks*:

> Всё кратко, по-пушкински, с самого начала, без психологических тонкостей, с короткими фразами ... Картузов принес мне одну (?) деловую бумагу – безграмотный. Он был ужасно необразован. (Dostoevskey, 1974: 44)

Everything briefly, *à la* Pushkin, from the very beginning, without psychological subtleties, in short phrases ... Kartuzov brought me one piece of official correspondence ... quite illiterate. He was terribly uneducated. (Dostoevsky, 1968: 42)

The importance that Dostoevsky attributed to Lebyadkin makes much more puzzling the fact that Bakhtin, in his book on Dostoevsky's poetics, in which he dedicated a whole chapter to the concepts of the carnivalesque and the grotesque, basing it on the unexpected personality of the protagonists, does not mention Lebyadkin at all (Bakhtin, 1929 [1963]: ch. 4). It is also noteworthy that, apart from the song of Ivan in *The Nose*, which is taken from *The Brothers Karamazov*, this is the only musical setting of Dostoevsky's texts to which Shostakovich had set music. Shostakovich compiled and re-arranged the texts of the captain's verses, which are scattered throughout the novel. The texts for the first song of the four, 'The Love of Captain Lebyadkin', appear in three different chapters of *The Possessed*. Shostakovich also used some of the prose text before and around the verses, and inserted it into his musical settings.[21] The final version of op. 146 is a grotesque mixture of beauty and ugliness, of repellent images and pseudo-philosophical remarks, of poetic imagination and blatant illiteracy:

The Love of Captain Lebyadkin

Любви пылающей граната
Лопнула в груди Игната.
И вновь заплакал горькой мукой
По Севастополю безрукий.

A blazing cannon-ball exploded
In Ignatius' breast with love corroded.
And, armless, in an agony of pain,
For Sebastopol he wept again.

(Хоть в Севастополи не был
и даже не безрукий,
но каковы же рифмы!)

(Though I was never at Sebastopol,
and though I never lost an arm;
but what rhymes!)

И порхает звезда на коне
В хороводе других амазонок;
Улыбается с лошади мне
Ари-сто-кратический ребенок.
Совершенству девицы Тушиной,
Милостивая государыня,
Елизавета Николаевна!
О, как мила она,
Елизавета Тушина,

A star goes riding graciously
In a throng of amazons wild;
And from her horse she smiles at me
The aris-tocra-tic child.
To the paragon of Ladies,
Dear Madam,
Elizaveta Nikolayevna!
Oh, what grace,
In Miss Tushin's face,

Когда с родственником на дамском
седле летает,
А локон её с ветрами играет,
Или когда с матерью в церкви
падает ниц,
И зрится румянец благоговейных лиц!
Тогда брачных и законных
наслаждений желаю
И вслед ей, вместе с матерью, слезу
посылаю.

When with her cousin on side-saddle forth she sallies,
And playful zephyr with her tresses dallies,
Or when with her mother in church she bows low,
And on devout faces a red flush doth show!
Then for the joys of lawful wedlock I yearn

And after her, with her mother, never a tear I spurn.

В случае, если б она сломала ногу,
Краса красот сломала член
И интересней вдвое стала,
И вдвое сделался влюблен
Влюбленный уж немало.
Составил неученый за спором.

(Достоевский, 1872 [1974]: 95, 106, 210)

If She A Leg Should Break ...
If this beauty of beauties broke a leg,
she would be more interesting than ever before
And far more I love her, my sweet, and I beg
Her remember how I loved her of yore.
Composed by an untutored man during an
argument.
(Dostoevsky, 1872 [1953]: 128,140, 271–272)

It is difficult to separate the satirical from the grotesque in Shostakovich's musical settings. There are many satirical devices that are aimed at ridiculing Lebyadkin's lumpish verses. Thus Shostakovich emphatically uses the dilettante device of accommodating the text into the music by crowding many syllables into one bar, resulting in its filling with short rhythmic-value notes (Ex. 12.13). The simplistic musical rhyming, echoing the textual one, is satirical, too (Ex. 12.14).

Ex. 12.13
'The Love of Captain Lebyadkin', bars 27–33: 'Though I was never at Sebastopol, and though I never lost an arm; but – what rhymes!'

Ex. 12.14
'The Love of Captain Lebyadkin', bars 5–8 and 88–91

(A blazing cannon-ball exploded
in Ignatius' breast with love corroded)

(Oh, what grace
in Miss Tushin's face)

Shostakovich's musical setting is even more blatant when it presents the captain stumbling over difficult, long words. Here Lebyadkin has some problems with the pronunciation of the word 'aristocratic', a word which in this specific context makes his struggle even more ludicrous. The victorious melodic leap at the end of the phrase, concordant with other musical phrases' endings in this song as well as with his sense of triumph after he manages to pronounce the whole challenging word, supplies the music with the extra irony needed to avoid the simplistic burlesque just by a hair's breadth (Ex. 12.15).

Ex. 12.15
'The Love of Captain Lebyadkin', bars 66–73: 'aristo … aristo … aristocratic child!'

Lebyadkin's self-admiration for his own readiness to marry Lisa 'even if she breaks a leg' provides yet another satirical tinge (Ex. 12.16). His self-satisfied remarks are echoed by the heroic march (bars 152–164), which, in an exaggerated mockery of musico-dramatic style, is contrasted with her horrible, yet fictitious doom (bars 137–151). A further emphasis is put on the satirical towards the end of the song, in which the extremes of self-subjugation and overpowering victory are juxtaposed: in a sudden outburst of ostensible humility Lebyadkin seals his poem with the inscription 'written by an untutored man', while the music is, accordingly, immediately subdued to minor seconds in piano, in the lowest register (bars 165–176), only to leap abruptly again, in a subito fortissimo, to the final triumphant chords of Lebyadkin's ostensible conquest. All these satirical musical remarks have more than a tinge of the grotesque: Lebyadkin's ludicrous clumsiness bears a concealed threat.

The Russian concept of the grotesque, like other European perceptions of it, is connected with chaos. However, while the German grotesque seems to be focused on existential chaos, the Russian version seems to perceive chaos through more tangible descriptions of the uncontrollable mob.[22] Uncontrollable masses of people are always characterized in Russian literature and art both by their absurd ludicrousness as well as by the threat of violence that is felt to be inherent in any human gathering.

In Russian literature the power of the crowd is always related to violence, whether festive or furious. The sudden and unexpected changes in its mood that foretell destruction are symbols of chaos; when combined with descriptions of ridiculous aspects, the result is almost always grotesque, and as such it consistently appears in the works of Shostakovich.[23]

Ex. 12.16
'The Love Song of Lebyadkin'

'If this beauty of beauties would break a leg, she would be more interesting than ever before. And far more I love her, my sweetheart, and I beg her remember how I loved her of yore.'

This trait, so prominent in his music, is apparently connected with Shostakovich's more general dread of masses. In his memoirs he tells how he preferred to walk for more than an hour, every morning and evening, instead of pushing his way on the bus, as everybody else did (Volkov, 1979: 5). This characteristic perception, which associates an accumulating crowd with fear, violence and insanity, is also tangible in the works of writers from Shostakovich's circle of acquaintances, who belonged to the formalists and to the Serapion Brothers.[24] Viktor Shklovsky, in his *A Sentimental Journey* (1923), describes with his typical dry, laconic and repetitive sentences the events and results of the civil war.[25] In Shklovsky's writing the gradual process of mass accumulation is often mixed with other characteristics of the grotesque, such as the loss of boundaries between the animate and the inanimate. For instance, he describes a machine gun as a small animal, scared by the mass of people that is accumulating around it:

> Пулемет, как маленький звереныш, прижался к мостовой, тоже сконфуженный, его обступила толпа, не нападающая, но как-то напиравшая плечом, безрукая. (Шкловский, 1923 [1990]: 28)

> The machine gun, equally embarrassed, hugged the pavement like some little animal. The crowd clustered around it, not attacking or using their hands, but somehow pressing with their shoulders. (Shklovsky, 1923 [1984]: 10)

Shklovsky used a situation that had been described before by Mayakovsky in his poem 'Kindness to Horses' (1918), which Shostakovich referred to as his favourite (Volkov, 1979: 190). Here the grotesque 'inanimate', mechanistic element is represented by the faceless mob, which is not referred to as human but as an inanimate entity – 'Kuznetsky Street':

... Лошадь на круп грохнулась, и сразу за зевакой зевака, штаны пришедшие Кузнецким клешить, сгрудились, смех зазвенел и зазвякал: – Лошадь упала! – – Упала лошадь! – Смеялся Кузнецкий. ...	... On the roadway a cob toppled, and immediately, loafer after loafer, sweeping the Kuznetsky with trousers bell-bottomous, came mobbing. Laughter rang over and over, 'Horse flopped! Boo, hippopotamus!' The Kuznetsky guffawed.
Подошел и вижу глаза лошадиные ... Улица опрокинулась, течет по-своему	... I came up, glimpsed in the horse's eye: the street, up-turned, swam in all its reality. ...

Все мы немножко лошади,   we're all of us a little bit horses,
Каждый из нас по-своему лошадь.   each of us in his own way's a horse.
(Маяковский, 1918 [1956]: 10–11)   (Mayakovsky, 1918 [1985]: 75)

The feeling of the threatening power of an accumulating crowd, 'loafer after loafer' that 'comes mobbing', governs the whole process. Human and animal, the animate and the inanimate, all are mixed; beyond and above them the crowd, which always appears as a mass, always in the hunt, be it after a woman, Jews, a machine, a horse or a nose – always an impending, tangible menace. This sense of danger and evil is felt not only in the process of accumulation, but also in the very nature of the chosen musical cells. Shostakovich achieves this effect by using several musical elements, such as pitch, rhythm and timbre.

This is felt even in his small-scale works. The violence is already present in the opening bars of Lebyadkin's song, in the bass register, which, combined with certain rhythmical patterns and a rather dancing motion, seems to be associated, in much of Shostakovich's music, with a violent grotesquerie (Ex. 12.17).

Ex. 12.17
The opening bars of 'The Love of Captain Lebyadkin' introduce a violent dance

This opening remarkably resembles the choir of the servants in *Lady Macbeth of the Mtsensk District*.[26] In a unison, heavy, stamped waltz, the servants of the Izmaylov Estate express their compulsory sorrow about the departure of their master. The number of incongruities that construct this waltz – incongruities in topic, in musical style, and in text versus music – point to a combination of irony, satire and the grotesque. However, it is particularly the heavy basses which imply the violence and the dread hidden in this bitterly grotesque, self-satirizing singing.

More than other cultures, Russian thought seems to associate dance and the feeling of overcrowding. This leads to the combination of the amusing aspects of dance with the chilling fear that is connected with an accumulating crowd. Horror, sarcasm, irony and grotesquerie are intertwined in an accumulative process, and arrive at their climax in Shklovsky's characteristically laconic description of a dance in time of war:

С пересадками, везя с собой сыпнотифозных, переехал в Херсон.

…

Приехал первого мая. вело все и уже отцветало.
Жена болела сильно.

…

Вешают людей на фонарях и расстреливают людей на улице белые из романтизма.
Так повесили они одного мальчика Полякова за организацию вооруженного восстания. Ему было лет 16–17.
Мальчик перед смертью кричал: 'Да здравствует Советская власть!'
Так как белые – романтики, то они напечатали в газете о том, что он умер героем.
Но повесили.

…

Я лежал в гамаке, спал целый день, ел. Не понимал ничего.
Жена болела.
Неожиданно зашевелилось. В городе показались солдаты. Кто-то начал упаковываться.

…

Рвались к лодкам. На берегу лежали горы вещей.

…

К вечеру Алешки были заняты разбездом черкесов.
Началась лезгинка. Белые – народ танцевальный.
(Шкловский, 1923 [1990]: 206–208)

Changing trains, and taking some typhus cases along, I finally got to Kherson.

…

When I arrived on the first of May, everything had bloomed and already faded.
My wife was very sick.

…

The Whites hang men from the lamp posts and shoot them out of romanticism.
They hanged a boy named Polyakov for organizing an armed rebellion. He was about sixteen or seventeen.
Before he died, the boy shouted: 'Long live the Soviet regime!'
Since the Whites are romantics, they printed in the newspaper that he had died as a hero.
But they hanged him.

…

I lay in a hammock, slept the whole day and ate. I understood nothing.
My wife was very sick.
Suddenly things got lively. Soldiers appeared in town. People started to pack their things.

…

People were trying frantically to get at the boats. Heaps of things lay on the bank.

…

That night, Aleshki was occupied by a mounted patrol of Circassians.

They promptly began to dance the lezginka. The Whites love to dance.
(Shklovsky, 1923 [1984]: 200–202)

The associative link between an accumulating mob and a dance appears in
the paintings of Kustodiev and Chagall, in the literary works of Gogol and
Dostoevsky (the ball described in Dostoevsky's *The Double*, for example, has
clear associations with the protagonist's growing state of insanity) and in the
music of Shostakovich, where rhythmical heavy basses always have a threatening purport of violence, recalling strongly the 'crashing of heels' in the
governor's ball, from Gogol's *Dead Souls*.[27] When superimposed on dancing,
manifested either in a triple metre or in light musical elements like staccato,
regular melodic skips, etc., such basses convey a purport of the grotesque.
Incongruous mixtures of gruesome musical elements with light dance topics,
particularly triple metered scherzos and waltzes, also appear in Shostakovich's
instrumental works, where they seem to bear the same implications.

Ex. 12.18
A stamping waltz points at a grotesque obsession in Shostakovich's scherzo from his
Eighth String Quartet

A most obvious instance of such a grotesque dance appears in the Scherzo
of the Eighth String Quartet (Ex. 12.18). Here the waltzing accompaniment is
similar to that of 'The Love of Captain Lebyadkin' and the servants' waltz
from *Lady Macbeth of the Mtsensk District* (though here it is harmonized,
while in the other works it appears just in octaves). This accompaniment,
which begins with a heavy forte, supports a dancing melodic figure which

conveys signs of an alleged musical lightness: staccato and high pitch. On top of this basic incongruity the melodic figure obsessively repeats itself until it reaches a point of a chromatic fall, blurred by the trill in the second violin. This is an image of a compulsive, almost insane motion rather than of a lighthearted dance. The last semantic point is the melodic cell, made upon Shostakovich's musical acronym D–S–C–H motif, thus identifying himself with the miserable, grotesque dancing figure.

These characteristics, which appear in the songs and chamber works on a smaller scale, are enlarged and highlighted in the symphonic music. In the third movement of the Tenth Symphony the heaviness of the accompaniment and the shrill high pitches create an almost hellish waltz (Ex. 12.19).

Ex. 12.19
A heavy, violent waltz in Shostakovich's Tenth Symphony

The influence of Mahler's music is apparent in these examples, particularly in the use of pitch contrasts and of the minor modes, attached to waltzing accompaniments and dotted, light melodic figures. Nevertheless, obsessive repetitions that emphasize the purport of compulsive attitude and its relation to the grotesque are even more characteristic of Shostakovich (Ex. 12.20).

In the fourth movement of the Seventh Symphony obsessive repetitions are combined with extreme pitches and with heavy, steady stampings in the bass (bars 228–237). Abrupt, unexpected brass outbursts only stress the uncanny feeling, while the falsity of the ostensibly cheerful dance, in the top register, becomes more and more obvious. These grotesque double messages are

Ex. 12.20
The Scherzo from the Fifth Symphony

sometimes achieved by quite subtle devices, as in the Presto from the Sixth Symphony, in which the dubious waltzing effect emerges from the constant heavy stamping just as a result of a timbre change (bars 202–218). The closest instance of symphonic grotesque in Shostakovich's works seems to be in his Fourth Symphony. This is one of the earliest examples, as well as one of the most extreme, and perhaps it is no coincidence that it was written approximately at the same period as *Lady Macbeth of the Mtsensk District*.[28] Curiously enough, the orchestration is exclusively based on strings, as if it was written for an enlarged string quartet. Nevertheless, the heavy stampings, all of them with down-bow movement, bear no signs of chamber-music style. They support a quasi-Viennese melody, which is further distorted by an awkward tonality (Ex. 12.21).

The layers of the grotesque are nowhere clearer than here: the melody itself, with its strongly topical waltz features, yet with the apparent inability to match the Viennese stylistic tonal norms, could be perceived as a satire. Yet the heavy, stamping accompaniment adds to its ludicrous purport an under-tone of a violent threat, thus transforming it into a clear, transparent musical grotesquerie.

Sixty-two bars anticipate the climax of the grotesque dance in the third movement of the Sixth Symphony. A gradual accumulation of instruments and a gradual shift of emphasis to the higher pitches are combined with the

Ex.12.21
An early instance of waltzing violence in Shostakovich's Fourth Symphony

use of an ostinato pattern, an obsessive clinging to the beats, and specific rhythmic patterns that push forward the general musical momentum to a general sweep, bursting into the mad, grotesque 'waltzing'. The whole section begins with three instruments playing in unison, in a very narrow and low register. During the next 62 bars instruments are gradually accumulated and the pitch-range is broadened and pulled upward to the very high pitches of the piccolo. Two musical elements are almost constantly present. In the background there is an ostinato pattern, while in the foreground melodies and repeated rhythmic patterns add to the feeling of accumulated excitement, as does the fact that the whole section should be played in fortissimo and marcatissimo to its most grotesque heaviness.

The 57 bars (bars 176–233) in the fourth movement of the Seventh Symphony present a cumulative process, at the end of which twenty instruments burst into a mad, repetitive, very high-pitched fortissimo whirling dance. Here not only the density, pitch-ascent and dynamics, but also the metric and rhythmic elements, are of utmost importance: in this passage there are constant metric shifts from duple to triple meters and vice versa, so that when the music finally bursts into a constant triple-metre 'waltz' the feeling of a sweeping dance motion is much more emphasized. The rhythmic patterns used in the duple-metre sections are all dotted, rendering a stronger rhythmic drive. Whatever the specific chosen musical devices, in all these cases there is a sense of accumulated tension that actually explodes into those specific 'grotesque waltzes', analogous to the poetical, literary and even physical sensations of the tension caused by an accumulating, uncontrollable mob.

The grotesque in the Russian theatre

In the Russian theatre, more than in any other field of art, there were a number of artists, authors, painters and musicians who dealt with the grotesque. Both natural tendencies of the grotesque towards the terrifying and repellent on the one hand, and the ludicrous and satirical on the other, could not have been welcomed by the dominant trend in revolutionary Russian art. This trend was represented particularly by futuristic artists, like Alexander Rodchenko (1871–1956), Kazimir Malevich (1878–1935) and Lyubov Popova (1889–1924) and not by the new Marxist aesthetics, which preferred realist and 'positive' art to the grotesque's 'fantastic nihilism'.[29] Since Malevich, Rodchenko and Popova became the political leading artists of the 1920s, it is quite clear why the grotesque in Soviet art survived not as an independent trend of the fine arts, but was rather attached to the theatre (Clark, 1995: 103). Thus it appears in stage-settings and costumes for various productions. Chagall argued that everything that is painted is, eventually, a 'thing' and that therefore art is essentially figurative. 'A triangle is no less an object than a chair,' he stated, emphasizing that art needs to be elevated by the spiritual values it conveys and not by technicalities (Meyer, 1964: 272).[30] The 1920s Russian artists, whose art tended towards the grotesque, such as Altman, Chagall, Kustodiev, Goncharova and Mayakovsky, became mainly engaged in theatrical productions. Goncharova prepared the grotesque set-designs for Rimsky-Korsakov's opera *The Golden Cockerel* (1914), Kustodiev prepared the settings and costumes for Mussorgsky's opera *Sorochintsy's Fair* (1919) and for Leskov's *The Flea* (1924), and Chagall for *The Government Inspector* (1919) and Sholem Aleikhem's *Three Miniatures: The Agents, The Lie* and *Mazeltov* (1920). Vakhtangov's 1922 production of *Haddybuk* had grotesque set-designs, costumes and make-up; Meyerhold's 1926 production of *The Government Inspector* and the first part of Mayakovsky's *The Bedbug* (1928) had grotesque costumes and make-up (partly designed by Rodchenko). Mayakovsky himself prepared grotesque, caricatural costumes for his own play *Mystery-Bouffe* (1918). The Russian conception of the grotesque found its most overt expression in the theatre. Both Vsevolod Meyerhold (1874–1940) and Yevgeny Vakhtangov (1883–1922) developed theories of the grotesque in the theatre, and regarded it as its most important characteristic, a *sine qua non* of this art.

It is hard to over-estimate Meyerhold's influence on Shostakovich, whose music often seems to be saturated with the grotesque, up to the point at which it becomes its major element (for example in *The Nose* or in the Finale of the Second Piano Trio). Therefore, it seems of major importance to devote some space to Russian theories of the theatrical grotesque, and especially to Meyerhold and Vakhtangov, who were its initiators and enhancers.

In 1928, the year in which he wrote *The Nose*, Shostakovich was working as the musician – composer and piano-player – in Meyerhold's theatre in

Moscow. Here he initiated a long and significant work relationship that turned into a close friendship. During this year he lived in Moscow with Meyerhold and his wife, the actress Zinaida Raikh, who had the leading female role in the director's famous production of Gogol's *The Government Inspector* (1926). Thus Shostakovich practically lived in the environment of Meyerhold's 'theatrical theory of the grotesque'.

The Russian stage at the turn of the century was dominated by Konstantin Stanislavsky (1863–1938) and his 'method'. This method enabled actors to discard exaggerated theatrical mannerisms and render more realistic and credible interpretations of their dramatic roles. Stanislavsky worked in close collaboration with Anton Chekhov (1860–1904), whose dramatic writing focused on subtle psychological traits and processes and was therefore suitable for Stanislavsky's theatrical approach. However, this demand for theatrical realism went further and further. Stanislavsky's idea 'to bring life to the theatre' and the degree of accuracy that it demanded not only in the style of dramatic acting but also in the settings, the make-up, the background noises, etc., almost blurred the boundaries between theatre and life, and the art of theatre, *qua* Art, seemed to be threatened. This tendency was scorned mainly by Stanislavsky's two most outstanding pupils: Vsevolod Meyerhold and Yevgeny Vakhtangov. Several symbolist attempts by Meyerhold, presenting Ibsen and Maeterlinck, did not satisfy him; he did not want to present some metaphysical, mystical reality, but life itself, though, in an artistic way, making use of 'theatricality'. Dissatisfied with the lack of 'theatricality' in the theatre, Meyerhold and Vakhtangov left Stanislavsky's theatre (although both, particularly Meyerhold, remained attached to their teacher personally as well as to his method), and began a new, revolutionary approach to the theatre. It was the elder, Meyerhold, who began to formulate a 'theory of the Grotesque in the Theatre', a notion which influenced Vakhtangov, who transformed the expression 'fantastic realism' into a synonym of the grotesque.

New plays that made extensive use of the grotesque were written by the poet Aleksander Blok (1880–1921), whose *Balaganchik* (*The Puppet-Show*) was, apparently, the first overt manifestation of the grotesque on the Russian modern stage, and by Mayakovsky, who mixed his grotesqueries with a popular agitprop atmosphere (in his 1918 *Mystery-Bouffe*) and with social satire (in *The Bedbug* and *The Bathhouse*, written in 1929 and 1930, respectively). A renewed fascination with Gogol was in vogue: Meyerhold's 1926 production of *The Government Inspector* was a milestone in Russian theatre's history, and was one of the main stimulants for Shostakovich's opera *The Nose*, after Gogol's short story, as well as for Bulgakov's stage adaptation of Gogol's novel *Dead Souls*. A renewed fascination with Shakespeare swept the Russian theatre, with new interpretations of his plays that focused on their satirical aspects and on their grotesque figures. *King Lear* was a favourite for productions in which the grotesque figure of the fool received special attention. *Hamlet* went through many interpretations, from Gordon Craig's symbolist interpretation (1905), through Mikhail Chekhov's 'anthroposophic' production, to Nikolay Akimov's highly controversial 1932 production, in which Hamlet was portrayed as a fat hedonist who invented the ghost as part of his cunning plan to seize the crown.

While in Vakhtangov's productions the grotesque seems to be attached to his general expressionistic approach, by calling the grotesque 'fantastic realism' Meyerhold transformed it into an independent device that became the theoretical basis of his directing technique. The grotesque's main attraction for Meyerhold was its eccentricity. Shortly before his production of Blok's *Balaganchik*, Meyerhold went to Berlin, where he saw the productions of Max Reinhardt. Reinhardt's influence might have been mainly in Meyerhold's predilection for cabaret's culture, also easily discerned in Shostakovich's music from the 1920s and 1930s. However, his revolt against theatrical realism was mainly expressed by the search for unrealistic or fantastic ways of presenting dramatized realities (Symons, 1971: 29). Meyerhold's first experiment in the style of the theatrical grotesque was Blok's *Balaganchik* (*The Puppet-Show*), first performed in 1907. This was an instance of 'a play within a play', in which the former is not literally a play but a scenario inspired by the *commedia dell'arte*. The protagonists are puppets playing the traditional *commedia dell'arte* roles of Pierrot, Columbine and Harlequin. The plot is partly based on the inventory of the *commedia dell'arte*'s scenarios and partly on the puppets' own 'reality', which is presented to us as the encompassing play. The author of this play (the one which the audience experiences as 'theatre') enters the stage from time to time, demanding his authorial rights, which the puppets simply ignore: a fashionable philosophical hint at the idea of Man as a puppet which rebelled against its creator.

This particular situation, in which the boundaries between theatre and life, puppet and Man, are manifestly blurred, was further loaded with grotesque situations, such as Harlequin's alleged suicide, after which he remains hanging outside the window through which he has jumped, screaming that he is bleeding cranberry juice, or Pierrot's discovery that Columbine is just a cardboard figure. The whole production was a strange mixture of mockery on symbolist dramatic devices, coarse jokes, layers of reality, imagination and theatrical reality, artificial sentimentality and genuinely moving moments.

The influence of this play on Meyerhold's conception of the grotesque is evident in the title of his essay, a great part of which is dedicated to his ideas about the grotesque. The name of Blok's play is *Balaganchik* (*The Puppet-Show*) while Meyerhold's title for his essay is 'Balagan' (Meyerhold, 1911–12 [1969]: 119–162). The play was central to Meyerhold's theory: in 1914 he revived the play in his cabaret–theatrical studio, where he directed avant-garde plays under the name of Doctor Dapertutto (Braun, 1969: 115). His ostensibly paradoxical approach, which on one hand wanted to remain faithful to reality, while on the other strove toward breaking the barriers of naturalism in favour of 'artfulness', found itself compelled to exaggerate dramatic situations. It was these exaggerations of a formerly naturalistic approach that created the first Theatre of the Grotesque. This is the source of the notions of 'stylized reality' and 'fantastic reality'.[32]

Musically educated, Meyerhold highlighted the function of music in his productions, in a number of which Shostakovich was responsible for the performance of the incidental music. Following Meyerhold's demands, Shostakovich appeared on stage in some of the productions, most significantly in the Moscow production of *The Government Inspector*, where he posed as one of the guests in the ball (Volkov, 1979: 159).

It is worth remembering that in Gogol's original play no real ball is mentioned, but just a gradual accumulation of guests coming to congratulate the mayor's daughter on her engagement to the alleged government inspector. In his willingness to enhance the grotesque effects of the play, Meyerhold turned these scenes into a ball held at the mayor's house. Much of the ball-scene, particularly the incidental music written to it, seems to be inspired by Gogol's description of the ball in *Dead Souls*. However, the specific musico-dramatic import of the grotesque incongruities in this scene, including the idea of using a Jewish band playing Jewish wedding-dance music, has its roots in the opening scene of the third act of Chekhov's *The Cherry Orchard*, which likewise presents a ball in which a Jewish band plays dance music, as a metaphorical description of a society on the edge of a calamity.[33] Meyerhold was particularly impressed by the grotesque aspects of that ball-scene, as he wrote in a letter to Chekhov:

> Your play is abstract, like a Tchaikovsky symphony. Before all else, the director must get the 'sound' of it. In the third act, against a background of the stupid stamping of feet – this 'stamping' is what he must hear – enters Horror, completely unnoticed by the guests. (Meyerhold, 1969: 33. The letter is dated 8.5.1904)

In his later analysis of the play, criticizing Stanislavsky's naturalistic production of *The Cherry Orchard*, Meyerhold wrote about the same scene in a much more explicit way:

> The author intended the act's leitmotiv to be Ranyevskaya's premonition of an approaching storm (the sale of the cherry orchard). Everybody else is behaving as though stupefied: they are dancing happily to the monotonous tinkling of the Jewish band, whirling round as if in the vortex of a nightmare, in a tedious modern dance devoid of enthusiasm, passion, grace, even lasciviousness. They do not realize that the ground on which they are dancing is subsiding under their feet. Raneyevskaya alone foresees the disaster; she rushes back and forth, then briefly halts the revolving wheel, the nightmare dance of the puppet show. (Meyerhold, 1969: 28)[34]

The buds of Meyerhold's own interpretation of the last scene of *The Government Inspector*, twenty years later, and the stress he put on the incidental music for it, can already be noted in these words. Meyerhold's production of *The Government Inspector* made a special impression on Shostakovich, who was then working on his first opera, *The Nose*, also based on Gogol's work (Volkov, 1979: 159).[35] Although he disliked the musical pastiche of nineteenth-century Russian romances by Dargomyzhsky and Glinka, which Meyerhold had chosen to include in the ball-scenes, Shostakovich highly appreciated the original music especially written for the production by the Jewish composer Mikhail Gnesin (ibid.).

Jewish music in the Russian theatre of the grotesque

Gnesin was Meyerhold's close collaborator in the establishment of his first St Petersburg theatre studio in 1908, which was the director's first attempt at formal teaching of his theatre theories. Gnesin participated in the planning of the curriculum, taught music and rhythmical declamation in the studio, and collaborated in several of Meyerhold's productions (Braun, 1979: 95, 125, 221).

Shostakovich met Gnesin in those years and then, again, in 1943, when both lived in Ivanovo, a small suburb near Moscow, where composers were accommodated during the war, allowing them to continue with their work. Composers like Prokofiev, Khachaturyan, Gnesin, Myaskovsky, Kabalevsky and Shostakovich, who lived in the same neighbourhood, met in the evenings for music-making and exchange of ideas (Shneerson, 1984: 253). There is a considerable influence of Gnesin on Shostakovich's 'Jewish works', for example, in his Second Piano Trio (1944) and in his *From Jewish Folk Poetry* (1948). In these works Shostakovich does not ridicule or satirize, but deals in total earnest with the horror of the grotesque, with the awareness of death that has to be borne in life, with the Meyerholdian 'nightmare dance'. In several instances it seems that Shostakovich used the Jewish fate as a symbol of human fate, which, without any choice, dances toward its own death.

Gnesin's interest in traditional Jewish music as well as his fascination with the grotesque connects him, on one hand, with the traditional Jewish grotesque self-mockery, as expressed in the contemporaneous writings of Sholem Aleikhem, the art of Marc Chagall, and to East European Jewish folklore in general; on the other hand his work is related to the *commedia dell'arte* tradition, with its own characteristic grotesqueries and parodies, which were at the centre of Meyerhold's attention. The title of the music he wrote for the last scenes of *The Government Inspector* is revealing: *The Jewish Orchestra in the Ball at the Mayor's House: A Grotesque.*

Answering a series of questions about this work, Gnesin referred to his conception of a musical grotesque:

В целом, это произведение, названное 'Гротеском', относится
к области музыкального юмора: забавное, комическое доводится
здесь местами до 'смеха сквозь слезы', однако – по самому
заданию – не доводится нигде до границ той серьёзности,
которая характеризует постановку вопросов в 'серьёзных'
юмористических или глубинных сатирических произведениях.
(Гнесин, 1961: 197)

On the whole, this work, entitled 'Grotesque', is related to the area of
musical humour: the amusing and the comical are accompanied here, in
some places, by 'the laughter through tears', though – at the same time –
it does not trespass the borders of seriousness, which characterizes the
presentation of subject-matters in 'serious' humorous or deep satirical
production.

This 'laughter through tears' is achieved by a complex structure of dramatic and musical incongruities, resulting in ironical, parodic and grotesque
imports. The scenery purports two types of incongruity: the irony of the
dramatic incongruity between the dance and the forthcoming shame that is
pending on the participants of the ball, and the cultural incongruity of a
Jewish wedding musical band in a Russian gentiles' ball. The music, too,
bears a double incongruity: the parodic stylistic incongruity of Jewish *kleizmer*
music, trans-contextualized and patterned into nineteenth-century social dance-
forms, and the intrinsic incongruities between the musical correlations of
cultural units which are structured into East European Jewish music. This
results in a complex structure of ironic, parodic and grotesque incongruities
that may overlap each other, offering simply different viewpoints of the same
phenomenon (Fig. 12.1).[36]

The use of a Jewish musical band in non-Jewish social events is a historical
fact (Idelsohn, 1944: 455–460; Gnesin, 1961: 198). The Russian gentiles
often preferred the Jewish musicians, not only because of their higher musi-
cianship, but also because of their 'modesty and sobriety' (Idelsohn, 1944:
456). However, it is not for historical accuracy that Meyerhold, who was
known for his anti-naturalistic aesthetics, had chosen a Jewish band to supply
the music for the ball in his production of *The Government Inspector*, but
rather because 'the style of this kind of music intensified the tragi-comic
situation in the final scenes of the play' (Gnesin, 1961: 198). It was for its
eerie, surrealistically incongruent feeling of inappropriateness that Jewish
band music was inserted here.

Yet there are other more intrinsic reasons that led Meyerhold and Gnesin to
choose the Jewish band of *kleizmers* as a musical source for this ball, enhancing its grotesque effects: these are the very musical incongruities that abide in
the typical Jewish *kleizmer* music itself. Gnesin refers to this intrinsic incongruity, which makes the very music of the Jewish bands sound 'grotesque',
calling it, again, 'the laughter through tears' (ibid.: 201). This effect is apparently achieved in two coexisting areas: the area of the parodic–allusive and

Fig. 12.1
Dramatic and musical incongruities

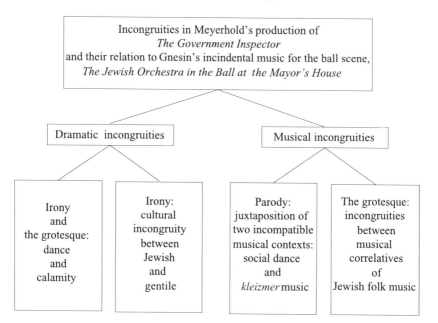

the area of the musical correlative. In the first area, the incongruities are a result of the superimpositions of two incompatible cultural contexts. Here the quadrille, a highly popular ballroom dance of the nineteenth century, serves as the parodied context, on which the Jewish *kleizmer* music is superimposed. Structured in a set of five distinct parts, the quadrille actually functioned as a kind of dance-suite, made up of the most popular dances of the period, which usually included a waltz, a galop, a mazurka and a polka. The quadrille is explicitly referred to in Chekhov's *The Cherry Orchard*; while the Jewish band is playing, the company, guests and hosts, are dancing the 'grand-rond', a characteristic figure of a quadrille.

Faithful to this source, Gnesin wrote his *The Jewish Orchestra in the Ball at the Mayor's House* for Meyerhold's production as a 'quadrille', in which he included the dance-forms from the ball in Gogol's *Dead Souls*, by which his quadrille parody seems to be inspired. To these he added a gavotte, probably to enhance the parodic impact of the whole piece. His choice of mainly heavy, fast dances (the polka and the galop) also enhances the feeling of the grotesque by contrasting the topical grace of a ballroom dance with the heaviness of these particular dances. The quadrille was played, uninterrupted, during the last scene of the production, after the mayor and his wife were carried off the stage. The dance, then, appears at the apex of ridicule and horror, coinciding with Meyerhold's own words about the ball-scene in Chekhov's *The Cherry Orchard*, about 'the dissonant accompaniment of the monotonous cacophony of the distant band and the dance of the living corpses' (Meyerhold, 1969: 28).

In his reconstruction of Meyerhold's *The Government Inspector*, Nick Worrall writes about the last scene of the production:

> As if in belated response to the mayor's cry about his disgrace being 'sounded from the steeples', the town bells suddenly began to ring out. The noise increased as the policemen began beating drums and blowing whistles. Underneath the cacophonous din, the Jewish orchestra could be heard playing a dance melody. Accompanying the din with their own shrieks and wails of horror, the entire cast cavorted and pranced across the open stage with their hands linked together, in a snaking, dancing file led by a fiddler. They looked like figures in a medieval Dance of Death. Across the stage they danced and through the lighted auditorium; into a medieval market place. (Worrall, 1972: 94)

Referring to the waltz in his quadrille, Gnesin describes the stylistic incongruity between ballroom dance and Jewish music as 'terrifyingly humouristic' (Gnesin, 1961: 205). Since there are no waltzes in Jewish folk music, he claims, a *kleizmer* band, accustomed to playing in duple metre but still insisting on playing a waltz, will necessarily generate a strange hybrid, which in fact is a non-waltz (ibid.: fig. 20). The incongruity between the two musical styles is apparent in all the musical elements: it is ridiculously obvious in the metrical clash between the duple and triple metres, abiding in the intra-beat level, where the oboe, clarinet and cymbals are doing their best, however unsuccessfully, to cope with the unfamiliar triple metre, as well as in the slightly ambiguous 6/8 metrical division. It is apparent in the melodic stumbling between the characteristic waltz-like chordal melody and the unavoidable falling back into more familiar melodic gestures of augmented fourths and seconds (bars 6–8). The parodic stylistic clash continues through the orchestration, in which the clarinet begins the melodic line (typical in *kleizmer* tunes) and hesitates there for a while until the violins take over their stylistically characteristic lead, then ends with the awkward harmonic clumsy cadence, in which the melodic sequence (bars 4ff.) is artificially resolved.

Gnesin emphatically noted that there is no musical satire here. To explain this point he compares the resulting effect of his waltz with Mozart's *Ein Musikalische Spass*, in which a non-fugal subject is used as a 'fugue', thus satirizing the dilettantism of the *Dorfmusikanten Sextett*.[37] In this waltz, writes Gnesin, there is no satirized dilettantism: the grotesque is solely created by the unresolvable clash between two incompatible musical styles that, because of historical and cultural constellation, were compelled to be juxtaposed. Such an artificially enforced combination inevitably results in a pitiful

Ex. 12.22
Mikhail Gnesin, quadrille from *The Jewish Orchestra in the Ball at the Mayor's House*: the waltz

and clumsy grotesque, evoking a mixture of compassionate alienation and frustrated self-repulsion (Ex. 12.22).

Another clumsy outcome of the superimposition of two alien musical styles is the gavotte. Although the duple meter and the relatively stressed first beat of the measure are common to both the Jewish folk style and to the gavotte, still the melodic gestures remain characteristically Jewish. The use of the eighteenth-century form of gavotte highlights even more its topical incongruities with the context into which it is inserted here. These can clearly be seen in the melodic level; however, several subtler (and more comical) hints are inserted in the rhythmical accompaniment (Ex. 12.23).

The rhythmic patterns, as well as the symmetrical structure of the phrase, are indeed 'well written' as a gavotte. However, Jewish music is full of unresolvable contradictory information, not only at the level of its musical correlatives, but also in its intrinsic nature. For example, the 'Jewish Dorian', i.e. a Dorian mode with a raised fourth, in which the gavotte is written, is in itself ambiguous, with its dysphoric minor third and raised fourth and

Ex. 12.23

Mikhail Gnesin, quadrille from *The Jewish Orchestra in the Ball at the Mayor's House*: the gavotte

euphoric raised sixth degrees.[38] Other ambiguities stem from certain processes which are based on the exaggeration of the musical units. In Gnesin's words, they have a natural tendency to extrapolarization (Gnesin, 1961: 201). The passage between musical units, that is from one polarity to the other, is achieved by transformative operations (ibid.). Gnesin explains and gives examples of the processing of musical elements in such transformations – using modifications of modes and of tempi and inserting pauses and 'sighs' – of the otherwise fluent musical message (ibid.: 202). The intended heterophonic effect of the melody played by the flute, oboe, piano and violins, which sounds so out of place in the strict context of the gavotte, clearly parodies the *kleizmer* improvisatory musical style. The last stroke of parody resides in the accompaniment, where the basses imitate as best they can the bass figurations of a gavotte, while the triangle and cymbals keep insisting on their customary (yet, in this case, considerably mutilated) 'oom-pah' patterns, the characteristic bass patterns of *kleizmer* music. These intrinsically incongruent musical entities served Gnesin as the basic material for further incongruities, located at levels closer to the surface of musical parody and dramatic situations. These were then moulded into larger grotesque scenarios in Meyerhold's production.

Another musical trait which is common to Jewish music and the musical grotesque is what Gnesin calls an 'ecstatic automatization' (ibid.: 201). This can be expressed either by constant musical motion, or by endless repetitions of relatively short musical units. Perpetual motion, which appears in the ritual music of many cultures, aims to bring the congregation into an ecstatic state of devotion, and is also one of the most important features of the grotesque (Jennings, 1963: 19). Constant repetitions can reflect an obsession, bordering on insanity, but they are also typical of Jewish Hassidic music, from which the *kleizmer* bands drew much of their musical material (Gnesin, 1961: 206; Braun, 1984).[39] Often both perpetual motion and endless repetitions will appear in combination. These musico-semantic units, frequently associated with the Dance of Death or with madness, are common to both the musical grotesque and to Jewish music. Gnesin's polka from his music for *The Government Inspector* is based on the characteristic Jewish musical descending gesture of 'iambic primas', in which each note is repeated, with a metrical stress on the repetition. It is presented in a perpetual motion, achieving after a while a mechanical, obsessive effect (Ex. 21.24).

Ex. 12.24
Mikhail Gnesin, Quadrille from *The Jewish Orchestra in the Ball at the Mayor's House*: the polka

This 'ecstatic automatization' correlates with two contradicting purports: on the one hand it is a grotesque reflection of the human puppet, whose helpless, mechanical Dance of Life was an ongoing subject in art and literature of the period; on the other hand it conveys, in its obsessive repetitions and modal peculiarities, an almost ecstatic state of soul, a mystical transfiguration that is the aim of the Jewish Hassidic dance, from which the Jewish East European *kleizmer* music drew much of its content. This perception of Jewish music and dance as an outlet for a grotesque *Übermarionette* functions as a cultural unit in twentieth-century Russian literature and theatre. As such it appears in Chekhov's *Cherry Orchard*, in Vakhtangov's production of *Haddybuk* and in Meyerhold's production of *The Government Inspector*.

The beggars' wedding-dance at Leah's wedding in *Haddybuk* is such a mixture of perpetual motion, whirled into endless, obsessive repetitions. They reflect both the surrealistic atmosphere of the mystic story about the possessed bride that surrounds the play, as well as the grotesque helplessness of the crippled human creatures that dance at the wedding. The impact of this production, and particularly of the beggars' dance in the second act, was overpowering. This act:

> began with the beggars' dance, which continued throughout, building to a frenzied pace ... Bent, crooked, some without noses, others suffering from dropsy, some idiotic, some consumptive or blind – they were like creatures from a nightmare ... (Worrall, 1989: 124)

Another critic was struck by its ritualistic aspects:

> This Habimah production is the only instance of extreme stylisation that
> I have encountered in which the whole of it seems inevitable. Here in it
> we get both the extreme stylisation that ritual can go to and at the same
> time the truth that worshippers bring to ritual. (Stark Young, quoted in
> Worrall, 1989: 126)

The music for the production of *Haddybuk* was written by Yoel Engel
(1868–1927), and is based on authentic Hassidic tunes. Here appear, without
exaggeration or modification, the characteristic repetitions of the main tune,
which is gradually accelerated and ascending in pitch: bars 3–4 are a repetition of bars 1–2, an octave higher and with a cadence; bars 5–8 are an exact
repetition of the first four, sequenced a third higher, and thus it continues,
always in ascending sequences, up to 'unreachable heights', thus evoking its
correlative cultural unit (Ex. 12.25).

Ex. 12.25
Yoel Engel's 'The Beggars' Wedding Dance' from Vakhtangov's production of
Haddybuk

This theme appears several times throughout the wedding-dance, in the
manner of a rondo's ritornello. Unlike a rondo, however, where the repetition
of the A section is a source of relief, here it is a source of growing tension.
Each time it appears higher, louder and faster, in an obsessive, ecstatic repetition, that reflects the mystical, spiritual uplifting of the wedding ritual while
simultaneously enhancing the sickly, frenzied dance of the crippled, monstrous beggars.

Engel's music faithfully follows the genuine lines of Jewish wedding music. Gnesin, however, modifies some authentic Jewish tunes by parodying
and intensifying the repetitious effect, using techniques of stylization, exaggeration, repetition and mechanization similar to those pointed by Tinyanov
in his article about Dostoevsky and Gogol (1921).[40] The musical theme in
Gnesin's 'Fantasia', which opens his music for the ball scene in *The Government Inspector*, is made up of four bars that repeat themselves six consecutive
times, with no addition of any other material or development except for
minute variations in pitch and orchestration (Ex. 12.26).

The tedious repetitions of the musical material reflect the accumulation of
guests on the stage, creating a musical correlative of an uncomfortably crowded
group of people, trying to make room for themselves while keeping their

Ex. 12.26

'Fantasia' from Gnesin's *The Jewish Orchestra in the Ball at the Mayor's House*

balance on the narrow moving platform, which represented the ballroom hall in Meyerhold's production:

> He [Meyerhold] wanted the effect of countless faces seen as if peering through the gaps of a rococo or pseudo-gothic background, and a feeling of nightmare … To the sound of the Jewish orchestra playing in the pit, small groups of guests begin to arrive at the mayor's house. Slowly, the platform began to fill as more and more guests arrived. Dressed in a multitude of brightly coloured dresses and shining uniforms, they soon filled the platform to capacity. (Worrall, 1972: 93)

The grotesque is ingrained in Shostakovich's music for the theatre. Grotesque parodies of social dances, particularly polkas and galops, abound in his incidental music for *The Bedbug*, *Hamlet* and *King Lear*, in his ballet music such as *The Golden Age* and *The Bolt*, and in his two operas.

Based on a mixture of the ridiculous and the horrifyingly insane, Jewish music was perceived by Gnesin, Engel and probably also by Shostakovich as the very embodiment of the grotesque in sound. For Shostakovich, however, Jewish music, as a particular instance of the grotesque that involves 'tears and laughter', may have symbolized a far larger idea: a representation of human fate, as portrayed in sound. This new aspect of the grotesque brings it to another level of ironic discourse, that of a positive existential irony, which accepts all discrepancies and contradictions not as mutually negating factors, but on the contrary, as parts of the rich, self-contradictory and yet all-accepting human existence.

PART VI
EXISTENTIAL IRONY

Alle Menschen sind etwas lächerlich und grotesk, bloß weil sie Menschen sind.
(Schlegel, 1796–1801 [1967]: 271)

People are all a bit ludicrous and grotesque, just because they are human beings.
(Schlegel, 1796–1801 [1957]: 145)

CHAPTER THIRTEEN

Compound messages

Satire, parody and the grotesque are three different techniques that overlap in many areas. Irony, whether satirical or not, is their shared purport; existential irony, in which the two layers of meaning contradict without necessarily implying any preferred solution, is their shared meta-structure.

Existential irony has a double nature: on one hand it uses contradictions to expresses the idea of *infinite negation*, which is the endless process of Socratic irony, as presented and analysed by Kierkegaard, and of romantic irony, as referred to by Schlegel.[1] In its second nature, on the other hand, it expresses precisely the contrary idea, that of *infinite accretion*, the process that accepts and affirms all contradictory data as part of one large, rich and varied picture, as expressed in Bakhtin's theory of the carnival and in his concepts of plurivocality and unfinalizability.[2]

Both natures of general, or existential, irony are represented in the works of Dmitri Shostakovich. Romantic irony seems to prevail in his non-satirical parodies. However, in certain instances the various stylistic layers, rather than contradicting, actually affirm, accept and reinforce each other, creating a texture that is more coherent than other parodies. Metaphorically speaking, it seems that the various elements create an amalgam rather than a mixture. Units that are normally separate from each other and belong to different cultural contexts become coherent contributors to something that is more than the sum of its parts; yet they never seem to lose their unique, separate identity. This kind of 'carnivalistic celebration of contradictions' is particularly apparent when Shostakovich uses Jewish musical idioms where both euphoric and dysphoric musical elements create a plurivocal, unfinalizable purport of infinite accretion.

Shostakovich's 'Jewish musical idiom': an amalgam of significations

The impact of Jewish music and its connotations within the thought and works of his artistic milieu is substantial in Shostakovich's music (Braun, 1986). This is not confined to vocal works, like the song-cycle *From Jewish Folk Poetry*, or to explicit reference to Jewish elements, as in the Finale of the Second Piano Trio. The intrinsic grotesque character of Jewish music as used in the theatre productions of Vakhtangov and Meyerhold seems to have penetrated a deeper layer, becoming an integral part of his more general musical output. Since the characteristics of Jewish music had for Shostakovich

a wider significance than their immediate 'Jewish' reference, his purely instrumental works have a remarkable number of 'Jewish music' moments.[3]
For example, the Piano Prelude in F♯ minor from his *24 Preludes and Fugues*
op. 87 is a work that has no direct political or any other extrinsic connotations. Nevertheless, it does reference, almost as an 'exercise', Jewish musical
idioms (Ex. 13.1). From its very start it seems that all characteristics of
Jewish *kleizmer* music are accumulated in the first 16 bars of the prelude: the
typical accompaniment figure, in duple metre; the repetitions of small melodic cells, both in an ostinato bass fashion (bar 1ff. and 7ff.) and in the
melody (bars 2–4, 6, and then again in bar 8, bars 12–13); the modal distortions of an augmented fourth (bar 16), and the typical 'iambic prima' (bars
10–11).[4]

Ex. 13.1
Prelude in F♯ minor from the *24 Preludes and Fugues for Piano*, op. 87

All these recall many other instances in Shostakovich's music, and not
only in the characteristic accompaniment, but also in the modal distortions,
that became part of his compositional language.[5] However, there is more in
this prelude than just the use of a folkloric idiom. These musical elements
correlate with both a semantic dysphoric purport (the mode, the melodic
descent, the obsessive repetitions that lead nowhere) and a semantic euphoric
one (the staccato articulation, the slurs on the semiquavers, the comfortable
register). Thus a mixture of euphoric and dysphoric purport is conveyed,
pointing to an ironical message. Additional musical information that relates it
to the grotesque is given from bar 21: a hopping melody, very similar to the
violin melody in the Finale of the Second Piano Trio and to melodic cells in
the 'Song of Poverty' in *From Jewish Folk Poetry*. It is interesting to note the
further distortion of this motif: in bars 21–24 the melody is congruent with
the modal F♯ minor, although it does not always converge with it, relating to
it more like an ostinato. In bars 31–34, on the other hand, the motif seems to
deflect completely from the mode, resulting in a tonal disorientation and in a
heightening of the tension. To this end Shostakovich uses conventional

musical correlatives of tension: a heightening of the general pitch-range
(particularly in the left hand), and a contrapuntal figure rather than a purely
accompanying one in the left hand. The general dynamic also rises, although
throughout the prelude it will never exceed piano. The focal point here is not
in the folkloric elements, but in the musico-semantic ironic purport of 'amused
tension'; Shostakovich uses elements characteristic to Jewish music that suit
this purport in order to achieve his own musical agenda (Ex. 13.2).

Ex. 13.2
Shostakovich's expression of existential irony through the combination of musical
Jewish characteristics and the musical grotesque in his Piano Prelude in F♯ minor,
op. 87

His own remarks on the subject, according to Volkov, sound like an almost
literal repetition of Gnesin's words:

> I think, if we speak of musical impressions, that Jewish folk music has
> made the most powerful impression on me. I never tire of delighting in
> it; it is multifaceted, it can appear to be happy while it is tragic. It is
> almost always laughter through tears.
>   This quality of Jewish folk music is close to my idea of what music
> should be. There should always be two layers in music. Jews were
> tormented for so long that they learned to hide their despair. They
> express despair in dance music … I can say that Jewish folk music is
> unique … This is not a purely musical issue, this is also a moral issue.
> (Volkov, 1979:118)[6]

The interesting point here is not Shostakovich's interest in Jewish music.
His interest was not folkloric or purely political. This is how he thought that
music should be. 'There should always be two layers in music': the grotesque
elements of Jewish music served Shostakovich in transmitting a wider purport that was very important to him: that of an emotional *mixture*, of a
musical double message, in short, of existential irony in music.

An amalgam of techniques

More than anything else, Shostakovich's music is a double-layered musical discourse. This fact has been widely acknowledged, but almost as a rule it was related to the political context in which he lived. Irony as the main message of Shostakovich's music has been detected only by a few, and even then it always remains attached to a political purport (Fanning, 1988). Nevertheless, it seems that, taken as a whole, this is a major, if not the foremost, purport of his artistic persona and his art. Shostakovich expresses irony through a mixture of satire, parody and the grotesque in his music. In order to convey existential irony Shostakovich superimposes on these mixtures musical cultural units that intrinsically contradict each other, particularly those inspired by the Jewish musical idiom.[7]

While parody was used by Shostakovich mainly in the Russian formalist sense, as a technique to enhance his own creative ideas, the combination of the Russian theories of parody and the grotesque, as presented by Shostakovich's contemporaries, mentors and friends, were used by him for the musical rendition of the more comprehensive idea of existential irony.

Shostakovich does not use mere musical analogies, since his musical structures are never devoid of significant content. His structures of irony, which may seem at first sight akin to analogies, are actually musical correlatives of structures, i.e. its elements correlate with elements that are not only contradictory to each other, but also bear a definite purport in themselves.

Shostakovich parodied folk music, popular dances, composers such as Bach, Rossini, Wagner and Mahler, taking from each source and then stylizing, parodying and developing those elements that agreed with his own agenda. The music of Mahler and Jewish East European music proved to be a particularly useful source for these manoeuvres due more to their intrinsically musical self-contradictory nature than to any ideological or political commitment.[8] The ironic structure serves him as a frame into which he inserts musical correlatives of semantic units, the combination of which result in musical amalgams that lend his music its unique character.

His mock 'non-waltz' from the first movement of the Tenth Symphony is such an amalgam. Its metrical basis is, indeed, that of a waltz. However, paraphrasing Wittgenstein's terminology, in the 'family of waltzes' this waltz is just a distant cousin, since it lacks many of the characteristic rhythmical gestures of a waltz. This unsure waltz is further 'self-negated' by a series of hemiolas that stay unresolved and nearly bring about the waltz's self-destruction, were it not for the repetition of the theme in an almost despaired act of self-assertion (Ex. 13.3).

Structurally, this theme is an ironic utterance, the metrical units of which endlessly deny each other. The direct correlative of a 'waltz that is not a waltz', which points to the topical correlation of 'a dance that is not a dance',

Ex. 13.3

The 'waltz–non-waltz' from Shostakovich's Tenth Symphony

which further correlates with the purport of 'a euphoric dysphoria'. As a structure, however, it is not a musical correlative but an analogue of existential irony, because the metrical incongruity by itself cannot convey the immediate impact of the *significance* of existential irony. In order to convey this particular significance through musical correlatives as well, Shostakovich inserts additional musico-semantic melodic and harmonic units into the basic ironical structure.

The waltzing melodic theme of the Tenth Symphony has been positivistically described as 'a pivotal melody' in which 'everything grows out of an oscillating semitone, G–F♯–G' (Roseberry, 1989: 70). This description seems to underrate the melodic cell's musico-semantic content, thus doing an injustice to its expressive potential. This 'growing out' is far more than a mere development of a melodic cell; the point is not that it develops just from one semitone, but that it develops *chromatically* and *downwards* while remaining *attached* to the melodic starting-point. It does not convey 'a development of a musical motif' so much as a musico-semantic manipulation of a cultural unit, the meaning of which points towards a dysphoric, helplessly dependent and disoriented sensuality, which is conveyed by its respective musical correlations: a melodic *descent*, its *oscillation* between a *fixed axis* and a widening melodic gap that grows *chromatically*. This musico-semantic amalgam, which can be loosely described as 'a tragically disoriented sense of life', is thus superimposed on the ironical structure of the 'waltzing non-waltz'.

The harmony is equally ambiguous: the melodic theme, which seems to start on a C major tonality, soon loses even this weak harmonic directionality due to the consistently blurred harmony in the accompaniment. Finally, Shostakovich adds to all the above incongruities, as a further stroke of genius, the use of the characteristically Jewish 'iambic prima' (Braun, 1984). This musical gesture is in itself ironical, combining the insistent melodic repetition of the stressed beat, which musically correlates with an assertive gesture, with the musical correlative of an incongruent empathic gesture: the sigh.

Existential irony as Shostakovich's meta-message

Artists, writers and composers do not necessarily express their immediate physical and emotional torments in their works. In spite of that, most biographies of Shostakovich seem to insist on such a direct reflection.

Virtually all the written material about Shostakovich has lingered on his historical and political contexts and the alleged ways in which they were reflected in his music.[9] Nevertheless, it seems that his cultural context had no less, and perhaps even much more, influence on the form and content of his musical output.

Shostakovich was, first and foremost, an artist. This statement, however, is not as straightforward as it may seem, since he was part of more than one artistic culture. His professional upbringing occurred in a revolutionary context, at the beginning of which 'art for art's sake' was the prominent idea. In a way, he remained faithful to this context: his principal attention and highest commitment were to his art. On the other hand, Shostakovich was very Russian in his approach to art in general and to music in particular. This cultural tradition appreciates literature, art and music in relation to the ethical messages they embody. Shostakovich's music, like the music of his Russian predecessors, is fully committed to referential expression, much of which has strong ethical connotations.

Ethical messages, however, need not be inevitably political. Shostakovich was a humanist. Recent biographies have stated and restated that he does not 'tell about' Stalin, Hitler or Khrushchev, but delivers a far more general satirical message condemning human stupidity and cruelty (Glikman, 1993; Wilson, 1994). I believe that Shostakovich is saying much more than that.

Søren Kierkegaard regarded irony as a matter of the utmost ethical consequence. To him, irony is not a mode of speech, but a basic attitude towards life and human existence. Taking this ideological position towards irony as the greater subject of his music and dealing with its ideological and ethical consequences, Shostakovich is no less referential than any other Russian traditionalist who states his ethics through his artistic work (although in most cases they reflect another kind of ethics, namely the political ethics of nationalism). In his music Shostakovich conveys the correlative of existential irony, i.e. *the referential idea of existential irony*.

Consequently, Shostakovich's music speaks about human nature as horrifying and ludicrous, simultaneously repellent and cruel, cowardly and loving, humorous and courageous. This very presentation adorns his music with the bitter-sweet smile of human compassion, which embraces, with helpless resignation as much as with ironical acceptance, the view that all people are grotesque, simply because they are human beings. When he inserted his own musical initials into several of his whirling, frenzied dances of life and death, he showed his awareness of being as human as those to whom his music was addressed.

Subtly, without rebellious manifestos or provocative credos, his parodies generate new musical utterances, walking in ways that have never been travelled before. Even Mahler, arguably the only composer with whom Shostakovich could be compared, eventually grants the pathetic and banal humankind the gift of divine grace; Shostakovich, on the other hand, grants us the gift of human compassion achieved through ironic acceptance. The love of the pathetic and the banal does not prevent him from expressing the most touching and tender subtleties of feeling; indeed, it only stresses his humane intention, transmitted through a compassionate irony and self-irony. Like a half-smiling, resigned Pierrot, Shostakovich's music seems to dance on a tightrope, letting its unresolvable incongruities express the infinite provisionality of existential irony.

More often than not, music not only expresses feelings and ideas, but actually does so better than words. This happens in Shostakovich's Waltz from the First Jazz Suite (1938). Written at the peak of the Stalinist terror years, it fuses the bitterness of satire, parody and the grotesque with the gracefully compassionate, telling of the ironical acceptance of the despicable, the ridiculous and the beauty of human existence. At such a point it is perhaps better to leave words behind and let the music utter its own discourse:

Ex. 13.4

Notes

Introduction

1. Seroff (1943) and Martynov (1947).
2. Sabinina (1959) and Rabinovich (1959).
3. Khentova (1964, 1975, 1979a, 1979b, 1980, 1982, 1985–86, 1986a, 1986b, 1990 and 1993).
4. Volkov (1979); Sollertinsky (1979); Luk'yanova (1980) and Gabrilovich (1983).
5. Roseberry (1981); MacDonald (1990); Wilson (1994); Meyer (1994). Collections of correspondence are a relatively new trend in Shostakovich studies, for example by Isaak Glikman (1994); a collection of his letters to Edison Denisov may be published by Nigel Osborne and Marina Adamia (personal communication).
6. For Russian publications see Dolzhansky (1956, 1958, 1963 and 1965); Sabinina (1965, 1976 and 1985); Martynov (1980); Mazel (1981); Khentova (1979a, 1979b, 1984 and 1993). For others, see Heyworth (1971); Ottaway (1978); Blokker and Dearling (1979); Norris (1982a); Roseberry (1989 and 1995); Longman (1989); Merrill (1990); Huband (1990); McCreless (1995); Redepenning (1995) and Taruskin (1995 and 1997: 468–511). An extreme example of ideological bias is the recent publication by Feofanov and Ho, *Shostakovich Reconsidered* (1998, London, Toccata Press). This book, published after the completion of the present study, does not disprove any of its points or conclusions.
7. Dolzhansky (1945, 1959 and 1966); Fyodosova (1980); Levando (1984); Bretanitskaya (1983); Fanning (1995b) and Kholopov (1995).
8. Norris (1982b, particularly the articles by Dearling and Stevenson) and Fanning (1995a, particularly the articles by Taruskin, Kholopov, McCreless and Redepenning: see the entries under the specific authors in the Bibliography).
9. Fanning (1988); Longman (1989) and Roseberry (1989).
10. Norris (1982b); see the articles by Norris, MacDonald, Dearling, Stevenson and Stradling. Others that relate to this trait in Shostakovich's music are Braun (1986), MacDonald (1990), Roseberry (1981 and 1989), Merrill (1990), Redepenning (1995) and Kholopov (1995).
11. Sollertinsky (1979); Vishnyevskaya (1984); Wilson (1994).
12. Fanning (1988: 6, 39, 47, 58, 70 and 77).
13. The well-known works by Langer (1942 and 1953), Zuckerkandl (1948 and 1959), Meyer (1956 and 1967), Cooke (1959), Coker (1972), Imberty (1973, 1975 and 1976), Kivy (1980, 1984, 1988, 1989, 1990 and 1993) and Cook (1992) are just a part of the vast literature on the subject.
14. The first attempts were made by Ruwet (1962, 1966, 1967a, 1967b, 1972 and 1975). After his came many others, of which it is worth mentioning the work of Nattiez (1973a, 1973b, 1975, 1987), Stefani (1974), Jackendoff and Lerdahl (1980), Lerdahl and Jackendoff (1983) and Mâche (1986).
15. To this trend, which deals mainly with musical topics, belong the works of Noske (1977), Ratner (1980), Allanbrook (1983) and Agawu (1991).
16. For example, Allanbrook (1983).
17. Eco builds his terminology on Schneider's concept of *units* (Eco, 1979a: 67; Schneider, 1968: 2).

18. To this approach contributed the writings of Francès (1958), Nattiez (1974), Doubravova (1984), Sheldon (1986), Kramer (1990), Staubman (1991) and Sheinberg (1992 and 1996a).
19. This view was enhanced by the writings of McCredie (1983), Net (1993a–e and 1994), Sheinberg (1995), Monelle (1990, 1991, 1992 and 1998) and Hatten (1994a).
20. In this he is referring to the Peircean infinite chain of signification, pointed out by Monelle (1992: 194), where he refers to Granger (1968: 114) and Greenlee (1973: 26). See also Eco (1979a: 71).
21. This quotation was taken from an early draft of Raymond Monelle's paper, and therefore is not identical with the reference. Further discussion of this point can be found in Hatten (1987: 410).
22. The studies by Nattiez (1990), Tarasti (1994), Hatten (1994a) and Monelle (2000) are prominent in this sense.
23. Recent works still try to overcome this problem, sometimes avoiding apparently unresolvable problems by a kind of theoretical bypass that eventually might prove itself to be useful for musico-semantic analysis (Cambouropoulos, 1996).
24. This time stressing his concern with narrativity. See Tarasti (1984, 1985, 1987b and 1987c, 1988 and 1994).
25. See Hatten (1985 and 1994a).
26. Tarasti (1979, 1982, 1985 and 1987a) and Grabócz (1986).
27. Greimas (1966 and 1970).
28. For an illuminating explanation of Greimas's semiotic square see also Monelle (1992: 244–252).
29. Robert Hatten chooses to use a general term and describes both 'happy vs sad' and 'tragic vs non-tragic' as 'semantic oppositions' (Hatten, 1994a: 30); however, for a study that focuses on structures of ambiguity, a sharper definition of the nature of semantic differences is imperative.
30. E.g. in Mozart's *Le Nozze di Figaro* (see Allanbrook, 1983: 66–67).
31. The fact that a known topos will tend simultaneously to function in the axis of musical topoi obviously complicates the structure; however, this, would be the more common situation.
32. A more detailed discussion of *markedness* can be found below, pp. 12–14.
33. R. Milgram, lecture given at the Tel-Aviv University, School of Education, November 1982.
34. I am well aware that Hatten might not be using the term 'cultural unit' in the same way that Eco does, a phenomenon which points to the term 'cultural unit' as culture-bound in itself.
35. In rare cases a semantic ambiguity could serve both functions. Such cases will be analysed further on in this study.
36. The concept of a structure as the source of meaning is further developed by Lotman (1995), who suggests a process of projection of a 'piloting structure' on signifiers, not to interpret, but moreover, to create the signified.
37. I base this statement on the definition of ambiguity as 'a word or phrase susceptible of more than one meaning: an equivocal expression' (*The Oxford English Dictionary*, 2nd edn, 1989, Oxford, Clarendon Press).
38. It should be rememberd that this 'past' is a cultural unit in itself. Even in the case of 'a dead metaphor' or a 'mere convention', their past is still functioning due to the *potential awareness* of their users on both sides of the communication channel of their existence. Therefore, no metaphor nor any other cultural units can be really 'dead', and no convention is 'mere' convention.

39. This correlation is already a second-level one, since the first level correlates 'high position in space' with what we call 'high pitch' and 'low position in space' with what we regard as 'low pitch' (Francès, 1958; Sheinberg 1995 and 1996a).

40. Compare with Hatten (1994a: 57–63). There is a notable difference between my description of this correlation, which is based on the *physical* gesture of 'reaching out', and Hatten's chain of descriptions of the very same musical gesture as 'upward', 'yearning', 'reaching', and then – the *spiritual* as well as the *encultured* – 'reaching for a higher existence' (ibid.: 57). Hatten aims here at *moral culturally favoured particularities*, while I am aiming at *pre-cultural biological generalities*. This difference stems from our different markings of the opposition 'encultured vs unencultured'. Both of us regard this opposition as privative (i.e. 'presence of A vs absence of A' – Battistella, 1990, referred to by Hatten, 1994a: 34). However, Hatten's depiction of markedness is phenomenological, while mine is historical. Therefore, while Hatten sees the 'unencultured' pole as the marked one (i.e. all correlations are based on encultured oppositions, and some of them also have unencultured elements), I see the 'encultured' pole as marked (i.e. all correlations are based on unencultured oppositions, and some of them have further encultured *oppositional tokens* that are therefore marked). This implies that correlations of oppositions that are based on encultured motivations tend to function as tokens of more general, unmarked oppositions. This idea, however, does not directly relate to the main point here, and therefore will not be further developed.

41. A hermeneutic interpretation would perhaps point to three different states of the psyche: youthful 'bravura', mature 'arioso' and the major-mode, 'nostalgic' part of the 'tarantella', all united under the human common gesture of 'reaching out'. To support this assumption it is interesting to point out that the only theme in the sonata that does not share this gesture is the 'tarantella' itself, associated with the cultural unit of the Dance of Death. This might be interpreted as a comment on the 'reaching-out' characteristic of human life that does not exist in death, and thus points to a yet higher level of meaning, 'life vs death' or even 'hope vs despair', which might be the meta-significance of the whole work. It is interesting to compare this hypothesis with Hatten's analysis of 'abnegation' in Beethoven's later works, pointing perhaps to the musical reflection of Beethoven's personal, spiritual and psychological growth.

42. For contrary examples, in which the Dance of Death is used to satirize the living (very much as in the original medieval Dance of Death), precisely by using triple-metre forms, see Mahler's description (in regard to the scherzo of his Second Symphony) of 'this ever-moving, never-resting, never-comprehensible bustle of existence' (in Cooke, 1980: 53) as well as the 'Immer zu! Immer zu!' of Marie while dancing the waltz in the second act of *Wozzeck*.

43. This principle is also applicable to a whole style that is in itself a parody of another style, like Russian neo-classicism.

44. An extremely high pitch-range also correlates, in many cases, with mental illness. It would be worth examining the many instances of insanity in musical literature, from the depiction of mental illness in *Wozzeck* to instances of general human insanity in Penderecki's *Threnody to the Victims of Hiroshima,* to discover how many of them make use of extremely high pitches.

45. Likewise, the concept of norm is particularly significant in studies of art, where both naturally and culturally motivated norms are constantly challenged as an inherent part of art's nature. This could lead to further studies that would

examine the role of ambiguities as indicators of historical change-points in style.

46. I regard here 'norms' as vectors that run along semantic axes. Therefore, topics or gestures are not norms, at least not in the sense used here, but at the most can be regarded as 'normative signs'. The difference is imperative, since a norm tends to be quantitative, in the sense that an element can be exaggerated beyond normative boundaries while still expressing the same topic and/or gesture.

47. A projection happens when a human biological or psychological quality is coordinated with a perceived element, imposing on it its own pattern (for example, when we tend to see the front of a car as a human face: its lights as eyes, etc.). A detailed discussion of musical correlations and bodily projections can be found in Sheinberg (1996a).

48. Kierkegaard (1841) is still the most comprehensive and insightful on this subject.

49. For various definitions and analyses of satire see Worcester (1940), Highet (1962), Kerman (1965), Hodgart (1969), Pollard (1970) and Blum (1979).

50. The classical studies on the grotesque are Kayser (1957) and Jennings (1963). During the 1970s and early 1980s there was a renewed interest in the grotesque, and quite a few studies tried to further sharpen and refine the definitions formerly achieved. Notable among them are Steig (1970), Barasch (1971), Thomson (1972), Geoffrey (1976), Henning (1981), Harpham (1982) and Fingesten (1984).

Chapter 1   The concept of irony: philosophical background

1. In other translations irony appears as more 'liberal' or 'nobler' than buffoonery.

2. These three translations reflect various ideas about irony that are characteristic of nineteenth-century thought.

3. 'Ethik [ist] der eigentliche Mittelpunkt der Kunst.' *Philosophiche Fragmente*, Zweite Epoche, I 13. in *Kritische Friedrich Schlegel Ausgabe*, 1967, Munich, Ferdinand Schöningh, Band 18: 198. Quoted by Handwerk (1985: 20).

4. These two kinds of irony, which are here described as 'finite' and 'infinite', are correspondingly named by Muecke as 'simple' and 'general' and by Booth as 'stable' and 'unstable'. However, they have roughly the same meanings, and all of them, so it seems, follow Kierkegaard's division.

5. Bakhtin (1941 [1984]). A more detailed account of Bakhtin's theories is given in the chapters on parody and the grotesque (Chapters Six to Twelve).

6. See below, pp. 298–302.

7. Morris translates '*Geist*' as 'intellect'; but, since the term '*Geist*' represents all the spiritual potential of the human being, I preferred to use the term 'moral' in the lines above.

8. Blok's formal 'return to Marxism' culminated in his poem *The Twelve* (1908). However, he was never fully accepted by the Soviets, nor regarded as a communist by his admirers in Russia, even at the height of the Soviet regime.

9. This is the technical basis for parody, also named 'trans-contextualization' (Hutcheon, 1985). See also the chapter on parody below (Chapter Nine).

10. In this respect there is not much difference between Marxist and several other systems of aesthetic thought.

11. For a detailed description of this interchange see Schwartz (1972 [1983]: 64) and Glenny (1966: 11).

12. These techniques are also characteristic of the later theatre of Brecht, who might have been influenced by the Russian formalists (Eaton, 1985: 21–22).
13. The relation between Bakhtin's ideas and Blok's *Balaganchik* are dealt with by Westphalen (1993).

Chapter 2   Incongruities as indicators of irony

1. In this respect the relation between 'irony' and 'metaphor' is analogous to the relation between 'S vs (-S)' and 'S vs non-S' in Greimas's semiotic square (Greimas, 1966).
2. Therefore, any statement, regardless of its structure, could be at least suspected of irony.
3. A further complicating factor is the reversed relation between the informative and the aesthetic value of irony, since uncertainty seems to be one of the measures of the aesthetic value of an ironic remark (Hatten, 1994a: 173). The subtlest (and therefore the most aesthetically valued) messages, in which the clues for irony will be few and ambiguous, will thus remain questionable precisely in their being ironical, the very measure according to which their value is estimated.
4. The work in question is Beethoven's *Grosse Fuge*. Longyear quotes Kirkendale, who described the 'unprecedented, almost exaggerated employment of contrapuntal artifices' in this work, and points to the 'deliberate highlighting of a contrapuntal artifice' (Longyear, 1970: 154, quoting Kirkendale, 1963: 23).
5. There are even studies about irony in musical works that completely ignore their musical aspects, and focus exclusively on dramatic situations (Vulpi, 1988).
6. In the last sections in this book, which analyse the grotesque and existential irony, I develop the idea of an infinite irony which is not based on negation (see Chapter Thirteen below).
7. The problematics of defining the norms is, as far as I know, not solved as yet. In the 1970s there were many attempts at statistical measurement of style, trying to apply the newly acquired device of computer analysis, but the problem proved to be far more complicated, since it involves a set of criteria that belong to widely divergent areas such as sociology of music, musical theory and musical cognition – to mention just the most prominent among them. The question has been raised again by Hatten (1996: 95). In the following chapters on musical satire and on the musical grotesque I shall suggest a set of criteria that may serve as a starting-point for renewed efforts in this direction.

Chapter 3   The structure of satire

1. It is interesting to compare this monologue with the captain's monologue in Georg Büchner's *Woyzeck* and with Berg's musical setting of this text, which emphasizes the satire on the captain's set of norms of what 'ein guter Mensch' is.
2. Voltaire's manuscript adds at this point 'Qu'en effet elle ne l'était pas' (Voltaire, 1959 [1758]: 131).
3. Characteristically, Gogol takes advantage of this opportunity simultaneously to satirize the socially fashionable discussions of Voltaire's ideas, exposing their pseudo-intellectual nature. Here he uses Voltaire as an example of the general

lack of norms, and not, as might seem on the face of it, to criticize Voltaire's scepticism of God.

4. All English translations of the Bible are taken from *The New Oxford Annotated Bible, with the Apocryphal/Deuterocanonical Books*, edited by Bruce M. Metzger and Roland E. Murphy, new revised standard version, Oxford University Press, 1989.

Chapter 4   The structure of musical satire

1. My attention was drawn to Stravinsky's satirical devices in *Pulcinella* by Joanne Towler (personal communication). Mussorgsky's *Rayok* and Prokofiev's *Classical Symphony* are discussed below, pp. 116–118 and pp. 100–101, respectively.
2. See discussion below, on pp. 112–115.
3. The satirical purport of this song is superimposed with the terrifying, and therefore it is fully discussed in Part V on the grotesque.
4. Mahler's satirical treatment of musical banality is discussed below, pp. 94–97 and 110–112.

Chapter 5   Satirizing techniques

1. In this it differs from the grotesque distortion, in which the focus is not on the distortion *of* a component, but on distortion *as* subject (see below in Part V on the grotesque).
2. This point is also related to the question of informative redundancy vs aesthetic redundancy, which has been dealt with elsewhere (Moles, 1958; Meyer, 1956 and 1967).
3. Ed. by Don Randal, London, Harvard University Press, 1986.
4. 'Хамите', 'Хо-хо!', 'Знаменито', 'Жуть', 'Не учите меня жить', 'Кр-р-расота!' and 'Ого!'
5. In using this quotation from a literary work of the 1920s there is obviously no intention to see any pejorative or racial remark in a positive light, but simply as a cultural phenomenon of its time and place. Such expressions, which regard black people as the epitome of the ignorant and primitive, are anything but rare in Western literature and art. An immediate instance that comes to mind, from the same cultural context as Ilf and Petrov's, is Stravinsky's almost ape-like 'black Moor' from *Petrushka* (I am grateful to Bish Sharma, for calling my attention to this point). I regard these expressions simply as a part of their cultural context, in the same way that I regard the 'greedy Jew' image of Shakespeare's Shylock and Dickens's Fagin (although not Cruikshank's *illustrations* of Fagin, see further on pp. 120–122).
6. For example, Alfred Schnittke recalled that his parents nicknamed their landlord 'Ostap Bender', after the famous charming-villain character from Ilf and Petrov's novels (Ivashkin, 1996: 37).
7. The similarity to Mahler's musical satires on the banal, which greatly influenced Shostakovich, is here more than obvious.
8. Such a drone figure is also often used by Haydn in his minuets, satirizing both the peasant clumsiness and the aristocratic audience which indirectly flatters itself in regarding minuets as a highly sophisticated dance.

9. The result of such explicit quotations may often degrade the music to the level of a simple burlesque, like the one Shostakovich actually made in his unpublished Satirical Cantata *Rayok: A Learner's Manual*, apparently written around 1948 (recorded by Erato, ECO 75571, 1990).

10. The sixth theme appears for the first time earlier, in bar 149. However, since it is written there in rather disconnected semiquavers, in the high strings accompanied by snare drum, I have preferred to copy here its second appearance, which is its popularly known form.

11. Mahler's scherzos or Shostakovich's burlesques could not be perceived as grotesque if the banal element in them were not perceived as ridiculous, which demands its former satirization within the given context (see Chapter Ten for a definition of the grotesque).

12. See the full analysis of this musical example below, pp. 131–136.

13. These four bars have aroused many assumptions concerning their original source, beginning with the above-mentioned passage from Lehár's operetta, through Tchaikovsky's Fifth Symphony, to the German anthem *Deutschland über Alles*. According to some of these, any descending scale could be regarded as the source of this 'quotation'. The most likely seems to be the first, particularly since it shares with the march passage, apart from the melodic contour, a similar kind of melodic sequence, has the same metrical structure and the same harmonic functions. Moreover, it seems that it had been a kind of private joke in Shostakovich's household, where it was sung to the original words, perhaps because Shostakovich's son was named Maxim (and not as a translated Russian song, as MacDonald had wrongly understood – MacDonald, 1990: 160).

14. See the music example on pp. 101 and 145–146.

15. There are, indeed, some accounts of Bartók's bitterness towards Shostakovich's success, but none of them is really cogent (for example, Milne, 1982: 102, Cooper, 1996: 80, Tallián, 1995: 112). Thus, before judging Bartók's set of norms and his musical applications of them, a more exacting analysis of his own work (and his sets of norms) is due, which is beyond the scope of the present study.

16. See further in Chapter Eight on parody, pp. 162–163 and 176–186 about Shostakovich's techniques of transferring compositional devices between various contexts.

17. See Chapter Twelve on the Grotesque, p. 300.

18. Some of the most popular translations are assembled in a special anthology, published in 1985, together with commentaries, analyses and historical reviews, and including the original in English: *Shekspir U. Gamlet: Izbrannïe Perevodi*, Ed. K.N. Atarova, Moscow, Ruduga.

19. This point is missed by Rowe (1976: 130), Law (1977: 106) and MacDonald (1990: 82). Unfortunately, all three based their commentaries on Yelagin's book without checking the music itself.

20. I could not get hold of Akimov's original text; the quotation is thus taken from Shostakovich's score.

21. As for particular characteristics of this song, and the way melodies were to be written in a 'Russian' style, see the analysis of another characteristic Soviet march, Knipper's *Stepnaya Kavaleriyskaya*, below on pp. 132–136. All the characteristics mentioned there also appear here. However, here it is the particular song and the censure it represents that is satirized, and not so much its style.

22. 'I love *Hamlet*. I went through *Hamlet* three times from a professional stand-

point, but I read it many more times than that, many more. I read it now'
(Volkov, 1979: 63).

23. More on this specific example is to be found in Chapter Nine on parody.

24. This definition may raise many problematical points: if accuracy is the criterion
for both a successful portrait and for the definition of a caricature, how could an
unsuccessful portrait be discerned? Other theoretical problems are the definition of 'defects' when the set of norms is unknown to the analyst, and the
ever-problematic question of authorial intention – how 'the purpose of fun and
mockery' could be definitely ascertained by analytical procedures. However,
since the main purpose here is to deal with satirizing techniques, I will continue
the analysis with the inspection of just one part of the definition, i.e. the subject
of 'overloading', the exaggeration and its manifestations.

25. See the reference to John Cage's *4'33"* above, p. 84. Indeed, it is highly
unlikely that it should be regarded as a satire; however, our only indication for
this is Cage's verbal account, and not the work in its own musical context.

26. Robert Samuels expands on this particular aspect to a discussion of Mahler's
structural 'gaps' in this first movement, which he claims reveal the ironic
purport of the movement. His argument refers to a particular moment before the
double bar, after the second subject; a sense of imitation is achieved by dividing
the descending scale, in itself a characteristic classical gesture, between the
violins and the bass strings, 'emphasising not the tonal function, but the fact
that it *is* tonally functional' (Samuels, 1995: 141–142; also in Pople, 1994:
154–157). Consequently, the familiar musical gesture, which often functions as
a structural component in eighteenth-century musical narrative, is transformed
here into an implicit commentary about the narrator, thus functioning in this
new context as an ironic remark.

27. Czerny, *School of Velocity*, Volume I, lesson 13.

28. See above, pp. 116–118.

29. Here, too, the device of condensation is used: most of the stereotyped 'Jewish'
physical characteristics – dark hair, long curved nose, large ears and thick lips
are also associated with evil: the dark is associated with the 'forces of dark-
ness'; the long curved nose with old age, witches, and ugliness as well as, by
gestural empathy, the 'nosy', 'grabbing' gesture; the thick lips are associated
with lust and coarseness (Gombrich, 1963: figs. 112–115 in the appendix;
Gilman, 1995: 99; Murray, 1995: 56 and 63). The condensation creates a
double meaning that equates physiognomic 'facts' with ethical and moral defects.

30. *Mausche* is explained in Heinz Küpper's dictionary as a derogative for '*Jude*',
specifying that it is derived from the Hebrew name *Moses*. All in all he lists five
usages of *mauscheln*, one of which, traced back to the year 1600, is 'fraudulent
commerce'. The Brothers Grimm's *Deutsches Wörterbuch* (1885), on the other
hand, defines *mauscheln* as 'to behave like a *Schacherjude*'. '*Schacherjude*'
means 'a haggling, cheating Jew'. Similar definitions also appear in the
Brockhaus Dictionary and Kluge's *Etymologisches Wörterbuch*, the latter trac-
ing the use of the word back to 1561, and confirming its stemming from
'Moysche', i.e. the Yiddish form of 'Moses'. The other four usages mentioned
by Küpper are: (2) to speak like a Jew (traced back to the 1600s); (3) nagging,
grumbling; secret grudging; to make a plot or plan an intrigue (used since the
1900s); (4) to tax, to take financial interest (this usage was popular in the
1960s!), and (5) unclear, unintelligible, blurred speech, mixed with Yiddish
words. The other sources also specify *mauscheln* as Yiddish speech, or a speech
of someone who 'sounds like a Jew'. Other dictionaries mention more mean-

ings: to cheat or haggle; to use Jewish gestures. Finally, *Mauscheln* is also a name of a specific card game, traced back to the Thirty Years War, in which the players try to cheat their opponents. (Part of this information was supplied by Dr Heather Valencia from the University of Stirling, who also helped me with the translations.)

31.   The two other prominent Jewish characters in the opera, Herodias and Salomé, are correlated with the evil not through their Jewishness, which is a rather background fact, but through their femininity. Their sexuality is not caricatured, but seriously depicted as the epitome of evil. The connection between evil and feminine sexuality and its musical correlations is, of course, a vast subject, and far beyond the scope of this study. Interesting steps toward such an analysis were made by Anne Suvoja-Gunaratnam in her paper about 'Kundry as Abject', presented in the Sixth International Congress of the ICMS, Aix-en-Provence, December 1998.

32.   The *Grove Dictionary of Music and Musicians* simply divides its article about the music of the Soviet Union into eleven different articles according to its different cultural territories, each one of them subdivided into art and folk music. Nearly all were written by different scholars (Grove, 1980, vol. 19: 334–424).

33.   For a comprehensive list of such collections see the Grove article on Russian folk music (1980, vol. 19: 398).

34.   On a more personal level, it is quite possible that in his memoirs Shostakovich is referring specifically to Lev Knipper's music. Knipper was of the same generation as Shostakovich, and developed along the same lines. He, too, began as a modernist, and his opera *The North Wind* was attacked in 1930 by party criticism together with Shostakovich's *The Nose* (MacDonald, 1990: 75). Unlike Shostakovich, Knipper immediately turned to writing mass-song symphonies and began to work with the Red Army Choir, with which he was, from then on, associated. Shostakovich became highly critical of Knipper's music (MacDonald, 1990: 105). Knipper's insistence, together with that of Asafyev and Dzerzhinsky, on helping Shostakovich 'to straighten out' after the *Lady Macbeth of the Mtsensk District* crisis, made possibly with the best of intentions to save him from danger in the terror-laden atmosphere of 1936, might have hurt Shostakovich's self-esteem even more. (MacDonald, 1990: 127). This, however, cannot be inferred from the analysed musical passage from *The Nose* (see pp. 132–136 below), since it was written when both Shostakovich and Knipper were still considered 'Modernist'.

35.   See note on p. 12 above. The inspiration for these dissonances might have its source in the following story, told by Shostakovich:

> [Voroshilov] loved choral singing. He sang himself, he was a tenor, and that's probably why he felt he was as much a specialist in music as Zhdanov. He longed to give valuable advice to composers and performers. His favourite works were Ukrainian folksongs. He used to sing them with his puny tenor voice. One of my actor friends told me how he sang with Stalin, Voroshilov, and Zhdanov after a reception. The soloists of the Bolshoi modestly sang along with the leaders. A horrible dissonance hung in the air. (Volkov, 1979: 75)

Chapter 6   Definitions of parody

1.   All major works about the theory of parody agree on these points (Tïnyanov, 1921 [1979]: 104; Bakhtin, 1963 [1984]: 195; Shlonsky, 1966: 797; Karrer, 1977: 39; Rose, 1979: 13–14; Golopentia-Eretescu, 1984: 130; Hutcheon, 1985: 6–7; Dane, 1988: 72–73).
2.   See above, pp. 43–49. In the case of parody, however, since it deals exclusively with intertextual commentary, the two last types of irony converge. Thus the analysis of 'parody as an ironic parabasis' refers to both romantic and existential irony.
3.   For two summaries reflecting contradictory opinions see Rose (1979: 20–36) and Hutcheon (1985: 54–60). Both relate to the infinite mirroring and multi-layered discourse that are the essence of parody, but while Rose sees the comic as a necessary element of parody, Hutcheon goes to great lengths to pinpoint the relative irrelevance of the comic to parody's structure and definition.
4.   See Shklovsky (1921) and Tïnyanov (1921 and 1927).
5.   See also the commentary on Kristeva in Rose (1993: 177ff).
6.   Cakewalk apparently began as parodical dances of American slaves, which imitated the slow, clumsy, self-important walk of their white masters (Hitchcock, 1980). Therefore, Debussy's choice of cakewalk rather than ragtime already bears satirical insinuations.
7.   Golliwogg, the black rag-doll, was the main protagonist in a series of children's books written by the American writer Bertha Upton and illustrated by her daughter Florence. Although written in the US (between 1895 and 1906), the series gained an enormous popularity in Britain and France, and the manufacturing of Golliwogg dolls became a prosperous industry in itself.
8.   See pp. 99–100 above.
9.   Compare with the analysis of Bartók's passage as a satire; see Ex. 5.12 above.
10. A repeating interval of a major second seems to be a traditional imitation figure of mocking laughter. Compare, for example, with the mocking chorus of villagers in the first act of Weber's *Der Freischütz*, where the same repeating major seconds figure is literally sung as laughter.

Chapter 7   The structure of parody

1.   It is interesting to note that none of the works on parody deals with its structure as a separate topic. This peculiarity is particularly apparent when compared with theoretical works on irony in which chapters devoted to structural questions abound.
2.   Dane (1988) supplies a detailed historical account of ancient and medieval parody, and Rose (1979 and 1993) gives a thorough overview of its etymology, based on its historical origins.
3.   Although Hutcheon does not use these terms in a structural sense, I find this terminological opposition useful to make my point about the prevalent, albeit misconceived, theoretical equation between structure and content.
4.   This equation is fallacious because parody, as any ironic structure, is potentially *but not necessarily* open-ended.
5.   Examples of this approach can be found in, among others, Tïnyanov, 1921 [1975]: 12–16 and 1927 [1971]: 69; Shklovsky, 1921 [1965]; Karrer, 1977: 60–68 and Riffatterre, 1984: 87.

6. See also Bakhtin 1934–35 [1981]: 362, regarding the structure of stylization.
7. This might be the source of Bakhtin's later fascination with the 'reversal of hierarchies' and the carnivalistic chaos to which such a process, that annihilates structural hierarchies, might lead (Bakhtin, 1941).
8. Bakhtin implicitly acknowledged this difficulty when he used the word 'parody' almost exclusively to denote the satirical type of parody, while open-ended manifestations of parody he regarded as heteroglossia.
9. At this point I am dealing with structure only, and therefore not describing the nature of the parodied object. However, it is worth mentioning that as far as it imitates the original, it must also be different enough to pinpoint the parody. On the other hand, if it distorts the original, it must be only to the extent to which the original is still recognizable, so the connection with its original context can be asserted.

Chapter 8 Historical background

1. Thorough accounts of his social background in those years are given in MacDonald (1990: 41); Volkov (1979: xxi); Sollertinsky (1979 [1980]): 42–46; Seroff (1943: 171) and Wilson (1994: 20–27).
2. Katerina Clark (1995) devotes her book to the description and analysis of the seventeen years between 1913 and 1930 in St Petersburg, displaying a highly complex network of interrelations between artists, writers, theatre directors and the politics of their time and place.
3. Quoted from the Serapion Brothers' manifesto (1921), in Slonim (1953: 295). The name was inspired by one of E.T.A. Hoffmann's characters, the count who, in detaching himself from the world, ended up believing he was the hermit Serapion, who could only live 'the real life' when disconnected from reality. It is probably no coincidence that this group chose as a model one of Hoffmann's most ironic personages, who chose personal insanity as an escape from the 'general insanity' of reality.
4. Kasack's word ordering of the original is misquoted; he missed the greeting's rhyming pun.
5. Zoshchenko is a main character in Shostakovich's memoirs. The inscription written on the photograph given to Solomon Volkov by the composer reads: 'To dear Solomon Moisyevich Volkov with affection, D. Shostakovich, 13/xi/1974. A reminder of our conversations about Glazunov, Zoshchenko, Meyerhold. D.S.' (Volkov, 1979, in the illustrations section).
6. For Shklovsky's article see Lemon and Reis (1965) and Sher's translation in Shklovsky (1929 [1991]). The first part of Tïnyanov's article is translated in Meyer (1989) and the second in Erlich (1975).
7. The fact that Shostakovich was by then only fifteen may seem confusing. However, he was a student at the St Petersburg Conservatoire from the age of thirteen, and his friends were, almost as a rule, far older than him (Wilson, 1994: 21 and 24). For the importance of oral performances and non-written communication in Petrograd in those years, see Clark (1995: 105).
8. Shpet was active in Moscow in the 1920s. His last publication is dated 1927. In the early 1930s his writings were banned; he was subsequently arrested and died in a Stalinist prison camp. A short survey of his life and theories appear in Zen'kovsky (1950 [1953]: 829–833) and Edwards (1972).

9. The translation of the Russian *ostranenye*, sometimes translated as 'estrange-
    ment' or 'defamiliarization' and sometimes as 'alienation', is problematic and
    deserves a separate discussion (Rose, 1993: 104). The associations of the first
    two terms are practical, and relate to art and literature criticism. 'Alienation',
    on the other hand, is an overcoded term which has complex philosophical and
    historical roots. However, as long as its implied ramifications are kept in mind,
    'alienation' should not necessarily be banned from use in discussions of parody
    (or any other ironic structure); on the contrary, it can give useful insights into
    the wider implications of artistic devices.

10. Some of Shklovsky's works appeared in several anthologies, some about Rus-
    sian formalism and others about other literary subjects. His 'Art as Technique'
    (1917) and 'Sterne's *Tristram Shandy*: Stylistic Commentary' appeared in Lemon
    and Reis's anthology about Russian formalist criticism (1965), chosen from
    Shklovsky's own Russian anthology, *Theory of Prose* (1929). The article about
    Tristram Shandy appeared in yet another anthology, about Lawrence Sterne,
    edited by Howes (1974). Shklovsky's whole anthology was translated by
    Benjamin Sher in *Theory of Prose* (1991), using slightly different terminology.
    The works of Tinyanov suffered an even more peculiar fate: his historical
    article 'Dostoevsky and Gogol: Towards a Theory of Parody' appeared in a split
    form: the first half of it was translated by Meyer and Rudy in their anthology
    about Dostoevsky and Gogol (1979), while the second half was published four
    years earlier in Erlich's anthology of *Twentieth Century Russian Literary Criti-
    cism* (1975). His *The Problem of Verse Language*, of 1924, on the other hand,
    was fully translated by Sosa and Harvey (1981), and his 'On Literary Evolu-
    tion', which is closely connected with ideas expressed in 'Dostoevsky and
    Gogol', was translated by Matejka and Pomorska for the anthology of *Readings
    in Russian Poetics* (1971). Thus not only did the formalists themselves create a
    new terminology that was inconsistent, but the English reader is further con-
    fused by the various translations of those terms, which sometimes overlap and
    sometimes discount each other. The 'luckiest', in this sense, is Mikhail Bakhtin,
    whose works are translated by people who belong, at least, to the same school
    of thought, mainly Michael Holquist, Saul Morson and Caryl Emerson. (See
    Bakhtin, 1981 and 1984, and Morson and Emerson, 1990.) Despite this more
    consistent approach, a scrupulous examination of the Russian original may
    reveal problematic points, mainly due to Bakhtin's own unclear terminology,
    but also due to the lack of clear parallel terminology in English, as a compari-
    son with Emerson's translation of Bakhtin's *Problems of Dostoevsky's Poetics*
    and an earlier translation, by Rotsel (1973), may show.

11. Given that the Russian language lacks articles, it is impossible to know whether
    Shklovsky meant to say 'a technique of defamiliarization' or 'the technique of
    defamiliarization'. The difference could be significant, but the question, it
    seems, must remain open. See also the explanations of *ostranenye* in Erlich
    (1955: 171–191) that discuss the basic concepts of the formalists, Terras (1985:
    152–153) and Sher (Bakhtin, 1981: xviii).

12. It is interesting to note that Sher (Shklovsky, 1990) refrained from translating
    Shklovsky's glossary.

13. The detailed analysis of these techniques appears below, in the section dealing
    with the techniques of parody.

14. Yevgeny Zamyatin is mentioned as one of the libretto writers, together with
    Alexander Preis and Georgi Ionin, both in Shostakovich's *Collected Works* vol.
    18, and in Hulme's catalogue (Hulme, 1982: 37). However, in *Testimony*

Shostakovich denied that Zamyatin had contributed anything to the libretto, and claimed that although he was approached to that end, he eventually failed, even in the one and only monologue he wrote for the opera (Volkov, 1979: 158).

15. If the role proves to be too stressful for the singer, Shostakovich allows this whole scene to be performed a minor third lower.

16. Shostakovich never admitted that Berg had any influence on him, nor that he had made a parody on *Wozzeck* in *The Nose*. However, Berg, Mahler and Stravinsky are composers whose music he admits 'he liked' (Volkov, 1979: 30). Nevertheless, the examples showing the connections between the works speak for themselves.

17. This is an important point, since this approach would change in the 1930s, after which Shostakovich might have been acquainted with Bakhtin's writings on parody. See below, pp. 168–186.

18. On the role of the captain in *Wozzeck* see the chapter on the grotesque below, pp. 223–225.

19. See below in the chapter on the grotesque, pp. 218–220.

20. Edison Denisov, who was acquainted with Shostakovich during the early 1960s, claimed he had never heard Shostakovich mention Bakhtin's name, nor seen a book of his in the composer's bookshelves (personal communication). However, it should be remembered that their relationship was never close, and towards the end of Shostakovich's life it worsened. On the other hand, Solomon Volkov did confirm Shostakovich's acquaintance with Bakhtin's writings and ideas (personal communication). Still, here too it must be admitted that Volkov is not a totally impartial source of information, particularly not after the controversy surrounding his book on Shostakovich.

21. I have omitted from the translation of the first quoted paragraph the additions of 1963.

22. Bakhtin's concept of unfinalizability is a complicated one, and has far-reaching philosophical and ethical repercussions. It is probable that this concept, too, does find expression in Shostakovich's music, but since it does not belong to parodic utterances it is not dealt with here. A full discussion of Bakhtin's concept of unfinalizability can be found in Morson and Emerson (1990: 36–40).

23. Eventually, he received an academic degree for that book, but not a *doktorat*. *Rabelais and His World* was published more than twenty years later, in 1963 (Morson and Emerson, 1990: xiv).

24. These were the accusations also addressed to Shostakovich's *Lady Macbeth of the Mtsensk District*.

25. The English translation of Bakhtin's *Problems of Dostoevsky's Poetics* was made from the 1963 Russian edition, which was revised by Bakhtin. For the Russian I preferred to work with the 1929 edition, since this is the one, I believe, that Sollertinsky and Shostakovich read. Whenever a quotation is given, I have carefully checked the 1929 edition in comparison with the translation. When I have found it necessary, I have made slight changes in the translation. These changes are always specified in a footnote. For example, the first two sentences of the above quotation do not appear in Emerson's translation, and I have translated them from the 1929 edition.

26. Although the scheme might recall Schenkerian schemes, there is no pretence here of making a traditional Schenkerian analysis. I use some of the traditional graphic tools only because I find them helpful and they clearly show the main harmonic relations in the work.

27. Such a modulatory ambiguity is present here, too; for example in bar 15, where the Bm chord acts as a II, in a process that began in bar 13, and also as a modulatory axis in which II=I, i.e. the cadence on Bm that is finally resolved in bar 22.

28. Of course, this beat could be also interpreted as V7–9–11 of E♭. However, this seems to be a bit out of place in the context of simple triads. Another interpretation of the very same progression could relate it to relations of seconds, since two series of parallel consecutive chords can be detected here.

29. See below, in the discussion of the Phrygian mode.

30. Consequently, the process in bars 13–17 could be also perceived as a modulation (a parody on classical and pre-classical modulations which were frequently based on a sequential progression) from the minor tonic to its major relative.

31. This is, of course, an 'altered' Neapolitan, since the traditional Neapolitan is a major chord. However, during the nineteenth century the use of a minor chord on the lowered II degree, considered as 'leading to the dominant of the subdominant', became more and more frequent, and by the time Shostakovich uses it here it is quite prevalent. B♭ major does appear in the prelude, but never in the context of the II degree (bars 10 and 23–24).

32. See below, pp. 195ff.

33. See Chapter Five on satire, pp. 87–88.

34. See above, in Ex. 8.4, the green patches that indicate the various uses of the Phrygian mode.

Chapter 9   Techniques of parody

1. Markiewicz quotes Quintilian's *Institutio Oratoria* 9, 2, 35, where he writes that the word *parode* 'ductum est a canticis ad aliorum [canticorum] similitudinem modulatis'.

2. A non-exhaustive list includes Tinyanov (1921 [1979]: 102); Bakhtin (1936 [1984]: 185); Shlonsky (1966: 797); Karrer (1977: 60); Rose (1979: 22); Deguy (1984: 4); Hutcheon (1984: 13 and 1985: 37). For inconsistencies within one work compare Karrer (1977: 60 and 98) and Hutcheon (1985: 6 and 37).

3. Bakhtin's translator, Caryl Emerson, pointed out that Bakhtin's translation was inaccurate, and gave the correct translation on p. 266 (note 4) of the translation. However, I chose to use Emerson's translation of Bakhtin's Russian version, since I am interested here in his ideas and his own emphasis of the quoted material.

4. I have modified Emerson's translation of this sentence.

5. A further parodic point here is Haydn's thematic allusion to Handel's *Harmonious Blacksmith*. However, this point is not necessarily connected to the comic effect of the sheer repetition.

6. Susanna's uneasiness (and/or amusement) is also expressed in her questioning 'Sotto i pini?', hinting at the sexual allusion of the particular suggested meeting place, under the pine trees.

7. The vowel 'O', when unstressed, is pronounced in Russian as 'A', thus resulting in a full rhyming sound between 'пела' and 'дело', which the music emphasizes.

8. Hutcheon solves this problem by including all borrowing phenomena under the umbrella term 'parody', thus denying the necessary structural element of semantic incongruity, limiting parodic incongruity to the work's syntactic level.

9.   The number of research works on the subject of musical quotations is vast. An annotated bibliography on musical borrowing is in progress (Giger: 1994).
10. The first approach can be seen in the writings of Tïnyanov (1927 [1971]: 69), Bakhtin (1963 [1984]: 194–195; see quotations above) and Hosokawa (1985: 184). Karrer (1977: 84–85), Hutcheon (1985: 40–41), Rose (1993: 77–78) and Burkholder (1994: 855–857) support the second view.
11. An ironical approach was, apparently, a natural tendency in Shostakovich's character, outside his musical activities (Volkov, 1979: 5–6; MacDonald, 1990: 23–24).
12. Mahler's influence on Shostakovich, particularly as manifested in his Fourth Symphony, is largely discussed by Roseberry (1989).
13. A separate study on the various manifestations of the waltz in the music of Shostakovich is in preparation.
14. Just to mention a few: Roseberry (1981: 173); Norris (1982a: 167, 182); Stradling, (1982: 211, 214); MacDonald (1990: 240–244); Wilson (1994: 435).
15. Although there have been attempts to interpret Rossini's theme as alluding to a 'mechanical macabre' motion and/or to a 'betrayal' motif, they don't seem quite feasible, and may not be totally devoid of an artificial enforcement of the critic's own ideas (e.g. MacDonald, 1990: 242–243).
16. See above, pp. 164–168.
17. See above, pp. 132–136.

Chapter 10   Definition, structure and content of the grotesque

1.   The definition of the grotesque as an unresolvable hybrid was suggested by Madeleine Şechter (personal communication; see also Şechter, 1994).
2.   See the section on infinite irony above, pp. 35–43.
3.   See the following section on existential irony.
4.   Bakhtin dedicates a considerable part of his chapter on 'The Grotesque Image of the Body' to a comparison between the 'normative', 'literary' canons of the body and the grotesque body, the impact of which is directly sensual (1941 [1965]: 319–322).
5.   See below, pp. 244–247.
6.   In his memoirs, Shostakovich repeatedly satirizes Stalin's predilection for the *Lezghinka* (Volkov, 1979: 108–109).
7.   See also p. 229–234 below
8.   See also pp. 234–238 below.
9.   This coincides with Gombrich's theory of projection, according to which we tend to project our bodily image onto whatever we perceive. (For the theory's implications for music, see Sheinberg, 1996a).
10. This scene in itself is a grotesque parody of the subject of *The Last Supper*.
11. See above, p. 219.
12. Other productions based on the *commedia dell'arte* masks seem to have engulfed the Russian stage in these years: Meyerhold's *Columbine's Scarf* (1916) and Tairov's *The Veil of Pierrette* (1916) were two distinctly different interpretations of the same play: Meyerhold presented it as a grotesque comedy, while Tairov saw it as a tragedy.
13. In one of his articles Meyerhold explains the connection between the grotesque

vaudeville shows and 'the art of the folk song and the folk theatre' (Braun, 1969: 123).

Chapter 11   The satirical grotesque

1. In order to be consistent, I kept Magarshack's translation for this excerpt, as with all other excerpts taken from *Dead Souls*. However, the translation is not completely loyal to the original, first in its use of 'Mr Chichikov' instead of the more familiar (and thus satirized, in this context) 'Pavel Ivanovich', and then in the subtle nuances of endearing expressions that are not translatable, and express an overly exaggerated affection, inappropriate to the described occasion.
2. The original songs did not have titles; their titles in op. 79 were all chosen by Shostakovich himself (Braun, 1989: 25).
3. For a discussion of Jewish jokes about Jewish parents' ambitions and pride concerning the intellectual achievements of their children see Davies (1986: 79–80).
4. Shostakovich had both the Russian translation and the Yiddish original, which was explained to him by Natalia Mikhoels, the daughter of the actor Solomon Mikhoels (who was himself executed by Stalin), and with whom he had a close friendship (Braun, 1989: 24).
5. This change, as well as the change of 'doctors' for the original 'engineers', was made by Dobrushin and Yuditsky, who translated the songs (Braun 1984: 264).
6. 'Oy' is an untranslatable typical Jewish exclamation. Its meaning changes according to context and intonation, semantically ranging from an expression of content satisfaction to the most desperate feeling of catastrophe. However, it usually signals a kind of resigned, sometimes even slightly smiling, despair.
7. One of my harshest teaching experiences was in a talk I gave about propaganda music, when not only I but also the students themselves were horrified to realize that in listening to a Nazi march, in spite of their following the text and being acquainted with its context, they also unknowingly stamped their feet along with the musical beat.

Chapter 12   The grotesque at the beginning of the twentieth century

1. The translation is taken from Patterson, except for the four last lines, which were translated by Raymond Monelle.
2. The translation is partly based on Mackendrick's (1979: 21).
3. *Wozzeck*, act II, scene 3: 'Man is an abyss, it makes one dizzy looking into his inner depths … I'm dizzy.'
4. The plates of Kustodiev's works are taken from M.G. Etkind, *Boris Kustodiev*, Moscow, Sovetskiy Khudozhnik, 1982. Those of Chagall are taken from Franz Meyer, *Marc Chagall*, New York, Harry and Abram Inc. Publishers, 1971. The reproduction of Picasso's 'Harlequin' is taken from Denys Sutton and Paolo Lecaldano, *The Complete Paintings of Picasso: Blue and Rose Periods*, Harmondsworth, Penguin, 1971. Bosch's 'Ecce Homo' was taken from Carl Linfert, *Hieronymus Bosch*, Köln, Verlag M. DuMont Schawberg, 1970.
5. Kustodiev made the illustrations for the printed edition of Nikolay Leskov's story, on which the opera is based.

6. The motif has been omitted from Exs 12.1 and 12.2 in order to illustrate the incongruity between the general purport of the music and this motif, which is reinstated in the next musical example.

7. This peasant 'Da!' will be echoed by Sergey in the next scene, thus emphasizing even more his simple-mindedness in contrast to the dream-like sensuality of Katerina.

8. The overt, almost coarse enjoyment of the basic functions of the body is also one of the most apparent aspects of the grotesque, and is much celebrated in Russian culture (Bakhtin, 1941: chs 5 and 6; see also Clark and Holquist, 1984: 306).

9. The scene with the passengers does not appear in Gogol's original story. It was incorporated by Preis, Ionin and Shostakovich, who used quotations and protagonists from other of Gogol's stories (Volkov, 1979: 157–158).

10. Shostakovich consulted with Natalia Mikhoels about the right pronunciation of certain words in the original Yiddish poems, the Russian translations of which he set to music in his song-cycle *From Jewish Folk Poetry*. The first (unauthorized) performance, in 1948, was at the Mikhoels' house (Braun, 1989: 24). There is a remarkable kinship between Shostakovich's so-called 'Jewish' works, particularly the last movement of his Second Piano Trio op. 67 (1944), written in memory of Sollertinsky, the Scherzo and the Burlesque, from his First Violin Concerto (1947–48), in which he inserted his musical acronym D–S–C–H, and this song-cycle, which was completed after the murder of Mikhoels (Braun, 1986: 737).

11. This potential of the Jewish culture in Russia for the grotesque was also used by Vakhtangov in his Moscow production for *Haddybuk* (1922); see the section on the grotesque in the Russian theatre, pp. 308–309 below.

12. For descriptions of significant traits of Jewish music in general and in the music of Shostakovich in particular, see Braun (1984, 1986 and 1989) and Sheinberg (1994).

13. This 'Jewish mode' is, in fact, only one of the many *steigers* (modes) used by Jewish cantors in prayers, and, subsequently, in Jewish folk music. The structure of this mode, characteristic of East European Jewish music, and called in *Hazzanic* literature the 'Ahava Rabba' mode, is similar to the Dorian church mode with a heightened fourth degree.

14. It could also be a kind of indirect allusion to Georg Grosz's '*Ecce homo*' (1920–21). Both Bosch's and Grosz's works are classic examples of the grotesque in art; Chagall's work, however, is also an example of parody through stylization. His imitation of certain elements, such as the raised hands, the angles of the rifles, and even the religious hint in the crossed flags, echoing the cross behind Jesus (which continues with an arm of a figure leaning on the post near him), point to a parody of techniques rather than a parody of the object. It seems as if he is applying Dostoevsky's literary techniques of parody, as suggested by Tinyanov and Bakhtin, to pictorial art.

15. It is interesting to note that the bottom left figure in Chagall's drawing seems to be a self-caricature.

16. See pp. 243–247 above.

17. It is interesting to note the difference, also in Chagall's works, between a faceless mob, like the proletariat in *The Revolution* (Pl. 12.20), and in the second one, in which every individual has a different face, in a similar vein to Bosch's famous grotesque '*Ecce homo*'.

18. A detailed analysis of this process, which examines the techniques by which

Shostakovich creates these two different types of 'mob music' is in preparation for a forthcoming paper.

19. Yelagin was wrong about the placement of the song quotation in the play. See above, p. 103–105.

20. In his *Notebooks for The Possessed* Dostoevsky called the personage that eventually became Captain Lebyadkin by several names: 'Kartuzov', 'Merzavstsev', 'The Captain', 'The Poetaster', etc. The amount of Dostoevsky's writing, in the notebooks, about and in the name of Lebyadkin is far beyond the figure's share in the actual novel, and points to a considerable amount of thought and importance ascribed to him.

21. The text of the first song is compiled from two verses that appear in the third chapter of part 1 of the novel, including a phrase in prose said after the first (in parentheses, in the text below); the next verse is taken from the fourth chapter, and the last one is compiled from its title, mentioned in a conversation in the first chapter of part 2 of the novel, and the verse that follows that conversation. The ending phrase was originally attached to the third verse.

22. For the German perception of the grotesque as the representation of existential chaos see, for example, Kayser (1957, esp. 13–27).

23. See, for example, pp. 277–282 above.

24. See pp. 155–157.

25. The title, of course, is a parody on Lawrence Sterne's novel that bears the same title.

26. See pp. 89–90 above.

27. See pp. 229–234 above. Musical 'stamping' does not necessarily have to be associated with the violent or the threatening; for example, it does not have such connotations in the 'stamping' Minuet from Haydn's Symphony No. 104, or in the Scherzo of Schubert's Seventh Symphony. In Shostakovich's music, however, the accumulation of musical correlatives of the violent unequivocally point to this purport.

28. The dating of the Fourth Symphony is complex, since it was apparently completed in 1936, but its publication, with some corrections, waited for 25 years, until 1961. One draft of the first movement is dated as early as 1934 (Hulme, 1991).

29. Chagall had bitter arguments and lengthy resentment with Malevich, who was, apparently, the main reason for Chagall to leave Vitebsk in 1920.

30. This attitude is in accordance with Bakhtin's ideas about 'Art and Answerability', Bakhtin's first published article (1919). Chagall was the Commissar for Art, he worked and taught in Vitebsk in the years 1918–20; Bakhtin was there in 1920–24, and had lectures and meetings there.

31. The employment of the *commedia dell'arte*'s figures was a commonplace in Russian puppet-shows. An obvious example is Stravinsky's Petrouchka, who is actually the Russian counterpart of Pierrot.

32. However, stylization does not explain the preference of the grotesque over, for instance, the burlesque, which is definitely an exaggeration of a simple comic situation, or over the extremely tragic, as happened, for example, in the theatre of Tairov (Worrall, 1989: 22–23).

33. See pp. 216–218.

34. This analysis was written in 1906, the same year as his first production of theatrical grotesque, in Alexander Blok's *The Puppet-Show* (*Balaganchik*).

35. Although Shostakovich denied any influence of Meyerhold's production on *The*

Nose, his own descriptions of the two works nevertheless do point to such an influence.

36. For example, the 'juxtaposition of two incompatible musical contexts' is the parodic manifestation of the ironic idea of 'cultural incongruity'.

37. See Mozart, *Dorfmusikanten Sextett (Ein musikalische Spass)*, K522. fourth movement, bars 28 ff.

38. Euphoric and dysphoric significations of intervals are, of course, culturally bound. The minor third has dysphoric connotations and the major sixth euphoric ones within Western culture because of their belonging, respectively, to the minor and major modes that culturally bear these significations. The raised fourth degree, on the other hand, bears dysphoric signification because it is alien to Western culture. Thus it is correlated with the unfamiliar and bizarre, which have dysphoric connotations. This is particularly true when it appears in a minor mode, both because of the dysphoric reinforcement of the mode itself and because of the resulting augmented second that is formed between the third and fourth degree, which is also alien to this culture.

39. Numerous repetitions, as correlatives of compulsion and obsession, can also convey a state of insanity.

40. See pp. 163 and 166.

Chapter 13   Compound messages

1. See Chapters One and Two.

2. See Chapter Seven.

3. For a full list of these works see Braun (1986).

4. See also Braun (1986) and Sheinberg (1994).

5. Obviously, Shostakovich's modal language is not solely based on Jewish modes. The point is that the kind of inflection characteristic to these modes went hand in hand with his other characteristic modal inflections, and he incorporated it as a part of his modal language (Dolzhansky, 1945 and 1963; for a more general outlook on Shostakovich's use of modality see Carpenter, 1995).

6. The question that is connected to the controversy about Volkov's publication – of whether Shostakovich did indeed say these very words or not – is quite immaterial. The impact of Jewish music can be seen directly in Shostakovich's works, and the above quotation only supports this finding.

7. This does not mean that Shostakovich had no sympathy or support for the Jewish cause, nor that he did not feel some identification with the persecuted Jewish people. My point is that these feelings are inseparable from his perception of Jewish music's characteristic (and also general ethos) of 'laughter through tears' as a fundamental metaphor of art (and probably also of the human condition).

8. As already stated, such ideological and political commitments might have been present (and in the case of Jewish music, indeed they are). However, Shostakovich's continuous elaboration of musical Jewish motifs and elements went far beyond social sympathies.

9. I find it necessary to refer here to the recent publication by Richard Taruskin. Expanding ideas he had expressed before (Taruskin, 1995), he pointed to the superficial approach of such studies (Taruskin, 1997: 468–497). I believe that, although not directly, the present study not only does not contradict, but actually supports Taruskin's ideas and interpretation, and vice versa.

Bibliography

Abbate, Carolyn (1991) *Unsung Voices: Opera and Musical Narrative in the Nineteenth Century.* Princeton, Princeton University Press.

Adler, Kathleen (1995) 'John Singer Sargent's Portraits of the Wertheimer Family', in Linda Nochlin and Tamar Garb (eds) (1995) *The Jew in the Text: Modernity and the Construction of Identity.* London, Thames and Hudson.

Adorno, Theodor W. (1971) 'Mahler: Eine musikalische Physiognomik', in *Theodor W. Adorno: Gesammelte Schriften* (1985), vol. 13: 149–309.

———— (1971) *Mahler: A Musical Physiognomy*, trans. by Edmund Jephcott, 1992, Chicago, The University of Chicago Press.

Agawu, V. Kofi (1991) *Playing with Signs: A Semiotic Interpretation of Classic Music*. Princeton, Princeton University Press.

Allanbrook, Wye J. (1983) *Rhythmic Gesture in Mozart: 'Le Nozze di Figaro' and 'Don Giovanni'.* Chicago, University of Chicago Press.

Apicella, Enzo (1993) *Mouthfool: A Gourmet Collection of Culinary Cartoons.* London, Grub Street.

Aristotle *Aristotle's Rhetoric*, trans. by J.E.C. Weldon, 1886. London, Macmillan.

———— *The Rhetoric of Aristotle*, trans. by R.C. Jebb, 1909. Cambridge, Cambridge University Press.

———— *The Works of Aristotle*, ed. by W.D. Ross. vol. XI: 'Rhetorica', trans. by W.R. Roberts, 1924. Oxford, The Clarendon Press.

———— *Poetics*, trans. by John Warrington, 1963. London, J.M. Dent & Sons.

At'ayan, Robert (1980) 'Armenia, folk music' in *The New Grove Dictionary of Music and Musicians*, ed. by Stanley Sadie, vol. 19: 336–349.

Austern, Linda Phyllis (1986) 'Sweet Meats With Sour Sauce: The Genesis of Musical Irony in English Drama After 1600', *Journal of Musicology*, vol. 4: 472–490.

Bakhtin, Mikhail (1919) 'Art and Answerability' in *Art and Answerability: Early Philosophical Essays by M.M.Bakhtin*, ed. by Michael Holquist and Vadim Liapunov. Trans. by Vadim Liapunov. Supplement trans. by Kenneth Brostrom, 1990. Austin, University of Texas Press, pp. 1–3.

———— (1929) *Problems of Dostoevsky's poetics*, trans. by R.W. Rotsel, 1973. Ann Arbor, Michigan, Ardis.

———— (1929, 1963) *Problemi Poetiki Dostoyevskovo*. 1963. Moscow, Sovetskii Pisatel'.

———— (193?) 'From the Prehistory of Novelistic Discourse' in *The Dialogic Imagination: Four Essays*, ed. by Michael Holquist, trans. by Caryl Emerson and Michael Holquist. Austin, University of Texas Press, 1981 (University of Texas Press Slavic Series, no.1).

———— (1934–35) 'Discourse in the Novel' in *The Dialogic Imagination: Four Essays*, ed. by Michael Holquist, trans. by Caryl Emerson and Michael Holquist, 1981. Austin, University of Texas Press (University of Texas Press Slavic Series, no. 1).

———— (1941) *Rabelais and His World*, trans. by Helene Iswolsky, 1984. Bloomington, Indiana University Press.

———— (1981) *The Dialogic Imagination: Four Essays*, ed. by Michael Holquist; trans. by Caryl Emerson and Michael Holquist. Austin, University of Texas Press (University of Texas Press Slavic Series, no. 1).

———— (1984) *Problems of Dostoevsky's poetics*, ed. and trans. by Caryl Emerson. vol. 8 of the series *Theory and History of Literature*, Manchester, Manchester University Press.

Baldinucci, Filippo (1681) *Vocabolario Toscano dell'Arte del Disegno*. Firenze, Santi Franchi al Segno della Passione.

Barasch, Frances K. (1971) *The Grotesque: A Study in Meanings*. The Hague, Mouton.

Batley, Edward Malcolm (1969) *A Preface to The Magic Flute*. London, Dennis Dobson.

Baudelaire, Charles (1852) 'De l'essence du rire, et généralement du comique dans les arts plastiques' in *Charles Baudelaire: Critique d'art*, text compiled and presented by Claude Pichois, 1965. Paris, Librairie Armand Colin.

Bauer-Lechner, Natalie (1923) *Recollections of Gustav Mahler*, trans. by Dika Newlin, 1980. London, Faber and Faber.

Bekker, Paul (1911) *Beethoven*. Berlin, Schuster & Löffler.

Berio, Luciano (1985) *Two Interviews with Rossana Dalmonte and Bálint András Varga*. New York, Marion Boyars.

Blok, Aleksandr (1906) Pis'mo k V.E. Meyerkhol'du. 22 Dekabrya 1906. *Sobranie Sochineniy*. Tom 8, 1963. Moscow, Gosudarstvennoye Izdatel'stvo. pp. 169–170.

———— (1908) 'Ironiya', *Aleksandr Blok Sochineniya*. Tom 2, 1955. Moscow, Gosudarstvennoye Izdatel'stvo.

Blokker, Roy and Dearling, Robert (1979) *The Music of Dmitry Shostakovich: The Symphonies*. London, The Tantivy Press.

Blum, Edward Alan (1979) *Satire's Persuasive Voice*. Ithaca, Cornell University Press.

Bonds, Mark Evan (1991) 'Haydn, Laurence Sterne, and the Origins of Musical Irony', *Journal of the American Musicological Society*, vol. 44, no. 1: 57–91.

Booth, Wayne C. (1974) *A Rhetoric of Irony*. Chicago, University of Chicago Press.

Branscombe, Peter (1991) *W.A. Mozart: Die Zauberflöte*. Cambridge, Cambridge University Press.

Braun, Edward (ed.) (1969) *Meyerhold On Theatre*. London, Methuen & Co.

———— (1979) *The Theatre of Meyerhold: Revolution on the Modern Stage*. London, Eyre Methuen.

Braun, Joachim (1977) *Jews in Soviet Music*. Hamerkaz Lemekhkar al Yehudey Brit-Hamoetsot uMizrakh Eiropa, research paper no. 22.

———— (1984) 'Shostakovich's Song Cycle *From Jewish Folk Poetry*: Aspects of Style and Meaning' in *Russian and Soviet Music: Essays for Boris Schwarz*, ed. by Malcolm Brown. Ann Arbor, UMI Research Press.

———— (1986) 'The Double-meaning of Jewish Elements in Dmitri Shostakovich's Music' in *Le Musique et le Rite Sacre et Profane*: vol. II, ed. by Marc Honegger and Paul Prevost. Strasburg, Association des Publications près les Universités de Strasbourg, pp. 737–757.

———— (1989) *Shostakovich's Jewish Songs*. Tel-Aviv, World Council Yiddish and Jewish Culture and Institute Yad Lezlilei Hashoa.

Brauner, Charles S. (1981) 'Irony in the Heine Lieder of Schubert and Schumann', *The Musical Quarterly*, vol. LXVII: 261–281.

Bretanitskaya, A.L. (1983) *'Nos' D.D.Shostakovicha*. Moscow, Muzyka.

Büchner, Georg (1836–37) *Woyzeck*, trans. by John Mackendrick, 1979, London, Eyre Methuen.

———— (1967) *Dantons Tod und Woyzeck*. Manchester, University of Manchester Press.

Bulgakov, Mikhail (1925) *Sobachiye Serdtse*, in *Sobraniye Sochineniy, v pyati tomakh, tom vtoroy*, 1989. Moscow, Khudozhestvennaya literatura, pp.119–208.

———— (1925) *The Heart of a Dog*, trans. by Michael Glenny, 1968. London, The Harvill Press.

Burkholder, J. Peter (1994) 'The Uses of Existing Music: Musical Borrowing as a Field', *Notes*, vol. 50: 851–870.

Cambouropoulous, Emilios (1995) 'A Computational Model for the Discovery of Parallel Melodic Passages' in *Proceedings of the XI Colloquium on Musical Informatics, Bologna 8–11 November 1995*.

———— (1996) 'A Formal Theory for the Discovery of Local Boundaries in a Melodic Surface', paper presented at the JIM'96 Computer Music Conference in Caen, France, May 1996.

Carpenter, Ellon D. (1995) 'Russian Theorists on Modality in Shostakovich's Music' in *Shostakovich Studies*, ed. by David Fanning. Cambridge, Cambridge University Press.

Chekhov, Anton Pavlovich (1904) *The Cherry Orchard*, trans. by Michael Frayn, 1978. London, Eyre Methuen.

Clark, John Richard (1991) *The Modern Satiric Grotesque and Its Traditions*. Lexington, Lexington University Press of Kentucky.

Clark, Katerina (1995) *Petersburg, Crucible of Cultural Revolution*. Cambridge, Mass., Harvard University Press.

Clark, Michael (1970) 'Humour and Incongruity', *Philosophy*, vol. 45: 20–32.

———— (1987) 'Humour, Laughter and the Structure of Thought', *British Journal of Aesthetics*, vol. 27, no. 3: 238–246.

Clark, Katerina and Holquist, Michael (1984) *Mikhail Bakhtin*. Cambridge, Mass., The Belknap Press of Harvard University Press.

Coker, Wilson (1972) *Music and Meaning: A Theoretical Introduction to Musical Aesthetics*. New York, The Free Press.

Conrad, Peter (1987) *A Song of Love and Death: The Meaning of Opera*. New York, Poseidon Press.

Cook, Nicholas (1992) *Music, Imagination and Culture*. Oxford, Clarendon Press.

Cooke, Deryck (1959) *The Language of Music*. London, Oxford University Press.

———— (1960) *Gustav Mahler, 1860–1911: A Companion to the BBC's Celebrations of the Centenary of His Birth*. London, BBC Publications.

———— (1980) *Gustav Mahler: An Introduction to His Music*. London, Faber Music.

Cooper, David (1996) *Bartók: Concerto for Orchestra*. Cambridge, Cambridge University Press.

Dane, Joseph A. (1988) *Parody: Critical Concepts Versus Literary Practices, Aristophanes to Sterne*. Norman, University of Oklahoma Press.

Daverio, John (1990) 'Reading Schumann by Way of Jean Paul and His Contemporaries', *College Music Symposium*, vol. 30, no. 2: 28–45.

Davies, Christie (1986) 'Jewish Jokes, Anti-Semitic Jokes and Hebredonian Jokes' in *Jewish Humor*, ed. by Avner Ziv. Tel-Aviv, Papyrus, Publishing House of Tel-Aviv University.

Dearling, Robert (1982) 'The First Twelve Symphonics: Portrait of the Artist as Citizen-Composer' in *Shostakovich: The Man and His Music*, ed. by Christopher Norris. London, Lawrence and Wishart.

Deguy, M. (1984) 'Limitation ou illimitation de l'imitation' in *Le singe à la porte: vers une théorie de la parodie*, ed. by GROUPAR: P.B. Gobin, J.J. Hamm, M.L. Kaitting, C. Thomson, M. Vernet and A. Wall. New York, Peter Lang: 1–11.

Dill, Heinz J. (1989) 'Romantic Irony in the Works of Robert Schumann', *The Musical Quarterly*, vol. 73, no. 2: 172–195.

Dolzhansky, Alexander (1945) 'O ladovoy osnove sochineniy Shostakovicha', in *A. Dolzhanskii: Izbrannie Stat'i* [1973]. Leningrad, Muzyka: 37–52.

———— (1956) 'O kompozitsii pervoyi chasti syedmoyi Simfonii Shostakovicha' in *A. Dolzhanskii: Izbrannie Stat'i*, 1973. Leningrad, Muzyka: 52–66.

———— (1958) 'Kratkie zamechaniya ob Odinnatsatoy Simfonii' in *A. Dolzhanskii: Izbrannie Stat'i*, 1973. Leningrad, Muzyka: 66–76.

———— (1959) 'Iz nablyudeniy nad stilem Shostakovicha (razroznennie repliki)' in *A. Dolzhanskii: Izbrannie Stat'i*, 1973. Leningrad, Muzyka: 76–86.

———— (1963) *24 Preludii i Fugi D.D. Shostakovicha*. Leningrad, Sovetskii Kompozitor.

———— (1965) 'Kamerno-instrumental'niye proizvedeniya D. Shostakovicha' in *A. Dolzhanskii: Izbrannie Stat'i*, 1973. Leningrad, Muzyka: 120–150.

———— (1966) 'Alexandriiskiy pentachord v muzyke Shostakovicha' in *A. Dolzhanskii: Izbrannie Stat'i*, 1973. Leningrad, Muzyka: 86–120.

Dostoevsky, Fyodor (1872) *Besï*, in *Polnoye sobraniye sochineniy v tridtsati tomakh*, 1974. Leningrad, Nauka, Tom 10.

———— (1872) *The Possessed*, trans. by David Magarshack, 1953. Reprinted 1971. London, Penguin Books.

———— (1872) *Besï: Glava 'U Tikhona'; Rukopisnïye redaktsii,* in *Polnoye sobraniye sochineniy v tridtsati tomakh*, 1974. Leningrad, Nauka, Tom 11.

———— (1968) *The Notebooks for The Possessed*, ed. with an introduction by Edward Wasiolek, 1935, Moscow. Trans. by Victor Terras. Chicago, University of Chicago Press.

Doubravova, Jarmila (1984) 'Musical Semiotics in Czechoslovakia and an Interpersonal Hypothesis in Music', *International Review of The Aesthetics and Sociology of Music*, vol. 15/1: 31–38.

Dyson, J. Peter (1987) 'Ironic Dualities in Das Rheingold', *Current Musicology*, vol. 43: 33–50.

Eaton, Katherine Bliss (1985) *The Theater of Meyerhold and Brecht*. London, Greenwood Press.

Eco, Umberto (1967) *Opera aperta: forma e indeterminazione nelle poetiche contemporanee*. Milano, Bompiani.

———— (1979a) *A Theory of Semiotics*. Bloomington, Indiana University Press.

———— (1979b) *The Role of the Reader: Explorations in the Semiotics of Texts*. Bloomington, Indiana University Press.

Edwards, Paul (ed.) (1967) *The Encyclopedia of Philosophy*. Reprinted edn 1972. New York, Collier Macmillan.

Eikhenbaum, Boris Mikhailovich (1918) 'How Gogol's "Overcoat" was made' in Robert A. Maguire (ed.) (1974) *Gogol from the Twentieth Century: Eleven Essays*, trans. with an introduction by Robert Maguire. Princeton, Princeton University Press: 269–291.

Eisenstein, Sergei (1929) 'A Dialectical Approach to Film Form' in Berel Lang and Forrest Williams, *Marxism and Art: Writings in Aesthetics and Criticism*, 1972. New York, David McKay Company Inc.

Elleström, Lars (1996) 'Some notes on irony in the visual arts and music: the examples of Magritte and Shostakovich', in *Word and Image*, vol. 12, no. 2: 197–208.

Ellis, Jack C. (1979) *A History of Film*. 3rd edn, 1990. London, Prentice Hall Inc.

Emerson, Caryl and Oldani, Robert William (1994) *Modest Musorgsky and*

Boris Godunov: Myths, Realities, Reconsiderations. Cambridge, Cambridge University Press.

Empson, William (1930) *Seven Types of Ambiguity: A Study of its Effects in English Verse.* London, Chatto & Windus.

Erlich, Victor (1955) *Russian Formalism: History – Doctrine.* 2nd rev. edn, 1965. The Hague, Mouton.

———— (ed.) (1975) *Twentieth Century Russian Literary Criticism.* New Haven, Yale University Press.

Fanning, David (1988) *The Breath of a Symphonist: Shostakovich's Tenth.* London, Royal Musical Association.

———— (ed.) (1995a) *Shostakovich Studies.* Cambridge, Cambridge University Press.

———— (1995b) 'Leitmotif in Lady Macbeth' in *Shostakovich Studies*, ed. by David Fanning. Cambridge, Cambridge University Press.

Fingesten, Peter (1984) 'Delimiting the Concept of the Grotesque', *Journal of Aesthetics and Art Criticism*, vol. 42, no. 4: 419–426.

Fletcher, M.D. (1987) *Contemporary Political Satire: Narrative Strategies in the Post-modern Context.* Lanham, University Press of America.

Francès, R. (1958) *La Perception de la Musique.* Paris, Librairie Philosophique J. Vrin.

Freeborn, Richard, Donchin, Georgette and Anning, N.J. (1976) *Russian Literary Attitudes from Pushkin to Solzhenitzin.* London, Macmillan.

Fyodosova, Eleonora Petrovna (1980) *Diatonicheskiye ladï v tvorchestve D. Shostakovicha.* Moscow, Sovetskiy Kompozitor.

Gabrilovich, Evgeny Yosifovich (1983) *The Fifth Quartet*, trans. from the Russian by Frances Longman. Moscow, Progress.

Gammond, Peter (1979) *The Magic Flute: A Guide to the Opera.* London, Breslich & Foss.

Geoffrey, H. (1976) 'The Grotesque: First Principles', *Journal of Aesthetics and Art Criticisms*, vol. 34: 461–468.

Gifford, Bill (1995) 'They're playing our songs', feature the online journal *Feed*, <http: //www.feedmag.com/feature.html>.

Giger, Andreas (1994) 'A Bibliography on Musical Borrowing', *Notes*, vol. 50: 871–874.

Gilman, Sander L. (1991) *The Jew's Body.* New York, Routledge.

———— (1995) 'Salome, Syphilis, Sarah Bernhardt and the Modern Jewess' in Linda Nochlin and Tamar Garb (eds) *The Jew in the Text: Modernity and the Construction of Identity.* London, Thames and Hudson.

Glenny, Michael (ed.) (1966) *The Golden Age of Soviet Theatre.* London, Penguin Books.

Glikman, Isaak (1993) *Pis'ma k drugu: Dmitry Shostakovich – Isaaku Glikmanu.* St Petersburg, Kompozitor.

———— (1994) *Lettres à un ami: Correspondance avec Isaac Glikman 1941–1975*, trans. by Luba Jurgenson. Paris, Albin Michel.

Gnesin, Mikhail (1961) 'O yumore v muzyke' in *Stat'i, Vospominaniy, Materiali*, ed. by R.V. Gl'ezer. Moscow, Sovetskii Kompozitor.

Goethe, Johann Wolfgang von (1801–30) *Goethes Faust*, Gesamtausgabe, no date. Leipzig, Im Insel Verlag.

———— (1801–30) *Faust (Part I)*, trans. by Philip Wayne, 1949. London, Penguin Books.

Gogol, Nikolai Vasilevich (1832) 'Ivan Fyodorovich Shponka and his Aunt' in *Diary of a Madman and Other Stories*, trans. with an introduction by Ronald Wilks, 1972. London, Penguin.

———— (1832) 'Ivan Fyodorovich Shpon'ka i yevo tyotushka' in *Vechera na khutore bliz Dikan'ki: Sobraniye Sochinenii*, vol. I, 1976. Moscow, Khudozhestvennaya Literatura.

———— (1834) 'How Ivan Ivanovich Quarrelled with Ivan Nikiforovich' in *Diary of a Madman and Other Stories*, trans. with an introduction by Ronald Wilks, 1972. London, Penguin.

———— (1836) 'The Nose' in *Diary of a Madman and Other Stories*, trans. with an introduction by Ronald Wilks, 1972. London, Penguin.

———— (1836) 'Nos' in *Sobraniye Sochinenii v shesti tomakh, tom 3: Dramaticheskiye proyizvedeniya*, 1952. Moscow, Gosudarstvennoye Izdatel'stvo.

———— (1836) 'Revizor' in *Sobraniye Sochinenii v shesti tomakh: tom chetvertiy: Dramaticheskiye proyizvedeniya*, 1952. Moscow, Gosudarstvennoye Izdatel'stvo.

———— (1836) 'The Government Inspector', in *The Government Inspector and Other Tales*, trans. by Constance Garnett. 1926, London, Chatto and Windus.

———— (1842) *Dead Souls*, trans. with an introduction by David Magarshack, 1961. London, Penguin.

———— (1842) 'Myertvye Dushi' in *Sobraniye Sochineniy v shesti tomakh, tom pyatiy, Myertvye Dushi: poema*, 1953. Moscow, Gosudarstvennoye Izdatel'stvo.

———— (1842) 'The Overcoat' in *Diary of a Madman and Other Stories*, trans. with an introduction by Ronald Wilks, 1972. London, Penguin.

———— (1842) 'Shinel' in *Sobraniye Sochineniy v shesti tomakh, tom tretii. Povesti*, 1959. Moscow, Gosudarstvennoye Izdatel'stvo.

Golopentia-Eretescu S. (1984) 'Parodie, Pastiche et Textualité' in *Le singe à la porte: vers une théorie de la parodie*, ed. by GROUPAR: P.B. Gobin, J.J. Hamm, M.L. Kaitting, C. Thomson, M. Vernet and A. Wall, 1984. New York, Peter Lang: 117–133.

Gombrich, Ernst H. (1960) *Art and Illusion: A Study in the Psychology of Pictorial Representation*, 3rd edn, 1968. London, Phaidon Press.

——— (1963) *Meditations on a Hobby Horse and Other Essays on the Theory of Art*, 4th edn, 1985. Oxford, Phaidon.

Gotuški, Dragutin (1977) 'Réalité, Musique, Langage: Contribution à l'Etude du problème de la Signification', *International Review of the Aesthetics and Sociology of Music*, vol. 8/1: 49–72.

Grabócz, Márta (1986) *Morphologie des Œuvres pour Piano de Liszt: Influence du Programme sur l'Evolution des Formes Instrumentales*. Budapest, MTA Zenetudományi Intézet.

Granger, Gilles-Gaston (1968) *Essai d'une Philosophie du Style*. Paris, Armand Colin.

Greenlee, Douglas (1973) *Peirce's Concept of Sign*. The Hague, Mouton,

Greimas, Algirdas Julien (1966) *Sémantique structurale: recherche de méthode*. Paris, Larousse.

——— (1970) *Du Sens*. Paris, Seuil.

GROUPAR: P.B. Gobin, J.J. Hamm, M.L. Kaitting, C. Thomson, M. Vernet and A. Wall (eds) (1984) *Le singe à la porte: vers une théorie de la parodie*. New York, Peter Lang.

Hamm, J.J. (1984) 'Parodie, pastiche: de l'écriture à la lecture' in *Le singe à la porte: vers une théorie de la parodie*, ed. by GROUPAR: P.B. Gobin, J.J. Hamm, M.L. Kaitting, C. Thomson, M. Vernet and A. Wall, New York, Peter Lang, pp. 105–116.

Handwerk, Gary (1985) *Irony and Ethics in Narrative*. New Haven, Yale University Press.

Harding, James (1965) *Saint-Saëns and His Circle*. London, Chapman & Hall.

Harpham, Geoffrey Galt (1982) *On The Grotesque: Strategies of Contradiction in Art and Literature*. Princeton, Princeton University Press.

Harrison, Daniel (1994) *Harmonic Function in Chromatic Music: A Renewed Dualist Theory and an Account of Its Precedents*. Chicago, University of Chicago Press.

Hatten, Robert (1985) 'The Place of Intertextuality in Music Studies', *American Journal of Semiotics*, vol. 3, no. 4: 69–82.

——— (1987) 'Style, Motivation and Markedness' in *The Semiotic Web*, ed. by Thomas A. Sebeok and Jean Umiker-Sebeok. Berlin, Mouton de Gruyter: 408–429.

——— (1994a) *Musical Meaning in Beethoven: Markedness, Correlation and Interpretation*. Bloomington, Indiana University Press.

——— (1994b) 'Twelve observations about musical gestures', part A of a presentation at the Fourth International Congress on Musical Signification, Paris.

——— (1995) 'Metaphor in music' in *Musical Signification: Essays in the Semiotic Theory and Analysis of Music*, ed. by Eero Tarasti. Berlin, Mouton de Gruyter.

————— (1996) 'John Rink, ed. *The Practice of Performance: Studies in Musical Interpretation*. Cambridge, Cambridge University Press, 1995', book review, *Indiana Theory Review*, vol. 17/1. Bloomington, School of Music, Indiana University.

Hauser, Arnold (1965) 'Alienation as the Key to Mannerism' (first published in *Mannerism: The Crisis of the Renaissance and the Origin of Modern Art*) in Berel Lang and Forrest Williams, *Marxism and Art: Writings in Aesthetics and Criticism*, 1972. New York, David McKay Company Inc.

Haweis, H.R. (1884) *My Musical Life*. London, W.H. Allen & Co.

Hegel, G.W.F. (1842) *Vorlesungen über die Aesthetik in Werke*, ed. by D.H.G. Hotho. Berlin, vol. X.

————— *Aesthetics: Lectures on Fine Art by G.W.F. Hegel* vol. I, trans. by T.M. Knox, 1975. Oxford, The Clarendon Press.

Henning, Sylvie Debevec (1981) 'La Forme In-Formante: A Reconsideration of the Grotesque', *Mosaic*, vol. 14, no. 4: 107–121.

Heyworth, Peter (1971)'Shostakovich Without Ideology' in Gervase Hughes and Herbert van Thal (eds) *The Music Lover's Companion*. London, Eyre and Spottiswoode: 198–206. (Originally published in *High Fidelity Magazine*, Oct. 1964.)

Highet, Gilbert (1962) *The Anatomy of Satire*. Princeton, Princeton University Press.

Hinchliffe, Arnold P. (1969) *The Absurd*. London, Methuen.

Hitchcock, H. Wiley (1980) 'Cakewalk' in *The New Grove Dictionary of Music and Musicians*, ed. by Stanley Sadie, vol. III: 611.

Hodgart, Matthew (1969) *Satire*. London, Weidenfeld and Nicolson.

Hoshovsky, Volodymyr (1980) 'Ukraine, folk music' in *The New Grove Dictionary of Music and Musicians*, ed. by Stanley Sadie, vol. 19: 408–413.

Hosokawa, Shuhei (1985) 'Distance, Gestus, Quotation: *Aufstieg und Fall der Stadt Mahagony* of Brecht and Weill', *International Review of the Aesthetics and Sociology of Music*, vol. 16/2: 181–199.

Houdebine, Anne-Marie (1984) 'Parodie et identité' in *Le singe à la porte: vers une theorie de la parodie*, ed. By GROUPAR: P.B. Gobin, J.J. Hamm, M.L. Kaiting, C. Thomson, M. Vernet and A. Wall. New York, Peter Lang, pp. 57–64.

Howes, Alan B. (ed) (1974) *Sterne: The Critical Heritage*. London, Routledge and Kegan Paul.

Huband, Daniel J. (1990) 'Shostakovich's 5th Symphony: A Soviet Artist's Reply...?', *Tempo*, no. 173, June: 11–16.

Hulme, Derek C. (1982) *Dmitri Shostakovich: A Catalogue, Bibliography and Discography*, 2nd edn, 1991. Oxford, The Clarendon Press.

Hutcheon, Linda (1984) 'Authorised Transgression: The Paradox of Parody', in *Le singe à la porte: vers une théorie de la parodie*, ed. by GROUPAR:

P.B. Gobin, J.J. Hamm, M.L. Kaitting, C. Thomson, M. Vernet and A. Wall. New York, Peter Lang: 13–26.

———— (1985) *A Theory of Parody: The Teachings of the Twentieth Century Art Forms*. New York, Methuen.

Idelsohn, A.Z. (1944) *Jewish Music in its Historical Development*. New York, Tudor Publishing Company.

Ilf, Ilia Arnol'dovich and Petrov, Evgenii (1928) *The Twelve Chairs*, trans. from the Russian by John Richardson, 1971, London, Sphere.

———— (1928) 'Dvenadtsat' stul'ev' in *Sobranie Sochineniy* vol. 1, 1961. Moscow, Gosudarstvennoye Izdatel'stvo.

Imberty, Michel (1973) 'Introduction à une sémantique musicale de la Musique Vocale', *International Review of the Aesthetics and Sociology of Music*, vol. IV/2: 175–196.

———— (1975) 'Perspectives nouvelles de la sémantique musicale expérimentale', *Musique en Jeu*, no. 17: 87–109.

———— (1976) *Signification and Meaning in Music: On Debussy's 'Préludes pour le Piano'*, Montreal, Groupe de Recherche en Sémiologie Musicale, Faculté de Musique, Université de Montréal.

Ivashkin, Alexander (1996) *Alfred Schnittke*. London, Phaidon.

Jackendoff, R. and Lerdahl, F. (1980) *A Deep Parallel Between Music and Language*. Bloomington, Indiana University Press.

Jankélévitch, Vladimir (1964) *L'Ironie*. Paris, Flammarion, Nouvelle bibliothèque scientifique.

Jarman, Douglas (1989) *Alban Berg: Wozzeck*. Cambridge, Cambridge University Press.

Jennings, Lee Byron (1963) *The Ludicrous Demon: Aspects of the Grotesque in German Post-Romantic Prose*. Berkeley, University of California Press.

Jost, Peter (1990) 'Brahms und die romantische Ironie zu den *Romanzen aus L. Tieck's Magelone* op. 33', *Archiv für Musikwissenschaft*, vol. 47: 27–61.

Kant, Immanuel (1911) *Kant's Critique of Aesthetic Judgement*, trans. with seven introductory essays, notes and analytical index by James Creed Meredith. Oxford, The Clarendon Press.

Karbusicky, Vladimir (1986) *Grundriss der Musikalischen Semantik*. Darmstadt, Wissenschaftliche Buchgesellschaft.

Karrer, Wolfgang (1977) *Parodie, Travestie, Pastiche*. Munich, W. Fink.

Kasack, Wolfgang (1988) *Dictionary of Russian Literature Since 1917*, trans. by Maria Carlson and Jane T. Hedges. New York, Columbia University Press.

Kayser, Wolfgang (1957) *Das Groteske: Seine Gestaltung in Malerei und Dichtung*. Oldenburg, G. Stalling.

———— (1957) *The Grotesque in Art and Literature*, trans. by Ulrich Weisstein, 1981. New York, Columbia University Press.

Kerman, Alvin Bernard (1965) *The Plot of Satire*. New Haven, Yale University Press.

Khentova, Sofia Mikhailovna (1964) *Shostakovich – Pianist*. Leningrad, Muzyka.

——— (1975) *Molodye godi Shostakovicha*. Leningrad, Sovetskii kompozitor.

——— (1979a) *Shostakovich v Petrograde–Leningrade*. Leningrad, Lenizdat.

——— (1979b) *D.D. Shostakovich v godi velikoy otechestvennoy voinï*. Leningrad, Muzyka.

——— (1980) *Molodye godi Shostakovicha*, 2 vols. Leningrad, Sovetskii kompozitor.

——— (1982) *Shostakovich Tridtsatletyï, 1945–1975: Monografiya*. Leningrad, Sovetskii kompozitor.

——— (1984) *Podvig, voploshchenniy v muzyke*. Volgograd, Nizhne-Volzhskoe Knizhnoe Izdatel'stvo.

——— (1985–86) *Shostakovich, zhizn' i tvorchestvo*. Leningrad, Sovetskii Kompozitor.

——— (1986a) *Shostakovich na Ukraine*. Kiev, Muzichna Ukraina.

——— (1986b) *Shostakovich v Moskve*. Moscow, Moskovskii Rabochii.

——— (1990) *Shostakovich i Sibir'*. Novosibirsk, Novosibirskoe Knizhnoe Izdatel'stvo.

——— (1993) *Udivitelnyi Shostakovich*. St Petersburg, Variant.

Kholopov, Yury (1995) 'Form in Shostakovich's Instrumental Works' in *Shostakovich Studies*, ed. by David Fanning. Cambridge, Cambridge University Press.

Kierkegaard, Søren (1841) *The Concept of Irony, With a Continual Reference to Socrates*, ed. and trans. with an introduction and notes by Howard V. Hong and Edna H. Hong, 1989. New Jersey, Princeton University Press.

Kirkendale, Warren (1963) 'The "Great Fugue", op.133: Beethoven's "Art of Fugue"', *Acta Musicologica*, vol. XXXV.

Kivy, Peter (1980) *The Corded Shell: Reflections on Musical Expression*. Princeton, Princeton University Press.

——— (1984) *Sound and Semblance: Reflections on Musical Representation*. Princeton, Princeton University Press.

——— (1988) *Osmin's Rage: Philosophical Reflections on Opera, Drama, and Text*. Princeton, Princeton University Press.

——— (1989) *Sound and Sentiment: An Essay on the Musical Emotions, Including the Complete Text of The Corded Shell*. Philadelphia, Temple University Press.

——— (1990) *Music Alone: Philosophical Reflections on the Purely Musical Experience*. Ithaca, Cornell University Press.

——— (1993) *The Fine Art of Repetition: Essays in the Philosophy of Music*. Cambridge, Cambridge University Press.

Kracauer, Siegfried (1947) *From Caligari to Hitler: A Psychological History of the German Film*. Princeton, Princeton University Press.

Kramer, Lawrence (1990) *Music as Cultural Practice: 1800–1900*. Berkeley, University of California Press.

Kris, Ernst and Gombrich, Ernst H. (1952) 'The Principles of Caricature' in Ernst Kris, *Psychoanalytic Explorations in Art*. New York, International Universities Press.

Kristeva, Julia (1966) 'Word, Dialogue and Novel', in *Desire in Language: A Semiotic Approach to Literature and Art*, ed. by Leon S. Roudiez and trans. by Thomas Gora, Alice Jardine and Leon S. Roudiez, 1980. New York, Columbia University Press.

La Grange, H.L. (1979) *Gustav Mahler, vol. ii, Vienna: The Years of Challenge* (reprinted 1995). Oxford, Oxford University Press.

Lamb, Andrew (1980) 'Galop' in *The New Grove Dictionary of Music and Musicians*, ed. by Stanley Sadie. London, Macmillan, vol. 7: 132–133.

Lang, Berel and Williams, Forrest (1972) *Marxism and Art: Writings in Aesthetics and Criticism*. New York, David McKay Company Inc.

Lang, C.D. (1988) *Irony/Humor: Critical Paradigms*. Baltimore, The Johns Hopkins University Press.

Langer, Susanne Katherina (1942) *Philosophy in a New Key: A Study in the Symbolism of Reason, Rite and Art*. Cambridge, Mass., Harvard University Press.

———— (1953) *Feeling and Form: A Theory of Art Developed from Philosophy in a New Key*. London, Routledge & Kegan Paul.

Law, Alma H. (1977) 'Hamlet at the Vakhtangov', *The Drama Review*, 21 December, 4 (T76): 100–110.

Léger, Fernand (1952) 'Satie inconnu' in *La Revue Musicale*, June: 137–138.

Lemon, L.T. and Reis, M.J. (eds) (1965) *Russian Formalist Criticism: Four Essays*. Lincoln, University of Nebraska Press.

Lerdahl, F. and Jackendoff, R. (1983) *A Generative Theory of Tonal Music*. Cambridge, MIT Press.

Lessem, Alan Philip (1982) 'Schönberg, Stravinsky, and neo-classicism: the issues reexamined', *The Musical Quarterly*, vol. 68: 527–542.

Levando, Pyotr Petrovich (1984) *Khorovaya faktura*. Leningrad, Muzyka.

Lineff, Eugenie (1905) *The Peasant Songs of Great Russia: As They Are in the Folk's Harmonization*. St Petersburg, Imperial Academy of Sciences.

Longman, Richard M. (1989) *Expression and Structure: Processes of Integration in the Large-scale Instrumental Music of Dmitri Shostakovich*, 2 vols. New York, Garland Publishing Inc.

Longyear, Rey M. (1970) 'Beethoven and Romantic Irony' in *The Creative World of Beethoven*, ed. by Paul Henry Lang. New York, W.W. Norton & Co. Inc.

Lotman, Mikhail (1995) 'Sound and Meaning in Poetry', paper presented at the Summer Seminar of the International Institute of Semiotics, Imatra, June 1995.

Luk'yanova, N.V. (1980) *D.D. Shostakovich*. Moscow, Muzyka.

MacDonald, Ian (1990) *The New Shostakovich*. London, Fourth Estate.

MacDonald, Malcolm (1982) 'Words and Music in Late Shostakovich' in *Shostakovich: The Man and His Music*, ed. by Christopher Norris. London, Lawrence and Wishart.

McCredie, Andrew D. (1983) 'Some Concepts, Constructs and Techniques in Comparative Literature and Their Interface with Musicology', *International Review of the Aesthetics and Sociology of Music*, vol. 14/2: 147–165.

McCreless, Patrick (1995) 'The Cycle of Structure and the Cycle of Meaning: The Piano Trio in E minor, Op. 67', in *Shostakovich Studies*, ed. by David Fanning. Cambridge, Cambridge University Press.

Mâche, François-Bernard (1986) 'Les procédures d'analyse sémiologique', *International Review of the Aesthetics and Sociology of Music*, vol. 17/2: 203–214.

Maguire, Robert A. (ed.) (1974) *Gogol from the Twentieth Century: Eleven Essays*, trans. with an introduction by Robert Maguire. Princeton, Princeton University Press.

Malloy, Joseph Thomas (1985) 'Musico-dramatic Irony in Mozart's "Magic Flute"'. Dissertation, University of Virginia.

Mann, Thomas (1918) 'Ironie und Radikalismus' in *Politische Schriften und Reden. Vol. I: Betrachtungen eines Unpolitischen*, 1968. Berlin, Moderne Klassiker Fischer Bücherei.

——— (1918) 'Irony and Radicalism', *Reflections of a Nonpolitical Man*, trans. with an introduction by Walter D. Morris, 1983. New York, Frederick Ungar Publishing Co.: 419–435.

Markiewicz, Henryk (1967) 'On the Definitions of Literary Parody' in *To Honor Roman Jakobson: Essays on the Occasion of his Seventieth Birthday, 11 October 1996*. The Hague, Mouton.

Martynov, Ivan Ivanovich (1947) *Dmitri Shostakovich: The Man and His Work*, trans. by T. Guralsky. New York, Greenwood Press.

——— (1980) *O muzïke i yeyo tvortsakh: sbornik statey*. Moscow, Vsesoyuznoye Izdatel'stvo 'Sovetski Kompozitor'.

Mayakovsky, Vladimir (1960) *The Bedbug and Selected Poetry*, trans. by Max Hayward and George Reavey. London, Weidenfeld & Nicolson.

——— (1985–87) *Selected works in three volumes*. Moscow, Raduga.

Mazel, Leo (1981) *Simfonii D.D. Shostakovicha: putevoditel'* (enlarged 2nd edn). Moscow, Sovetski Kompozitor.

Merrill, Reid (1990) 'The Grotesque in Music: Shostakovich's Nose', *Russian Literature Triquarterly*, vol. 23: 303–314.

Meyer, Franz (1964) *Marc Chagall*. New York, Harry N. Abrams Inc.

Meyer, Krzysztof (1994) *Dimitri Chostakovitch*. Paris, Librairie Arthème Fayard.

Meyer, Leonard B. (1956) *Emotion and Meaning in Music*. Chicago, University of Chicago Press.

——— (1967) *Music, the Arts, and Ideas: Patterns and Predictions in Twentieth-century Culture*. New edn, 1994. Chicago, University of Chicago Press.

——— (1973) *Explaining Music: Essays and Explorations*. Berkeley, University of California Press.

——— (1989) *Style and Music: Theory, History and Ideology*. Philadelphia, University of Pennsylvania Press.

Meyer, P. and Rudy, Stephen (eds) (1979) *Dostoevsky and Gogol: Texts and Criticism*. Ann Arbor, Michigan, Ardis.

Meyerhold, Vsevolod (1911–12) 'The Fairground Booth' in *Meyerhold on Theatre*, trans. and ed. with a critical commentary by Edward Braun, 1969. London, Methuen & Co.: 119–142.

——— (1969) *Meyerhold on Theatre*, trans. and ed. with a critical commentary by Edward Braun. London, Methuen & Co.

Mikheyeva-Sollertinskaya, Lyudmilla (1988) *I.I. Sollertinsky*. Leningrad, Sovyetskii Kompozitor.

Milhaud, Darius (1973) *Ma Vie Heureuse*. Paris, Éditions Belfond.

——— (1987) *My Happy Life: An Autobiography*, trans. by Donald Evans, George Hall and Christopher Palmer. London, Marion Boyars.

Milne, Hamish (1982) *Bartók*. Sydney, Omnibus Press.

Moles, Abraham (1958) *Information Theory and Esthetic Perception*, trans. by Joel E. Cohen, 1968. Urbana, University of Illinois Press.

Monelle, Raymond (1990) 'A Semantic Approach to Debussy's Songs', *The Music Review*, vol. 51/3: 193–207.

——— (1991) 'Structural Semantics and Instrumental Music', *Music Analysis*, vol. 10/1–2: 73–88.

——— (1992) *Linguistics and Semiotics in Music*. Chur, Switzerland, Harwood Academic Publishers.

——— (1995) 'Music and Semantics' in E. Tarasti (ed.) *Musical Signification: Essays in the Semiotic Theory and Analysis of Music*. Berlin, Mouton.

——— (ed., with Catherine Gray) (1996) *Song and Signification: Studies in Music Semiotics*. Edinburgh, The University of Edinburgh Faculty of Music.

——— (1997) 'Binary Semantic Opposition in Instrumental Incipits' in *Proceedings of the Fifth Congress of the International Association for Semiotic Studies, Berkeley, 1994*. Berlin, Mouton de Gruyter.

——— (1997–8) *Musica Significans: Proceedings of the Third International Conference on Musical Signification*, Edinburgh, 1992. (Editor) presented in five issues of *Contemporary Music Review*.

———— (1998) 'Music Transparency', in Costin Miereanu and Xavier Hascher (eds) *Les universaux en musique: actes du quatrième congrès international sur la signification musicale*. Paris, Sorbonne, pp. 11–30.

———— (2000) *The Sense of Music*. Princeton, Princeton University Press.

Morson, Gary Saul and Emerson, Caryl (1990) *Mikhail Bakhtin: Creation of a Prosaics*. Stanford, Stanford University Press.

Morton, Brian (1990) 'How Not to Write for *Dissent*' *Dissent*, Summer. Reproduced in 'L'Isle de Gilligan', <http://www.anatpmy.su.oz.au/danny/danny/humour/Gilligan>.

Muecke, D.C. (1969) *The Compass of Irony*. London, Methuen.

———— (1970) *Irony*. London, Methuen.

Murray, Gale B. (1995) 'Toulouse Lautrec's Illustrations for Victor Joze and Georges Clemenceau and Their Relationship to French Anti-Semitism of the 1890's' in Linda Nochlin and Tamar Garb (eds) *The Jew in the Text: Modernity and the Construction of Identity*. London, Thames and Hudson.

Nattiez, Jean-Jacques (1973a) 'Linguistics: A New Approach for Musical Analysis?', *International Review of the Aesthetics and Sociology of Music*, vol. IV/1: 51–68.

———— (1973b) 'Sémiologie et sémiographie musicales', *Musique en Jeu*, no. 13: 78–86.

———— (1974) 'Sur les relations entre sociologie et sémiologie musicales', *International Review of the Aesthetics and Sociology of Music*, vol. V/1: 61–75.

———— (1975) *Fondements d'une sémiologie de la musique*. Paris, Union Générale d'Éditions.

———— (1987) *Musicologie générale et sémiologie*, Paris, Christian Bourgois.

———— (1990) *Music and Discourse: Toward a Semiology of Music*. Princeton, Princeton University Press.

Neţ, Mariana (1993a) 'Literature, Strategies and Metalanguage, Part 1', *Semiotica*, vol. 93/3–4: 241–267.

———— (1993b) 'Literature, Strategies and Metalanguage, Part 2: Grammar and Metalanguage', *Semiotica*, vol. 94/1–2: 55–84

———— (1993c) 'Literature, Strategies and Metalanguage, Part 3: Poetical Arts and Metalanguage', *Semiotica*, vol. 94/3–4: 253–293

———— (1993d) 'Literature, Strategies and Metalanguage, Part 4: Context, Cotext and Metatext', *Semiotica*, vol. 95/1–2: 75–99

———— (1993e) 'Semiotics and Interfictionality in a Postmodern Age: The Case of the Playbill', *Semiotica*, vol. 97/3–4: 315–323.

———— (1994) 'Mentalities and Cultural Interpretants', *Southern European Journal for Semiotic Studies*, vol. 6/3–4: 675–690.

Nichols, James W. (1971) *Insinuation: The Tactics of English Satire*. The Hague, Mouton.

Nichols, Roger (1987) *Ravel Remembered*. London, Faber and Faber.

Norris, Christopher (ed.) (1982a) 'Shostakovich: Politics and Musical Language', in *Shostakovich, the Man and His Music*. London, Lawrence and Wishart.

———— (ed.) (1982b) *Shostakovich, the Man and His Music*. London, Lawrence and Wishart.

Noske, Frits (1977) *The Signifier and the Signified: Studies in the Operas of Mozart and Verdi*. The Hague, Nijhoff.

Orledge, Robert (1995) *Satie Remembered*. French trans. by Roger Nichols. London, Faber and Faber.

Ottaway, Hugh (1978) *Shostakovich Symphonies*. London, British Broadcasting Corporation.

Patterson, Michael (1981) *The Revolution in German Theatre: 1900–1933*. London, Routledge & Kegan Paul.

Petro, Peter (1982) *Modern Satire: Four Studies*. Berlin, Mouton Publishers.

Plekhanov, Gyorgiy (1912) 'On Art for Art's sake' (first published in *Art and Society*), in Berel Lang and Forrest Williams (eds) (1972) *Marxism and Art: Writings in Aesthetics and Criticism*. New York, David McKay Company Inc.

Pollard, Arthur (1970) *Satire*. London, Methuen.

Pople, Anthony (ed.) (1994) *Theory, Analysis and Meaning in Music*. Cambridge, Cambridge University Press.

Posner, Donald (1971) *Annibale Carracci: A Study in the Reform of Italian Painting Around 1590*, 2 vols. London, Phaidon.

Pritchett, James (1993) *The Music of John Cage*. Cambridge, Cambridge University Press.

Quintilian (1922) *The Institutio Oratoria of Quintilian*, English trans. by H.E. Butler. London, William Heinemann.

Rabinovich, D. (1959) *Dmitri Shostakovich*. London, Lawrence and Wishart.

Ratner, Leonard C. (1980) *Classic Music: Expression, Form and Style*. New York, Schirmer.

Reaney, Gilbert (1960) 'Ars Nova in France' in *The New Oxford History of Music*, ed. by Don Anselm Hughes and Gerald Abraham. London, Oxford University Press.

Redepenning, Dorothea (1995) '"And Art Made Tongue-tied by Authority": Shostakovich's Song-Cycles' in Daving Fanning (ed.) *Shostakovich Studies*. Cambridge, Cambridge University Press.

Revill, David (1992) *The Roaring Silence – John Cage: A Life*. Edinburgh, Bloomsbury.

Riffaterre, Michael (1984) 'Parodie et répétition' in *Le singe à la porte: vers une theorie de la parodie*, ed. by GROUPAR: P.B. Gobin, J.J. Hamm, M.L. Kaiting, C. Thomson, M. Vernet and A. Wall. New York, Peter Lang, pp. 87–94.

Rose, Margaret A. (1979) *Parody/Meta-fiction: An Analysis of Parody as a*

Critical Mirror to the Writing and Reception of Fiction. London, Croom Helm.

———— (1993) *Parody: Ancient, Modern and Post-modern*. Cambridge, Cambridge University Press.

Roseberry, Eric (1981) *Shostakovich*. New edn, 1986. London, Omnibus Press.

———— (1989) *Ideology, Style and Thematic Process in the Symphonies, Cello Concertos and String Quartets of Shostakovich*. New York, Garland.

———— (1995) 'A Debt Repaid? Some Observations on Shostakovich and His Late-period Recognition of Britten' in David Fanning (ed.) *Shostakovich Studies*. Cambridge, Cambridge University Press.

Rosenberg, Wolf (1988) 'Paradox, Doppelbödigkeit und Ironie und der Dichterliebe', *Dissonanz/Dissonance*, vol. 15, February: 8–12.

Rowe, Eleanor (1976) *Hamlet: A Window on Russia*. New York, New York University Press.

Rudnitsky, Konstantin (1988) *Russian and Soviet Theatre: Tradition and the Avant-garde*, trans. by Roxane Parmer, ed. by Lesley Milne. London, Thames & Hudson.

Ruwet, Nicolas (1962) 'Note sur les duplications dans l'oeuvre de Claude Debussy', *Revue Belge de Musicologie*. vol. 16; reissued in *Language, Musique, Poésie*, Paris, Le Sevil: 70–99.

———— (1966) 'Méthodes d'analyse en musicologie', *Revue Belge de Musicologie*, vol. 20: 65–90.

———— (1967a) 'Musicology and Linguistics', *International Social Science Journal*, vol. 19/1: 79–87.

———— (1967b) 'Quelques remarques sur le rôle de la répétition dans la syntaxe musicale' in *To Honour Roman Jakobson*. The Hague, Mouton, pp. 1693–1703.

———— (1972) *Langage, Musique, Poésie*. Paris, Le Seuil.

———— (1975) 'Théorie et méthodes dans les études musicales', *Musique en Jeu*, vol. 17: 11–35.

Sabinina, M. (1959) *Dmitry Shostakovich*. Moscow, Sovetski Kompozitor.

———— (1965) *Simfonizm Shostakovicha: put' k zrelosti*. Moscow, Nauka.

———— (1976) *Shostakovich – Symphonist: dramaturgiya, estetika, stil*. Moscow, Muzyka.

———— (1985) 'Symfonizm D. Shostakovich v gody voiny', *Muzyka v Borbe s Fashizmom*. Moscow, Sovetski Kompozitor.

Samuels, Robert (1995) *Mahler's Sixth Symphony: A Study in Musical Semiotics*. Cambridge, Cambridge University Press.

Schaerer, René (1941) 'Le mécanisme de l'ironie dans ses rapports avec la dialectique', *Revue de Métaphysique et de Morale*, 48e Année, no. 3: 181–209.

Schlegel, Friedrich (1957) *Literary Notebooks 1797–1801*, ed. by Hans Eichner. London, Athlone Press.

———— (1963) *Kritische Friedrich Schlegel Ausgabe*. Abtl. 2: *Schriften aus dem Nachlass, Bd 18 Philosophische Lehrjahre, 1796–1806*. Munich, Verlag F. Schöningh.

———— (1967) 'Über die Unverständlichkeit' (1799) in *Kritische Friedrich Schlegel Ausgabe*. Zweiter Band: *Karakteristiken und Kritiken I (1796–1801)*. Munich, Verlag Ferdinand Schöningh. Band 2: 363–372.

———— (1967b) 'Athenäum – Fragmente' (1801) in *Kritische Friedrich Schlegel Ausgabe*. Zweiter Band: *Karakteristiken und Kritiken I (1796–1801)*. Munich, Verlag Ferdinand Schöningh.

———— (1971a) 'On Incomprehensibility' in *Friedrich Schlegel's Lucinde and the Fragments*, trans. with an introduction by Peter Firchow. Minneapolis, University of Minnesota Press, pp. 259–271.

———— (1971b) 'The Athenaeum Fragments' in *Friedrich Schlegel's Lucinde and the Fragments*, trans. with an introduction by Peter Firchow. Minneapolis, University of Minnesota Press.

———— (1985) *Kritische Friedrich Schlegel Ausgabe*. Abtl. 3: *Briefe von und an Dorothea Schlegel, Bd 24 Die Periode des Athenäums, 25 Juli 1797–Ende August 1799*. Munich, Verlag Ferdinand Schöningh.

Schneider, David (1968) *American Kinship: A Cultural Account*. New York, Prentice-Hall.

Schwartz, Boris (1972 and 1983) *Music and Musical Life in Soviet Russia: Enlarged Edition, 1917–1981*. Bloomington, University of Indiana Press.

Şechter, Madeleine (1994) 'Defining the Grotesque: An Aesthetics of Liminality', PhD thesis, Tel-Aviv University.

Seroff, Victor Ilyich (1943) in collaboration with Nadejda Galli-Shohat, aunt of the composer, *Dmitri Shostakovich: The Life and Background of a Soviet Composer*. New York, Freeport.

Shapiro, Michael (1983) *The Sense of Grammar*. Bloomington, Indiana University Press.

Sheinberg, Esti (1992) 'Hamashma'ut Sheme'ever Latslilim' ('The Meaning Beyond the Sounds'), *Makhshavot*, Tel-Aviv, IBM.

———— (1994) 'Jewish motifs in the music of Dmitri Shostakovich', *The Edinburgh Star*, no. 19: 22–25.

———— (1996a) 'An Application of Ernst Gombrich's Projection Theory in Art to Musical Semantics' in Raymond Monelle and Catherine Gray (eds) *Song and Signification*, Edinburgh, Edinburgh University, The Faculty of Music.

———— (1996b) 'Signs, Symbols and Expressive Elements in the String Quartets of Dmitri Shostakovich' in Eero Tarasti (ed.) *Musical Semiotics in Growth*. Imatra, The International Semiotics Institute.

———— (Forthcoming) *Dancing to the Grave: The Musical Semiotics of the Dance of Death*. Hillsdale, NY, Pendragon Press.

Sheldon, David A. (1986) 'The Fugue as an Expression of Rationalist Values', *International Review of the Aesthetics and Sociology of Music*, vol. 17/1: 29–51.

Shklovsky, Viktor Borisovich (1917) 'Iskusstvo kak priyom' in *O teorii prozi*, 1929. Moscow, Federatsiya.

———— (1917) 'Art as Technique' in L.T. Lemon and M.J. Reis (eds) *Russian Formalist Criticism: Four Essays*, 1965. Lincoln, University of Nebraska Press.

———— (1921) 'Sterne's *Tristram Shandy*: Stylistic Commentary' in L.T. Lemon and M.J. Reis (eds) *Russian Formalist Criticism: Four Essays*, 1965. Lincoln, University of Nebraska Press.

———— (1923) *Sentimental'noye puteshestviye*, 1990. Moscow, Novosti.

———— (1923) *A Sentimental Journey: Memoirs 1917–1922*, trans. from the Russian and ed. by Richard Sheldon, 1970. Revised edn, 1984. Ithaca, Cornell University Press.

———— (1929) *O teorii prozi*. Moscow, Federatsiya

———— (1929) *Theory of Prose*, trans. by Benjamin Sher, 1991. Elmwood Park, Dalkey Archive Press.

———— (1940) *Mayakovsky and His Circle*, ed. and trans. by Lily Feiler, 1972. New York, The Cornwall Press.

Shlonsky, Tuvia (1966) 'Literary Parody: Remarks on Its Method and Function' in *Proceedings of the IVth Congress of the International Comparative Literature Association*, ed. by François Jost. The Hague, Mouton, vol. II: 797–801.

Shneerson, Grigory (1984) 'At the Birth of Dmitri Shostakovich's Eighth Symphony', *Russian and Soviet Music: Essays for Boris Schwarz*, ed. by Malcolm Hamrick Brown. Ann Arbor, Michigan UMI Research Press: 253–257.

Shneyerson, Grigory Mikhaylovich (ed.) (1976) *D. Shostakovich: Stat'i i Materiali*. Moscow, Sovetskii Kompozitor.

Shostakovich, D.D. (1946) 'I.I. Sollertinsky: ko vtoroi godovshchine so diya smerti', *Sovetskaya Muzyka*, nos 2–3: 90–95.

Slobin, Mark (1980) 'The Volga–Ural peoples' folk music' in Stanley Sadie (ed.) *The New Grove Dictionary of Music and Musicians*, vol. 19: 401–406.

Sloboda, John A. (1985) *The Musical Mind: The Cognitive Psychology of Music*. Oxford, Clarendon Press.

Slonim, Marc (1953) *Modern Russian Literature: From Chekhov to Present*. New York, Oxford University Press.

———— (1977) *Soviet Russian Literature: Writers and Problems, 1917–1977*. 2nd revised edn New York, Oxford University Press.

Slonimsky, Nicolas (1953) 'Non-acceptance of the Unfamiliar' in *Lexicon of*

Musical Invective, ed. by Nicolas Slonimsky. Seattle, University of Washington Press: 3–33.

Sollertinsky, Dmitri and Ludmilla (1979) *Pages From the Life of Dmitri Shostakovich*, trans. by Graham Hobbs and Charles Midgley, 1980. New York, Harcourt Brace Jovanovich.

Sollertinsky, Ivan Ivanovich (1939) 'Zametke o komicheskoy opere', reprinted in *Istoricheskiye Etyudi*, 1963. Leningrad, Gosudarsvennoye Muzikal'noye Izdatel'svo.

——— (1941) 'Istoricheskiye tipï simfonicheskoy dramaturgii' in *Istoricheskiye Etyudi*, 1963. Leningrad, Gosudarstvennoye Muzykalnoye Izdatelstvo: 335–346.

Staubman, Helmut (1991) 'The Concept of Norm in Sociological Theory and its Application to Music', *International Review of the Aesthetics and Sociology of Music*, vol. 22/2: 119–125.

Stefani, Gino (1974) 'Progetto Semiotico di una Musicologia Sistematica', *International Review of the Aesthetics and Sociology of Music*, vol. 5/2: 277–289.

Steig, Michael (1970) 'Defining The Grotesque: An Attempt at Synthesis', *Journal of Aesthetics and Art Criticism*, vol. 29, no. 2: 253–260.

Stevenson, Ronald (1982) 'The Piano Works' in Christopher Norris (ed.) *Shostakovich: The Man and His Music*. London, Lawrence and Wishart.

Stradling, Robert (1982) 'Shostakovich and the Soviet System, 1925–1975' in Christopher Norris (ed.) *Shostakovich: The Man and His Music*. London, Lawrence and Wishart.

Swiderski, Edward M. (1979) *The Philosophical Foundations of Soviet Aesthetics: Theories and Controversies in the Post-war Years*. Dordrecht, D. Reidl Publishing Company.

Symons, James M. (1971) *Meyerhold's Theatre of the Grotesque: The Post-Revolutionary Productions, 1920–1932*. Coral Gables, Florida, University of Miami Press.

Tallián, Tibor (1995) 'Bartók's Reception in America, 1940–1945', trans. by Peter Laki, in Peter Laki (ed.) *Bartók and His World*. Princeton, Princeton University Press.

Tampere, Herbert (1980) 'Estonia, Folk Music' in Stanley Sadie (ed.) *The New Grove Dictionary of Music and Musicians*, vol. 19: 358–360.

Tanimoto, Kazuyuki (1980) 'Siberian folk music' in Stanley Sadie (ed.) *The New Grove Dictionary of Music and Musicians*, vol. 19: 398–400.

Tarasti, Eero (1979) *Myth and Music: A Semiotic Approach to the Aesthetics of Music, Especially That of Wagner, Sibelius and Stravinsky*. The Hague, Mouton.

——— (1982) 'Perice and Greimas from the Viewpoint of Musical Semiotics: An Outline for a Comparative Semiotics' in *Semiotics 1980: Proceedings of the 5th Annual Meeting of the Semiotic Society of America, 1980, Texas,* ed. by Michael Herzfeld and Margot D. Lenhart, New York, Research Center for Language and Semiotic Studies, Indiana University, Plenum Press, pp. 503–511.

———— (1983) 'Sur les structures élémentaires du discours musical' in *Actes sémiotiques*. Paris, EHESS, Groupe de recherches sémio-linguistiques, vol. 4: 6–13.

———— (1984) 'Pour une narratologie de Chopin', *International Review of the Aesthetics and Sociology of Music*, vol. 15/1: 53–75.

———— (1985) 'Music as Sign and Process' in *Analytica: Studies in the Description and Analysis of Music, in Honour of Ingmar Bengtsson, 2 March 1985*. Stockholm, Royal Swedish Academy of Music: 97–115.

———— (1987a) 'Some Peircean and Greimasian Concepts as Applied to Music' in Thomas A. Sebeok and Jean Umiker Sebeok (eds) *The Semiotic Web 1986*. Amsterdam, Mouton de Gruyter.

———— (1987b) 'Vers une grammaire narrative de la musique', *Degrés*, vol. 52: d1–d24.

———— (1987c) 'Le rôle du temps dans le discours musical', *Sémiotique en Jeu: Actes Sémiotiques.*Paris, EHESS, vol. 5.

———— (1988) 'On The Modalities and Narrativity in Music' in Veikko Rantala, Lewis Rowel and Eero Tarasti (eds) *Essays on the Philosophy of Music. Acta Philosophica Fennica 43*. Helsinki, Societas Philosophica Fennica.

———— (1994) *A Theory of Musical Semiotics*. Bloomington, Indiana University Press.

———— (1995) 'Après un rêve – l'analyse sémiotique d'une mélodie de Gabriel Fauré' in Eero Tarasti (ed.) *Musical Signification: Essays in the Semiotic Theory and Analysis of Music*. Berlin, Mouton de Gruyter.

Taruskin, Richard (1993) *Musorgsky: Eight Essays and an Epilogue*. Princeton, Princeton University Press.

———— (1995) 'Public Lies and Unspeakable Truth: Interpreting Shostakovich's Fifth Symphony' in David Fanning (ed.) *Shostakovich Studies*. Cambridge, Cambridge University Press.

———— (1997) *Defining Russia Musically: Historical and Hermeneutical Essays*. Princeton, Princeton University Press.

Terras, Victor (ed.) (1985) *Handbook of Russian Literature*. New Haven, Yale University Press.

Thomson, Philip (1972) *The Grotesque*. London, Methuen.

Tinyanov, Yury Nikolayevich (1921)'Dostoyevsky i Gogol: K teorii parodii', in *Arkhaistï i novatorï 1929*, Leningrad, Priboy: 412–455.

———— (1921) 'Dostoevsky and Gogol', (a translation of the first part of Tinyanov's 'Dostoyevsky i Gogol') in P. Meyer and Stephen Rudy (eds) (1979) *Dostoevsky & Gogol: Texts and Criticism*. Ann Arbor, Ardis: 101–117.

————— (1921c) 'Dostoevsky and Gogol' (a translation of the second part of Tïnyanov's 'Dostoyevskii i Gogol') in Victor Erlich (ed.) *Twentieth-century Russian Literary Criticism*, 1975. New Haven, Yale University Press: 102–116.

————— (1924) *The Problem of Verse Language*, ed. and trans. by Michael Sosa and Brent Harvey, 1981. Ann Arbor, Ardis.

————— (1927) 'O literaturnoy evolutsii' in *Arkhaistï i novatoryï*, 1929, Leningrad, Priboy: 30–47.

————— (1927) 'On Literary Evolution' in Ladislav Matejka and Krystina Pomorska (eds) (1971) *Readings in Russian Poetics: Formalist and Structuralist Views*. Cambridge, Mass., MIT.

Trotsky, Leon (1925) 'The Formalist School of Poetry and Marxism' (first published in his *Literature and Art*). Trans. in Berel Lang and Forrest Williams (1972) *Marxism and Art: Writings in Aesthetics and Criticism*. New York, David McKay Company Inc.

Tsitovich, Gennady (1980) 'Belorussia' in Stanley Sadie (ed.) *The New Grove Dictionary of Music and Musicians*, vol. 19: 354–357.

Vakhtangov, Yevgeny (1982) *Yevgeny Vakhtangov*, compiled by Lyubov Vendrovskaya and Galina Kaptereva, trans. by Doris Bradbury. Moscow, Progress.

Veselovsky, A.N. (1939) *Izbrannïye stat'i*. Leningrad, Khudozhestvennaya Literatura.

————— (1940) *Istoricheskaya poetika*, ed. with an introduction by V.M. Zhrimunskii. Leningrad, Khudozhestvennaya Literatura. (Also published in 1970 by Mouton, The Hague, Slavistic Printings and Reprintings.)

Vishnevskaya, Galina (1984) *Galina: A Russian Story*. London, Hodder & Stoughton.

Vītoliņš, Jēkabs, (1980) 'Latvia, folk music' in Stanley Sadie (ed.) *The New Grove Dictionary of Music and Musicians*, vol. 19: 369–372.

Volkov, Solomon (1979) *Testimony: The Memoirs of Dmitri Shostakovich, As Related to and Edited by Solomon Volkov*, trans. from the Russian by Antonina W. Bouis. London, Hamish Hamilton.

Volta, Ornella (1989) *Satie Seen Through His Letters*. London, Marion Boyars.

Voltaire (1758) *Candide, ou L'optimisme. Édition critique, avec une introduction et un commentaire par René Pomeau*, 1959. Paris, A.G.Nizet.

————— (1758) *The History of Candide, or All For The Best, translated from the French of M. de Voltaire. Ornamented by Martin Travers*, 192?. London, Chapman & Dodd.

Vulpi, Frank (1988) 'Irony in Verdi's Rigoletto', *The Opera Journal*, vol. 21: 21–31.

Wagner, Richard (1850) 'Judaism in Music' in *Richard Wagner's Prose Works*, trans. by W.A. Ellis. 1894, London, Kegan Paul, Trench, Trübner & Co., vol. III: 79–100.

————— (1852) 'Das Judenthum in der Musik' in *Gesammelte Schriften und Dichtungen von Richard Wagner*, 1872. Leipzig, Verlag von E.W. Fritzsch. Fünfter Band: 85–108.

Warner, Elizabeth A. and Kustovskii, Evgenii S. (1990) *Russian Traditional Folk Song*. Hull, Hull University Press.

Westphalen, Timothy C. (1992) 'The Ongoing Influence of V.S. Solov'ev on A.A. Blok: The Particular Case of *Belaja lilija* and *Balagančik*', *Slavic and European Journal*, vol. 36, no. 4, Winter: 435–451.

————— (1993) 'The Carnival-grotesque and Blok's The Puppet Show', *The Slavic Review*, vol. 52: 49–66.

Wilde, Alan (1981) *Horizons of Assent: Modernism, Post-modernism, and the Ironic Imagination*. Baltimore, The Johns Hopkins University Press.

Wilde, Oscar (1893) '*Salomé*', in Robert Ross (ed.) *The First Collected Edition of the Works of Oscar Wilde*, vol. 2, 1969. London, Dawsons of Pall Mall.

————— (1893) *Salomé* in *Plays*, 1954. Harmondsworth, Penguin.

Wilson, Elizabeth (1994) *Shostakovich: A Life Remembered*. London, Faber.

Wittgenstein, Ludwig (1953) *Philosophical Investigations*, trans. by G.E.M. Anscombe, 1972. Oxford, Basil Blackwell.

Woodley, Ronald (1995) 'Strategies of irony in Prokofiev's Violin Sonata in F minor Op. 80' in John Rink (ed.) *The Practice of Performance: Studies in Musical Interpretation*. Cambridge, Cambridge University Press.

Worcester, David (1940) *The Art of Satire*. Reprinted 1960. New York, Russell & Russell.

Worrall, Nick (1972) 'Meyerhold directs Gogol's *Government Inspector*: Reconstitution using director notes, designs and photographs of the original production', *Theatre Quarterly*, vol. II, no. 7: 75–95.

————— (1989) *Modernism to Realism on the Soviet Stage: Tairov-Vakhtangov-Okhlopkov*. Cambridge, Cambridge University Press.

Yelagin, Yury (1950 [1988]) *Ukroshenye Iskosstv* 1988. Leningrad, Ermitage.

Zemtsovsky, Izaly (1980) 'Russian folk music' in Stanley Sadie (ed.) *The New Grove Dictionary of Music and Musicians*, vol. 19: 388–398.

Zen'kovskii, Vasilii Vasilyevich (1950) *A History of Russian Philosophy*, 2 vols, trans. by Georg L. Kline, 1953. London, Routledge & Kegan Paul.

Zuckerkandl, Victor (1948) *Sound and Symbol: Music and the External World*, 1956. London, Routledge and Kegan Paul.

————— (1959) *The Sense of Music*. Princeton, Princeton University Press.

General index

Index of names